The History of
ROGERS' RANGERS

Volume I

The Beginnings
January 1755-April 6, 1758

Burt Garfield Loescher

HERITAGE BOOKS
2006

HERITAGE BOOKS
AN IMPRINT OF HERITAGE BOOKS, INC.

Books, CDs, and more—Worldwide

For our listing of thousands of titles see our website
at
www.HeritageBooks.com

A Facsimile Reprint
Published 2006 by
HERITAGE BOOKS, INC.
Publishing Division
65 East Main Street
Westminster, Maryland 21157-5026

Copyright © 1946 Burt Garfield Loescher

Other books by the author:

*The History of Rogers' Rangers, Volume II:
Genesis: Rogers' Rangers, The First Green Berets*

*The History of Rogers' Rangers, Volume III:
Officers and Non-Commissioned Officers*

The History of Rogers' Rangers, Volume IV: The St. Francis Raid

All rights reserved. No part of this book may be reproduced or transmitted in any form or by any means, electronic or mechanical, including photocopying, recording or by any information storage and retrieval system without written permission from the author, except for the inclusion of brief quotations in a review.

— Publisher's Notice —
In reprints such as this, it is often not possible to remove blemishes from the original. We feel the contents of this book warrant its reissue despite these blemishes and hope you will agree and read it with pleasure.

International Standard Book Number: 978-0-7884-4295-3

"*Like Durer's knight, a ghastly death stalked ever at their side. There were those among them for whom this stern life had a fascination that made all other existence tame.*"

                  Francis Parkman's:
  Montcalm and Wolfe, I, p 447;
Courtesy of Little, Brown & Company

TO
MY SON
DAVID ANTHONY LOESCHER
THIS BOOK
IS AFFECTIONATELY DEDICATED

ACKNOWLEDGMENTS

For their generous assistance in furnishing material for this Volume and for their words of advice and encouragement, the author is most deeply grateful to:-

My Wife, Helene Loescher, for her excellent and authentic illustrations.
Leslie Edgar Bliss, Director, Huntington Library, for his permission to publish Documents relative to the *Mutiny* and other excerpts from the Loudoun and Abercrombie Manuscripts.
Jacqueline La Bonte, Hull, Quebec.
Helene M. Bruner, Sutro Branch, California State Library, for her unfailing efforts in obtaining rare books.
Norma Cuthbert, Cataloguer, Dept. of Manuscripts, Huntington Library, for many clues.
Detmar H. Finke, Washington, D. C.
Colonel A. Gibson and Margaret H. Clees, Army War College, Washington, D. C.
Otis G. Hammond, Director, N.H. Historical Society
Florence S. Hellman, Chief Bibliographer, Library of Congress, Washington, D. C.
Robert W. Hill, Keeper of MSS, N.Y. Public Library
W. S. B. Hopkins, Worcester, Mass.
Edna L. Jacobsen, Head, MSS, N.Y. State Library.
John Jennings, Plymouth, New Hampshire.
J. E. Jones, Editor, 'The Prospector', Chicago.
Gustave Lanctot, Deputy Minister, Pub. Arch Canada
C. C. P. Lawson, London, England.
H. Charles McBarron, Jr, Chicago, Illinois.
Mrs. Frank L. Nason, Secy, Mass, Soc, Mayflower Desc.
Victor H. Paltsits, formerly Keeper of MSS N.Y.Lib
Stanley M. Pargellis, Librarian, Newberry Library, for 'deciphering' Loudoun's Diary entries.
Major Douglas Parmentier, A.U.S. Chief Pub. Branch.
Howard Peckham, Curator of MSS, Clements Library.
S. H. P. Pell, Director, Fort Ticonderoga Museum.
Anne S. Pratt, Reference Librarian, Yale Univ. Lib.
Robert Rea, past Librarian, San Francisco Pub. Lib.
Kenneth Roberts, Kennebunk Port, Me, for clues.
Anne Marie Sautour, San Francisco, California.
Secretary of State, Concord, New Hampshire.
St. George L. Sioussat, Chief, MSS, Lib. of Congress
Staff, Huntington Library, San Marino, California.
Superintendent, Public Record Office, London.
Colonel Frederick P. Todd, Secy, American Mil. Inst.
Anthony J. Wall, Jr., New York Historical Society.

CONTENTS

VOLUME I
JANUARY 1755 TO APRIL 6, 1758

	PAGE
FRONTISPIECE	ii
ACKNOWLEDGMENTS	vii
INTRODUCTION	xiv
PROLOGUE	17
CHAPTER ONE "WINNING THEIR SPURS"	23
CHAPTER TWO "FALCONS OF THE LAKES"	51
CHAPTER THREE "GROWING PAINS"	111
CHAPTER FOUR "A REGIMENT IS FORMED"	213

APPENDIX

I - ILLUSTRATIVE APPENDICES

APPENDICE:

A - DOCUMENTARY PROCEEDINGS OF ROBERT ROGERS COUNTERFEITING TRIAL	264 264
B - UNIFORMS AND EQUIPMENT OF ROGERS RANGERS 1755-1783	271
C - ROBERT ROGERS' "OWN" COMPANY AND THE SIX ESTABLISHMENTS	287
D - LOSSES IN ROGERS RANGERS to Apr 5 8"	290
E - ROGERS' FAMOUS RANGING RULES	291
F - ROGERS' CADET COMPANY	297
G - VARIOUS PAY ESTABLISHMENTS	304
H - THE WHIPPING POST MUTINY	304

II-SELECTIVE DOCUMENTS ON THE AM-
BUSCADES & BATTLES OF ROGERS RANGERS
SEPT 29, 1755-MAR 13, 1758

1 *ROGERS' AMBUSCADE NEAR ISLE AU MOUTON:
ROGERS' OFFICIAL REPORT TO COL. BLANCHARD (312)
ROGERS' JOURNALS ACCOUNT (312-13)
SETH POMEROY'S ACCOUNT (313)

2 *BATTLE OF THE ISLE OF MUTTON: (313-19)
PRIMARY REASONS FOR THE EXPEDITION (313)
JOHNSON'S GENERAL ORDER TO ROGERS (314)
JOHNSON'S INSTRUCTIONS TO ROGERS AFTER HIS NOTE
FOR REENFORCEMENTS; & ORDERS TO BILLINGS (314-15)
ROGERS' OFFICIAL REPORT TO JOHNSON (315-17)
ROGERS' JOURNALS ACCOUNT (317-18)
CAPTAIN ROGER BILLINGS' REPORT TO JOHNSON (318)
PROVINCIAL ACCOUNTS (318-19) CASUALTIES (319)

3 MASSACRE OF SERGT ARCHIBALD'S SQUAD: (319)

4 *THE RETALIATION SCOUT: (319-20)
ROGERS' JOURNALS ACCOUNT (319)
CAPTAIN DE LERY'S FRENCH ACCOUNT (320)

5 *THE OTTER CREEK MOUTH AMBUSCADE: (320-24),
ROGERS' OFFICIAL REPORT (320-24)
ROGERS' JOURNALS ACCOUNT (322)
ROGERS' LAST REPORT TO SHIRLEY (322)
PROVINCIAL AND NEWSPAPER ACCOUNTS (322-23)
FRENCH ACCOUNTS (323-4)

6 *LIEUTENANT JACOB'S AMBUSCADE: (324)

7 *CAPTAIN JACOB'S SCALP SCOUT: (324)

8 *THE BATTLE OF LA BARBUE CREEK: (324-45)
ROGERS' OFFICIAL REPORT TO ABERCROMBIE (324-8)
ROGERS' JOURNALS ACCOUNT (328-9)
LOSSES OF ROGERS' FORCE (329-30)
SERGEANT WILLIAM MORRIS'S ACCOUNT (330-31)
SERGEANT JAMES HENRY'S ACCOUNT (331)
PRIVATE THOMAS BROWN'S ACCOUNT (331-340)
CAPTAIN JOHN STARK'S ACCOUNT (340)
PRIVATES J. SHUTE'S & EASTMAN'S ACCOUNT (340-1)
BRITISH ACCOUNTS: EYRE'S (341-2); GEN. ABERCROM-
BIE'S (342); LOUDOUN'S (342); CAPT. ABERCROMBIE'S
(342-4); BURTON'S (344); RECOMMENDATION FOR BAK-
ER (344); MATRON BROWN'S ACCOUNT (344-5)

PROVINCIAL ACCOUNTS (345)
FRENCH ACCOUNTS: MONTCALM'S (345-6); MINISTER MORAS'S (346); ANONYMOUS (346-8); VAUDREUIL'S (348) FRENCH LOSSES (348-9); BOUGAINVILLE'S (349). LOCATION AND DESCRIPTION OF THE BATTLEFIELD (349) FATE OF THE 7 SLEIGHMEN CAPTURED BY ROGERS (350)

9 *FIRST DEFENSE OF FORT WILLIAM HENRY: (350-2)
10*STARK'S MARCH 21ST SORTIE: (350-2)
11*THE MARCH 22ND RUM SORTIE: (350-2)

12*RICHARD ROGERS' ATTACK ON COUTRE COEUR:(352)

13 THE JULY 1ST AMBUSCADE: (352-3)
GRIDLEY'S ACCOUNT (352); VAUDREUIL'S (352-3)

14*AMBUSCADE AT ISLE LA BARQUE: (353)
FRENCH ACCOUNTS: 2 ANONYMOUS (353); DORIEL'S (353)

15 SIEGE, SURRENDER & MASSACRE OF WM. HENRY:
SOURCES (354); LOSSES OF ROGERS' RANGERS (354) FATHER ROUBAUD'S ACCOUNT (354-5)

16*THE HUNTING SCOUT: (355)

17 STARK'S MISBEHAVIOUR SCOUT: (355-6)
BRITISH ACCOUNTS (355); MALARTIC'S (355-6)

18*ROGERS' XMAS EVE RAID ON TICONDEROGA:
ROGERS' JOURNALS ACCOUNT (356-7); THANKS NOTE (357) FRENCH ACCOUNTS: DOREIL (357); MONTCALM (357); MALARTIC (357); HEBECOURT (358-9); COURCEL (359); JEAN BOIS (359); ROGERS' TWO PRISONERS (360-1) PROVINCIAL ACCOUNT TO JOHNSON (357-8). BOSTON NEWS-LETTER (359). RANGER GOODENOUGH (360).

19*ARNOUX'S DEFEAT: (361)
COURCEL'S ACCOUNT (361); ROGERS' ACCOUNT (361)

20*SHANKS' AMBUSCADE AT LITTLE MARY RIVER:
RANGER SHANKS' ACCOUNT (361-3)

21*THE MORNING PATROL FIGHT: (363)

22 THE BATTLE OF ROGERS' ROCK: (364-388):
CAPTAIN EZRA CLAP'S PROPOSAL TO ABERCROMBIE (364) ROGERS' OFFICIAL REPORT (364-8). ROGERS' LOSSES (369-71). FATE OF PHILLIPS DETAIL (371). CROFTON'S ACCOUNT (371-2). FITCH (372). ROGERS ESCAPE BRITISH ACCOUNTS (374-82). FRENCH (382-388).

III-SOURCES AND NOTES FOR EVERY RECORDED SCOUT, EXPEDITION, AND INDIVIDUAL FIGHT 1755-MARCH 1758:

1755

1	*CONSTRUCTION OF FORT WENTWORTH	389
2	*ROGERS' FIRST RECONNOITRES	389
3	*ROGERS' HUDSON RIVER SCOUT	389
4	*CONSTRUCTION OF FT. LYMAN (EDWARD)	389
5	*THE GOPHER SCOUT	389
6	*THE DECOY SCOUT	389
7	*ROGERS' SCALP SCOUT	389
8	*THE SIXTH FRENCH FORT SCOUT	390
9	*THE NOVEMBER 11-15, ALARM	390
10	*RICHARD ROGERS' SCOUT	390
11	*THE FISHERMEN SCOUT	390

1756

12	*ROGERS' RAID AT FIVE MILE POINT	390
13	*A RANGER'S ODYSSEY	390
14	*ROGERS' FIRST CROWN POINT VILLAGE RAID	390
15	*ROGERS' SECOND CROWN POINT VILLAGE RAID	391
16	*THE THREE WEEK ALARM	391
17	*AKIN'S NIGHT SCOUT	391
18	*AKIN'S UPPER ISLAND SCOUT	391
19	*THE CATTLE TONGUE SCOUT	391
20	*RICHARD ROGERS' WOOD CREEK PATROL	391
21	*ROGERS' WOOD CREEK HUNT	391
22	*THE DISCIPLINE SCOUT	391-2
23	*ROGERS' HORSE RAID	392
24	*ROGERS' CANADA RAID	392
25	*PUTNAM'S POND BLOODHOUND SCOUT	392

26	*ROGERS' SEPT 7-13TH SCOUT	392
27	*WOOD CREEK-SOUTH BAY PATROLS	392
28	*THE QUI ETES VOUS SCOUT	392
29	*SECOND BLOODHOUND SCOUTS	393
30	*ROGERS-ABERCROMBIE SCOUT	393

1757

31	*STARK'S APRIL SCOUT	393
32	*MC CURDY'S SHORT SCOUT	393
33	SCOUT OF BULKELEY'S COMPANY	393
34	*RELIEF OF NUMBER FOUR	393
35	*LAWRENCETOWN BLOODHOUND SCOUT	393
36	*NORTHWEST NOVA SCOTIA SCOUT	393
37	*SERGT. SEVERANCE'S HUDSON R. SCOUT	393
38	*LIEUTENANT MC CURDY'S CAPTURE	393
39	*ROGERS-LORD HOWE SCOUT	393
40	*THE SMALLPOX SCOUT	393

1758

41	*'BILL PHILLIPS' ICE TESTING SCOUT	394
42	*STARK'S ICE TESTING SCOUT	394
43	SERGEANT COOPER'S MASSACRE AND ROGERS' PURSUIT OF LANGY	394
44	*LESLIE'S SNOWSHOE TEST	394
45	*PUTNAM'S TICONDEROGA SCOUT	394
46	PURSUIT OF LANGY'S INDIANS	394
47	*MARCH 9TH BLOODHOUND SCOUT	394

BIBLIOGRAPHY OF PRINCIPAL SOURCES	395
HISTORICAL NOTES (FOOTNOTES)	400
NOTICE OF SUBSEQUENT VOLUMES	438

*Designates successful Battles and Scouts.

COLORED PLATES by HELENE S. LOESCHER
Depicting the Uniforms and Gear of all Companies:-

PLATE I (Frontispiece) MAJOR ROBERT ROGERS
Officers Dress - all Companies 1758 (and Uniform of
Private men, minus silver sleeve looping, beaded
shoulder sash and black hat. Privates and Sergeants
wore Green Scotch Bonnets as shown in Plate II.
Sergeants wore the silver looping on sleeve button
holes like the officers).

PLATE II (Page 104. SERGEANT JAMES HENRY
Uniform of the two Roger.'s Companies 1756-7 (same
uniform worn by Shepherd' except color was brown)
Summer Campaign Dress of all Companies 1758-1760.

PLATE III (Page 105) PRIVATE SHANKS SHANKLAND
Uniform of Hobbs' and Speakman's (Bulkeley's and
Stark's) Companies 1756-! and back view of Summer
Campaign Dress and gear of all Companies 1758-60
(except color of hunting shirt which was green).

ILLUSTRATIONS:

ROGERS PLEA TO GARTE GILMAN   page 16
ILLUSTRATION.BY ROY F. HEINRICH
   FOR THE NATIONAL LIFE INSURANCE COMPANY   147
THE BATTLE OF ROGERS' ROCK BY J. FERRIS
   FOR THE GLENS FALLS INSURANCE COMPANY   252

MAPS BY THE AUTHOR:

BATTLE OF LA BARBUE CREEK   125
BATTLE OF ROGERS' ROCK   250
THE BATTLES OF ROGERS RANGERS 1755-58   441-443

INTRODUCTION

The purpose of this book is to set forth the first part of the History of one of the most remarkable corps of men that ever gathered under a similiarly remarkable leader; and also to establish facts on the important part they played in the most vital period of American, Canadian, British and French history in North America. An attempt has been made to set this History down with unbiased conclusions on any controversial subjects, such as lack of rigid discipline in Rogers Rangers, the down-right cussedness of certain officers and men on occasion and the prima-dona attitude of the mighty Rogers himself in certain instances. This has been done not because it has been enjoyable setting forth the worst as well as the good side of the Corps' character but because it would be a distortion of the true facts to do otherwise. Consequently it is hoped that British, Canadian and French as well as American readers will find this work an unbiased account by an American writer.

Much has been written in novel and fact of certain phases of Robert Rogers life but very little has been told of the history of his different Companies of Rangers whose exploits were world reknown. A corps as famous as "Rogers Rangers" certainly deserves a history of their organization, exploits and personnel.

Based on the actual documents (cited in the footnotes, Appendices, and Bibliography) this

History is as documentary as it could be. The Loudoun Manuscripts in the Huntington Library were the chief source for this volume. Every one of the 10,000 manuscripts have been gone through by the author for items on Rogers Rangers. A sentence here, a paragraph there in these unpublished documents have served to knit together the first part of the History in a narrative of men who verily personafied the spirit of 'rugged Americanism'. In an effort to relieve the relating of exploit upon exploit, the characterization of Rogers, his officers and men has been dealt with, and it is believed that the historian as well as the casual reader will discover characteristics of Rogers and his men that have never before been brought to light.

In closing this introduction the author would like to state that if this volume is well received he will go ahead and publish the other two which only lack a few missing links to complete them. The second volume should complete the History and the third volume will give the names and services of every officer and man that served in the Corps with a biographical sketch of every officer and certain men. This should be of special value to New England Geneologists. So please write giving your opinion of this volume and send any historical or biographical information that would amplify these volumes. *March 21, 1946*

Burt Garfield Loescher, 134 Appleton Ave,
San Francisco, 10, California, U.S.A.

Mr Gilman Sr for gods
sake do the work that you promised
that you would do by no means
fail or you will destroy me forever
& my Life Lay att your prudence in
this mone I agreeing or by your neglect
to do it for in lies should Such an one
ever be killed &c I am a sworn frend
Robert [—]

[illegible lower lines]

PROLOGUE

Rogers Rangers might never have been born had not an 18th Century Confidence man stealthily approached young Robert Rogers in the Fall of 1754. Rogers was hunting at Martin's farm, near Goffstown, New Hampshire when John McDaniel, alias, "Sullivan of Boston", a notorious maker of counterfeit notes, approached him. Telling Rogers he was in the market for three yoke of oxen, he confidentially showed Rogers a handful of new bills and gave him one for pasturing his horse on Rogers' farm. Rogers, always anxious to turn an honest penny- or not so honest, hoped to get a large quantity of the counterfeit money and glancing nervously about, ushered "Sullivan" into Martin's house and made a deal in the presence of the Martin brothers; telling Sullivan that he would obtain the oxen and have them at Martin's farm at an appointed time.

Rogers asked his friend, John Stark, if he had any oxen to sell and Stark told him John McCurdy had some. Rogers, with visions of getting rich quick, arrived at the rendezvous with the oxen, only to find that Sullivan, alarmed, had fled the country. His bubble now burst, Rogers was later heard to grumble to John Stark that "he was cheated". Rogers was further disgruntled by the fact that McDaniel had not even left him his horse but had sold it to Nathaniel Martin before he fled. Rogers

made Nathaniel produce his brother, Samuel,
who had been a witness to the transaction and
then he reluctantly turned the horse over to
Nathaniel.

But, unfortunately for Rogers, the Martin
brothers and others, who had felt the illegal
flutter of "Boston Sullivan's" homemade money,
were hauled into the New Hampshire Inferior
Court at Rumford and their houses searched
"for any such Counterfeit bills and for any
Plate or Places for making such bills and for
any tool or instrument for making, cutting
such plates and to bring them in with any one:
concerned in making or knowingly passing any
such bills". There was strong evidence that
Rogers was implicated, in not only knowingly
passing the faked bills but in making the
money as well. A farmer, Garty Gilman, was
later dragged in and confessed that he had received several bills from Rogers, some of
which he had passed; the others he had returned. From this evidence it appears that Rogers
was either making the money or receiving it
from someone else. "Boston Sullivan" was no
longer around but there seems to be a possibility that Rogers had met him again while in
Boston in January, 1755, engaging with Major
Frye to enlist New Hampshire men for his battalion of Shirley's Massachusetts Provincial
regiment. Rogers could very well have been
Sullivan's go-between and returned to the
Merrimac Valley loaded with counterfeit money
as well as a commission to raise recruits.

Undoubtedly he had immediately set about to dispose of his money and raise recruits. Twenty four men had been enlisted and ordered to assemble at Portsmouth when his various enterprises were rudely interrupted by his arrest on February 7th. Rogers was tried with fifteen other suspects before the Inferior Court at Rumford. The two Joseph Blanchards, John Goffe and Matthew Thornton, were the Justices who conducted the examination. In an effort to detract attention from himself during the hearing Rogers stated that he had asked one of the Justices, Joseph Blanchard, Jr., to become his partner to discover if he was concerned in the counterfeiting. Rogers close friend, John Stark, was among those examined as witnesses and he tried to stand by him. Torn between the desire to tell the truth and still save Rogers, he revealed Rogers' conversation to him: "that he was cheated for he intended [selling the oxen to Sullivan] for a large quantity of Counterfeit money". However, he tried to help by adding that Rogers "said he would not be concerned anymore in any such things".

The general impression to be gained from the answers of Rogers to the Justices questions is that he had been temporarily led astray, in part by native dishonesty, in part by a rural want of judgment, but had early forsaken his evil course in alarm.

In spite of this impression and the fact that he had pleaded not guilty, Rogers was in a bad spot. The crime was punishable by death and the evidence against him was very incriminating. Four of those who were tried with Rogers were sent to jail, and five others besides Rogers were admitted to bond. Placed under bond of 500 pounds, Rogers was to appear before the Superior Court at Portsmouth on February 12th. He was badly frightened. Even if he did escape the extreme penalty he might be branded and have "both his ears crop'd" which was the customary light sentence for like criminals tried in the neighboring province of Massachusetts.

Rogers had only four days to find means of clearing himself. The first thing he had to do was try to keep his principal customers quiet. He wrote one of them, Garty Gilman, a farmer of Exeter, to destroy his counterfeit notes. His letter to Gilman reveals how scared he actually was: "Mr. Gilman, for God's sake do the work that you promised me that you would do. By no means fail, or you will destroy me foreever. Sir, my life lies at your providence, once more I adjure you by your Maker to do it, for why should such an honest man be killed?".

Meanwhile the twenty-four men whom he had enlisted for Massachusetts had gathered at Portsmouth. When Rogers arrived and saw them a happy thought struck him. Finding that Governor Wentworth of New Hampshire was raising a Regiment to serve in the Crown Point Expedition, Rogers managed to secure a commission from Wentworth himself, and the next day turned over all his recruits to the New Hampshire

Regiment. When the hour of his trial arrived on the 12th, he had so wormed his way into Wentworth's favor that he was admitted as King's evidence, and escaped scot free.

His crisis over, Rogers returned to the Merrimac Valley and set about enlisting the balance of his company and met with such success that he was given the Captaincy of the first Company of Blanchard's New Hampshire Regiment. When Major Frye of Massachusetts heard of Rogers' abscounding with his twenty-four recruits, he secured Governor Shirley's backing and complained to Wentworth of his conduct, stating that Rogers had secured his first volunteers by the use of the King's money, and demanding that he be given exemplary punishment for treacherously and illegally returning them to New Hampshire. Wentworth, however, shielded Rogers and replied that Frye's agreement with him was utterly irregular, and that since Rogers "whom I am told is recognized for a capital offense," was out of his reach.

"Captain Rogers" had so embedded himself in Wentworth's favor by raising so many recruits that all his subordinates followed suit and accepted Rogers and when Garty Gilman was hauled into Court on April 24th producing fresh and definite evidence against Rogers being involved in passing counterfeit notes, he was not bothered any further.

Consequently, out of this dramatic interlude in Rogers' life and by his adroit method of untying the Gallows' noose from about him,

Rogers Rangers were born in this shadow to step into the fray of the French and Indian War to establish a history that has seldom been equaled by a partisan military corps, for its daring accomplishments, heroic defeats, and virsitility of characters.*

---

*See Appendice A, p 264 for Documents on Rogers' Counterfeiting Trial.

CHAPTER I

1755

WINNING THEIR SPURS

Freed of the uncomfortable burden of facing the gallows Rogers could breath easier, but not too easily for after all he was literally on a probational status. He must prove to his probation officer, and protector, Governor Wentworth that he was worthy of saving from a *crow's banquet*. This opportunity was not long in coming. Wentworth had not saved Rogers because of any humanitarian impulses. He had long cherished for a safe frontier in the Coos Meadows region so that he might open up this rich territory to settlers and thus obtain 500 acres of the choisest land from each grant for himself.[1] The appearance of ominous war clouds offered Wentworth the two-fold opportunity of manipulating in real estate, under the cloak of protecting his New Hampshire frontier, at the same time affording him the chance of being a "military Governor". Although far from being the central figure in Wentworth's schemes, Rogers was a bold useful man and such characters were needed for his enterprises.

Rogers' first Company of Colonel Joseph Blanchard's New Hampshire Provincial Regiment consisted of approximately 50 men. Since they all had considerable experience in defending their homes against Indian raids, particularly St.

Francis Indian raiders, and were well versed in the lore of the woods gleaned from trapping beaver, hunting and pursuing Indians, they were called "Rogers Rangers" and constituted the Ranging Company of the Regiment.

Rogers had his own choice of officers. At first he only had one Lieutenant, an Ensign and a Clerk to keep the muster rolls which, if they were kept, have not been preserved for posterity. The Lieutenant was John Stark, Rogers close friend. Abraham Perry was the Ensign and Hugh Sterling the Clerk.[2] On October 4, Rogers' younger brother Richard entered the Company and on November 28, became Lieutenant.

Rogers Rangers belied their name in their first enterprise, instead they should have been called "Rogers Engineers", for their first activity of consequence was the building of a *Ghost Fort*.

Colonel Blanchard's Regiment was ordered by Governor Wentworth to rendezvous at the Fort in Stevenstown, subsequently Salisbury, and in that part of the town next to the Merrimack River, now constituting a part of Franklin. This fort had been built as a defense against the Indians, and was afterwards known as the Salisbury Fort. It was located on the well known farm of Daniel Webster. So little was known at that time of the geography of the New Hampshire frontier, that the "Coos Meadows"[3] on the Connecticut, above Lancaster, were believed to be on the direct route from the "Salisbury Fort" to Crown Point. Wentworth hoped to establish himself as a militarist by pushing his Regiment through to French held Crown Point by this legendary short-cut.[4]

Supposing that there was to be the opportunity of traveling most of the way by water, by means of the Merrimac, Connecticut and unchartered tributaries, the Regiment in rendezvous was kept busily at work building batteaus for the transportation of troops and stores, while Captain Robert Rogers was sent forward to the Coos Meadows with his Company of Rangers to build a fort there, for the occupation of the Regiment, and for resort in case of disaster. Rogers executed his commission and built a fort at the junction of the Ammonoosuc with the Connecticut, on the south side of the former river. This was called Fort Wentworth. After Rogers' return, and the Regiment had spent some weeks in building batteaus that could not be used for want of water, Wentworth discovered his error, and ordered his Regiment to proceed across the Province to Number Four and then to Crown Point via Albany. This fort upon the Ammonoosuc should have been called *Fort Folly* instead of Wentworth, for the fort as well as the batteaus never was of any use.[5]

_{Construction of Fort Wentworth*1}

Rogers did not forget this *ghost fort* though he had it constantly in mind when planning a base for his St. Francis raid as later events will prove.

*Documentary footnotes for activities and actions titled and numbered in consecutive order in the margins will be seen in Appendix II and III.- See Table of Contents for Appendix page numbers.

As can be seen, Rogers Rangers at this time were not on a permanent establishment as a distinct Corps. They had volunteered for the summer campaign against Crown Point like the rest of the Provincial troops and were supplied with food and blankets. The majority of Rogers' men wore their hunting frocks of deerskin and brought their own muskets. [6]

Several days after the New Hampshire Regiment arrived at the Albany rendezvous of Johnson's Crown Point Army, Rogers was called before Colonel Blanchard and given instructions to escort the provision wagons to the Carrying-Place soon to be called Fort Edward. But more important to Rogers' future was the note of introduction that Blanchard gave him for General Johnson at his army base at Fort Edward recommending the young adventurer "as a person well acquainted with the haunts and passes of the enemy and the Indian method of fighting". [7]

Accompanied by his own Company and one other, Rogers left Albany on August 20, and escorted the provision train to the site of Fort Edward. Here he soon found himself in the presence of the new General. Without his shady past to darken his introduction, Rogers presented a refreshing figure to Johnson who was sorely in need of efficient scouts. Rogers' self-confidence attracted Johnson and he was immediately sent out with small parties on several scouts towards the possible routes that a French army might approach by. [9]

Rogers' First Reconnoitres [2]

Rogers was on one of these scouts with a

tatchment of his Rangers up the Hudson River on the 8th of September when Baron Dieskau was made prisoner, and the French and Indians under him were defeated at Johnson's camp at the south end of Lake George.[10]

Rogers Hudson River Scout [3]

After Johnson's victory at "The Battle of Lake George" the general idea was for the army to move forward and take Crown Point, but instead, Johnson remained on the defensive and allowed the French to build Ticonderoga at the northern end of Lake George. The only conspicuous achievements of units of his army were performed by Rogers and his Rangers.[11] During the remainder of the campaign Rogers Rangers made eight successful expeditions towards Crown Point[12] and the new French fort[13] and reported on its construction and the number of troops advanced there.

Having repeated their engineering abilities by helping the New York Regiment build Fort Lyman (Edward) Rogers' Ranging Company and the rest of the New Hampshire Regiment joined Johnson at Lake George a few days after the battle (viz., sometime between the 9th and 14th of September).

Construction of Ft Lyman [4]

Rogers proved his capabilities as a scout in his first reconnaisance into French held territory. On the 14th of September, Johnson ordered Rogers "to reconnoitre the strength of the enemy at Crown Point". Embarking in a batteau with four men (two of his party were Connecticut Provincials, the other two, his own Rangers) Rogers landed at dawn on the west

The Gopher Scout [5]

side of Lake George,[14] near Bald Mountain, about
25 miles from Johnson's camp. They hid the
batteau and Rogers entrusted the two Connecticut men to remain and guard it while he marched with his own two Rangers through the woods
for three days to Crown Point. At night they
crept through the enemies picket lines, squirm-
ed across a small village to a newly dug entrenchment on a small hill connecting with the
main fort only thirty rods away. Here they
audaciously ate a cold meal and spent the night
while Rogers made several notes on the fortifications. This audacity caused the French considerable annoyance when they later discovered
the signs of unwelcome guests spending the
night inside their very fortifications.

Before dawn the three human gophers moved to
a large hill a mile west on the other side of
the fort to ascertain it from that angle. Here
they had a complete view of all worth seeing
and spent the day languoring on their stomachs
while leisurely observing the motions of the
enemy. Rogers notes that "some of (them) were
hunting Pidgeons all round in the Woods. Some
of which came within about 15 rods of (my
party)". But luckily they were not discovered
and remained undisturbed until night fall when,
slipping off the hill they started back for
Johnson's camp.

On the way they passed within two miles of
Ticonderoga, but could not stop to find out
how much of the new fortress had been built
as their "provisions were expended". They made

their return trip in less than two days but to their "great mortification" found that the two Connecticut men and the batteau "were gone and no provisions left". Rogers states that "this circumstance hastened us to (Johnson's) encampment with all possible speed where we arrived September (23, late at night) not a little fatigued and distressed with hunger and cold".

The two Connecticut men undoubtedly had returned to camp as they were not captured. However there is no record of them being punished for neglecting their duty. Johnson was almost forced to make up his scouting parties with men from different Colonies so that none would feel slighted. A situation which caused a slackening of obedience especially when the men were under officers other than their own.

Four days later, on September 27, Rogers and his Rangers were again sent on a scout. This time in a party of five to Ticonderoga to find out how the new fort was progressing and also the numbers of the French and Indians there. Receiving his orders on the 27th, Rogers traversed Lake George that night passing several enemy campfires of Indian patrols. When he arrived at a point of land (now called Friend's Point) on the east side, near Isle au Mouton, he followed his former procedure and left three men with the canoe, while with the other two he launched forward and spotted a large advance guard at the end of Lake George. Crawling through the guards they counted close to one thousand men there. Slipping out they hur-

Rogers Ambuscade near Isle au Mouton[1]

ried on to Ticonderoga and saw them lay the foundation of a fort.

Remaining within the fortifications that night (of September 28th) they started back late the next morning. On their return they lingered at the north end of Lake George long enough to note a bark canoe with nine Indians and a Frenchman in it going up the lake. They kept sight of them until they passed the point of land where Rogers canoe was hid. When Rogers arrived at his canoe hideout his three Rangers there informed him that the enemy had landed on an island five miles to the south in the middle of the lake. In a short time they left the island and started back for Ticonderoga. Whether they had seen the flash of a musket barrel of one of Rogers' men, or actually intended to land at the point is not known; but the canoe headed straight for Rogers' party. However, Rogers Rangers were ready for them. Rogers says: "we put ourselves in readiness to receive them in the best manner we could, and gave them a salute at about 100 yards distance which reduced their number to four" and disabled two more. Then jumping into their own canoe the Rangers pursued the four survivors down the lake until three canoes filled with savages relieved them and Rogers and his small party were in turn pursued most of the way back to the American Army at the other end of Lake George. This little odyssey was the first skirmish of Rogers Rangers. Although, a mere ambuscade, it was the only brush of Johnson's army with the enemy since the Battle of Lake George and the whole army heard and repeated Rogers' latest adventure. Seth Pomeroy called it "a bold adventure".

The first scout of Rogers to Crown Point and his successful ambuscade on Lake George established him in Johnson's favor and although in the next week Rogers' Regiment returned to New Hampshire, the terms of the men's enlistments being up, Johnson prevailed on Rogers to remain "with a few of /his/ men", [15] to continue scouting and insure the safety of his army. Rogers' decision to stay not only insured the safety of the army but insured the growth of his fame as a Ranger. Although they knew that they might not be paid for their services, 28 men, half of Rogers' Ranging Company of Blanchard's New Hampshire Regiment were cajoled into remaining by Rogers' persuasive personality. Most of them were personal friends of Rogers and though they were now serving with him as volunteers they composed the nucleous of "Rogers Rangers". At the same time Sergeant Richard Rogers and Private Jonathan Sillaway of Captain William Simes tenth Company of Blanchard's resigned and joined Rogers' little Company swelling its numbers to thirty strong.[16]

Twelve of these thirty "originals" served with Rogers for the six years of the French and Indian War or until they were killed or captured. Rogers did not forget their willingness to remain with him and five of them became prominent officers in the corps of Rogers Rangers and the remainder all became Sergeants.[17] Rogers' former officers, Lieutenant John Stark[18] and Ensign Abraham Perry; and Clerk Hugh Sterling, left with the New Hampshire Regiment so Rogers unofficialy appointed his younger brother Richard to the Lieutenantcy and Noah Johnson to the Ensigncy of the twenty eight remaining Volunteers. This little Company of Rogers' original Rangers served as Volunteers from October 6, to November 25, 1755.

The fame of Rogers and his Rangers was growing after their first little ambuscade but unfortunately there were personages in the army and out who were jealous of Rogers justly rewarded praise. Men, who no doubt knew of his Counterfeiting Trial, for they were quick to drop sly inuendos against his character, some of them, as they were intended, reached the ears of Johnson. But to no avail, for he recognized Rogers as "the most active man in (his) army"[19] and repeatedly stood up for him. On October 13, Johnson in writing to Governor Fitch, calls Rogers "a brave and honest Man"[20] and again to Governor Sir Charles Hardy of New York, on October 13, his good opinion of Rogers is clearly set forth: "Captain Rogers whose Bravery & Veracity stands very clear in my Opinion & all who know him, though his Regiment is gone he remains here a Volunteer, & is the most active Man in our Army. Tomorrow he proposes to set off with two or three picked men to take a review if he can of Tionderogo & proceed to Crown Point for a prisoner. I have mentioned Captain Rodgers more particularly as I have Understood some Insinuations have been made to his Disadvantage. I believe him to be as brave & as honest a Man as any I have equal knowledge of, & both myself & all the Army are convinced that he has distinguished himself since he has been among us, superior to most, inferior to none of his Rank in these Troops."[21]

On October 7, one week after their safe arrival from their thrilling canoe chase, Rogers embarked with his complete force of 30 Rangers and ten others from various Provincial Regiments who virtually clambered to join the expedition.

The Decoy Scout

Johnson was alarmed at Rogers' report of the presence of enemy patrols upon Lake George. Consequently he sent "his most active man" to execute the following orders:

Orders "to Captain Robert Rodgers," from "Camp at Lake George, October 7, 1755...You are to embark with the party under your command, and land with them on one of the nearest and most convenient islands in the lake towards the carrying place and Ticonderoga and then send out three or four proper persons to reconnoitre the enemy thereabouts and make what discoverys they can; you are then to send out the Birch Canoe as a bait for the enemy, and to remain with the rest of the party, in order to succor and assist them if pursued, or to circumvent the enemy, for which purpose you are to be in constant readiness with your

Men and Battoes and keep a good lookout..."

The French were too alert after the Rangers last escapade and Rogers' expedition returned on the 12th without any success in trying to decoy the enemy into several ambuscades they had prepared.

Rogers' Scalp Scout[7]

This plan was put aside for awhile and two days later Rogers was again ordered to Crown Point with Israel Putnam and three Rangers to attempt to take a prisoner. Arriving within 300 yards of the fort, Rogers left his three Rangers in a thicket of willows while he and Putnam crept nearer to a large pine log and concealed themselves by holding bushes in their hands. Shortly after sunrise French soldiers came out of Crown Point in such numbers that they could not possibly re-join their comrades in the willows without being discovered. Rogers and Putnam were in great peril and could only hope to escape discovery by lying as quiet as the earth until the French re-entered the fortress, fortunately, this soon happened. But Rogers was determined to get a prisoner and although he and Putnam were now free, they lingered on behind the pine log. They were soon rewarded by a soldier coming out alone. When he was within ten yards Rogers sprang on him from behind the log and pointed his fusee at his chest demanding his surrender. But the Gaul was a huge fellow and preferred to fight it out. Calling to a nearby guard he pulled a dirk and a fierce fight took place. Rogers had been, and still was for that matter, the undisputed champion wrestler of northern New Hampshire, but here he had met his match. The two men were in a desperate death-hold when Putnam nearby saw the other guard approaching. He rushed to the aid of Rogers and ended the dual by striking the Frenchman a fatal blow over the head with the butt of his musket.

By now the garisson was aroused and Rogers and Putnam re-joined the three Rangers and beat a hasty retreat with the pursuers close on their heels, but not before Rogers whipped out his scalping knife and cut away the Frenchman's scalp. Rogers excited shocked horror among weak-stomached Provincials in camp when he displayed his grisly trophy.

Eight days after they arrived exhausted into camp Rogers received orders on October 29, to try again Johnson's plan to intercept the enemy canoe patrols which were reported by a French deserter as being sent out every day to advance as close to the American camp as they dared, to make what discoveries they could. Johnson in another letter to Governor Hardy on October 31, expresses his hope that Rogers would make a successful stroke against the enemy "if the enemy comes in his way". Battle of the Isle of Mutton[2]

Rogers was just as anxious to engage with them and he spared no pains in outfitting his expedition to make it as formidable as the weapons of the time permitted without sacrificing speed of movement. In each of four batteaus he mounted a miniature cannon called wall-pieces, which were a rare small-arm ordinarily used over parapets. They had a barrel of 4 feet 6 inches, a bore of .91, weighed 35 pounds, 2 ounces, and shot balls numbering 6 2/5 to the pound. It could be served very effectively on a batteau as Rogers soon proved.

Rogers' force consisted of acting Lieutenant Richard Rogers, acting Ensign Noah Johnson, and twenty six of his now thirty private Rangers (as private John Kidder and Nathaniel Smith of Goffe's second Company of Blanchard's Regiment had resigned on October 23, and returned to Johnson's camp to serve as volunteers with Rogers); besides, Captains Israel Putnam and Fletcher, Lieutenants Noah Grant and John Durkee of the Connecticut Provincials. At least one Indian of the four in Rogers Rangers, accompanied the expedition. Including himself, Rogers' party numbered thirty three chosen men.

Rogers received Johnson's orders on October 29, the 30th, he spent in outfitting his expedition and armoring his *flotilla* with the wall pieces. They embarked quietly that night to evade the daring day-patrols of the enemy.

Cruising down Lake George in the clear cold night, Rogers with his little amphibious force arrived shortly before dawn within half a mile of the advanced guard's camp on the west side of the lake. Landing his little force he had the Rangers hide the batteaus and sent Putnam, Durkee and Fletcher to reconnoitre the strength of the advanced guard. After posting sentries, Rogers told his men to try and get some sleep as they would probably see plenty of action in the next twenty four hours.

Captain Fletcher returned the following evening and reported that the enemy had no fortifications about their camp and that they lay open to an assault. Rogers immediately sent Fletcher with six Rangers as an escort to General Johnson with this information, asking for a sufficient force to attack them. One of Rogers' four Indian Rangers was included with the escort. He was sent especially to guide the relief force to Rogers. Further reducing Rogers' original force were six Rangers who were all sick. They crawled into the batteau and returned with Fletcher.

This left Rogers force at twenty men, besides himself. However, all of them were of Rogers' own Rangers with the exception of Grant; and, Putnam and Durkee who were still out scouting. Rogers states that "being un Easie with [Fletcher's] Report, I took [one of the three remaining] batteau with five men and went down within 25 Rods of their Fires, Discovered a Small Fort with Several Small Log Camps within ye Fort which I judged to Contain about ¼ of an acre. Said Fort being open towards ye Water, The rest Picketted. Made no further Discovery there and Returnd to My Party, found all well except Captain Putnam and ye Spie with him, who was not returned.."

The next morning about ten o'clock Putnam and Durkee returned to substantiate Rogers' reconnoitre. They had a narrow escape; but re-

vealed Rogers' position: The French campfires,
instead of being placed, according to the English
custom, round the camp, were grouped in
the center of it; their men were stationed
circularly, and the sentinels posted still
farther in the surrounding darkness. After
Fletcher left them they crept closer towards
the camp, expecting to see the sentinels within
the circle of fires, but suddenly found
themselves inside the hostile lines. The guards
discovered the scouts and fi d at them. In
their flight in the darkness, Putnam soon stumbled
into a clay pit. His companion, although
shot in the thigh, followed not far behind,
and he, too, fell into the pit. Putnam, supposing
his pursuer to be one of the enemy, was
about to strike him with his hatchet, but at
that moment recognized the voice of Durkee,
who inquired whether he had escaped, uninjured.
They leaped out of the pit together, and although
again fired upon reached a ledge not far
distant. "There they betook themselves to a
large log," by the side of which they lodged
the remainder of the night. Before they lay
down, Captain Putnam said he had a little rum
in his canteen, which could never be more acceptable
or necessary; but on examining the
canteen, which hung under his arm, he found
the enemy had pierced it with their musket
balls, and that there was not a drop left.

Soon after their return to Rogers' camp, two
Frenchmen appeared on the crest of a hill overlooking
the camp. They called, and receiving

no answer disappeared. In a few minutes, two canoes with 30 men in them were sent against Rogers. The war-canoes soon appeared and lay in the middle of the lake forty rods apart. From their behaviour, Rogers surmised that they were waiting for a land party to arrive and thus catch him between two fires.

For the first time in his young life, Rogers' ability as a commander of men in battle was put to the test. If his judgement proved wrong he and his whole force would probably be anihilated. He had three alternatives: to abandon the batteaus and breaking his twenty men up into small parties retreat by land to the American Army before the French land party arrived. If his parties were lucky enough to evade pursuit his judgement in retreating might be looked upon by Johnson and the Army as a cautious move. Then again it might not, if any of the retreating Rangers were cut off Rogers' jealous enemies would be quick to promote claims against his bravery. Rogers' second alternative was to place his men in a state of defence and attempt to hold off the enemy who would be on all sides of him, until Johnson's reenforcements arrived - if they could arrive in time.

It was obvious to Rogers that if he retreated his courage might be doubted, still the latter plan of defence might prove suicidal, for he had no idea how large a force might yet be sent against him. No, this crisis called for a daring aggressive manouvre, and Rogers' following decision cast the die and established his fame as "a bold usefull man".

Darting his eyes quickly over his seventeen Rangers and three Connecticut officers, he ordered Lieutenant Noah Grant and acting Sergeant, John McCurdy with five men into one of the batteaus while he launched another with Ensign Noah Johnson and five other Rangers aboard and proceeded to attack. To complete his manouvre, Rogers left seven men on shore (viz: Captain Putnam, Lieutenants Richard Rogers, and Durkee; and four Rangers).

In order to decoy the enemy within range of his wall-pieces mounted on the batteaus, Rogers steered his *ships* as if intending to pass by them. His ruse worked completely for the enemy canoes closed in to head him off. When they were within a hundred yards, Rogers' flotilla discharged their wall-pieces, killing several of the Indians and creating havoc among the two canoes, who in attempting to get out of range of Rogers' fire, came in too close to the shore, where they received a galling fire. from Putnam's detatchment. The Indian canoes had sprung several leaks from this deadly cross fire, and while half of their number were furiously bailing out the water, the remaining survivors were paddling desperately to get out of the range of fire. At this time, Rogers saw the French land party approaching Putnam. He shouted a warning to Putnam's force who, hurriedly stowing the wounded Durkee on the remaining batteau, they embarked under cover of Rogers' and Grant's fire. They held the superior force of the expected French land party at bay until Putnam's six men were afloat and out of range on the lake.

This was a close call for Rogers' land party. He reports that Putnam "had but Just time to Shove his Battoe into ye Water, and Gett into [it] Before ye Enemy appeared upon ye Waters Edge and Made a Brisk fire upon him Shot thro' his Blanket in Divers Places, and thro' ye Battoe".

Rogers' *navy* now pursued the Indian canoes and managed to get close enough to deliver another broadside into them which drove all thoughts of engagement from their minds and completely dispersed them, Rogers and his little squadron hotly pursued them down the lake to their landing, within eighty rods of their advance fort which the French called "Coutre Coeur". Here the two Indian canoes were received and covered by one hundred French Regulars, upon whom, Rogers discharged another broadside at forty rods distance, and drove them from the shore "into the bushes".

Due to the nearness of Ticonderoga and the superior force that he had temporarily dispersed, Rogers did not feel it wise to linger any longer in the neighborhood, and withdrew triumphantly to the American encampment at the end of Lake George. He had accomplished his assignment and successfully engaged the French advance guard of over 150 men and drove them from the lake with only twenty men. It was just such audacious and brilliant strokes that made Rogers and his Rangers famous, and also irksome in the extreme, to the French and Indians. Having squelched all thoughts of any pursuit of them, Rogers' victorious crews paddled serenely homeward. Rogers says "after we Got fairly into ye Lake [we] Lay upon our Oars and Inquired after the Circomstances of ye Party. Found none killed, but one Wounded, which Gave Joy to all of us after so Long an Engagement, which I Judge was near 2 Hours." About half way up the lake they met Johnson's reenforcement under Captain Billings, "but upon Consultation, Thought best to report [to Johnson] what had happened".

Rogers' victory definitly established him as the foremost, and only, for that matter, partisan fighter, of Johnson's army. His fame reflected likewise on his followers, and the name "Rogers Rangers" echoed from the army camp to firesides in New England in the letters and diaries of the literary minded Provincials who penned down what they saw and did. Although this little *Battle of the Isle au Mouton* had only the sole effect of dampening the frequency of enemy patrols on Lake George, still it was a brilliantly executed manouvre. There were no actions of Rogers Rangers at any future time that were more successfully executed, either in their completeness of victory of boldness of execution.

The *Battle of the Isle of Mutton* stands forth as the first Battle Honour of Rogers

Rangers. Though it was only a mere skirmish as far as numbers were concerned, still the numbers of the Rangers and the enemy throughout the war were frequently small and the term *Battle* must be considered by the intensity of the action rather than by the size of the forces engaged, if a list of Battle Honours is to be established for the Corps.

Johnson was well pleased with his young protege (Rogers was only 23 at the time of his first *Battle*). He immediately dictated to his secretary the news of Rogers' success and enclosed a copy of Rogers' official report to Governor "Sir Charles" Hardy. Although the packet was entrusted with a Provincial Sergeant, he somehow lost it with his pack of clothes enroute to Albany. But Johnson wrote others of the victory, including persons who had held doubts as to Rogers' veracity, among them Goldsbrow Banyar. Banyar was the Deputy Clerk of the Supreme Court of New York and he was in a position to know the details of Rogers' Counterfeiting Trial, and like others, had not overlooked this unfortunate incident of Rogers' career to justify jealous sentiments of Rogers' advancing fame. He seems to have particularly resented the fact that Johnson took the *Young Criminal* under his wing. When Rogers made his second scout of the campaign, towards the French forts (September 27-29,) he reported on the numbers of French at Ticonderoga, and their advanced guard at Lake George. But a French deserter left Ticonderoga a few days after this scout and informed Johnson that the numbers were considerable less than Rogers reported. Johnson notes this fact in writing to Governor Hardy. Banyar, being informed of it, writes Johnson from Albany, "I may be in error but don't believe a single Syllable of Rogers' explanation. The life of the deserter is in our Power, who might be forced to give an accurate account". But Johnson's excellent expression of his fine opinion of Rogers is revealed in his October 13th letter to Hardy already mentioned (on pp 32-33). On October 18th, Banyar made one last effort to blackball Rogers. He writes Johnson: "I don't know if it be from anything I have wrote that you conclude doubts are entertained here of Captain Rogers's veracity: I mean & still think he was imposed upon himself, & indeed to what cause can you impute his mistake, which made almost thousands instead of hundreds [at Ticonderoga]. I think you push the Point a little too far in your Letter in his behalf unless Sir Charles had given Occassion for it in any of his Letters.." However, after he received the news of Rogers' victory, Banyar seems to have given up his sly inuendos, for he writes to Johnson, November 11th: "..However exaggerated his accounts are thought here to be [of the numbers at Ticonderoga], every one says he is a bold usefull man, and deserves well of the Publick.."

This controversy, finally at an end,[22] shows, that although Rogers was legally freed of the

penalty for passing counterfeit notes, his
character, at the very beginning of his military career was shadowed with his crime. A
fact which made Rogers all the more anxious to
excel in partisan warfare,[23] in an effort to
obliterate the stains of his past. Fortunately,
he was gifted with the requisites of an energetic Ranger Chieftan, and this, coupled with
his desire to redeem himself, made it not surprising that his exploits were on the successfully daring side.

No longer than three days passed after he had returned from his successful engagement, than Rogers, with ten of his men, was again within the enemy lines at Ticonderoga, to determine their exact strength and progressing fortifications not to mention stopping off to take a curious peek at "Coutre Coeur", their last objective. *Sixth French Fort Scout*[8]

Returning to Johnson's camp about 9 o'clock at night on November 11, they were followed an hour later by two Mohawks who had been out for two weeks, supposedly scouting towards Ticonderoga, but they must have been laying up some place well removed from the French lines, for, anxious to create attention, they concocted a tall yarn of seeing a large French army advancing and only about fifteen miles from the American camp. This belied both Rogers' and Putnam's reports. Rogers firmly stated he had only seen ten men as an advance guard this side of the Second Narrows. Putnam had not come in yet with a similar report but until he did four *Nov 11-15, Alarm*[9] days later the camp was in an uproar. The complete American army stood on their arms that night and scouts were thrown out the next two days. On the fourteenth Rogers made a scout down the lake about fourteen miles and reported that the French advance guard there had been strengthened and because of this there was a probability of "a large army about that distance". Upon receiving this news fifty drums "beat to arms" and Johnson's army held themselves in readiness until the following day when Putnam returned from his two weeks scout with the relieving news "that there (was) no French army". He states that he "..saw no Enemy but saw large Incampments where they (had) Landed their Battos..". The alarm was now at an end. Nevertheless, Johnson wanted to keep an eye on the French to determine if, and when they were going into Winter quarters, or whether they might be considering advancing on him despite the lateness of the season. Accordingly, Lieutenant Richard Rogers was sent by Johnson, on November 16, to recoinotre Ticonderoga and Crown Point. Accompaning him were Daniel Claus, a trusted associate of Johnson's and two Mohawks, Hendrick and Henry. They successfully scouted Ticonderoga and hurrying on to Crown Point attempted to take a prisoner, but the coldness of the weather kept the French within their fortress, and no such opportunity presented itself. Returning to the American camp, they arrived on the 25th of November to find Rogers forming a distinct Company of Ran-

Richard Rogers' Scout [10]

gers for Winter service. Richard Rogers conveyed his report to General Johnson now in Albany, who breathed a sigh of relief when Rogers informed him that the bulk of the French were retiring to Canada leaving only garrisons at Crown Point and Ticonderoga. Returning to Fort William Henry on November 28, Richard Rogers stepped into the Lieutenantcy of his brother's Ranging Company,[24] which Rogers had held open for him.

While brother Richard was scouting northward Rogers "had a month's repose",[25] during which time his first distinct Ranger Company was formed. On November 25, drums were rolled to beat up for Volunteers to garrison Forts Edward, and William Henry (which Johnson named the new fort he built at his encampment).

Rogers describes the raising of his Company as follows: "It was judged that it would be of great use to have one Company of woodsmen or Rangers under my command to make excursions towards the enemy's Forts during the winter. I accordingly remained, and did duty the whole winter.."[25]

Rogers' officers were Richard Rogers, Lieutenant; Noah Johnson, Ensign. James Archibald and John McCurdy were the Sergeants. James McNeal and Nathaniel Johnson, Corporals. All of Rogers' Volunteer New Hampshire Rangers who had served the campaign, entered the Company forming the nucleous. The remaining ten were Provincial would-be-Rangers from Colonel Peter Gilman's lately arrived but short servicing

Second New Hampshire Regiment; five joined on November 26, one on the 28th, three others on December 13, and Private John Leighton joined on December 14, swelling Rogers' Company to forty three officers and men.[27]

This Company had no uniform. "They Cloath themselves and [were] very ragged [consequently] they catch cold..". Most of the men wore the Indian Leggings. Some wore the hunting shirt, while others sported jackets or coats with the long tails cut off. They carried whatever arms and camp equippage that they might own.[28] Although, like most Provincial troops they were nondescript in appearance, seventy five per cent of them were veterans of Rogers' daring odysseys and they soon imparted their woodland knowledge and partisan methods of warfare to the ten New Hampshire recruits.

The Fishermen Scout [11]
In spite of the forbidding weather, Captain Rogers went to Ticonderoga on one last scout for the year. In his typical unasuming style, Rogers gives his customary detailed "report of a Scout": "On the 19th [of December] I set out by Orders with three Men to make discoverys of the French and the Situation of their Fort at Tianderoga. We Paddled in a Battoe about 15 Miles down the Lake and saw a fire on an Island, then we turned our Course and landed our Battoe on the West side of the lake by the Great Mountain and Lodged there that Night.

The 20th day [of December] we Travelled by Land towards Tionderago about 20 Miles and Camped in a Pleasant Place between two Mountains, nothing remarkable happened this day.

The 21st we went on our Course towards Tionderogo and about 12 of the Clock we Came in plain sight of the French Fort, where we discovered their Men busy at Work all of them excepting the Guards, some were Sawing Boards, others Shaving Clapboards, some of them were at Work finishing their Barracks, some drawing stones with Horses, and others were Exercising themselves shooting at Marks with the Indians there. There are two large Barracks in said Fort and some small Houses and several on the outside of the Fort and Men living in some of them. On the North West Bastion were mounted two Cannon; two laid on Wheels by the Gate and four or five pointing towards the Lake. On the East and South East part of the Fort, I tryed to Number their Men but could not do it, they were going about their Secular Affairs so busy, but my Judgement was that there were about 500. In the evening we advanced nearer the Fort and way laid a Road in order to take a Prisoner or get a scalp. The said Road led towards Lake George. About half an Hour after we set our Ambush, there came ten Men by us within 8 Rods but we were so weak we durst not fire on them, and so let them pass. A few minutes after, there came a Company of Indians over from the East side of the Lake on the Ice loaded with Venison & Skins. Just about Sunset there went 5 Men with a Horse & Cart for a Load of Wood to the Northside of the Fort and went beyond the Clear Land into the Woods. Then we left our Ambush in order to fall upon said five, but before we could get near enough to them they had got their Wood and were returning to the Fort so we sat down till it was quite dark intending to wait till the Morning & try them again but it was so cold we could not sit still, and were oblidg'd to keep moving, and went softly down to one of their Hutts which they had left and went into it for a shelter from the cold, and about break of Day next Morning the Snow fell so fast that we were oblidged to retreat. [We] travell'd homewards that day about 25 Miles and Camped yet lay in fear of a pursuit and by Break of day next Morning set out homewards. Within about two Miles of our Battoe we Came upon a Flock of Deer and kill'd two of them. With the utmost Expedition dress'd them and made to our Battoe and Launched it ready to set homewards.. [We]. dugg up our Bottle which we had hid with about one Quart of Rum in it which revived our Spirits greately. Then set home with good Courage and about 2 of the Clock in the Morning Arrived at Fort William Henry in a good time to hold Christmas."

So ended the first campaign of Rogers Rangers. Out of eight scouts performed by Rogers and his men towards Ticonderoga and Crown Point, two of them were engagements with the enemy and most of the remaining six were so daring in their execution as to well establish the name of Rogers and "Rogers Rangers".[28] They had won their spurs and Rogers had wiped his slate clean.

CHAPTER II

1756

FALCONS OF THE LAKES

Like all northern New York winters, the winter of 1755-56 was fierce, and was not fit for "man nor beast" to be out in. But Colonel Benjamin Gleasier's scouting Company at Fort William Henry were neither man nor beast, but 'Rogers Rangers'. Consequently they did not remain phelegmatic at their winter station instead they stepped out of the fort into the forbidding weather and executed three daring excursions against the enemy.

Their prime objective was the taking of prisoners as they were the most valuable source of information in discovering what reenforcements Crown Point and Ticonderoga had received and what improvements had been made on their fortifications.

On January 14, Rogers marched out of the fort with seventeen of his men. At the lake's edge they put on ice skates and skimmed swiftly down Lake George. Arriving at the waterfall at the end of the lake on the second day, they remained in the bushes and ate a cold meal washed down with rum. As night descended they marched over the snow across the narrow neck that separated Lake George and Lake Champlain. Putting on their skates, the Rangers skated quietly by the lights of Ticonderoga and out

Rogers' Raid at Five Mile Point 12

over the frozen surface of Lake Chanplain.
Rogers' plan was to waylay any small parties
of the enemy that might be passing on the lake
between Ticonderoga and Crown Point. Strategically picking a point of land on the east
shore of the lake which would bring any passing parties within musket-shot, Rogers Rangers lay quietly in ambush – and waited.

They were rewarded shortly after sunrise by
the appearance of "two Frenchmen with a horse
and slay loaded with fresh beef" for Ticonderoga. The Rangers: "immediately made them
prisoners". "Rogers would have brought off the
sleigh with /its four or five quarters of beef/
but hearing a gun fire, and observing a number
of men coming upon him from Crown Point on
their skates, he sunk the sleigh with the
horse and beef, under the ice," and returned
unscathed to Fort William Henry where they arrived with the two prisoners on January 17th.

French held territory was not the only locale for the adventures of Rogers Rangers. On
January 21, one of Rogers' men was scouting
alone late in the afternoon, upon a mountain
west of Fort William Henry, when he was fired
upon by an Indian in ambush. The shot missed
him and the Ranger quickly returned the compliment killing the Indian. He had dug his
fingers into the Indian's greasy hair and was
on the point of scalping him when he saw eight
more Indians howling down upon him like so
many wolves. Relinquishing a *'Ranger's spoils
of war'* he managed to outrun the human wolf

A Rangers' Odyssey[13]

pack until darkness and a fortunate snow-fall covered his tracks. When dawn broke he found himself in the vicinity of Fort Edward and stumbled into the fort exhausted to mumble his harrowing escape to the commandant, Nathan Whiting, who, relating the story to Johnson, aptly remarked: "may they always be so disappointed in all their attempts upon us".

Nine days after his return, Rogers set out again for Crown Point, with orders from Commandant Gleasier to "take a view of that fortress". "If you meet Indians or any enemy in your way you are to take them prisoners or kill them, or distress them any other ways or means your prudence shall direct you". Rogers' party consisted of his Company of Rangers and six volunteers. This was the first expedition of his complete Company and proved the most successful excursion of Rogers' own winter campaign. *Rogers' First Crown Point Village Raid*[14]

Arriving within sight of the fort, they climbed a steep mountain and Rogers made a map of the fortifications. In the evening they descended and formed an ambuscade on each side of the road that led from the fort to a village half a mile away. One prisoner was captured and two more were almost taken but managed to out-run the Rangers to the fort, although some of Rogers Rangers pursued them to within musket-fire of the gate. The whole garrison was aroused, drums were rolling the call to arms and a strong party was sent out. In the meantime Rogers had hurriedly ordered his party to set fire to the houses and barns of the village, which contained large quantities of grain. They also managed to slaughter fifty cattle and retire safely, leaving most of the village in flames. The next morning one of Rogers' party was taken sick and Rogers dropped behind with seven Rangers to cover his slow retreat. The bulk of the party he sent on ahead. The next day, on February 6, he arrived at Fort William Henry with his rear-guard to find all of his party safe.

The gaps between these daring raids were punctuated by the *minutie* of Provincial garrison life recorded by Captain Jeduthan Baldwin: On January 22, they "had a dance". On February 1, Lieutenant Woodwell and 16 of the carpenters were sent home; and five days later three Provincials including a future officer of Rogers Rangers, Samuel Shepherd of Canterbury, New Hampshire, got homesick and deserted. On the 14th, Provincial Private John Doty, got the same longing but was caught and "put under guard". The next day he was "tried & received 10 lashes". This put a stop to any more outward expressions of homesickness. On the 17th, the garrison "shot at marks" and two Frenchmen came in from Crown Point. The 19th, saw Captain Baldwin at Captain Rogers' quarters for dinner, which probably consisted of fresh venison or ration fare of Salt Beef, peas, rice, bread and butter, washed down with rum; cooked and served by Rogers' orderly or *servant*.

The customary New England piety seems to be

lacking for Baldwin notes in his *Diary* with shocked italics on a Sunday entry: "Being Lord's Day,..*Hardly anything of religion to be seen*.." When the weather permitted the garrison were able to indulge in their New England sport of fishing on a frozen lake. A hole was cut in the frozen surface of Lake George. A fire-pot was set to keep the fisherman from freezing while he dangled his line in the hole. All hands served in gathering wood for fuel. Another necessary task was that of salting down fresh beef. Beef was the principal meat rationed to the men and there are frequent entries of them "salting beef". Several excursions were made across the lake to the west side to obtain copper which had been discovered there. Even cedar-cutting forays were made for the construction of whaleboats; a craft much used in the near future by Rogers Rangers.

Like preying falcons Rogers Rangers made yet another swoop on Crown Point during a season when all normal mortals would have been forced to remain indoors. On the last day of February Rogers started his third foray of the year. The day before, on the 28th, Fort William Henry buzzed with excitement as busy preparations were made "for a Scout of 15 days". *Rogers' Second Crown Point Village Raid* 15

Rogers' force consisted of Captains Israel Putnam, Parker and Jeduthan Baldwin, and sixty two men including the bulk of his Rangers.

Marching down the west side of Lake George they continued directly north for six days. Interesting details of the march are revealed in Captain Baldwin's *Diary:* The first day, the 29th, they marched twelve miles. March 1, five men were reported sick and they were sent back. The expedition continued northward for fourteen more miles and Baldwin notes that they saw a wolf chase a deer into the [lake]". March 2, they arose at sunrise marched over "Parker's Mountain" chalking up ten more miles they camped on the low lands of Lake George "not on feather beds but on hemlock boughs". March 3, marched thirteen miles over mountains in four inches of fresh slippery snow. The 4th travelled northeast eleven more miles. On the 5th they marched northeast until eleven a.m. when they came opposite to Crown Point, eight miles away to the east. Then altering their course they marched about six miles north until they had cut across to Lake Champlain.

Rogers' Ranger Indians had informed him that he would find an inhabited village about here. But to their disappointment they found nothing but virgin wilderness. It seems that at this time Rogers' knowledge of the country directly above Crown Point was limited. However, his quick perception and ability to remember landmarks made it necessary for him to travel over a strange piece of terrain but once to remember it. No party of Rangers led by Rogers ever became lost. His men had complete confidence in his uncanny *homeing pigeon* instinct.

Camping in sight of Crown Point without any fires they held a council of war and it was decided to try and cross the lake in the dark and way-lay the St. Johns' road on the east side. About 2 a.m the next morning they started out with Rogers in the lead, but when they reached the craggy shore Rogers slipped and plunged twenty-six feet into the thinly ice covered lake. "With much difficulty he got out, but it prevented [their] crossing [that] morning as the ice was too weak". They lingered out of sight all that day and that night at 3 a.m Rogers and three men gingerely tried again to see if the ice would bear them but found it still too thin. The plan to cross the lake was now abandoned and it was decided to waylay a possible road from Crown Point to Ticonderoga. Accordingly they marched south 12 miles to the road and lay in the woods directly outside of the outlying barns and houses on the outskirts of the little village that Rogers had fired on his last visit. Remaining in the woods until nightfall they slipped foreward to within a mile and a half of "the upper village". Hiding their packs in a barn on the Point, they went through the plowed fields making a large track. Dividing forces, Captain Baldwin with twenty-three men posted themselves in a house while Rogers, Parker and Putnam hid in the barn about eighty rods distance with thirty-four men.

All day they waited in ambush expecting the labourers out to tend their cattle and clean their grain, of which there were several barns full. No one appearing, Rogers and Parker went forward to reconnoitre but could find no French outside of the walls. Rogers and the three Captains decided not to wait around any longer in their precarious position. That night at 9 p.m they fired two houses and nine barns filled with eight hundred bushels of wheat, peas and oats. Unfortunately, one of Rogers' Indians was asleep in the second barn set afire and he was mortally burned before they could drag him out. He had to be carried in the four mile march homeward they made after firing the farm buildings. That night, March 8, Rogers' Raiders "Lodgd in wet land". The following day they marched eighteen miles according to Baldwin, and during the day they came to La Barbue or Putnam's Creek, waded across, and followed it southwest for several miles carrying the burned Indian Ranger. That night they again "Lodgd without fire".

A conference was held and it was decided to leave Captains Rogers and Putnam with seven men including the other Indian Ranger in the expedition, "in order to find a good wagon road to or by the Carolong [Ticonderoga] rapids". Which, if one existed, would be of good use to the expected American or English assault in the summer. Captain Baldwin was to lead the rest of the detail home and send down batteaus on the lake for Rogers' detatchment.

Baldwin relates the progress of his detail to Fort William Henry: They marched southward fifteen miles that day reaching Trout Brook; marched down the brook six miles crossing a day old track of a French and Indian scout of one hundred and sixty men. Evidently this party had seen the raging fire on Crown Point's horizon and suspected that Rogers Rangers had made another visit, for Baldwin found angry warnings written on the trees at their last camp stating that "if they caught [them] they would burn [them] or [Rogers] should [burn] them directly". The French were not far from wrong in the latter part of their philosophical warning, for this second raid of Rogers' on Crown Point village had practically wiped out all the outlying settlements near the fortress (the first raid had literally levelled the village proper while the second raid had destroyed most of the outlying farm buildings).

These two raids were not attacks against fortified works, still they were directed against military objectives for the vast food supplies they destroyed were essential to the feeding of the French garrison at Crown Point and Ticonderoga. Crown Point, because of its former security (until Rogers Rangers came along), was the supply depot for Ticonderoga.

Captain Baldwin continues in his *Diary:* On March 11, his detatchment marched the remaining eighteen miles to Fort William Henry, arriving about 2 p.m; "The men very weak & faint having had nothing to eat for some time".

Meanwhile, Rogers, with his detatchment had reconnoitred the defenses at Ticonderoga. In order to obtain a better view of their works, Rogers crept into the trench beneath the walls and looking up could see the sentries directly

above him on the ramparts. After obtaining all
the information on their fortifications that
he desired, Rogers, with a sardonic smile,
left tell-tale evidence of his presence in the
trench, then slipping away, returned to Fort
William Henry with his Rangers, arriving on
Sunday, the 14th of March, about 1 a.m, after
being out in the freezing weather for 15 days.

Rogers' total loss in this very successful
expedition, was the Indian Ranger who was so
badly burned. He died on the march homeward.

In these three winter expeditions, Rogers
Rangers had managed to obtain knowledge of all
the improvements that had been made on the
fortifications of the two French forts; also
the condition and numbers of the troops; besides audaciously destroying most of the food
supplying settlements outside of Crown Point
and intercepting a much needed food supply for
the garrison at Ticonderoga. When the garrisons of both the French and Americans had been
confined to the restricted limits of their
forts, looking out discontentedly on the bleak
and wintry horizon, Rogers and his Rangers had
made three successful expeditions within two
months. It was these brilliant winter forays –
carried on at a time when all normal campaigning had ceased that made Rogers Rangers most
famous. The Provincial newspapers rang with
detailed notices of their raids and "a number
of officers at Albany made a collection and
presented Captain Rogers with a handsome suit
of clothes; and about 161 shillings of New

York Currency, to be laid out in refreshments, for him and his men".[30]

The New York Assembly, in February, showed their appreciation of Rogers' efforts by voting him 125 Spanish milled pieces of eight as "a gratuity for his extraordinary courage, conduct and diligence against the French and their Indians".[31] A proposal for a similar measure: "was made in New Hampshire."[32] While Shirley, quite forgetting his old score against Rogers, knew that he must continue the services of Rogers and his Company for the ensuing campaign.[33] Accordingly, he had a letter penned to Rogers on February 26, summoning him to Boston. No sooner had Rogers returned from his last scout than he received Shirley's letter on March 15th.[34] Leaving the command of his Company of Rangers to Ensign Noah Johnson, as his second, Richard Rogers, was already in Boston, having been sent there previously with dispatches, Rogers left Fort William Henry for Boston on March 17th.[35]

This was Rogers' first *leave* since Blanchard's New Hampshire Regiment marched up the Connecticut River valley last spring, and the young warrior must have been just a little anxious to see what kind of a reception he would receive in Boston. After all, this was the seat of the Government that he had thwarted the provincial recruits from. But he soon relaxed, for his journey from Fort William Henry via Fort Edward, Albany, then cross-country to Boston was a continuos shout of welcome and congratulation. His personage excited whisperings among both sexes whenever he was pointed out as *the* Captain Robert Rogers who made those daring excursions against Crown Point and Ticonderoga. Places which personafied, in the most nervous Provincial eye, hornest's nests of French and Indians erupting forth in ever growing strength to threaten the very seaboard cities. Rogers' self-confidence, height of stature, and, commanding in countenance, in spite of his youth, must have seemed to the provincials who had never seen a battlefront, and never would, a bulwark of strength, who would surely keep the plague of a French and Indian invasion from their doors.

In his new suit of clothes, Rogers shone with the attention bestowed upon him and his face radiated until he approached the council chamber of the old Province House in Boston. *How would Shirley receive him?* After currying his animosity a year ago, he expected anything. Still, what about the reception he had received during his seven days journey? His youthful brow knotted unaccustomly as he was ushered into the Commander-in-Chief's presence. His worried face must have registered surprise when Shirley rose and gave him "a very friendly reception" and "soon intimated his design of giving [him] the command of an Independent -- Company of Rangers".[36] *This was it* - This was what Rogers wanted more than anything else. To command such a Company, would put him above a Provincial officer, and on the way to that final goal he longed for -- a commission as a British *Regular* officer. The fact that Shirley was giving him this command, showed Rogers, that the old score against him had been forgotten. Yes, his continuos, almost desperate attempts to distinguish himself as a Ranger, had borne fruit. Shirley, and no one else, for that matter, any longer looked upon him dubiously and instinctively felt for their money bags. Rogers must have issued from the Province House bursting with joy. It is not to be doubted that he and brother Richard, who had preceded him to Boston, celebrated. Although it is possible they may have waited until the next day after Robert received his commission and set of instructions.

Rogers' new command had a unique status. His Company was not a *Regular* or *Provincial* Company. It was *independent* of either. Hence the official title of *His Majesty's Independent – Company* (and later Companies) *of American Rangers*. Or, Rogers' and the Provincial's title: *Rogers' Independent Company* (and later Companies) *of Rangers*. Since they were paid and: - feed by the King they were subject to orders from British officers directed through Rogers. It was on this status that all future Companies of Rogers Rangers were raised. They were *free of the line* and consequently enjoyed more freedom and laxness than Regulars. But unlike Regulars, their organization lacked the permanentcy of a *Regular Corps*. They were raised and maintained out of contingent funds which the King and Prime Minister granted the Commander-in-Chiefs. Consequently, Rogers Rangers were subject to disbandment at any time by whim or reason of either the King, Prime Minister or the Commanding General in North America. This disturbing factor, was in itself, sufficient excuse, for Rogers to execute daring feats to insure the continued establishment of himself and his Corps.

On March 24, 1756, Rogers received his commission as Captain of an Independent Company of Rangers and was authorized to raise a Company of 60 Privates at 3 shillings New York Currency per day; 3 Sergeants at 4 shillings; an Ensign at 5 shillings; 2 Lieutenants at 7 shillings each; and Rogers received as Captain 10 shillings per day. Ten Spanish dollars were allowed each man towards providing clothes, arms and blankets.[37] Rogers was ordered to raise this Company as quickly as possible and to enlist only men who were experienced in hunting, tracking, long marches, and endowed with courage and loyalty that could be relied upon. The men were to be subject to military discipline and the articles of war. The Second and Sixth sections of the Articles of War were read to the recruit, and he took the oath of fidelity. For every Indian or French prisoner, or *scalp*, that he brought in, he was to receive five pounds sterling.

Rogers Rangers were henceforth considered as an Independent Corps of *Independent Companies* attached to the British Army, on an establishment of their own; a very expensive one, paid out of contingencies. The officers received almost the same pay as officers in the British Regular Army. Privates received twice the pay of Provincial Troops, which was considerably more than that of Regular Privates. The men were enlisted for one year and later for the War.[38]

The requisites for the Rangers which Shirley had set forth in his instructions could not be found in a community like Boston. But Rogers knew where he could get these new Rangers with ease and he reluctantly left hospitable Boston with Richard for the sparsely settled frontier towns of New Hampshire.

Arriving at Dumbarton they meet John Stark, one of Rogers' best friends and his Lieutenant in the old New Hampshire Regiment. As Stark had a yen to throw in his lot with the Rangers Robert made him his Second Lieutenant. Richard was still the First Lieutenant, while Noah Johnson, Rogers decided, could still be Ensign.

Rogers' command from March 24, to June 6, 1756, now consisted of two Companies (his original Company at Fort William Henry and the new Company he was raising). Over half of the Rangers of his original Company had promised to reenlist when their time was up on June 6, 1756. When the new Company was completed in the townships of the Merrimac Valley they marched for the Lake George front by two different routes. Among the recruits was Garty Gilman, who had been released after being forced to reveal the most incriminating evidence against Rogers in the Counterfeiting Examinations. Rogers readily signed him up as a Private to get him out of New Hampshire and away from any future inquisitiveness of the law.[39]

Rogers sent part of his new Company to Fort William Henry by way of Albany under the command of Lieutenant Richard Rogers.[40] With the remainder, Rogers was ordered to march to Number Four, the most advanced frontier town and fort in the Connecticut Valley, greately exposed to the enemy.[41] Lingering here awaiting an expected St. Francis Indian Raid, Rogers received orders on April 28, to march to Crown Point for a reconnaissance and then return to his station at Fort William Henry.

The Cattle Tongue Scout[19]

As in the Campaign of 1755, the reconnoitering of Ticonderoga and Crown Point and the catching of prisoners for the sake of information were primary objectives. Carefully feeling the Connecticut Valley for the expected St. Francis Raiders they advanced cautiously up the Connecticut River. Although not ordered to do so, Rogers had in mind a raid on a small settlement "between Crown Point and Montreal". Stark was supposed to have been there and consequently would pilot Rogers' party. However on the second day of the march Stark fell sick and was obliged, with a guard of six men, to repair to Fort Edward. Within a half-mile of the Fort they fortunately missed meeting a scouting party of French and Indians numbering over one hundred.[42]

Arriving opposite to Crown Point with only nine men, Rogers lay in hiding, hoping to capture any small parties crossing the lake. Unsuccessful in this endeavor they turned their attention to killing 23 head of cattle and cutting out the tongues to sustain them on their return trip. No sooner had this been done than they noticed eleven canoes loaded with French and Indians coming directly toward them across the lake. Rogers ordered each Ranger to take a different route and to meet at Lake Champlain where they had concealed their packs. This method of eluding pursuers was adopted numerous times by Rogers Rangers. Gathering at the designated rendezvous, Rogers and his Rangers built a raft and crossed the lake. On the return march they had a look at the French advanced guard in the valley that lay between the foot of Lake George and Ticonderoga. This valley was four miles long and guarded by four different outposts or fortified camps. The strongest of these was the stockade at the edge of Lake George called "Coutre-Coeur".[43] Watched as it was at all points and ranged incessantly by Indians in the employ of France, Rogers and his Rangers however, knew every yard of the ground. This fact, along with their successful methods of attack and retreat, made Rogers Rangers the only Corps that could successfully cope with this unseen enemy of virtually *red demons*.

The War was now on in earnest and after Braddock's tragic Defeat in 1755, it was found necessary to raise a force that was capable of meeting the enemy Indians and Canadians on their own grounds and who were versed in their manner of fighting, tracking and scouting; to act as advance guards to armies and frontier garrisons; to procure intelligence of enemy movements and to protect working parties or baggage trains from surprise attacks. For such purposes, Indians, if they could be trusted, were most valuable, but the Six Nations were never reliable and were prone to remain neutral during the war, as they had numerous relatives that were fighting for the French and were not anxious to take up the hatchet against them. Also, the opening years of the War were victorious ones for the French and the Six Nations were inclined to the victorious side. This was especially true of the Senecas.

However, in May, 1756, Shirley made an arrangement with the friendly and dependable tribe of Stockbridge Indians from Massachusetts, to raise a Company of fifty men, with a Captain, Jacob Cheeksaunkun, a Lieutenant, Jacob Naunauphtaunk, and, an Ensign, Solomon Uhauamvaumut; this Company was enlisted for the campaign.[44] It was raised anew in the Spring of each year of the War for the ensuing campaign and disbanded in the late Fall when the campaign was over.[45] The warriors would then return to their village and do the hunting for the tribe for the Winter; taking time out to squander their wages, viz., if they had managed to keep away from the Sutlers' huts with their temptations of rum, etc. At first the Stockbridge Indian Company was put under Colonel Burton, commanding at Fort Edward; but later they were attached to Rogers Rangers and were under Rogers' command throughout the War. They proved a great help in forming an advance guard of scouts for the Rangers themselves. Rogers realized that the capacities of the Indians were limited in the way of discipline, so he was careful to supplement their numbers with Rangers when they were sent out on a scout and usually a Ranger officer commanded.

Lord Loudoun intended early in 1757 to form a whole Regiment of Indians, of about 500 men, with field officers, to cost the Crown, including provisions, over 30,000 pounds a year.[46] The scheme fell through because Indians either would not enlist, or would not remain in service after they had joined. The dependable Stockbridge Indians were a small tribe and could not raise over 50 to 60 warriors. The Mohegans, a Connecticut tribe, who entered Rogers Rangers in 1758, could not muster many more.

So in place of Indians, the chief reliance was placed on Rangers, since Robert Rogers had proved that they were the only Corps capable of serving as a buffer for the Regular as well as the Provincial troops. Contrary to popular belief the average Provincial was not a traditional *Deerslayer* as Cooper would have us believe. The average Provincial soldier knew less what to do if he fell into an ambush than a British Regular, for he had never been trained either in the discipline of arms or in frontier warfare. Most of the men who composed the Provincial Army came from long settled communities which had never seen an Indian in war paint. There were some exceptions: men from northern New Hampshire, western Massachusetts and northern New York were raised to the hardships and dangers of frontier life and were excellent woodsmen and shots.[47] Consequently these advanced settlements furnished the bulk of Rogers Rangers. The Companies raised in New Hampshire consisted mostly of men of Scotch-Irish descent. Especially was this so of the Rangers from the Merrimac Valley.[48]

Rogers arrived safely with his party at Fort William Henry on the 11th of May,[49] after almost a two months absence from the fort. His welcome arrival was dampened by the harrowing account of Ensign Johnson of the first defeat of his Rangers.

Massacre of Sergt Archibald's Squad[3]

On Sunday, April 11, Sergeant James Archibald was sent with a squad of five Rangers on a scout down Lake George. Archibald's squad consisted of Corporal James McNeal, Privates John Mitchel, Isaac Colson, Jonathan Sillaway & Elisha Bennett. They only covered two miles on Sunday and encamped on an island in the First Narrows. The next morning at exactly "10 minutes past 4 a.m the sentries [at Fort William Henry] heard 3 or 4 guns fired down the Lake, & soon after a volley of 30 or 40 guns. After that several scattering shots." Lurking eyes on the lake's shore had followed Archibald's short journey on the lake and their landing on the island. True to form, the French Indians, numbering close to two hundred, made a pre-dawn attack, overan the island and Archibald's men.

Apparently, Corporal McNeal and Privates Colson and Bennet awoke in time to fire one volley, for they were "shot, stript and scalped in the most awful manner". While Sergeant Archibald and Privates Mitchel and Sillaway were carried prisoners to Montreal. This accounts for only three or four guns being heard before the larger enemy volley.

When the firing was heard at William Henry, Lieutenant Poor of the Provincials with nine men were sent down the lake in two batteaus as soon as it was light at six o'clock. Cautiously landing on the ominous isle, they proceeded to Archibald's camp and found the scalped remnants of McNeil, Colson and Bennet. One of them "the barbarous Indians had cut quite across his breast and turn'd it under his chin, and left his inwards exposed to the wild beasts." Archibald managed to make his escape from Montreal in September and brought with him valuable information on the illicit trade carried on with the French by Provincial merchants.

When Lieutenant Poor returned to the fort at 2 a.m with the bodies, Commandant Gleasier ordered the garrison to prepare for a possible attack. A Sergeant was sent down to Fort Edward for help and the guards were doubled at

The Three Week Alarm Apr 12- May 3[16]

night. The next morning Private Akin (now acting Sergeant in lieu of Archibald) of Rogers Rangers returned from a night patrol. That evening before dark a Provincial Sergeant went out with another night patrol. They saw many of the enemy down the lake and heard more who soon followed them up within half a gunshot of the fort. That night at 8:15 an alarm gun was fired so that Fort Edward would hear it and send reenforcements. The next morning two men arrived from Fort Edward and more arrived at three in the afternoon. "The enemy appear[ed] very bold and daring and another alarm gun was fired at 4:30 p.m. Meanwhile the garrison "Cleaned up the arms, filled sand bags, and made all possible preparations for an attack".

A five day rain storm started the next morning keeping the enemy well under cover, but the vigil was maintained. Even "All the officers of the garrison agreed to take their turns to stand, one in each bastion, 2 hrs. at a time every night, all night." On April 22, acting Sergeant Akin of Rogers Rangers took a scout out to the east Mountains and got close enough to "the upper island" to take a pot shot at the enemy there. The enemy, after their success against Sergeant Archibald's party had taken post on the island and later on the side of the east Mountains. Occasionally, one of their dogs could be heard barking.

Two days later on April 24, Lieutenant Richard Rogers arrived with his detatchment of 20 men of the new Company of Rogers Rangers to

Akin's Upper Island Scout [18]

provide a welcome relief; and altho ~~gh~~ enemy batteaus and canoes were seen going off from the upper island on the 28th, and Indian canoes were espied down the lake as late as May 2, still no attack came and the alarm had faded away by the time Lieutenant Stark arrived on May 8, with another detatchment of Rogers' new Company. Stark brought the disquieting news of seeing fresh tracks of over 100 French Indians near Fort Edward on the 6th. Lieutenant Rogers was sent with a scout of Rangers to Wood Creek and South Bay to see if they or other parties were lurking in that neighborhood. *Richard Rogers' Wood Creek Scout* [20]

Nine days after his arrival at Fort William Henry, Rogers was ordered by General Shirley to reconnoitre the French "advanced guards". After making his observations, Rogers and his scout of eleven men lay in ambush on a path between the fort and the nearest fortified camp in an effort to retaliate for the massacre of Sergeant Archibald's detatchment. A large body of 118 French soldiers passed and the Rangers lay close in their hiding place. Soon after, came a smaller party of 22, the time of vengeance was at hand. The Rangers fired on them, killed six, and captured their leader. This party was an armed working detail of 20 Canadian militia and 1 Indian commanded by a Cadet, the Sieur de Fontenay. They had been sent with axes to clear the portage trail. The French claim that they were fired upon while resting from their work and sitting in a circle smoking the Indian calumet. This does not conform with *The Retaliation Scout* [4]

Rogers' account. Who says that Fontenay's party came along a few minutes after the first detail of 118 men. The alarm gun sounded at Ticonderoga as soon as the Canadian survivors burst in. A large party sallied out but Rogers Rangers had melted away like so many phantoms.

    Returning to Fort William Henry with their prisoner the Rangers breathed less angrily, for in part, they had retaliated for Archibald's disaster. Upon Cadet Fontenay's report that a large party of French and Indians were preparing to attack the environs of Fort Edward, Rogers, in spite of his just returning from an active scout, issued forth the next morning with 78 men "to scour the woods" as far as South Bay to intercept them. Unfortunately the raiding party managed to slip thru Rogers' net before he had it completely laid.

Rogers Wood Creek Hunt 21

    This was the first and last scout that the effective men of Rogers' two Companies served in together, for shortly after their return, the old Company was disbanded on June 6th. However, fourteen of them stayed on swelling the strength of the remaining Company to 67 officers and men.[50]

The Discipline Scout 22

    On June 13, Rogers embarked with 37 Rangers in batteaus to revisit the French advanced guards at Ticonderoga. A Ranger named Samuel Eastman unfortunately became lost in this scout. Having left his knapsack upon the hill where they had overlooked the French camps Eastman left camp and returned for it without notifying Rogers. But he did tell one of his mess-mates before he left and when Eastman did not return before day-break the Ranger became worried and told Rogers. Rogers immediately sent a party after him but to no avail. Returning to their batteaus Rogers' party waited all day but still no Eastman. While nervously waiting, the Rangers had ample time to contemplate on the folly of wandering from camp. Many visions of the horrible fate of Eastman must have passed through their minds. Leaving enough provisions to last Eastman until he reached Fort William Henry, Rogers' men embarked and measuring the depth of the Second Narrows found them deep enough for British invasion barges of 100 tons to pass, Returning to Fort William Henry, Eastman was returned as lost, but fortunately he staggered sheepishly in five days later (on June 23rd), "almost famished for want of substinance".

This incident is characteristic of the independent nature of the men of Rogers Rangers. A fact which estranged them so with the British officers. Because of their lack of a sense of rigid discipline, Rogers could not enforce the same tactics as the British officers upon their Regulars, namely, that of whipping the men at the whipping post. Instead, he was almost forced to *cajole* them into obedience. Calling on their friendship for each other (Rogers knew personally, practically all the men of his Company). He did not dare use the whip for the victim *and* his friends would more than likely tell Rogers to go to hell and march home, in spite of the fact that they had agreed when signing up not to Mutiny or Desert. In their minds, they would not consider their actions as such. Rogers realized this and his form of punishment, though not one of violence, was effective.

Unlike other Corps commanders, Rogers set the pace for his men, and his dashing, daring strokes were related with pride by his Rangers and although "following him was hard service", as one veteran Ranger aptly put it,[51] they all clambered to go out with him whenever he was forming a scouting party; and if Rogers thought a man needed chastising he would refuse to take him along. This was discipline enough, and could be worked effectively as long as Rogers Rangers consisted of only one Company. But when the Corps was later expanded Rogers had a serious problem on his hands.

Proof of the sound logic of Rogers' discipline is revealed in the muster rolls of the Rangers for 1756. They show that only two privates deserted, not to the enemy, but to return home.[52] However, this could not be boasted of in later years when the corps consisted of four or more Companies.

Upon their return from their last scout Rogers Rangers found six light whaleboats that had just arrived from Albany.[53] They were built expressly for Rogers Rangers and were made light but strong. The preying falcons soon made good use of their comparitive lightness in making a big catch.

Rogers' next exploit greately perplexed the French and was probably his most incredible feat of the year. He embarked on June 28, with fifty men in five of the new whaleboats. Rowing about ten miles down Lake George they landed on the east side, *carried the boats six miles over a gorge of the mountains*, launched them again in a tributary of South Bay. This herculean effort took three and a half days to accomplish in the intense heat of summer. Rogers Mouth of Otter Creek Ambuscade[5]

Resting part of July 3, after their backbreaking feat, they started out that night and rowed down the narrow body of South Bay and Wood Creek. At dawn they were within six miles of Ticonderoga. Landing, they hid the boats and lay concealed all day. Embarking again that night, they rowed with muffled oars under the shadow of the eastern shore, and passed so close to the French fortress that they heard the voices of the sentinels calling the watchword. In the morning they were six miles beyond Ticonderoga. Again they landed and hid their boats, and lay hidden all day in the woods. Crown Point was only five miles farther on but when night fell there was a moon and they dared not venture on the lake that evening.

From their hideout the next day they saw nearly a hundred boats pass before them on the narrow neck of Lake Champlain. This was Montcalm's army on their way to Ticonderoga. About noon boats appeared and stood a few yards off on the lake while two officers argued. One of them wanted to land where the Rangers were hidden, but the other officer finally prevailed and the party landed within musket-shot of Rogers Rangers and innocently ate their lunch with 51 pairs of eyes upon them. The unsuspecting French embarked after their meal.

That night was darker; embarking at nine that evening they passed Crown Point unseen, and hid themselves during the day as before, ten miles beyond the fort. Thirty boats and a schooner passed them on their way to Canada.

The next night they rowed eight miles further to the mouth of Otter Creek. Rogers then sent scouts to reconnoitre along the shore to the southern point of Buttonmould Bay. Returning to Rogers, the scouts reported a schooner at anchor about a mile off. Lightening their whaleboats they were preparing to launch them and set out for the schooner to board her when two armed batteaus appeared, coming up the lake a short distance from the shore, from their course it appeared that they intended to land at Otter Creek. Rogers Rangers gave them a volley and called on them to surrender; but the crews put off and made for the opposite shore. The Rangers hastily shoved their whale boats into the water, pursued, and seized them. Out of twelve men, the Rangers fire had killed three and wounded two, one of whom was mortally wounded and could not march, so they put an end to him to prevent discovery. Rogers' buccaneers sank the *vessels*, which were laden with wheat, flour, rice, wine and brandy. The wine and brandy Rogers' men "hid in very secure places" with the whaleboats on the west shore and returned on foot with their prisoners.

These prisoners had informed Rogers that they had been part of a force of 500 men who were only six miles off. So the attack on the schooner had to be abandoned and the Rangers could not return with their whaleboats but were forced to leave them for the present. The whole party arrived safely at Fort William Henry on the 15th of July, with four scalps and eight prisoners. Once again Rogers Rangers had turned marintime and made another victorious *Commando Raid*. Rogers' *navy* was unique in its tactics, if water lanes ended due to the presence of an enemy force, and the desired goal lay on the other side of a range of mountains, notwithstanding, the boats were immediately carried bodily across these barriers, much to the amazement of the French, who could not understand how English whaleboats were found above Ticonderoga and Crown Point. Rogers' raid stirred up an anxious geographical interest in the French and numerous exploring parties were sent out to discover the new water passage from Lake George to Lake Champlain. The more they looked the more confused they became.[54]

Upon his return, Rogers asked for an audience with the new temporary Commander-in-Chief, General Abercrombie, who, arriving at Albany the 25th of June, had succeeded Shirley to the command of the British and Provincial forces in North America and was plugging for Loudoun until he arrived. Rogers and his brother Richard, were granted an audience to discuss augmenting the Rangers. Arriving at Abercrombie's headquarters in Albany with his prisoners and report of his latest and most daring exploit of the year, Rogers presented them as a worthy token of introduction. Abercrombie ordered a new Company of Rangers to be raised and gave the command to Richard Rogers on July 24th.[55]

From this date Robert Rogers was no longer called *Captain Rogers* by the Provincials, instead, *they* breveted him a Major and he was now called *Major Rogers* in spite of the fact that he was technically still a Captain.[56]

This Company was one of three which Shirley had planned to be raised.[57] Abercrombie, upon his ascension to command had fulfilled his plan.[58] The other two Companies, Captained by Hobbs and Speakman, Shirley had ordered Winslow to raise in May. They were slow in recruiting however, and did not take the field until August. But Richard Rogers completed his Company in 28 days, partly in the vicinity of Rumford, New Hampshire, but mostly while on the march to Albany.[59]

The new Company, upon their arrival at Albany, found Lord Loudoun on the scene. They were immediately ordered to act as the scouting arm for General Webb's troops that were posted in the small stockades up the Mohawk River awaiting confirmation of the reports that Oswego had fallen.[60]

Noah Johnson, Rogers' former Ensign, was

promoted and appointed Captain Richard Rogers' First Lieutenant; (there was no Second Lieutenant[61]) and Caleb Page, his Ensign. John Stark, who had been Rogers' Second Lieutenant, was promoted to his First Lieutenant, and Sergeant John McCurdy succeeded to Stark's place. Jonathan Burbank was appointed Rogers' Ensign. All of these names were to become famous in Rogers Rangers and all but Caleb Page were to become Captains, the covetted command of all Ranger officers.

The Campaign for 1756, as originally planned by Shirley was to have been a very extensive one. Troops were to embark from the British fort, Oswego, and capture Fort Frontenac and then turn about and take Fort Niagara at the other end of Lake Ontario, and thus gain possession of the Great Lakes and sever the French Provinces. This was a renewal of the same plan of 1755 that delay had held up. Meanwhile, an attack was to be made against Ticonderoga and Crown Point. Unfortunately, Shirley was superseded in his command by Major General Abercrombie who was shortly followed by the Earl of Loudoun. By the time Loudoun arrived from England it was too late to carry out the designs on Fort Frontenac and Niagara. Instead, the situations were reversed and Montcalm, who commanded the French Regulars in New France, with the help of Canadians and Indians and Colony Regulars, attacked Oswego in August and compelled the Oswego forts to surrender. After destroying them, Montcalm hastened to Ticonde--

roga, where he awaited an attack by the English. Loudoun now abandoned any attempt against Frontenac and prepared to advance on Ticonderoga until he received word that Montcalm was advancing with 14,000 men. But Montcalm only had 5,300 Regulars and Canadians and they were in a strong position where they could defy three times there number. Montcalm had no idea of advancing against the 10,000 men of Loudoun's army stationed from Albany to Lake George. So each army stood watching and waiting for the other, with Lake George between them, until the season closed.[62] General Winslow, who commanded the Provincials, was at Fort William Henry with 3,000 of them including Robert Rogers' Company. Richard Rogers' Company served in the Mohawk Valley until September 16th when Loudoun recalled them to Fort Edward when he feared Montcalm was advancing.

Once again the shadows of Robert Rogers shady past hovered about him. General Winslow was the same John Winslow who commanded Shirley's Provincials in Nova Scotia the preceding year. It was from this Regiment that Rogers had adroitly *absconded* with the 24 recruits he had raised in 1755. Rogers, in spite of his unfaltering self-confidence, must have felt ill at ease in Winslow's presence. Whatever Winslow's personal feelings towards Rogers were, he did not reveal, instead, he seems to have accepted Rogers, but not with open arms. In his reports on Rogers' various scouts to Shirley and later Loudoun, he dryly reports them offering no comment on Rogers' extraordinary services. No, Rogers was not commended in *official reports* as far as Winslow was concerned. Rogers was never directly under Winslow's command. While stationed at Fort William Henry, Rogers had almost a free rein, to go and come as he pleased and he says that he received his orders from General Shirley himself.[63] Although justified, this high-handiness must have irked Winslow.

The rest of the Campaign was conspicuous by the operations of partisan bands such as Rogers Rangers in several brilliant forays, while Marin and Langy, almost equally famous Canadian partisans, and less known Captain Columbiere and Ensign Meloise, conducted several excursions against the English posts, that were in no way less galling than those of their rival Robert Rogers.

Ticonderoga was a hornet's nest, pouring out swarms of savages to infest the highways and byways of the wilderness. Loudoun did not have the numbers of Indian allies that Montcalm had; he only had the Company of 50 Stockbridge Indians, but he kept them and the rest of Rogers Rangers in continuous active service.

Loudoun and Abercrombie even employed members of Rogers Rangers as couriers or dispatch carriers from Fort Edward to the various posts on the Hudson and even as far south as New York and Boston. Sergeant Severance of Robert Rogers' own Company made a regular run south on the old Hoosack road.[64]

Rogers Rangers were only too glad to launch

forth on their various scouts and expeditions. Fort William Henry was a hotbed of disease and sickness due to the unhealthy condition of the camp, the large number of troops encamped there and the kitchens, graves, and places for slaughtering cattle were all inter-mixed about the rim of the Rangers' hut-village; and the insidious fragrance drifted in along with the dreaded smallpox.[65]

Rogers' Horse Raid[23] Rogers Rangers did not rest on their laurels after their recent Lake Champlain raid, for on August 2, Rogers set out with 25 of his Company and 50 Provincials under Captain Larnard to reconnoitre the French forts and advanced guards. Larnard's party returned to Fort William Henry after a reconnoitre of Ticonderoga with Rogers. Rogers and his Rangers, skirting the hordes of Indians in the valley of Ticonderoga, continued on towards Crown Point to where they had destroyed the village during the last winter. Here, failing to waylay any French soldiers, they killed forty horses before they were discovered and were forced to hastily retire to Fort William Henry with hordes of Canadians and Indians on their trail.

On this expedition Rogers had taken along as a guide, a supposedly French deserter, who, attempting to betray Rogers while they were lying in ambush, was discovered in time. Inside his waistcoat Rogers discovered carefully drawn plans of Forts Edward and William Henry. Upon their return he was sent to Albany to be hanged.

Returning to Fort William Henry, Rogers
found that thirty privates and Lieutenant Jacob Naunauphtaunk of the Stockbridge Indian
Company had been attatched to his command.[66]
Half of these with a Ranger and a Provincial
Sergeant had been sent out by Lieutenant Stark
on their first scout as *Rogers Rangers*.

Lieutenant Jacob left Fort William Henry on
August 8, with sixteen Stockbridges, a New
York Provincial Sergeant and one Ranger as a
guide. They slipped through the *hornet's nest*
of the Valley of Ticonderoga and waylaid three
Frenchmen. Jacob sent three of his braves to
reconnoitre Ticonderoga and they brought back
a fairly accurate report of the strength and
disposition of the French. In retiring to Fort
William Henry Jacob lost the New York Sergeant
and two old Stockbridges who had wandered from
the camp and were lost. Jacob could speak English but not write it, so he dictated to a Secretary who penned a *Journal* of his scout and
it was sent to Lord Loudoun.

Jacobs Ambuscade[6]

Rogers now determined to fulfill his attempt
to raid the settlements on the Richelieu River
that he had planned to do in his first scout of
the year. Another reason for Rogers almost
anxiety to make this expedition was the fact
that Lieutenant Kennedy of the Regulars was
organizing a similar expedition and Rogers and
his men felt slighted. If they only realized
it, Rogers Rangers, by their daring scouts had
made the British and Provincials feel insignificant and desirous of emulating their ac-

Rogers Canada Raid[24]

complishments in the arts of partisan warfare.
On August 11, Rogers petitioned Loudoun for permission to make this raid, but Loudoun was either to busy to answer or he wanted Kennedy to get a head start, for he did not give Rogers the order to proceed. The Ranger Chieftan, after waiting restlessly for five days, impetuosly took the matter in his own hands. He excused himself to Loudoun when writing him again on the 16th, by stating that the eagerness of his Company to go on the scout had forced him to comply with *their* wishes. To avoid the possibility of a negative opinion by Loudoun, Rogers embarked the same day in whale-boats in two sections. One section, commanded by Lieutenant Stark, had preceded him by starting in the morning. Rogers led the other section which started that evening. The next morning the two sections joined forces and hiding their boats proceeded by land to where they had cached their whaleboats on Lake Champlain. Fortunately the French had not yet discovered their boat-hideout and the Rangers found them and the stowed wine and brandy very acceptable after their long march. Travelling by night, they rowed northward for two nights. At midnight on the second night, they approached Isle la Motte and discovered a schooner sailing towards them. They prepared to board her but a brisk wind was with the schooner and she raced by to quickly for the Rangers to attempt a boarding.

Chagrined, but not discouraged, Rogers party

preyed slowly northward for two more nights and landing at *Wind-Mill-Point* on the east side of Lake Champlain and the Richeleiu River they perched in ambush ready to swoop down upon any enemy traffic passing through the narrow waterway. But their grim watchful waiting proved fruitless and since their provisions were running out they returned to a small cove on the east side of the lake, eight miles from Crown Point. Hiding the whale-boats, the Rangers took prisoners near the fort, a French family of three, and slipped back to Fort William Henry.

A glimpse at the detatched service that Richard Rogers' Company had been on reveals that on August 31, two days after their arrival in Albany from their record-breaking on-the-march mustering, Loudoun paraded them at seven o'clock in the morning with 250 of the 42nd Highlanders and a detatchment of Artillery.[67] They were all sent up the Mohawk Valley to reenforce Webb's command at Burnet's Field where he was anxiously awaiting confirmation of the fall of Oswego. It was necessary to send scouts out to try and determine Oswego's fate but none of Rogers' Rangers were sent that far as Webb notes they were not very well acquainted with the country so that they could scout but at a very little distance from him.[68] However, in the short two weeks that they were with Webb, young Richard Rogers exerted himself to disciplining his Company into a respectable Ranging body worthy of the name

Rogers Rangers. A difficult job at its best. Fresh in the field, in an utterly strange terrain, undisciplined, and reluctant to embrace any discipline even from their own officers, Richard Rogers and his seconds, the veteran Noah Johnson, and the young, good-looking, Ensign Caleb Page had their hands full. The new Company had hardly time to settle themselves when Loudoun, fearing a push by Montcalm from Ticonderoga, penned a rush order to Webb to hurry them back to Fort Edward via batteaus to Schenectady and then cross over quickly to Saratoga to receive orders from Lieutenant-Colonel Burton.[69]

Meanwhile brother Robert, returning to Fort William Henry with his French family of prisoners found orders awaiting him from Loudoun to wait upon Colonel Burton at Saratoga to receive a special assignment, which in reality were orders to stay in the field and watch out for Montcalm's rumoured advance. Although flattered at the attention and confidence put in him, Rogers wanted a furlough and he told Colonel Burton as much. He disguised it by saying that he wanted to go down to Albany "to settle his accounts, and to get some money". However, Burton's thoughts did not run in cohesion with the Ranger Chieftan's and he told Rogers that this was an improper time and how desirous Loudoun was of having the motions of the enemy thoroughly watched. Although Rogers had just taken three prisoners near Crown Point, a prisoner taken now from Ticonderoga or the advanced guards would establish him very favorably in his Lordship's eyes. Especially since an advance was so seriously expected from that quarter at this time. If Rogers had asked for his furlough a month sooner he might have gotten it. As it was, it was now to late and even his indirect approaches to it were to no avail. This evasiveness in his character, of getting to the point by a roundabout method became a marked characteristic of Rogers as his fame developed.

To Rogers' surprise Burton responded to his statement that he needed money. He told Rogers that he could borrow what he pleased from him "upon account". Rogers asked for forty dollars and set off (September 15th) "very well pleas'd to joyn his Company at Fort William Henry and ..immediately to send a party of six, to try for a prisoner, and with the rest of his Company to reconnoitre from opposite Ticonderoga along the Pine Ridge and so down to Saratoga", to keep as much as possible in the general war paths that the French Indians used.[70]

It took just such judicious handling of Rogers as Colonel Burton employed to obtain the maximum of efficiency out of this indispensable but temperamental Ranger Chieftan. After all, Rogers' fame was still fresh and being so young and inclined to be boastful, the excessive attention bestowed upon him occassionaly turned his head and he needed to be ingeniously restrained but still not offended. Rogers' nature called for the guidance of

a phsycologist, which breed, there were very
few to be found amongst the British Regular
officers. Colonel Burton was an exception. His
tact completely won Rogers' confidence, and the
two had a complete understanding throughout
the war. If more of Rogers' superiors had employed Burton's methods, Rogers' abilities
could have been expanded instead of retarded
as they continually were by the tactless and
arrogant attitude of the Regular officers who
misunderstood Rogers' boastful countenance for
that of a braggart and an upstart Provincial.
Generally speaking, their minds were not shrewd
enough to pierce this disturbing first impression which Rogers often gave, to see the sparks
of genius smouldering within.

Putnams Pond Blood Hound Scout[25] Rogers returned from his reconnaisance with four prisoners, but not French prisoners. His expedition had fallen short of its original intent and developed into the unwelcome task of capturing a party of Irish Catholic Regulars who had deserted with their priest to make their way to the more reciprotive French. Of the six deserters, the priest and one soldier eluded Rogers to later give themselves up. Rogers' men took the other four captive while they were crossing a pond near Wood Creek.

Several of Rogers Rangers had dogs (particularly the officers) who accompanied them on:
their scouts and in their battles. These dogs
were usefull in these *Bloodhound Scouts* as
well as fighting the enemy in battle. Cadet
William Stark, who became a Captain in Rogers

Rangers in 1758, had a Wolf Dog named Sergeant Beaubier, who became famous. He accompanied Stark on all his Ranging expeditions and was present in several of the Rangers' Indian battles, and it is said, assisted in the destruction of more of them, than any individual of the Corps. When he became a Ranger Captain, Stark returned "Sergeant Beaubier" on his muster roll, and drew pay and rations for him.[71]

Returning to Saratoga with his deserters, *Major* Rogers met brother Richard and received orders from Loudoun through Burton to proceed to Fort Edward with his two companies and the Stockbridge Indian Company and form an encampment for his Corps on the island opposite the fort in the Hudson River.[72] As Loudoun was more afraid of Fort Edward being attacked by Wood Creek than Fort William Henry by Lake George, he concentrated the elite of his army at Fort Edward. "Rogers' Island",[73] as the Rangers' new post was soon called, served as the base and headquarters for the operations of Rogers Rangers for the balance of the campaign and the site for their winter quarters. A large block-house was built on the island for the Rangers by Colonel Meserve's New Hampshire Carpenters. However, the roof was not put on until late November, when boards were gathered from the dismantled Fort Miller. Until this time, Rogers Rangers threw up temporary bark huts for their quarters.[74] These huts were favoured by the Rangers, who, would rather live in them than in the army-like block-house.

They liked the mountain shack atmosphere of their huts and usually four Rangers of a congeniality would bunk in a hut. Turns would be taken in cooking the rations and keeping the place tidy; and although, the huts fairly rocked some nights with carousals, the men, with these exceptions, were orderly enough. When it came time to move into the block-house the men put up such a cry that it was decided to allow them to remain in their huts if they wished and the blockhouse developed into a hospital:- for smallpox victims who had to be isolated.

From "Rogers' Island", Rogers Rangers "ebbed and flowed", as General Abercrombie (commanding at Fort Edward) aptly put it.[75] Part of Jacob's Stockbridges under Captain Jacobs were sent on the east side of Wood Creek to harass the enemy at Ticonderoga; while Rogers, with a detatchment made another scout down Lake George in a whaleboat. The remainder of the Corps were employed in patrolling between Forts Edward and William Henry and Wood Creek, besides serving as flankers to the parties that guarded provisions to Fort William Henry.[76]

As they "ebbed and flowed" from their Island base they presented a barbaric, cut-throat, tide of men. Un-uniformed as they were at this time and with the parties frequently sprinkled with Stockbridge Indians, the British sentries at Fort Edward must have stirred nervously more than once when one of these wild looking bands flowed by. Sometimes emerging from the ford between their Island and the fort in a splashing, shouting horde, not unlike a collection of demons being cast upon the shore; then again, returning on the ebb from their various and frequent startling interludes with death, sometimes in the dead of night or pregnant morning, flowing back like so many wild phantoms. It is no wonder that the frightened sentries took occasional pot shots at them and sounded an attack alarm. Finally, a rigid system of paroles and passwords had to be established.

The Corps continued to make successfull swoops into the valley of Ticonderoga. Captain Jacob, Rogers notes, "returned [five] days before me with four french scalps, which they took opposite to Ticonderoga on the eastside". *Jacobs Scalp Scout Sept. 2-8*[7]

On September 7, Rogers returned to Ticonderoga in his unrelenting campaign of harassment and reconnaisance. Accompaning him was young Ronald Chalmers, an English gentleman sent to Rogers by Sir John St. Clair (the deputy quartermaster general) to learn the Rangers art of warfare. Rogers was shrewd enough to cultivate the friendship of these eager aspiring warriors. He realized that by so doing, they would put in a good word for him to their British superiors and relatives in high places. He guessed wisely, for the correspondence and petitions of Rogers' Cadets always contained admiring mention of their Ranging instructor.[77] *Rogers Sept. 7-13th Scout*[26]

Upon his return, Rogers was ordered by Abercrombie to send out alternately, three parties of Rangers consisting of one officer and twenty men each to patrol the Wood Creek-South Bay *Wood Creek South Bay Patrol*[27] region, the direction which Loudoun most feared an approach by Montcalm. This continuos patrol was maintained for sometime.[78]

Again, on October 22, Rogers was *on party*,[79] this time to execute an incredible bit of audacity. He embarked in two whaleboats from Fort William Henry with 20 Rangers. Cautiously approaching Ticonderoga they left the boats and penetrated the valley until they came near the fort. Spotting a sentinel on the forest road within shouting distance of the fort, Rogers, followed by five of his Rangers, walked directly towards him. The man challenged him, and Rogers answered in French. Perplexed for a moment, the soldier in his confusion allowed them to come closer, until seeing his mistake, he called out in amazement: "Qui etes vous?"; "Rogers", was the answer; and the sentinel was seized, led in hot haste to the boats and spirited away to Fort William Henry, coatless and pantless so that he could move faster. He gave much important information including the news that Rogers' four whaleboats were found in Lake Champlain much to the amazement of the French.

Qui Etes Vous Scout[28]

From November 1, to the 19th the Rangers restricted their activities to patrolling the woods about the two British forts to retard the last flickering stings of the partisan hornets of the enemy.[80] Their objective was varied on the 16th, for two parties of Rangers were sent in pursuit of deserters from Webb's Regiment, but with no success.

Second Blood Hound Scout[29]

On the 19th, with General Abercrombie's

nephew and aid-de-camp, James Abercrombie and, James Dunbar, also kin to Abercrombie and first cousin to an English Lord, Rogers made one last scout of the year to Crown Point. But nothing was effected in a military way, beyond obtaining a view of the French garrison and noting the important fact that Montcalm had retired for the winter. Winter was now on in earnest and the snow forced Rogers' scout to return "sooner than they proposed". While on this scout, Rogers had the opportunity to instruct his two volunteers and study them at close range. In James Abercrombie he must have recognized the boastful arrogance which he felt towards any troops other than Regulars. But Rogers, anxious to promote his own interests, realized the opportunity of creating friendships with Abercrombie's aid-de-camp and kin. Consequently he humoured both Abercrombie and Dunbar. However, his teachings to young Dunbar were especially rewarded, for three years later when he made his St. Francis Raid, Dunbar, though not a Ranger officer, volunteered to accompany him and proved most usefull and courageous.

<small>Rogers-Abercrombie Scout[30]</small>

Before their return, and the last prisoner's report that Montcalm had withdrawn to winter quarters had been confirmed by Rogers' scout, Loudoun had drawn off the main body of his army from Fort Edward to be quartered from Saratoga to New York for the winter. Rogers found orders to remain on at *Rogers' Island* with his Corps which consisted now of only his and Richard Rogers' Company as Captain Jacob Cheeksaunkun's Stockbridge Company was disbanded on November 11th.[81] Three days later, Jacob received 743 pounds and 12 shillings New York Currency without deductions to pay for the balance due his warriors for their service during the campaign, that is, from May 27, to November 11, 1756.[82] There was considerable trouble in settling their accounts for when it came time to compile a list of the mens' names and their time the Company Clerk, John Wauwaumpequunaunt could not be found. This stymied Loudoun so much that he gave express orders for Wauwaumpequunaunt's name to be struck off the roll.[83] Without the Clerk to spell the mens' difficult names and to furnish a record of their length of service Loudoun and his agents had a wearisome time in settling their accounts.[84]

Already, Rogers had formulated the idea of his St. Francis Raid. On October 19, 1756, when Loudoun was at Fort Edward he grasped the opportunity to petition him to allow him to double the strength of his two Companies to 200 Rangers by enlisting picked men from the frontier towns of New Hampshire. Rogers asked that he might be stationed for the winter with this detatchment of 200, either at Number Four (Charlestown, N.H.) or forts adjacent, which could have meant the uninhabited Fort Wentworth, which he and his men had built in 1755. His plan was to make a winter raid into Canada and to destroy the St. Francis Indian settlements. For this service he required "the flower of his own Rangers, in all 200 men.." and more than three months time. Fort Wentworth or Number Four would have been an ideal base for an expedition to this notorious Indian town and would have eliminated the necessity of rossing the Missisquoi swamps by the Lake Champlain approach. This original plan of Rogers for attacking St. Francis was the main reason for his being so well versed in the Lake Memphremagog-Coos Meadows region. The raid was a pet project of his and he devoted much time in planning his itinerary in this direction. Because of his thorough study of this route Rogers was able to use it and guide his Rangers to safety in their harrowing retreat from St. Francis in 1759.

Rogers even goes so far as to state that Loudoun would not be disappointed in him and his Rangers if he would grant him his petition. Rogers' plan was sound and practical,[85] and though Loudoun realized the plausibility of a daring St. Francis Winter attack, his hands were tied as the Provincial Assemblies were reluctant to raise any men for Winter service to replace Rogers Rangers in their absence, and as Abercrombie put it: Rogers was the chief man they could depend upon for intelligence and could not be dispensed with for so long a time without risking too much.[86] Rogers must have put up a stiff argument for Abercrombie writes to Loudoun that if it was so important to New Hampshire and Massachusetts

for St. Francis to be destroyed that they had
enough Provincial troops (now that the campaign was over on the Lake George front) to
undertake it and if they succeeded they could
be taken into the service as Rangers. However,
if Loudoun thought that Rogers should be allowed to undertake the raid he would send for
him and give him orders to go ahead.[87] But
Loudoun did not give the order for Rogers to
proceed. He was too worried about a French incursion against Forts William Henry and Edward
so the town of St. Francis was allowed to pour
forth its hordes of savages upon the frontiers
of New England for three more years before
Rogers was finally ordered to wipe it out.

Going into retrospect we find that in the
middle of September two new Companies of prospective Rangers had arrived at Albany. As early
as April 1756, Shirley had ordered General
Winslow to form three such Companies out of
the 2,000 New Englanders who returned from the
1755 campaign in Nova Scotia.[88]

A little further dwelling on the raising and
composition of these new Companies would not be
amiss for after all they were soon to form a
part of Rogers Rangers and were to serve in
the Corps for a time under their following
original enlistment status which was different
than that of the two Rogers's Companies.

The enlistment terms and authorized strength
of each Company were: that they consist of 2
Sergeants, 2 Corporals, and 58 Private men.
The Officers (a Captain, one Lieutenant an a

Ensign), were to have the same pay as the officers in the British Army. The men upon enlisting were to receive six dollars bounty money and to be paid the same as the troops raised by Massachusetts for the expedition against Crown Point. This pay amounted to 10¼ d, sterling a day (against 8 d. which a British Regular received). A good hunting coat, vest and breeches, a pair of Indian stockings, shoes and a hatchet were to be delivered to each man gratis after they arrived at Albany.[89] Firelocks were to be issued to them at Boston, which they were to return at the end of their service.[90] They were to receive the same provisions as the King's regular troops. Out of their bounty money they were to provide themselves with blankets. A reward of five pounds sterling was to be given for every Indian scalp.[91] The Companies were to be enlisted for the 1756 Crown Point campaign and were to be discharged as soon as it was over, whether successful or not.[92] As the Rangers were to be raised chiefly, if not wholly out of Winslow's Nova Scotia Battalion of Massachusetts Provincials:-They had just arrived at Boston on April 30, having been kept in service in Nova Scotia throughout the winter of 1755-56 against their will; to assure them that this would not happen again, Shirley authorized Winslow to print up a number of discharge certificates to issue to the non-coms and private men upon their enlistment.[93]

Shirley wanted Proctor and Humphrey Hobbs

to Captain two of the Companies and either
Adams or Thomas Speakman to command the other.[94]
Leaving the choice of the latter to Winslow,
as also the choice of the subalterns who were
to be good officers, with a knowledge of the
wood service, and reliable. Shirley also "en-
treated" that none but picked private men,
with experience in the scouting service should
be enlisted. The Companies were to be enlisted in Boston and the vicinity if necessary.
The rendezvous was to be Albany where the officers would pick up their commissions and the
men their hatchets and clothes.[96] Shirley's
intentions were good enough, but those of Winslow's disembarking battalion were not, at
least they were not in cohesion, for the ragged battalion swarmed off the Nova Scotia transports and headed like pigeons for their various homes. If Winslow (then in Boston) had
only received Shirley's orders a few days before he might have been able to induce enough
of his disgruntled battalion to enlist and fill
up the two Ranging Companies. As it was, Shirley at New York, did not write Winslow his
orders until the 30th of April, the same day
that the battalion arrived in Boston harbour.
By the time that the orders were received and
the proclamations printed the battalion had
landed and reached their homes.[97]

 Instead of the three Companies originally
intended by Shirley, only two were raised,[98]
and proper woodsmen could not be gotten for
these. Although the men were principally a

wild band of adventurers, still, the officers were of the best. The Captains who accepted commands were Humphrey Hobbs and Thomas Speakman, both veterans of the Beajour Campaign and the expulsion of the Acadians in 1755. Very few of the picked woodsmen that Shirley had asked for could be found. Instead, the old seaman's recruiting method of *pressing* was employed and the Boston waterfront was beat up for recruits. As a result, the two Companies consisted of Sailors, Spaniards and an occasional Irish, or Spanish Catholic.[99] An interesting fact, especially since it has been the popular belief that Rogers Rangers were made up solely of Protestant New Englanders. Another factor that slowed down the growth of these Companies was the fact that several of the Rangers who were pressed into service gave respectable amounts of money to others to serve in their places. These "premiums" offered were usually more than the established six dollars bounty money. Accordingly, Hobbs' and Speakman's attempts to enlist men were greately stymied by these *premium offerers*.[100]

A glimpse at the officers reveals that Captain Humphrey Hobbs was a famous fighting Congregational Deacon Ranger from Souhegan (now Amherst), New Hampshire. His military career began in King George's War and his many successful fights, particularly about Number Four, won for him, from the chagrined Indians, the phrase "Souhegan deacon no very good, he fight Sabbath-Day". Hobbs was a Captain in Winslow's expedition to build Fort Halifax on the Kennebec River in 1754, and acted as guide.[101]

Captain Thomas Speakman was a trusted friend of Winslow. He had well established his fame as a warrior in the Nova Scotia campaign; particularly distinguishing himself on October 10, 1755 at Peticodiac in a desperate fight against Boishebert and a superior party of guerrilla Acadians and Indians, finally being forced to retire to the British ships after making a most stubborn defense.[102]

Hobbs' officers were Lieutenant Charles Bulkeley, a most capable Massachusetts fighter, later to become one of the most famous but ill fated Captains of Rogers Rangers. Hobbs' Ensign was James Rogers, elder brother of Robert Rogers. Receiving word, possibly from Robert, of the raising of the new Ranging Companies, James left his widow mother's house at Rumford, New Hampshire and arriving at Boston he convinced Hobbs that he was the most likely man for his Ensign. It is probable that Hobbs had known James Rogers' father, both having been early settlers of the New Hampshire frontier. This factor along with the growing enchantment of the name Rogers paved the way for a third member of the family to join the Corps of Rangers. James was not heralded by any brilliant military exploits of the past. He had only served in minor scouting parties in King George's War. Nevertheless, James rounded out into an invaluable Ranger officer.

Speakman's seconds were Lieutenant Samuel

Kennedy, a noted surveyor. He had acted as a surveyor for Winslow in 1754 on the Kennebec and had a knack for detail in describing terrain.[103] The Ensign was Jonathan Brewer, a brave enough officer, but headstrong as later events proved. He had more the traits of a subordinate buccaneer who believed in acquiring promotion by brute force which will be dwelled upon later. Brewer, because of his ranging ability had been assigned to make many daring scouts when he was serving as an Ensign in Shirley's Provincial Regiment in Nova Scotia during the winter of 1755-56.[104]

Out of these six officers, only two, James Rogers and Jonathan Brewer, survived the war. Hobbs died of Smallpox. Bulkeley and Kennedy died in battle and Speakman after being mortally wounded was scalped alive and decimitated.

Returning to the early history of these two Companies, documents reveal that finally two skeleton Companies were formed. On August 23, Captain Hobbs began his march from Boston with his 32 nondescript Rangers for the rendezvous at Albany and the next day Captain Speakman followed with his Company of 40 men.[105] Shirley had intended for the mens pay to start from May 27, but due to the lateness of their raising and arrival, Loudoun started their musters from August 1, which saved the Crown considerable, as he boasted to the Ministry.[106] Although the new Companies had two months of the Campaign left in which to distinguish themselves there is little mention of any part of them being

PLATE II
See p xiii

PLATE III
See p. xiii

sent out on a scout. The only singular service performed by them that has been recorded was a convoy duty:- On September 28, Abercrombie ordered Captain Speakman with his meagre Company to convoy General Lyman's Provincial supply train to Fort William Henry and to bring back the wagons so that Winslow's army at the lake would not be diminished by sending back an escort with the empty wagons to Fort Edward.[107]

Before Winslow's force withdrew from William Henry, Hobbs' and Speakman's Companies were moved up in October to form part of Major Eyre's winter garrison at that post and additional huts were built for them outside the fort. These two Companies did not come under the direct command of *Major Rogers* when they first stepped into the fray. There were several insinuations that he, being the Senior Captain of Rangers, had the command of them as early as December 1756, for Abercrombie mentions "..the flower of his own Rangers, in all, 200 men". All the four Companies (Robert and Richard Rogers' and Hobbs' and Speakman's) would just about comprise the "200 men".[108] However in January 1757, Hobbs' and Speakman's Companies definitly came under Rogers' command.[109]

After Loudoun withdrew his army he wrote Abercrombie, commander of his advanced posts, on November 11, to "make a clear bargain with the Ranging Companies as to the pay of the Officers and Private men, and as to their Cloathing, and being Mustered Regularly, and everything they can claim on any occassion".[110]

Apparently Abercrombie had a little trouble in fulfilling this order for he writes back on November 16,:-"I had your Lordship's letter of the 11th by Appy, in relation to the Rangers to whom I have given all the information I am able and therefore I shall not trouble your Lordship on that head, they are like their countrymen, so tedious and difficult to settle points that this messenger has been detained longer".[111] The "tedious and difficult..points," seem to be the uncompromising fact that the Hobbs' and Speakman's Officers were receiving the same pay as Regular Officers whereas the Rogers's Officers were not. Another bone of contention arose over the fact that the new Companies, according to the terms of their enlistment, received clothes, arms, and equipment, whereas Rogers' Companies had to provide their own. But this was compensated by the fact that the Rogers's Privates received twice as much pay as those of Hobbs' and Speakman's. Rogers' Privates received 3 shillings New York currency per day; whereas Hobbs' and Speakman's received approximately 1 shilling 6 pence. One can well imagine the grumblings that must have arose in the Rogers's Companies as they noted the new gear and uniforms that were issued to the two new Companies. The short stay of Hobbs' and Speakman's Companies at Fort Edward while enroute to their station at Fort William Henry was long enough to stir up the disatisfaction of these differences in their establishments. The new Privates were equally disgruntled when they learned that their brethern in the Rogers's Companies were receiving twice as much pay as they. Composed as they were, in a large part, by pressed men, it is doubtful if a wholesale desertion could have been avoided in the new Companies, if Loudoun had not nipped it in the bud by ordering Abercrombie to put them on the same footing as the Rogers's.[112] Although this decision quieted the new Companies, the Rogers's Privates now complained that they were getting more than they because of the new Companies clothing, arms and equipment allowance. The bewildered Abercrombie compromised and promised Rogers new blanket material. This had the desired phsycological effect for the men of the old Companies now got a new blanket free whereas the new Companies had to buy their own.[113] Another point of quibiling which arose to add to Abercrombie's headache was the fact that the new Companies had been promised that they would serve in Winslow's Crown Point Army of Provincials and not with the Regulars. Loudoun and Abercrombie settled this by moving them up to Fort William Henry where they joined Winslow's Army but not for long as the army was soon disbanded. However, Hobbs' and Speakman's Ranger Companies had to remain for they had enlisted for one year.[114] So they were forced to serve with Regulars after all for Regulars formed the Winter garrison of Fort Wm. Henry.

So ended the campaign of 1756, a strictly defensive one except for the minor swoops of Rogers Rangers in their daring penetrations into the heart of French held territory.[115] Loudoun realized as he anxiously awaited Montcalm's advance the indespensability of Rangers and although he considered them a big expense, he writes to Prime Minister Fox in November that he could not do without them; for it was only by them that he could learn what the French were doing. He relied on them to safeguard his camps and marches. Loudoun expresses the correct assumption that until the British had won a few victories they could not depend on much help from the Six Nations. He states that until that time his army could not exist in the forests of America without the protective eyes of Rangers; and for that reason he planned to partly garrison his northern forts with five Companies of Rangers.[116]

Accordingly, Loudoun's whole Winter plan of defense was built around Rangers, and he maintained the five Companies that he had planned. Four of these Companies constituted Rogers Rangers before the Winter was over. The other was a detatched Company of the New York Provincial Regiment at Saratoga commanded by Captain Jonathan Ogden. Loudoun's strategy of defense was as follows:- After Rogers' capture of the French sentry and his confirmation of the enemy drawing off from Ticonderoga, Loudoun immediately made plans for putting his troops into Winter quarters also. At Fort William Henry he posted Major Eyre with 400 of the 44th and 48th (mostly Irish) and Hobbs' and Speakman's Ranging Companies of 43 and 55 officers and men, "to get them intelligence in order to prevent sudden surprises".[117] At Fort Edward he stationed Major Sparks with 500 Regulars and the two Rogers's Companies of Rangers of approximately 50 men each. Loudoun hoped by these four Ranger Companies and Ogden's New York Rangers at Saratoga, to prevent any Winter incursions of the French. He hoped to have intelligence in time by his Rangers to be able to concentrate a strong force at any threatened fort.[118] Loudoun further reveals that he was counting on Rangers for his winter defense:-He writes Governor Hardy on November 9, that although the French were reported to have 200 Indians at Ticonderoga for winter raids he expected to be informed by his Rangers of every move they made. If the enemy detatchments proved to numerous for the Rangers, Regulars were to join them, and intercept the raiders. Loudoun was convinced that "one rebuff of this kind will put an entire end to that sort of War".[119]

Loudoun did not know it at the time but his own Rogers Rangers were the ones to receive the *rebuff* but not before they had conducted one of their most hardy and devastating Winter campaigns of the War.....

CHAPTER III

1757

GROWING PAINS

From a climatic and routine point of view it appeared that it was going to be a dreary uneventful winter for Rogers Rangers. The long bleak months from January to May started out in a series of wood-cutting forays and road-repairing projects not to mention the local reconnaisances all within a few miles of the British forts.[120] Time in camp, on Rogers' Island, was punctuated by endless *Spruce Beer* and *Laced Rum* routes which were inevitable for quite a few of the Rangers when inactive.[121] In all, it started out to be a long monotonous winter for the Corps until the commanding officer at Fort Edward decided that a large scale scout by Rogers and his men would not be amiss.

Ever since his petition to raid St. Francis had been shelved, Rogers had stirred restlessly. Even though the past year had been marked with the singular daring of his numerous scouts, still they had been of a small nature and he was anxious to do something big. Either in the form of a large scale raid or engagement with the enemy. The next few days not only satisfied this desire but elevated Rogers Rangers from the status of a scouting Corps to that of a fighting body.

On January 15, 1757, Major Sparks, Rogers'

Battle of La Barbue Creek[8]

commanding officer at Fort Edward, issued the order that launched Rogers Rangers on the first of their famous Winter battles on snowshoes. British commanding officers were uneasy as to what might be brewing at the ominous French fortress's Ticonderoga and Crown Point. Consequently, Rogers marched from Fort Edward on January 15, with his Lieutenant, John Stark; Ensign Caleb Page of Richard Rogers' Company, and fifty Rangers from the two Rogers's Companies. Arriving at Fort William Henry that night, Rogers informed the Commandant, Major Eyre, that he had been ordered to reconnoitre the French forts with eighty-five Rangers, and to harass the enemy in any way that he saw fit. Major Eyre assigned Captain Speakman to choose thirty-three of the best officers and men from his and Hobbs' Companies at Fort William Henry. "All were Voluntiers that went on this Scout" but Speakman had many aspirants. Besides himself, sixteen officers and men from his Company were accepted; while Ensign James Rogers with fourteen men of Hobbs' Company also volunteered (Captain Hobbs, *the fighting Deacon*, was in the hospital with smallpox). Robert Baker, a Volunteer in the 44th Regiment was also taken.

From this date, January 15, Hobbs' and Speakman's Companies came under Rogers' command, and, although as yet unofficial, they constituted part of Rogers Rangers.

The next two days were busily spent in preparing snowshoes and provisions for the expedition. It appears that the Rangers whom Rogers brought from Fort Edward all had snow-shoes:- for as early as November 11, 1756, Loudoun had transmitted orders through Richard Rogers for the Rogers's Companies to construct them. But Hobbs' and Speakman's Companies at William Henry, being new Companies, had never engaged in any winter campaigns, which were so characteristic of Rogers Rangers; naturally the new Companies were not complete in this very essential winter gear, and it remained for the seasoned veterans of the Rogers's Companies to instruct them in the making of snowshoes.

A glimpse at the officers and men comprising this first *major expedition* of Rogers reveals a strange but deadly potent conglomeration of fighting men:- Of the officers, Captain Thomas Speakman, second in command to Rogers, was a seasoned fighter as well as a Ranger. Rogers' Lieutenants, John Stark, and Samuel Kennedy were veterans as scouts but as yet had never been in a heated action. His Ensigns (present in the expedition) James Rogers, Jonathan Brewer and Caleb Page were also skilled scouts but unbaptised by battle, with the exception of Ensign Brewer, who had seen considerable action in Nova Scotia. Two Volunteers, Andrew Gardiner, and Robert Baker, had joined the expedition with the prime thought of distinguishing themselves and thus win promotion. Gardiner was from the frontier town of Number Four, New Hampshire and was serving as a Cadet in Rogers' own Company. His goal was an Ensigncy in Rogers Rangers, while Baker, a Cadet in the 44th Regiment, strove for an Ensigncy in the Regulars.

The Sergeants:- James Henry, and a Dutch-Indian half-breed, William Hendrick Phillips of Robert Rogers' Company had served with Rogers in his various exploits of 1756; but James Henry alone could boast of being one of the original thirty Rangers of Rogers' nucleous Company in 1755, and unlike Phillips, had served in Rogers' first victorious action at "The Isle au Mouton". Stephen Holland, the only Sergeant of Richard Rogers' Company in the expedition, was an industrious individual, but as yet had not had the opportunity to distinguish himself. Sergeants Charles Joseph Walter and John Howard of Hobbs' Company were also inexperienced in battle. The same could be said of Sergeant Increase Moore of Speakman's Company.

The Corporals:- a status which existed in Hobbs' and Speakman's Companies exclusively, were represented by Ebenezer Perry and John Edmonds of Hobbs' and Samuel Fisk of Speakman's who were also novices.

Among the Privates were:- William Morris of Robert Rogers' Company who had been a Sergeant from July to September 1756, when he was demoted to his enlistment status of a Private for a breach of discipline. He had prevailed on Rogers to let him serve in the Scout and was determined to recover his non-com status if events permitted. Other staunch characters were Thomas Burnside of Rogers' Company and Joshua Martin and John Shute of *Dick* Rogers', who, though frequently distinguishing himself, served the length of the war as a Private, not desiring anything higher. Like many of the veterans of Rogers Rangers, Shute was happy enough to serve in the ranks and not take on the responsibilities of an advancement. Among other individuals, Hobbs' Company furnished a Spanish Catholic, Emanuel la Portuga, who was soon to die heroicly. Among the many young men in Speakman's Company was Thomas Brown, a 16 year old boy, who, as a consequence of this expedition went through an incredible period of harrowing captivity. Practically all the above mentioned individuals who survived the forthcoming *battle* were promoted as a reward for their outstanding services and deeds of valour.

A few notes on the gear of these four Companies reveals that Rogers Rangers went into this *battle* dressed in greenish buckskin (viz., the two Rogers's Companies); the other two Companies of the Corps (Hobbs' and Speakman's) were the only Rangers who were in uniform which consisted of a grey duffle coat and vest, and buckskin breeches and leggings. Arms consisted of individually owned muskets, flintlocks and firelocks in the Rogers's Companies as well as privately owned scalping-knives and hatchets (or tomahawks). Hobbs' and Speakman's carried regulation muskets, cartouch boxes, and wore regulation shoes from the King's stores, and were supplied hatchets by a contractor. Unlike the Rogers's Companies they did not all have the Corps' most prolific weapon, the *scalping knife.* The Rogers's Company officers carried compasses in the large end of their powder horns. This excellent practice was later imitated by all the officers of Rogers Rangers. Ammunition per man consisted of 60 rounds of powder and ball. Provisions consisted of two weeks supply of dried beef, sugar, rice and dried peas and cornmeal. In their wooden canteens each Ranger carried rum. The food rations were carried in a knapsack strapped over the shoulder.

As Rogers desired that the utmost secrecy be maintained in regard to his expedition, he did not start until the evening of the 17th. Shortly before dark eighty-five well picked and equiped Officers and Rangers assembled on the fort-parade. Rogers personally inspected each and every man to see that he was properly equipped with a musket, sixty rounds of powder and ball and two weeks rations of food. As quickly as darkness descended to form a protective screen, the expedition filed out of the fort into the quiet frosty night wrapped in blankets (a Rangers' winter-campaign coat) resembling a long line of ghostly phantoms wending their ghastly way to some theater of death.

Marching only a few miles down the lake to the first narrows of Lake George they made their camp on the east side of the lake at a point where the steep slope of a mountain covered their rear, and the frozen surface of the lake lay unbroken and free of any obstruction as far as the eye could see in the clear night. In spite of the strength of t. is position, Rogers fixed strong sentries at intervals about the encampment. They were not to be relieved from the main body until morning. As Rogers most aptly put it, "profound secrecy and silence being often of the most importance in these cases". Each sentry therefore, consisting of six men, two of whom were constantly alert, and when relieved by their companions did it without noise; and, in the event of those seeing or hearing anything to alarm them, they were not to speak, but one of them was to silently retreat and notify Rogers. The strategy of these tactics were, of course, to warn the main body as noiselessly as possible so that they might deploy themselves quietly to repulse a night attack. If any noisy alarm was given the enemy would rush in before the Rangers had time to form for battle, and so catch them at a disadvantage.

The night passing tranquilly, Rogers' men were up at the break of dawn as that was the usual time for the French Indians to make a surprise attack. During the night Rogers had allowed small fires to be built in the heavy part of the woods, in pits about three feet deep. The coals were now rekindled and the Rangers quickly made themselves a gruel of cornmeal, which was washed down with rum from their wooden canteens. As they ate, Rogers went from man to man asking if they were lame from their first days march on the ice, as several new men had slipped on the first nights march; but none would admit their disability and it was not until the days march had started that Rogers, standing to one side, picked out eleven lame men as the column filed past. In spite of protests Rogers sent them back to Fort William Henry, under the charge of one of their number, a Corporal. Alarmed as he was at this loss of nearly fifteen per cent of his force, Rogers must have smiled as he watched them stumble back up the lake muttering their disappointment at not being allowed to stay, even though their halting steps revealed their total ineffectiveness as capable fighting men.

Rogers' detachment, now reduced to seventy four officers and men, started out after small reconnoitring parties had scouted around the encampment for any signs or tracks of an enemy. The Rangers marched in extended order, single file, keeping enough from each other to prevent one shot from killing two men in case of an ambush from the wooded shore. Keeping close in against the shore the expedition was less likely to be seen from the hills on either side of Lake George. As long as the sun remained behind the crest of the eastern ridge the traveling was easy going and they had little difficulty in scanning everything that lay ahead on the frozen lake. But when the sun rose and topped the trees, its slanting rays beat down upon the smooth ice ricochetting up into the Rangers' eyes. An advance guard preceded the column and flanking parties skirted the main body on each side at a distance of about twenty yards. Before the first narrows of Lake George, with its islands had been traversed, the expedition had cut across to the western shore and encamped three miles south of Sabbath-Day-Point. By this means, Rogers had conducted his second days march under the protective screen of the narrow neck of the lake, and the shady side, thus minimizing the possibility of the French or Indians observing his party from a high mountain at the other end of the lake.

The next morning they left the lake at Sabbath-Day-Point. Taking the snowshoes from their backs they strapped them on their feet and plodded northwest through the hills. According to Rogers' official report they "encamped about eight miles from the lake. The 20th, continued our course till night and encamped opposite to Lake Champlain about three miles westward from it. The 21st, marched East till we came on Lake Champlain about midway betwixt Crown Point and Ticonderoga". Immediately upon their arrival, with Rogers calling a council of war with his officers, the scouts reported two sleighs coming towards them from Ticonderoga. This was exactly what Rogers wanted. It was at this very same spot that he had ambushed two sleighs the preceding winter, and it did not look like his men would have to freeze any toes waiting for them now.

Lieutenant Stark, with twenty men of Rogers' Company were sent through the trees along the shore, towards Crown Point, to head the French sleighs. His orders were to get as far as he could down the lake, before the sleighs got opposite to Captain Speakman, who was to remain in the center with his men. When the sleighs were opposite to Speakman, Stark "was to push on the lake to head em"; meanwhile Rogers, with about thirty men, hurried towards Ticonderoga to cut off their retreat. But for the shape of the shore line, Rogers Rangers might have effected a brilliant surprise attack and captured ten sleighs, eighty horses and 30 men. Unfortunately for Rogers' manoeuvre, the lake shore-line came to a point where Captain Speakman's detachment was poised in the center. At this point the La Barbue Creek (Putnam's Creek) joined with the lake. Because it was almost exactly half-way between the French forts, Ticonderoga and Crown Point and *five miles* from each, it was frequently called "Five Mile Point". Rogers and Speakman could see the sleighs coming down the lake but Stark's party, due to the *point*, could not, until they were directly opposite to Speakman. To this jutting point of land and "it being a rainy day" may be laid the blame for the initial factors that led to one of the Rangers' bloodiest battles.

The reason for the caravan of French sleighs on the lake is revealed in French documents. At 9 on the morning of January 21, De Rouilly, an officer of the Colony Regulars, acting as Major at Ticonderoga, received orders from De Lusignan, the Commandant, to proceed to Crown Point and have some brandy and forage loaded there on eight sleighs, with eight horses harnessed to each, under an escort of fifteen soldiers and one Sergeant; De Liebot, an officer of the Royal Rousillon Regiment, an Varennes, a Colonial Cadet. Two other sleighs with ten men had gone ahead and these were the ones that Rogers Rangers saw first while lying in ambush. The two advanced sleighs had passed Rogers' party and were almost directly opposite to Captain Speakman's detachment when Rogers saw De Rouilly's other eight sleighs approaching from their cover of falling rain.

Rogers' thoughts must have raced exultant at the prospect of this more promising coup. Well might his fame be more elevated if he could turn in a report of ten sleighs, and more than eighty horses captured and destroyed; thirty men captured, including three probable officers; particularly since it would be executed five miles within the French lines and between two French forts. But weather and a jutting point of shore line had other plans.

As Rogers counted the strength of the caravan as it slowly emerged from the blanket of rain he must have cursed the weather for hiding the true state of things. His exultant face clouded as he thought of Lieutenant Stark's party beyond the point at that very moment ready to swoop down upon the two advanced sleighs. From the excited murmurings of his Rangers, Rogers sprung into action "and immediately dispatched two men to tell Lieutenant Stark not to discover himself and let the first Sledges pass". The two Rangers, picked for their agility on snowshoes, hurried through the woods bordering Lake Champlain. Passing Captain Speakman, they gasped out Rogers' order and clumped on to warn Stark. *But they were too late.* Stark's unsuspecting party had waited until the two sleighs were opposite to Speakman when they dashed from the north side of Five Mile Point and spreading fan-wise headed the two sleighs. *The die was now cast.* There was a blood curdling shout as Rogers Rangers cut loose with their terrifying war cry, hardly discernable from that of an Indian war party. Bolting from the lake's shores Stark, then Speakman and Rogers surrounded the two sleighs. Seven of the ten men in charge of them were captured. The other three, desperately cutting the traces from three of the horses, leaped on their backs and broke through to Ticonderoga. Having removed their snowshoes while waiting to attack, Rogers Rangers raced over the smooth ice after the fleeing enemy. Major De Rouilly, with the main part of the caravan had approached opposite to Presqisle, a small isle near Ticonderoga, when, witnessing Rogers' capture and the Rangers bearing down on him, ordered his caravan to retreat to Ticonderoga.

Rogers wisely did not pursue when he saw that the unloaded sleighs were outdistancing his men. Gathering at their original position at Five Mile Point, an examination of the prisoners was made. Kept separately and brought before Rogers singly, so that they could not get together on a story, the information gleaned from all, revealed that 200 Canadians and 45 Indians had just arrived at Ticonderoga and were to be joined that evening or the following morning by fifty Indians from Crown Point. There were also 350 Regulars at Ticonderoga and 600 at Crown Point. More troops were expected in a short time at Ticonderoga to attack Fort William Henry in the Spring. Since they had large magazines of provisions and the Canadians and Indians were well equipped and ready to march at a moments notice, Rogers concluded that they would turn out to pursue him. Now the Ranger Chieftan had a problem on his hands. If he crossed the lake and returned by way of Wood Creek he would surely be seen by the French at Ticonderoga and a trap would be set for them. Yet he dared not wait until nightfall to do so, for this would give the enemy time to gather in force both from Ticonderoga and Crown Point. No, he could not wait for darkness and be caught in the middle. Despite the opposition of some of his officers he had only one other course open and that was to return by the same way he came in the hope that he could slip pass Ticonderoga.

This settled, Rogers ordered the detachment to march as quickly as possible to their last nights encampment and rekindle the coals of the fires and dry their guns. All morning it had been raining, soaking the Rangers guns and rendering them useless for a possible engagement. While drying their muskets, Rogers ordered Sergeant Walker, who had charge of the prisoners, to kill them if the Rangers were attacked, so that none of them could escape and inform the French of their strength. Inhuman though this seems, Rogers was in an extremely difficult position and was using every method to insure the safe return of his men. After drying their muskets and swallowing a hasty snack the Rangers wrapped their blanket-coats about them with their muskets and powder carried beneath them to keep them dry. They set out on the return march, in single file order, as they had come. Rogers, with Lieutenant Kennedy, took the front; Captain Speakman the center; and Lieutenant Stark and Ensign Brewer the rear. Ensigns Caleb Page and James Rogers were between the front and rear; the rear-guard and the prisoners were under the command of Sergeant Walter.

Meanwhile, Major De Rouilly, retreating precipately to Ticonderoga with his sleigh caravan, dispatched a soldier on horseback to inform De Lusignan at Ticonderoga, of Rogers' capture. De Lusignan, upon being informed that Rogers had attacked from the west, wisely surmised that he would return through the mountains west of Ticonderoga. Accordingly, he dispatched one hundred men, including Indians, Regulars, and Canadian Volunteers, under the command of Captains De Basserode, of the Languedoc Regiment, and La Granville, of the La Reine Regiment to intercept them. Subordinate officers were Lieutenant Dastrel of the Languedoc Regiment; and Ensign Langlade, a Colonial

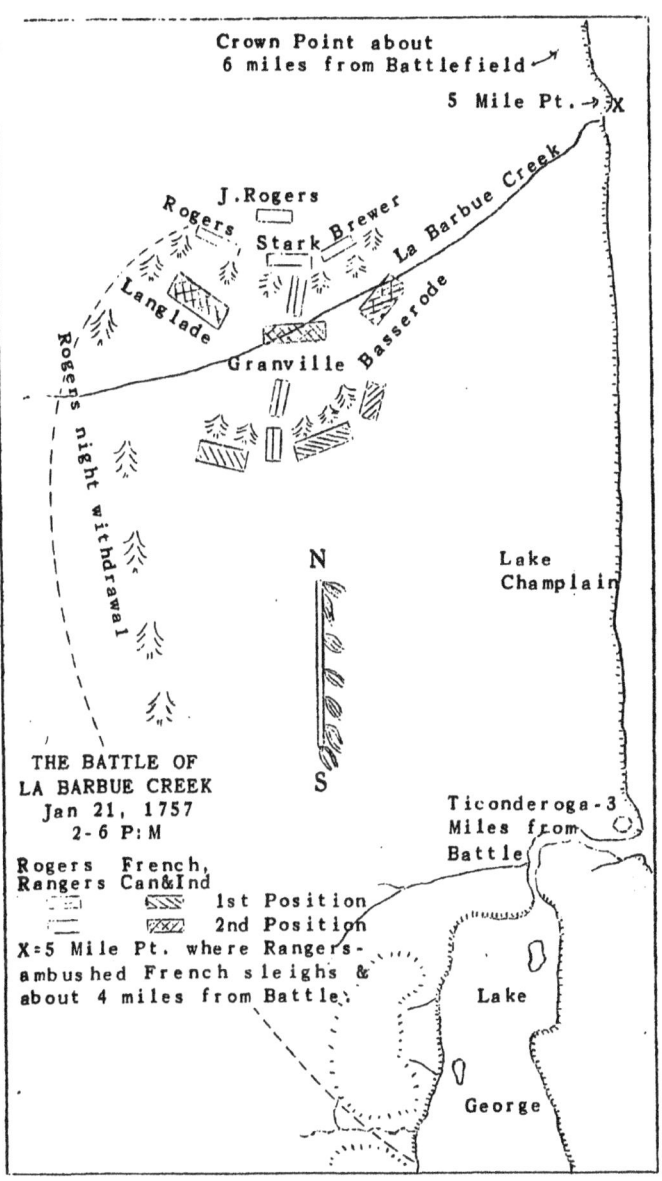

officer. Five Cadets, anxious to distinguish
themselves, volunteered and joined the expedition. Captain De Basserode, the senior officer, commanded the expedition. So anxious were
they to intercept Rogers that they hurriedly
filed out of Ticonderoga with only a few rounds
of ammunition and very few supplies. Lusignan,
however, in the next half hour loaded ten men
with ammunition and supplies and they were sent
to join Basserode. Basserode's Canadian and
Indian scouts located Rogers' column about two
in the afternoon three miles northwest of Ticonderoga. As the Rangers route of march would
bring them across a ravine about fifteen rods
in breadth between two steep hills with the
small frozen winter remnant of La Barbue Creek
running down the center (of the ravine); Basserode deployed his one hundred and thirteen
men in a crescent shape among the trees and
bushes bordering the crest of the gully, which
took a turn at this point.

After leaving the campfires, Rogers endeavored
to keep off the rising ground. He tried to follow a route through the ravines separating the
hills so that his party would not be seen. As
Basserode's ravine was the natural route to
follow without revealing themselves on the
surface: Consequently, Rogers Rangers, fell
into Basserode's trap. Shortly after two in
the afternoon about a mile and a half from
the start of their march the Rangers descended
the ravine. Basserode allowed Rogers and twelve
others to almost reach the ambushed summit of

the ravine, when he opened fire on the front
of Rogers' column. Speakman was crossing La
Barbue Creek on the floor of the ravine and
Stark's and Brewer's rear column on the opposite hill from Rogers had not descended into
the ravine. Fortunately, half of the one hundred and fourteen muskets fired at Rogers Rangers missed fire due to the rain. Nevertheless,
the barrage was deadly enough and it was only
because of the extended order of Rogers' march
that they did not suffer more in this first fire.
Several Rangers were wounded; and Lieutenant
Kennedy of Speakman's Company, and Gardiner,
the Volunteer from Rogers' own Company were
killed. Rogers was leading the column and he
only escaped death by a miracle. As it was he
received a glancing shot across his forehead.
He wiped the blood from his eyes and shouted
the order to fall back across the ravine to
Stark's column on the other hill. Accentuating
his orders, the enemy poured forth from their
ambuscade and charged down into the ravine
with bayonets set. They burst forth in a crescent shape and it is a miracle that Rogers'
and Speakman's columns were not completely cut
off from Stark in the rear and destroyed. As
it was, they were badly cut up. By the time
that Rogers' battered advance column fell back
unto Captain Speakman's center the enemy were
upon them in a crescent of stabbing, shouting,
exultant foe. There were French Regulars of :-
the seasoned Royal Rousillon, La Reine, and
Languedoc Regiments; Troupes de la Colonie,

the veteran French Colonial Regulars of New France; French Canadians in their buckskin attire; and intermixed with them, Indians, in all their hideous paint and grimaces. The little hollow, only fifteen rods wide, was a spot of hell as the fierce melee started. The enemy had not stopped to reload after their first deadly volley, instead, they had put their reliance on the cold bayonet of the Regulars, and the tomahawks of the Canadians and Indians. Rogers Rangers still had their loaded flintlocks and muskets to greet them when they poured down the ravine. The French outnumbered Rogers' force two to one and the Rangers were surprised and confused but like a haven in a fog, they heard a roar of musketry over their heads from Lieutenant Stark's and Ensign Brewer's rear column, who had formed themselves on the opposite hill to cover Rogers' retreat.

After discharging their muskets, Rogers Rangers, upon Rogers' command, broke like a covey of quail and ran as fast as they could on snow shoes, across the gulley and back up the hill to where Stark and Brewer had posted themselves so advantageously. In the race across the floor of the ravine they lost several men and the hollow rang with the harrowing screams of tomahawked and bayoneted men. Those that fought their way clear and left the floor of the ravine to clamber up the hill had the hardest time, for they could only run a few feet uphill in four feet of snow, then turn and fight off their pursuers. It was at this time that Stark served best, the survivors who managed to break out of the *hollow of death*. For his men could see over their heads better to fire over them into the enemy; whereas, it had been more difficult to do this when Rogers' men were in the fierce melee below. There were many fierce duels between the Rangers and their frenzied pursuers. Thomas Brown, the sixteen year old Private of Speakman's Company, relates on his remarkable escape. Having already received a wound through his body, he was clambering up the hill when he dodged behind a large rock hoping to throw off his pursuers, but an Indian sprung up from the other side. Brown threw himself backwards into the snow, and it being four feet deep, he sank so low that he broke his snowshoes. Quickly jerking them off, his shoes came with them, but he scrambled barefoot to safety with the Indian's tomahawk whistling close. Not all were as fortunate. Ensign Caleb Page, reputed the handsomest man in Rogers Rangers, fell fighting to a hideous death of knife stabs. Captain Speakman fell wounded but managed to crawl under a bush until the shouting horde passed by when he crawled down the creek out of the line of battle.

No sooner had Rogers and his survivors reached the summit and joined Stark's men, than Basserode, too close behind, tried to envelop them by a flanking movement on the Rangers' right. Lieutenant Stark, the first to discover it, quickly informed Rogers, who sent Sergeant "Bill Phillips", the noted half-breed Indian hunter, with a detachment to hold them. Phillips' men, all marksmen, hurriedly deploying themselves on the right of Rogers Rangers, delivered the first fire, which proved so fatal that the flank movement abruptly ceased and fell back to the main body.

Although this manouver failed, the French and Indians were too flushed with their initial success and a charge was begun along the Rangers' whole front. From the shelter of the bushes and pine trees on the slope the enemy worked their way up within range and began a crackle of fire-at-will, until they were within a few yards, when they ventured a charge. Rogers Rangers had the advantage of height of ground and denser cover "and [the French] were obliged a second time to retreat, as they could not stand the Rangers continual fire upon them". Finding it impossible to advance against the Rangers' constant fire-power, the French, hesitating for a few seconds, broke and raced down the slope. They dived behind convenient bushes and pine trees and the attack dissipated into their taking potshots from a distance. The secret of Rogers Rangers constant firepower was unique at that time and the tactic instigated by Rogers was practiced exclusively by his Corps. One-half of the Rangers would fire while the other half reloaded. A simple enough tactic but heretofore, never used to any appreciable extent by any armies.

There was now a lull in the action along the center and right of Rogers' line; but soon the

firing increased along Rogers' left flank and
the French could be seen moving up the hill
enmasse to turn this flank. Rogers immediately
sent his brother, Ensign James Rogers, with
twelve Rangers, to strengthen his left. Their
fire was so effective that Basserode was driven
off a third time. However, the veteran Ensign
Charles Langlade, a famed Canadian partisan
fighter, lingered as close as he dared with
the French Indians and Canadians and maintained
an effective bush-fight with Rogers Rangers,
both sides being adept at this game. Basserode
withdrew out of range to digest his failure.
He had tried to pierce the Rangers' line on
all sides and failed all three times. His men,
veterans though they were, did not have it in
them to make a fourth attack. Moreover, they
had suffered heavily from the Rangers deadly
fire-power and an overwhelming force could not
be mustered for a fourth assault. Accordingly,
two Canadians were sent to Ticonderoga for
reenforcements and more ammunition. Lusignan,
the Commandant, sent Le Borgne, a Colonial
officer, and 25 men to reenforce Basserode.

While waiting for relief, Basserode and his
officers attempted strategm. Calling to Rogers
by name they flattered him and the bravery of
his men, assuring him and his Rangers good
treatment if they surrendered, adding that
when their reenforcements arrived the Rangers
would surely be cut to pieces if they refused.
But Rogers assured them that he had plenty of
men and would do some scalping and cutting to

pieces himself if a fourth charge was attempted.

After the third attack had been beaten off, Rogers had a breathing spell in which he deployed his Rangers into a stronger battle formation. Rogers took the post of honor on the right; Stark, and the Volunteer Baker, were in the center; Ensign Brewer commanded the left; while Ensign Rogers with Sergeants Phillips and Walter, with twelve men were sent to the rear on the very summit of the hill, to act as a reserve, ready to throw themselves into any part of Rogers' thin line that might be attacked. There were not more than forty effective officers and men in Rogers' thin line from end to end. With the reserve of fifteen men, Rogers' force now numbered fifty-seven officers and men, out of the original seventy four at the beginning of the Battle. In the first fire from ambush and the retreat back across La Barbue Creek, Rogers lost ten men killed, and seven were captured or too badly wounded to have reached Stark's column. Two of Rogers' dwindled force of fifty-seven were too severely wounded to fire a gun. They were David Page of Richard Rogers' Company, who was shot through the side, and Eben Perry of Hobbs', who was wounded in the shoulder. The rest of the injured were able to hold a gun and fire. While deploying his men, Rogers could be seen talking earnestly to Robert Baker, the British Volunteer, trying to get him to retire to Ensign Rogers' rear-guard, a much more secure post. He declined and was later mortally wounded.

Creeping as near as they dared, the enemy; numbering one hundred and fifteen according to their accounts, or two hundred and fifty by Rogers Rangers' reports, maintained a bushfighting warfare with the fifty-five effectives of Rogers' force for the remainder of the afternoon. The fire on both sides was not without effect. Captain Basserode was mortally wounded, also Clapier, one of the French Regular Cadets. The French command now devolved on Captain La Granville. About sundown, Rogers himself was again wounded, he received a slanting wound along his hand and through his wrist which prevented him from loading his musket. One of his Rangers deftly made a rude turnquet from Rogers' own que-ribbon. Fearing that his men might be alarmed if an exaggerated account of his injury spread, Rogers sent a Ranger to inform his officers of the true nature of his wounds and not to be discouraged but maintain their ground. Jonathan Cahill of Speakman's Company, was shot in the arm; while Private Joshua Martin of Richard Rogers' was hurt badly, a shot entered his stomach and shattered his hip.

When darkness descended, Rogers called a council of war of his remaining officers, viz., Lieutenant John Stark, Ensigns James Rogers and Jonathan Brewer. "All officers were unanimously of opinion that it was prudent to carry off the wounded of [their] party and take the advantage of the night to return homeward, least the enemy should send out a fresh party upon them in the morning, [besides, their] ammunition being almost expended [they] were obliged to pursue this resolution".

Fortunately, the 7 wounded men that Rogers gathered together in the dark had no leg injuries. Three had arm wounds, two were wounded in the head, one in the mouth, and David Page, brother of the unfortunate Ensign Caleb Page, probably received the worst wound in his side. So, helped by their able comrades, they were able to make fairly good time during the night. Seeing a fire in the woods, which they supposed was that of a hostile party, Rogers Rangers made a long circuit and in the morning found themselves six miles south of the French advance guard on Lake George. The wounded were unable to advance much farther on foot and they were still forty miles from Fort William Henry. Lieutenant Stark volunteered with Thomas Burnside (despite his hand wound) and another Ranger Private, to travel as fast as they could in their exhausted condition, to the fort for a sleigh to convey the wounded. Casting off their snowshoes they took to the lake, and in spite of their fatigue from the Battle and the long march during the night, Stark and his companions reached Fort William Henry, a distance of forty miles, by evening. Stumbling exhausted into the fort they informed the surprised Major Eyre of the engagement. Lieutenant Charles Bulkeley of Hobbs' Company, was immediately dispatched with fifteen men to bring in the wounded. The following morning,

January 23, they met Rogers and his fifty-four survivors staggering through the first narrows of Lake George, and loaded the wounded on the welcome sleigh. After Stark had left Rogers' party at the second narrows, Rogers, not daring to wait, being so far from Fort William Henry, plodded slowly after Stark up the lake. Happening to look back on the ice, Rogers and his Rangers saw a dark object following them. Supposing it might be one of their stragglers Rogers sent men back to get him. It turned out to be Private Joshua Martin of Richard Rogers' Company, whose hipjoint had been shattered by a ball, from a bullet passing through his stomach. He had been left for dead on the field of battle, but recovering himself, he kindled a fire in the night and so, kept from freezing, he was enabled to drag himself painfully after Rogers to the lake. The fire that he had built was the one that the retiring Rangers had mistaken for that of the enemy. The loss of time demanded by the circuitous line of their retreat enabled Sergeant Martin, mortally wounded though he was, to overtake them. He was so exhausted that he collapsed the moment the Rangers reached him. This amazing feat was a characteristic example of the dogged determination of members of the Corps. His deed did not pass unrewarded. Transported with his wounded comrades to William Henry, Martin recovered from his wounds, much to Rogers surprise who thought he did not have a chance for survival. Rogers imagined that he would be shelved for the rest of the year at least. He was promoted to a Sergeant in Dick Rogers' Company and later received an Ensigncy in the Corps.

Not all the Rangers who had been accidentally left on the field of battle were as fortunate as Private Martin. Captain Thomas Speakman, after being mortally wounded, managed to crawl down the gully out of range of the battle. Here he was later joined by Baker, the British Volunteer, and Private Thomas Brown of his own Company, both severely wounded. Brown could just walk and with reckless abandon he built a fire for his Captain and Baker, who could scarcely move. Being out of range of the Battle, Rogers naturally overlooked them when gathering his injured before retiring. After Speakman called to Rogers and received no answer, "except from the Enemy at some distance;" the three unfortunates realized that they had been left. "All hope of Escape now vanish'd;" since they "were so wounded that [they] could not travel" without help. Aware of their deplorable condition, they decided to surrender to the French, if this could be done before the Indians found them. Just as they reached this decision, Brown relates in his *Narrative*, that he "saw an Indian coming towards us over a small Rivulet [La Barbue Creek] that parted us in the Engagement. I crawled so far from the fire that I could not be seen, though I could see what was acted at the fire; the Indian came to Capt. Sp[ea]kman, who was not able to resist, and stripp'd and scalped him alive; Baker who was lying by the Captain, pull'd out his Knife to stab himself which the Indian prevented and carried him away. Seeing this dreadful tragedy, I concluded, if possible, to crawl into the woods and there die of my wounds. But not being far from Captain Sp[ea]kman, he saw me and beg'd me for God's sake! to give him a Tomahawk [Brown's musket had been rendered useless by an enemy ball], that he might put an end to his life. I refus'd him, and exhorted him as well as I could to pray for mercy, as he could not live many minutes in that deplorable condition, being on the frozen ground, cover'd with snow. He desir'd me to let his wife know if I lived to get home the dreadful death he died". Later, Private Brown, in attempting to escape, was captured and experienced one of the most harrowing periods of captivity that has ever been related. Like many of Rogers Rangers though, he managed to escape, was recaptured, and later exchanged.

In this, the first *major* engagement sustained solely by Rogers Rangers, Rogers' losses were fourteen killed, nine wounded, and seven taken prisoners out of seventy-four men engaged. The French force under De Basserode, numbered anywhere from 145 to 250 men, including Canadians and Indians. Taking even the minimum number stated by the French as engaged, viz., 145, Rogers Rangers were outnumbered two to one, not to mention the fact that they were surprised at the outset of the engagement. Rogers, Lieutenant Stark, and Ensigns Rogers and Brewer had turned a desperate situation into a well conceived plan of defense and stubbornly repulsed every attack of Basserode's against their flanks and center until the losses of the enemy were so great that they were forced to resign themselves to firing from the woods. But the Rangers were well covered by large pines and suffered no great damage. Their only appreciable loss was in the first fire from ambush and while they were retiring out of the ravine and back up Stark's hill. The French reports state that their own losses at eighteen killed, including the seven prisoners which Rogers took at Five Mile Point. These were killed by the Rangers at the beginning of the Battle while Rogers was retiring up the hill. The wounded are stated at twenty seven. Thus making the total French losses forty five against the thirty of Rogers Rangers. It is probable that the French losses were greater. They had a habit of understating the true figures.

Both sides claimed a victory. When writing to the French Minister, Montcalm was naturally very generous in the praise he gave to the French Regulars part in the affair; and recommends Captain De Basserode for the Cross of St. Louis. The French claim a victory, no doubt due to the fact that Rogers retired from the field of Battle during the night. While Rogers claims a Battle Honour because he repeatedly beat off Basserode's attacks; and the

French retired out of range and ceased firing when darkness descended thus leaving Rogers Rangers in possession of the field of Battle. The fact that Basserode's losses were greater are other points in favor of the Rangers claim to victory. All factors considered, the Battle of La Barbue Creek might be considered an undecisive engagement with both sides a right to the claim of a victory.

When General Abercrombie heard of the affair he sent Rogers and his Rangers "thanks for their behaviour, and recommended both him and them strongly to Lord Loudoun". As the news of the Battle spread through the Colonies, it did much to bolster the Colonials drooping spirits at the apparent black aspects of the War.

On January 25, while the Rangers were recuperating from their Battle, Richard Rogers had arrived in Boston and was in conference with Lord Loudoun. He turned out to be a most able proxy for his brother, for in the true Rogers' manner he stated that in a fortnight he could raise 100 Rangers in New Hampshire to complete the two Rogers's Companies to 100 each. Fortunately, Loudoun was laying his plans for an attack on Louisbourg on Cape Briton Isle and they included a large body of Rangers to keep the Indians at bay while British Regulars conducted a siege. So Richard was told to talk to the prospective recruits before they started out for their seasonal beaver trappings the middle of February and definite recruiting instructions would soon follow.[122] Follow they did, for nine days after this discussion Lord Loudoun received Rogers' official report of the "Battle of La Barbue Creek" from Abercrombie. Rogers followed it up with a list of officers he recommended to fill up the vacancies in the four Companies.[123] He also offered to augment his Companies to 100 men each and enlist the Privates at 2 shillings and 6 pence New York Currency per day in lieu of the 3 shillings they were now receiving. Ever anxious to show the Crown that he was saving money, Loudoun grasped Rogers' offer and sent the following terms for enlistment to Rogers via General Abercrombie. Rogers had gone down to Albany to obtain better medical treatment for his wrist wound which had become worse.[124]

The new establishment and terms of Rogers Rangers were: that each of the four Companies consist of 100 Privates at 2 shillings and 6 pence per day New York Currency. One Captain, two Lieutenants, one Ensign, who received *English Pay*. The same as British officers of the same rank. Four Sergeants at 4 shillings each, New York Currency, which was the same as before. The new establishment terms went on to state that: "whereas there are some private men of your Companies [meaning the men already in service] serving at present upon higher pay than the above establishment, you are at liberty to discharge them, in case they refuse to serve at the said establishment, as soon as you have other men to replace them. If your men agree to remain with you and serve upon

the above establishment, you may assure them
they will be taken notice of, and be first provided for [in regard to promotion]; each man
to be allowed ten dollars bounty-money, and to
find their own clothes, arms and blankets, and
to sign a paper subjecting themselves to the
rules and articles of war, and to serve during
the War. You are to enlist no vagrants but
such as you and your officers are acquainted
with, and who are every way qualified for the
duty of Rangers; and you and your officers are
to use your best endeavours to complete your
companies as soon as possible, and to bring
them to Fort Edward."[125]

At last the chief bone of dissension between
the four Ranging Companies had been settled
and the officers of all four Companies now received the same pay. When Rogers arrived in
Albany to have his infected wrist wound cared
for he contracted the smallpox or probably
brought it with him from Forts William Henry
or Edward. Thus shelved for several weeks he
was personally unable to promote the interests
of himself and his Corps. But he could still
convey his schemes in writing which he did
through a secretary while still at Fort Edward
and later when he was hospitalized at Albany.

This letter-campaign of Rogers brought about
the above described establishment of Rogers
Rangers:- Writing to Abercrombie from Fort
Edward he offered to sign up his men at twelve cents a day less (about one-sixth less a
day than they were now receiving) if his and

Richard's Company officers would be given the same pay as those of Hobbs' and Speakman's.[126] Although Rogers must have realized that his men would not appreciate this cut in their pay still he knew it was the only way he could settle the *deplorable situation* of officers of the oldest Rogers' Ranging Companies receiving less pay than officers of the newest Companies; for he was aware that Loudoun would have to be shown a means of saving before he would condescend to raise his officer pay. Besides, Rogers shrewdly surmised, how would his men know that it was his idea to lower their pay. If his scheme was agreeable to Loudoun it would then appear that Loudoun himself had conceived the wage cut. In spite of this apparent *selling out* of his Private men, Rogers still had the best interests of his present Rangers at heart for he planned to promote the most desirable; and the new recruits coming in, who would comprise one-half of his augmented Corps, had never received the higher pay and consequently would not have reason to grumble.

Only 74 out of the 159 Privates of the four Companies remaining after La Barbue Creek accepted the wage-cut when Loudoun's new establishment was read to them. The men in Rogers' own Company, the oldest and most seasoned Company in the Corps, objected strenuously, and sixty-five per cent, 26 out of 40 Private men to be exact, refused to serve on the new establishment and were discharged in March and April as soon as new recruits had arrived to fill their places (pursuant to Abercrombie's February 24, order).[127] Richard Rogers Company did somewhat worse. More than two-thirds (32 out of 45 Privates) refused to accept the cut in pay.

A Private in Rogers Rangers now received six pence (12¢) less a day or approximately $7.71 (French and Indian War dollar valuation) a month instead of $9.25 (this was $1.54 or one-sixth less per month). In spite of the 12 cent deduction and the deduction of the $10.00 bounty money from their first pay warrants, this was very good pay for the times.[128] Rogers Rangers were kept on this establishment for the remainder of the War.

Fortunately for the growth of Rogers Rangers were the deaths of both the commanding officers of the new Ranger Companies. Captain Speakman being killed at La Barbue Creek and Captain Hobbs succombing to smallpox on February 22,[129] it was necessary to quickly fill their places. Although Hobbs did not die until after the "List of Commissions granted by Loudoun in the Independent Ranging Companies" were being drawn up, Rogers, anxious to definitly unify and consolidate the Fort William Henry Ranging Companies with his, had strongly recommended Lieutenant John Stark for Captain Speakman's vacancy.[130] The conspicuous role Stark played at La Barbue Creek cinched the Captaincy for him. This helped Rogers' scheme for a battalion size Corps of Rangers, still it started a profound jealousy which grew in a few months to an act of violence. The fact that John Stark was given the command of Speakman's Company infuriated Jonathan Brewer. Brewer, when he discovered that he was the only officer left alive in the Company after the Battle, had naturally hoped for the Captaincy of it. But Stark was the Senior Lieutenant of Rangers and Brewer was only an Ensign. Brewer was promoted though, to the First Lieutenantcy of the Company, but he never accepted St~~k, who he felt was holding his command. Brewer quietly served efficiently under Captain Stark but his jealousy smouldered on and he bided his time.

Now that the four Companies were on a new establishment it was necessary to increase the Lieutenants and Sergeants of each Company as the new status called for one more Lieutenant and Sergeant to each Company. Rogers' own Company, who had previously mustered two Lieutenants, now carried three; while Richard Rogers' and the two new Companies now mustered two Lieutenants instead of one. The supernumeracy of Lieutenants in Rogers' own Company seems to have been established due to the fact that Rogers, the Senior Captain, had to devote considerable time to the command and looking after of his complete Corps of four Companies. It was frequently left to the First Lieutenant of Rogers' Company to take care of the details of management, muster-rolls, and breaking in of new recruits for that Company. This was now ably done by Rogers' First Lieutenant, the veteran John McCurdy who had replaced Stark.[131]

There was no question now but that the former Hobbs' and Speakman's Companies were definitly under Rogers direct command and formed part of his Corps. After La Barbue Creek he quickly recommended outstanding participants to fill up the vacancies in all the Companies. This could not have been done if the new Companies were not under Rogers' command. Rogers' list of officers recommended to fill up the vacandies was followed by a very favorable letter to Loudoun by Abercrombie in which he states: "Captain Robert Rogers, whose behaviour upon this late occasion intitles him to marks of your Lordships favour and Countenance. His relation" of the Battle "by way of" his "journal is very modest.."[132]

Jonathan Brewer's natural expectancy to the Captaincy of late Speakman's Company showed how independent the recent Hobbs' and Speakman's Companies considered themselves from the two Rogers's. Stark's promotion to command Speakman's Company and Loudoun's commissioning of other recommendations of Rogers in the new Companies reveals how finally the four Companies (although still called Independent Companies) were definitly merged into one distinct body under Rogers' command. By all military ethics, Robert Rogers should have now been promoted and held at least a commission as Major over his *battalion* of 400 Rangers. Although he was already *dubbed* "Major" by his men and the Provincials (British Officers in camp still called him "Captain") he was, actually, still only the Senior Captain of Rangers. It was not until April 1758, that he finally received his Majority. Loudoun was very foolish in not promoting him sooner. Possibly he wanted to see first how the home office was going to swallow his increasement of the Rangers. This lack of promotion put Rogers in an awkward position and gave him the disturbing sense of holding a temporary command. How true this was, if he could have read the correspondence that passed between Loudoun and the Prime Minister stating their plans of employing Rogers' Rangers only long enough to teach the Regulars their tactics,[133] it is to be wondered if Rogers would have continued in his command, or, in disgust, have given it up and sought other pursuits. But Robert Rogers was young and consequently hopeful, and though he was not promoted, he had finally got an increase of command. His command, instead of being doubled as he had hoped for in his petitions of last Fall and Winter, was increased three hundred per cent and he was delighted.

Meanwhile, the growth and fame of his Corps was being increased by his able seconds Captains Richard Rogers and John Stark, while he was confined to his bed in Albany with smallpox wondering if he would be as unlucky in this ravaging disease as Captain Hobbs. Officers and Sergeants were sent into New England to recruit and they kept in touch with Captain Richard Rogers who managed this end of the recruitment service.

By Courtesy of the National Life Insurance Company.

Rogers' recruiting officers had an ample selection of worthy aspirants to choose from for the fame of *Rogers' Rangers* had spread far and wide and adventurous souls were eager to sign up.

Lieutenant Charles Bulkeley, now in line for a Captaincy since Hobbs' death, exerted himself to make a good showing and thus win his spurs. Even though he had been unlucky enough to miss making a name for himself at La Car'oue Creek, still, he more than fullfilled the prerequisites for a promotion by enlisting thirty two Privates in Massachusetts (his home Province) in less than two weeks. On April 25, following his good enlisting service and a very favorable recommendation from *Major* Rogers, he was commissioned Captain to succeed the late Deacon Hobbs.[134]

Not all the Ranger recruits were plucked in New England. *Ensign* "Bill Phillips", now in the late Hobbs' Company, set an unprecedented record by enlisting eleven Privates in one day in the Mohawk River Valley.[135] This speaks well for the growing enchantment of Rogers Rangers for it was not customary for natives of this region to serve in any Corps other than those raised and commanded by Sir William Johnson or his hencemen. The fact that five of Phillips' recruits were Dutch friends and one, John Phillips, was related to him, might have presented additional inducement factors besides the magnetic hypnosis of *Rogers Rangers*.

Meanwhile, the Rogers Rangers who were stationed at Fort William Henry were commanded by Captain John Stark in Rogers' absence, and while Richard Rogers was overseeing the growth of the Corps, Stark managed to increase their fame. Stark's command comprised the remnants of Hobbs' and Speakman's Companies consisting in all of about 82 officers and men. Ten of these were Privates on the sick list. One of them, John Cahill being a casualty of La Barbue Creek. John Fish, a Private was on furlough. Privates John Hays and Amariah Hildreth were on party, and the effective Privates were further reduced by the absence of William Mitchael who was confined in the provost at Albany for attempting to desert.[136]

The two Companies were forlorn bodies with both their Captains dead, still, the bulk of them revealed their desire to continue as Rogers Rangers when the terms of the new establishment were known to them. Almost two-thirds of the two Companies took the ten dollars bounty money and reenlisted; even though the terms of their original enlistments were up on May 27th. The other third, 27 Private men to be exact, were discharged at intervals from March 12th to May 31st 1757, when recruits had arrived to fill their places (pursuant to Abercrombie's orders).

When Stark arrived at William Henry he was still only the Senior Lieutenant of Rangers. A fact which started the feud between him and Jonathan Brewer. Though Loudoun dated the new commissions February 24, 26, or the 27th,[137] he shrewdly did not let the officers know that they had been promoted until after the eager candidates had completed the Companies to their newly authorized strength. However, immediately after Captain Hobbs' untimely death, Stark was sent up to command the two Companies until his Captaincy of Speakman's Company had been confirmed, and Hobbs' vacancy filled up. Fortunately, Stark's elevation to this temporary command was accepted by the majority of the officers and men of the two Ranging Companies at William Henry, for he had won their respect and admiration by his brilliant leadership at La Barbue Creek. The only strained relation existed between Ensign Brewer and Stark. Even though they had fought side by side at La Barbue Creek and together skillfully covered Rogers' retreat to a station of defense, still, Brewer inwardly fumed at Stark's assumption to the command of his Company. The month that he had commanded the Company after his return from the Battle and Stark's arrival had been long enough to give him a taste of the Captaincy and he liked it. When the December 24, to February 24, Muster Rolls were compiled for "the late Speakman's Company" he had signed and confirmed the names on the roll just like a Captain would have done.[138] Naturally he had developed a hopeful claim which he now saw crumbling, and Stark's taciturn nature did nothing to smooth things over. So things remained rather tense while all the prospective officers anxiously awaited news about their promotions. But they did not know until after March 24, of their promotions for Loudoun was busy in Virginia with the Provincial Assemblies and he did not sign their commissions until March 8, and dated them for February, and by the time the packet boats reached New York and Albany, then by foot-express to William Henry via Fort Edward, the officers discovered that they bore commissions dated a month old.[139]

Meanwhile, Stark had sent Lieutenant Bulkeley and Sergeant Charles Joseph Walter recruiting for their Company and Sergeants Robert Truett and Increase Moore; and Corporal Jacob Townsend recruiting in New England for his Company.[140] Outside of the repressed Brewer-Stark feud events at William Henry went their routine way until the middle of March when Rogers Rangers gathered new laurels and Fort William Henry was saved, to a great extent, by the forethought and vigilance of John Stark.

On the evening of March 16, Stark overheard that his Rangers were planning a celebration of St. Patrick's day, which was on the 17th. Knowing that the greater portion of British Regulars stationed at the fort were Irish and would be indulging in paying homage to their patron Saint in excessive quantities of rum and spruce beer; Stark foresaw the danger to which the fort would be exposed if both the Rangers and Regulars were in their cups. He knew that a large proportion of Rogers Rangers were Irish or Scotch-Irish, like himself, and, though they were not Catholic, they were all intending to celebrate, as this was to good an opportunity to break the monotony of garrison life not to be taken advantage of. Stark accordingly gave orders to the Rangers' Sutler, Levi, who had his storehouse among the Rangers'

First Defense of Fort William Henry[9]

huts, that no *spirituous liquors* should be issued, except by authority of written orders from himself; and when he was swamped for these orders he laconically pleaded the lameness of his wrist, from a sprain, as an excuse for not giving them. In this way he kept the greater part of the Rangers sober; though they protested loud and clear their grievance, and at the time actually hated their commander. The Irish Regulars were, for the most part, in a mellow stupor, at the close of the day, when the French appeared.

Governor-General Vaudreuil had sent a strong force of 1,600 men, under the command of his brother, Rigaud, to make an unexpected attack on Fort William Henry. The total force at William Henry under the able Major Eyre consisted of 346 Irish Regulars and Rogers Rangers. Of these, Stark's effective command consisted of sixty non-coms and men. Stark's officers were his colleague Ensign Jonathan Brewer, and his good friend and home-neighbor, Ensign James Rogers, the "Major's" elder brother, who commanded the late Hobbs' Company during Lieutenant Bulkeley's absence.

The Irish Regulars had their celebration after evening mess on the 17th and staggered heavily through the routine duties of the following day and that night fell into their beds in a deep sleep. The Rangers in their picketted fort on the east side of William Henry fumed and quietly cursed Stark as the sounds of the Regulars ribald celebration drifted down to them. As the night and following day passed without any visit from the enemy, Stark grew uncomfortable and began to wonder if he had done the right thing, for all the inhabitants of the little hut-village gave him black looks whenever he encountered them. But his emotions were soon quieted when that night one of his alert Ranger sentrys on the east side of their picketted hut-fort discovered a light moving on the lake. Stark immediately informed the Commandant, Major Eyre, who ordered the Rangers into William Henry. The Regulars were routed from their heavy sleep and hushed into silence as they took their places along the ramparts with Rogers Rangers who had reluctantly abandoned their picketted village.

"Soon after the enemy endeavoured to approach the Fort, but met with such a warm and unexpected reception as [to] soon oblige them to retire". At daylight and throughout the day "there was not the face of a Frenchman to be seen, but at night they returned..intending to scale the walls of the fort..but the defenders [kept] so good a look-out and constant fire on them as they approached that their design was frustrated."

The following morning, which was Sunday, the enemy's camp was discovered about a mile from the fort by their camp-fire smoke. Major Eyre immediately ordered Stark to send a reconnaisance party of Rangers out to view the strength of their encampment. They returned before noon and reported the French very numerous and about ready to make another attack. About twelve o'clock noon they marched their whole army in sight of the fort, two men deep, which extended more than a mile-and-a-half on the ice, in order to intimidate the garrison. Rigaud now sent Chevalier Mercer under a flag of truce to Major Eyre asking him to surrender. In spite of the sight of Rigaud's numerous force before his fort, the valiant Eyre flatly refused to surrender even on good terms. A general assault was now expected and when the news reached the sick Rangers and Regulars below the ramparts, who were suffering mostly from scurvy, those that could walk or crawl bravely made their way to a firing position on the ramparts.

The men of Rogers Rangers who so stoicly left their sick beds to defend the fortress against assault "to the last man" were Privates: Zebulon Bush, Zach Crow, James Dorey, Solomon Lopos, Dematres Seat and Peter Sleater of Stark's Company; and Joshua Dutton, Levi Gray, Jonathan Hodgkins, Charles Hanns and Charles Knowlton of late Hobbs' Company.

Much to the defenders disappointment, Rigaud did not order a general assault but waited until nightfall when they concentrated their attention on the Rangers' stockade and the British flotilla of lake boats in dry-dock near by. When the Rangers saw their huts going up in flames they begged to be allowed to make a sortie and divert the enemy away from them. Because of their hasty withdrawal to William Henry the Rangers did not have time to gather

their personal belongings, and now they were
forced to stand helplessly by for the huts
were out of range of even their most accurate
fire. But Eyre soon gave Stark permission to *Stark's*
sally out, for there was grave danger of the *March 21st*
whole fort catching fire and endangering William *Sortie*[10]
Henry proper. Stark had no trouble gathering
volunteers and he burst out of the fort with
an angry party of grey uniformed Rangers to
wreck vengeance on their home-destroyers. They
attacked with such determination that Rigaud's
men abandoned the Rangers' huts and Stark returned to William Henry before they could be
cut off. In spite of their efforts, the fire
consumed seventeen of the Rangers' huts before
it died out. In this fierce little sortie,
Rogers Rangers suffered three men wounded:
Privates William Annis and Jonathan Edmunds of
Stark's Company, and John Stark himself was
grazed by a bullet for the first and only time
in his adventurous life.

Rigaud now devoted his attention to the
British flotilla and managed to destroy most of
it in spite of a vigorous sortie of Regulars *March*
and Rangers who could not save them. But they *22nd*
did manage to save a considerable portion of *Rum*
the provisions, particularly rum, from the *Sortie*[1]
Rangers' storehouse and other sheds in the hut
village, which had been fired by the enemy.
Part of the sallying-party maintained a covering fire while the remainder quickly evacuated
all the kegs of rum and whatever other *subordinate* items that they had time for.

On the morning of March 23, Rigaud's army could be seen filing down Lake George back to Canada. His initial attempt a failure, Rigaud excused himself by saying that the thaw rendered it impossible to take the fort. But this was a poor excuse for the thaw did not start until after he returned. Rigaud lost fourteen men killed and three wounded, who were captured, being to wounded to make the return march. English losses were four Regulars; John Stark and two Rangers slightly wounded. Losses on both sides occurred mostly in the two sorties on the 21st and 22nd.

From the prisoners, the Rangers and soon the Colonies at large, learned that two of Rogers Rangers had turned traitor and offered their services to the French. Privates Benjamin Woodall and David Kimble of Richard Rogers Company had been prevailed upon to show Rigaud the way to William Henry and the most accessible places where they could make an attack with success and when Rigaud took the fort each of them was to be given a thousand Crowns. The two Rangers who had sold out to Rigaud had both been taken prisoners by the French in their first surprise attack at La Barbue Creek. Their survival instinct predominated after witnessing the barbarity inflicted upon their comrades. They had witnessed Lieutenant Samuel Kennedy's death by a barrage of tomahawks after he had been mortally wounded, besides being eve-witnesses to other Indian refinements; and when an opportunity arose to save their own necks they grasped it.

Another Ranger captive of La Barbue Creek who had been approached by Rigaud at Ticonderoga relates his own refusal and the scorn he felt towards Woodall and Kimble who weakened. Young Thomas Brown says that "the first of March General Rigaud came to" Ticonderoga with 1,600 men, "in order, as they said, to make an attempt on Fort William Henry. Their design was to scale the walls, for which purpose I saw them making scaling-ladders. The day before they marched the General sent for me and said, *Young Man, you are a likely fellow; it's a pity you should live with such an ignorant people as the English; you had better live with me.* I told him I was willing to live with him." Brown was willing to live with anyone but the Indians. "He answered, I should, and go with him where he went. I replied, perhaps he would have me to go to War with him. He said that was the thing, he wanted me to direct him to Fort William Henry, and show him where he might scale the walls. I told him I was sorry that a Gentleman should desire such a thing of a youth, or endeavor to draw him away from his duty. He added, he would give me 7,000 Livres on his return. I replied that I was not to be bought with money, to be a traitor to my country and assist in destroying my friends. He smiled, and said, in War you must not mind even Father nor Mother. When he found that he could not prevail with me by all the fair promises he made, he ordered me back to the" guard house; "and had two other

Prisoners"-Privates Benjamin Woodall and David Kimble,--"brought before him, to whom, he made the same proposals as he had to me; to which they consented. The next day I went into the room where they were, and asked them if they had been with the General; they said they had, and that they were to have 7,000 Livres apiece, as a reward. I asked them if that was the value of their Fathers and Mothers, and of their Country? They said they were obliged to go. I said the General could not force them; and added, that if they went on such a design they must never return among their friends, for if they did, and Baker [the British Volunteer] and I should live to get home we would endeavour they should be hanged. At this time a Smith came and put Irons on my feet. But the General gave those two men who had promised to go with him, a blanket, a pair of stockings and shoes. They were taken out of the Guardhouse, and marched with the French as Pilots. The General did not succeed; he only burnt our Battoes etc., and returned to Ticonderoga. The poor fellows never had their reward, but instead of that were sent to the Guard-House and put in Irons." The subsequent fate of the two Rangers who sold out are not definitly known but they were not among those that escaped or were later exchanged. It is probable they were given to the Indians to pacify them for Rigaud's failure. What fate they met at their savage hands can only be imagined. Thomas Brown reports that two Rangers suffered horrible deaths at their hands and it is possible that they were the two betrayers.

When Rigaud appeared before William Henry Major Eyre waited until the following day, the 20th, before he sent news of the attack to his superior in Albany. The message was entrusted to one of Rogers Rangers and he got through to Fort Edward. When Rigaud retired down the lake on the 23rd, Eyre sent another Ranger with the joyfull news. This Ranger because of the fierce weather could not make Fort Edward the same day and he built a fire at night to keep from freezing. Lying too close to the coals he burnt his pocket and the message while sleeping. However one of Rogers Rangers at Fort Edward sent to William Henry with the news that reenforcements were coming up, had returned to Fort Edward before the dejected Ranger tardily entered the fort and informed Colonel Monro of his excusable accident.[141]

Monro proceeded to William Henry with a strong reenforcement and relieved Eyre's scurvy ridden battalion, which returned with Eyre to Albany arriving there on April 2nd.[142] Rogers Ranger Companies at William Henry were not as fortunate to be relieved after their trying ordeals. They had to remain on and lick their wounds as best they could. With Monro's relief force arrived the colorful new Ranger *Ensign*, "Bill Phillips", and eleven Ranger recruits from the Mohawk Valley.[143] There also arrived Loudoun's belated commissions and promotions for the Ranger Companies.[144]

The officers berths of late Hobbs' and Speakman's Companies had been filled up by Loudoun (at Rogers' suggestion) as follows:-[145]

SPEAKMAN'S (now STARK'S) COMPANY:
CAPTAIN: First Lieutenant John Stark of Rogers' own. Commissioned Captain, February 24, 1757.
FIRST LIEUTENANT: Ensign Jonathan Brewer of Speakman's. First Lieutenant, February 24th.
SECOND LIEUTENANT: Ensign Jonathan Burbank of Rogers' own. Second Lieutenant, February 26th.
ENSIGN: Sergeant Increase Moore of Speakman's. Ensign, February 26th.

HOBBS' COMPANY (Captaincy still unfilled):
FIRST LIEUTENANT: Charles Bulkeley.
SECOND LIEUTENANT: Ensign James Rogers of Hobbs' First Lieutenant, February 27th.
ENSIGN: Sergeant William Hendrick Phillips of Rogers' own Company, February 27, 1757.

All of these officers, with the exception of Bulkeley, Burbank and Moore who were recruiting in New England, were at William Henry. Finally, by the end of April the Companies were swelled to their newly established strength when these officers returned with their recruits. Ensign Moore set a new high for recruiting by enlisting fourty Privates in New Hampshire for Stark's Company.[146] Lieutenant Burbank ushered his way into the same Company with fourteen Privates enlisted by him in New Hampshire;[147] while Lieutenant Bulkeley returned to Hobbs' Company with thirty-two men which he had mustered in Massachusetts.[148] A new Lieutenant gazetted to late Hobbs', Thomas Cunningham, and a new Sergeant, John Dinsmore, swelled the Company with twenty-seven Privates raised in

New Hampshire.[149] Two weeks after his return to William Henry, Charles Bulkeley received his Captains' commission to command the late Hobbs' Company. His commission was dated April 25th.[150] The officer berths of Hobbs' now Bulkeley's Company were:

Lieutenant Charles Bulkeley now Captain Apr. 25.
Second Lieutenant James Rogers now First Lieut.
Ensign Thomas Cunningham of Rogers' own now Second Lieutenant of Bulkeley's April 25, 1757.
Ensign 'Bill' Phillips remained as the Ensign.

The reason for Cunningham's promotion to Second Lieutenant over Phillips was due to the system of seniority which held in Rogers Rangers fairly rigidly. Cunningham was an Ensign three days before "Bill Phillips". He was also a Sergeant in Rogers' own before Phillips.[151]

Rogers' plan to infuse the Fort William Henry Companies with seasoned members of his own Company had succeeded. Half of the eight officers berths were filled by former officers and sergeants of his Company. Already the two Companies had profitted by Rogers' wise recommendations by Captain Stark's masterful handling of them before and during the attack on William Henry. With two Battle Honours under their belts and skilled officers at their heads, Stark's and Bulkeley's Companies were developing into skilled fighting Rangers. By fighting and winning two engagements within two months during the dead of Winter, they had proved themselves worthy of Rogers Rangers. All of the officers of the two Companies had served together at La Barbue Creek with the exception of Captain Bulkeley and Lieutenants Burbank and Cunningham. Still it was through no fault of theirs that they had not taken part in this first major testing ground of Rogers Rangers in a heated engagement. Lieutenant Burbank soon cemented himself well with the officers and men. Although he did not share the comradeship which drew men so close after serving together in a life or death struggle, still Burbank's paunchy good humour endeared him to his fellow officers and men. Captain Stark was well liked by his subordinates after they knew him for awhile. Because of his naturally tactless nature and grim countenance he was not one to be taken to immediately. His was a personality that won respect by deeds rather than words, and there was no question that he was a brave, capable commander, well able to lead men into battle besides skillfully managing the tedium of routine garrison life. Burbank and "Bill Phillips" were direct opposites in personality and there hail-fellow-well-met attitude did much to sooth Stark's grim impression.

While Stark's and Bulkeley's Companies had passed a stirring winter at William Henry since La Barbue Creek and the coming of Spring, events at Rogers' Island had been tranquil for the two Rogers's Companies. John McCurdy commanded Rogers' own Company during Rogers' illness while Lieutenant Noah Johnson took over the reins of Richard Rogers' Company while he recruited. Both of these men were of Rogers' original Rangers but McCurdy was the only one

of the two to profit by the new establishment
and be promoted. He was promoted from Second
to First Lieutenant of Rogers' Company. Captain
Richard Rogers returned from New Hampshire in
March with enough recruits to complete his
Company,[152] while Lieutenant William Stark,
Ensign Charles Walter; and Sergeants Bolton
and Lownsbury of Rogers' own, raised seventy
eight Privates for the "Major's" Company.[153]
The officer status of the two Rogers's Companies at Fort Edward were:[154]

ROBERT ROGERS' COMPANY:

CAPTAIN: Robert Rogers.

FIRST LIEUTENANT: John McCurdy, from Second to First Lieutenant.

SECOND LIEUTENANT: Cadet Wm. Stark of Rogers' own. Second Lieutenant, February 24, 1757.

ENSIGN: Sergt. Charles Joseph Walter of Hobbs' Ensign, April 1, 1757.

RICHARD ROGERS' COMPANY:

CAPTAIN: Richard Rogers.

FIRST LIEUTENANT: Noah Johnson.

SECOND LIEUTENANT: Civilian Nathaniel Abbot of N.H. Second Lieutenant February 25, 1757.

ENSIGN: Sergeant Stephen Holland of Richard Rogers'. Ensign, February 25, 1757.

Loudoun's plans for the year were to attack
Louisbourg, with the view of assaulting Quebec
afterwards. He accordingly, very unwisely,
drained all the interior Forts of the bulk of
their troops and gathered them at New York to
await embarkation for Halifax where he was to
meet Admiral Holbourne and 15 ships.[155]

Loudoun in a letter to the Duke of Cumberland shows that he realized the value of Rangers, and his original plan for the Campaign of 1757 shows that they were to play a conspicuous part. His letter also expressed his viewpoints on the so called Indian Allies of England, which were anything but favorable:- "I am afraid I shall be blamed for the Ranging Companies" (meaning his increasement of Rogers Ranging Companies, and the additional expense of keeping such a large body of Rangers in the field would necessitate) "but as really in effect we have no Indians, it is impossible for an Army to act in this country without Rangers; and there ought to be a considerable body of them, and the breeding them up to that, will be a great advantage to the Country, for they will be able to deal with Indians in their own way; and from all I can see, are much stronger and hardier fellows than the Indians, who are many of them tall, as most of the People here are, but have a small febble arm, and are a loose-made indolent set of People; and hardly any of them, have the least degree of Faith or honesty; and I doubt a good deal of their Courage; better times may show them in a different light."[156]

Part of Loudoun's dream for 1757 was to ask for 4,000 men, all Rangers, from the four New England Governors. His plan was to send them into French held territory by way of Number Four-Otter Creek-and Lake Champlain, "to make all the disturbance in their Power". They were to attack the settlements on the south side of the St. Lawrence and drive in the inhabitants; disrupt the flow of provisions sent to Quebec; and when Loudoun arrived before Quebec the Rangers were to be transported to the north side and continue their harassment and thus detract from Loudoun's siege operations.[157]

This was an amplification of Rogers' proposal to attack St. Francis but not once does Loudoun mention his name or give him the least bit of credit. It is too bad that the demon hand of delay had held up Loudoun's dreams for a fast dashing Campaign, so that he was not able to develop this scheme, sound as it was, in the hands of such a partisan as Robert Rogers the execution of it could be assured, and in all probability carried through to success; and who knows but that the conquest of Canada might have been completed in 1757, instead of 1760.

On April 15, Rogers dragged his cured but fever-weakened body from the room where, for forty days, he had been battling with smallpox that to prominent disease of the times.[158]

Seven days later he received orders to prepare the bulk of his now fully recruited Corps for "Foreign Service".[159] The men of the two Rogers's Companies were still considered the most experienced Rangers of the Corps because of their longer length of service. Consequently one of them, Richard Rogers' Company, was moved up to William Henry to serve as the eyes of Webb's army left to guard the Lake George front. Stark's and Bulkeley's came down from William Henry and embarked with Rogers' own

Company at Albany for New York to await orders to proceed to Louisbourg via Halifax.[160]

Stark's April Scout[31] Captain Stark, shortly after Rigaud's withdrawal, had led a scout to reconnoitre Ticonderoga. He returned unscathed to report a state of inactivity at the fortress.

McCurdys Short Scout[32] Lieutenant John McCurdy with thirteen men of Rogers' Company were scouting towards Crown Point when their scout was rudely interrupted by a Ranger from William Henry who had been sent to find them and tell McCurdy to abandon his quest for a prisoner and make a forced march to Albany or they would miss their boat.

Scout of Bulkeley's Co.[33] Another scout out from Bulkeley's Company at William Henry lost Private John Robertson on May 11th.

Arriving at New York Rogers Rangers were augmented by a new Company of New Hampshire Rangers under the command of Captain John Shepherd. The officers for this Company had been recommended to Loudoun by Colonel Messerve "the Carpenter",[161] who was high in Loudoun's favor. Even though Rogers had nothing to do with its creation, Shepherd's Company came under his command when they met at New York and from then on it constituted part of his Corps.[162] Shepherd's Company came to life on February 25, 1757, when Loudoun commissioned him Captain. James Neal was commissioned his First Lieutenant on February 28; and the next day, Samuel Gilman, Second Lieutenant. No Ensign was appointed at this time.[163]

Raising his Company in New Hampshire, Shepherd

was ordered to help Colonel Messerve convey three cannon to strengthen the defences of Number Four, who feared an Indian attack from St. Francis.[164] Much to the uneasiness of the Number Four inhabitants, Shepherd's Rangers were almost immediately ordered to follow Messerve's Company of Artificers to Long Island and join the Louisbourg Expedition.[165] Crossing the woods on snowshoes Shepherd's men arrived at Middleton and embarked for Flushing Bay on Long Island where they joined Rogers Rangers when they arrived from Albany.[166]

Rogers Rangers had expected their stay in New York would be somewhat on the status of a furlough but they soon discovered differently. Arriving in New York harbour they came to anchor a half-mile from the transports while their sloops were searched for smallpox victims. Among others removed to the Hospital was Captain John Stark who had fallen prey to the disease while enroute to New York.[167] After the smallpox search the Companies were assigned to the following transports:[168]

Rogers' Company to the Sheffield.
Stark's Company to the brig Betsey.
Bulkeley's Company to the snow Tarter.
Shepherd's Company to the Delight.

Fortunately the Rangers received a much needed addition at this time in the form of Doctor Ammi Ruhamah Cutter of Portsmouth, New Hampshire, who became Surgeon to Rogers Rangers for the Campaign. He had arrived at New York with Colonel Messerve and together they waited on Loudoun's office on May 6, and secured a

Relief of Number Four 34

commission for Cutter to act as Surgeon to the Rangers and Messerve's Company of Carpenters at five shillings a day. He had his Medicine Chest fitted out at a cost of ten pounds New York currency which he borrowed from Rogers. Luckily for Surgeon Cutter, all he had to do while the Corps was in New York was to diagnose the sick Rangers and have them sent to the Hospital if they showed symptoms of smallpox. While at sea, and at Nova Scotia, he had to care for his own patients and administer "blood purgings", the accepted cure-all of the times.[169]

A Provincial Company of 100 Rangers under Captain John Titcomb had been raised in New Hampshire. They were assigned to Rogers' command but were paid and equipped by the New Hampshire Government. They were *not* Rangers though, in the status that Rogers Rangers were (viz., His Majesty's Independent Companies of American Rangers; maintained out of contingent funds); and were not under Rogers' command when the expedition was over.[170]

While waiting on board the transports, the Rangers were galled and considerably restricted by Loudoun's various General Orders of the Day.[171] They were allowed ashore only during the day and could not bring on board any "Spiritous Licquors" and if any were found on board they were to be destroyed.[172] While ashore they were not allowed to gamble or watch any one else cast the rolling dominoes;[173] and five days before they sailed, they were forbidden ashore unless an officer accompanied them as several complaints had been reported of robberies committed by drunken soldiers and the *Lorelei* camp women.[174] Being denied their liquid and gaming pleasures the Rangers turned to fishing and swimming off the transports but several men were attacked by sharks and a General Order forbade any more swimming.[175]

Finally, on June 18, the ships dropped anchor an sailed for Halifax, arriving there on July 1st. The next day, Rogers Rangers were detatched from the army by being quartered on the Dartmouth side of the harbour "in houses left by the people". There were many cases of small pox in the Corps, and Surgeon Cutter was kept very busy. On the 4th, he spent all day visiting the sick.[176]

At Long Island, on the night of their sailing, occurred one of the most audacious acts committed by an officer of Rogers Rangers. It was the second act of the Brewer-Stark drama. Captain Stark, at almost the last hour, having recovered considerably from the smallpox, decided that he was well enough to sail with his Company. But not so Lieutenant Jonathan Brewer who had commanded in Stark's absence. Brewer had expected that Stark's illness would last until after they had sailed at least. Now he saw all his hopes of commanding the Company for at least the campaign shattered and his smouldering resentment came flaming to the surface in an act of violence. Meeting his Captain on shore he locked the surprised Stark up

and by the time he got free the transports had
sailed. Furious, Stark penned an account of
his rough treatment to Rogers and sent it by
the first packet-boat bound for Halifax. Rogers
confined Brewer and informed Loudoun of the incident. The precocious Lieutenant was tried by
a Court-Martial in Halifax on July 21, presi-
ded over by Lieutenant Colonel Thomas Gage,
who had no love for the rugged individualism
of Rogers Rangers. Brewer was judged guilty of
"confining his Captain illegally" and the Court
Martial sentenced him to be cashiered. Loudoun
approved of the sentence but on July 26, in
consideration of his former good services,
particularly at La Barbue Creek, pardoned him
(It is probable that Rogers intervened in his
behalf, hoping that the fiery, but valuable
Brewer had been sufficiently chastised).[177]

Stark had a relapse from his attack of smallpox and could not join his Company.[178] When he
again assumed active command when his Company
returned, the feud between him and Brewer had
been considerably softened. Rogers, fully aware
of the value of the two officers, had intervened. He assured Brewer that he would receive
the Captaincy of the next Company of Rangers
raised. At the same time Captain Stark was
told to take it easy on him. When the two meet
Brewer must have apologized, and though the
situation was tense for awhile, time, and active service together, smoothed it out.[179]

While Loudoun waited for the arrival of the
British fleet from England to support his ad-

vance on Louisbourg, Rogers Rangers were employed on various services but not before another feud had been nipped in the bud, this time by the quick intervention of Loudoun. When the Corps arrived at Halifax on July 1, Rogers exploited his shaky brevet of *Major* and left the immediate command of his Company to First Lieutenant John McCurdy. Rogers' assumed rank, and the fact that he commanded five Companies (including Titcomb's temporary Rangers) irked Joseph Goreham, who was Captain of the ancient "Goreham's Rangers" of Nova Scotia. Goreham had been a Captain of this Independent Company of Rangers since King George's War and he strongly resented Rogers taking over. He must have stated as much to Rogers for a "Holler" started between Rogers' and Goreham's Rangers. It was apparent that the Rangers would come to blows unless some sort of seniority was settled. Consequently Rogers and Goreham marched into Loudoun's headquarters to have him determine the Senior Captain of Rangers.[180] How Loudoun settled this delicate situation has not been recorded, but we do know that he never made the catastrophic mistake of sending them scouting together. He wisely separated these two rugged personalities by ordering Rogers the same day with a large party of his Rangers to Lawrencetown and Shitzcook to cut and stack hay in the meadows for the army horses.[181] By these tactics Loudoun quieted the controversy, but the "Holler" would never have occurred if he had given Rogers his Majority which his command warranted.

    While on their "hay assignment" turns were taken in cutting and standing guard. Small scouts were thrown out to spot any partisan bands lurking in the vicinity. In spite of these precautions, three Rangers were taken prisoners at Lawrencetown "by ye Indians" on July 29th.[182]

Lawrence Town Blood Hound Scout[35]   On July 5, two privates of Lassel's 45th Regiment deserted from Halifax. They were seen going in the direction of Lawrencetown, and Loudoun ordered after them, a Sergeant and a party of Rangers from Rogers' base at Dartmouth. He gave the Sergeant a letter with express orders to Rogers to take them dead or alive, but not to pursue them more than twelve miles from where he was cutting hay as he might meet an enemy band to strong for his detatchment. Rogers threw out a dragnet which was effective and the hapless deserters were seized and brought in.

North West Nova Scotia Blood Hound Scout[36]   The only other singular service of Rogers Rangers occurred on July 13, when forty Rangers were sent across the isthmus of Nova Scotia to the settlements on the Bay of Fundy and a party of sixty Rangers under Captain Bulkeley were sent down the north-west arm to scour the woods for deserters and enemy Indians. They found no Indians but by the end of the month brought in several deserters from both the army and the navy.

    Finally the British fleet arrived, "upon which all scouting parties were called in", and the troops were embarked on August 1st and 2nd.[183] All was in readiness when word came that 22 French ships of the line, besides several frigates had united in Louisbourg harbor, and that the fortress of Louisbourg had been heavily reenforced. So, any attempts to take Louisbourg this year were decidedly risky and the expedition was abandoned.[184] Loudoun sailed with his troops back to New York to protect the menaced Colonies, and Rogers Rangers returned to Fort Edward.

* * * * * *

While Loudoun with the best part of the army and the bulk of Rogers Rangers were at Halifax, Montcalm had not been idle. He determined to attack and destroy Fort William Henry and possibly Fort Edward as well. While Montcalm was assembling his army at Ticonderoga prior to his advance, Richard Rogers and his Company gave a good account of themselves. A Company of New Jersey Dutch Batteaumen under Captain Philip Burgin had induced Loudoun to sign them up as *Rangers* for the Campaign and they were sent up to Fort William Henry to be instructed by Richard Rogers in the different scouts and patrols that were maintained for the safety of the fort. It was soon discovered that they were inadequate for the exacting and ardous Ranging duties.[185] They were sent to Fort Edward and Captain Ogden's New York Company of Provincial Rangers came up to relieve them and they fought side by side with Rogers' Company in the forthcoming Siege.

Captains Richard Rogers and Ogden soon made

Richard Rogers' Attack on Coutre Coeur [12]

a notable scout which included a skirmish with the French advanced fort of Coutre Coeur. This was a noteworthy expedition in the history of Rogers Rangers for it was the first *battle* that Richard Rogers commanded in, and the last one that he ever fought. Richard had been in numerous scouts since the creation of the Corps but he had missed being present at La Barbue Creek and at William Henry during its first attack. However he was with his brother in the Corps' first engagement at the "Isle of Mutton" in 1755, when Coutre Coeur was their objective. He now conceived the idea of returning to the scene of his first fight and attempt to destroy the French stockade which was a thorn in the side of all scouting parties sent towards Ticonderoga. Arrangements all made, Richard Rogers and Ogden filed out of Fort William Henry with a detatchment from their respective Companies of Rangers. Approaching the end of the lake in boats before daybreak of June 6, Richard stealthly approached Coutre Coeur. His men caught the French by surprise and shot three sentinels on the ramparts of the stockade while rushing in to the attack. The small garrison rallied and manned the walls in time and the Rangers were forced to retire to the bushes on the edge of the clearing but not before a Ranger marksmen brought down a French officer who revealed himself while exhorting his men. He fell dead onto the outside of the stockade. Alarm guns were fired and a strong party sallied out from Ticonderoga. Rogers Rangers kept firing at Coutre Coeur until they arrived, then gave the relief party one good volley and fell back in good order to their boats and rowed unmolested to William Henry. In this action, Richard Rogers' losses were four men wounded; while the French lost at least one officer and three men killed, besides several wounded.

This little undecisive victory of Rogers' and Ogden's earned for them considerable fame. Provincial Diaries recorded it and Colonial Newspapers gave lengthy notices and even Loudoun, on board *H.M.S. Sutherland*, the day before his expedition left New York harbour, penned an account to Prime Minister Pitt. Robert Rogers, also, proudly heard of his brother's exploit before sailing but was soon to hear again of his brother, this time of his death, for almost immediately after his return to Fort William Henry, Richard came down with the smallpox and died on June 22,[186] only two weeks after his last battle. So ended the brief career of the second in command of Rogers Rangers. Next to Robert, he had been the most valuable man in the Corps. He was well liked by everyone and his sudden passing was felt by all who knew him. Lieutenant Noah Johnson now commanded the Company and during the month of July he hurled numerous scouting parties towards Ticonderoga and even Crown Point.

Unfortunately, they were not always lucky for one party penetrating as far as Crown Point was ambushed on July 1, and suffered seven Rangers killed before the balance extricated them-

July First Ambuscade 13

selves and escaped out of the trap.

As Montcalm's army ominously grew at Ticonderoga, Monro, commanding at William Henry, kept out continual patrols of Rogers' and Ogden's Rangers towards Wood Creek and Lake George. One spot in particular which Rogers Rangers frequented was an island opposite to Sabbath Day Point, for it offered a commanding view of the lake and was still readily accessible to both shores since it was in the narrow part of the lake. Later, when General Webb was trying to find a scapegoat for the fall of Fort William Henry, he accused the Rangers of lying and sleeping for two weeks on the island during the Summer heat of July, when they were supposed to be reconnoitering the enemies position at Ticonderoga.[187] However, it seems that there presence there on July 16, was fortunate, for they ambushed a prowling French patrol. Lieutenant De Saint Ours of the Colony Regulars, had been sent out from Coutre Coeur with ten men to scout towards William Henry. An alert Ranger sentry on the tip of La Barque Island spotted his boat approaching the isle. The commanding officer of the Rangers on the Island was warned and he quickly formed a detail in ambush at the spot where it appeared Saint Ours would land. The rest of Rogers Rangers stood by their boats and made ready to shove off and cut off the French retreat. Saint Ours fell neately into the trap. Upon landing, his patrol was immediately surrounded and two Canadians were killed; four wounded, one, a

Ambuscade at Isle La Barque[14]

Cadet, mortally, before they managed to fight their way back to their boat and escape the boatloads of Rangers pursuing them. The Rangers soon rested on their oars for they feared a trap.

Two weeks later, Montcalm advanced on Fort William Henry with 7,600 men. Arriving at William Henry, the advance guards proceeded to destroy several outbuildings and the Rangers picketed camp. Part of Rogers Rangers desperately held back the French and Indian hordes while the rest of them hurriedly evacuated most of their belongings from their huts. For a time the firing was hot until all the Rangers, Regulars, and Provincials had retired safely to the fort or a fortified entrenchment outside. Monro's complete force, Regulars, Provincials, and Rogers' and Ogden's Rangers, consisted of 2,200 men. When the brave Scot saw the size of the army opposing him he sent a hasty note to General Webb, who was at Fort Edward, to send him reenforcements, and the next night three of Rogers Rangers were sent to Fort Edward begging for reenforcements before William Henry was invested and cut off. But Loudoun, in stripping the frontier of troops for his abortive Louisbourg expedition, had left the whole frontier open to attack, and Webb, though condemned for not making an attempt to march to the relief of Fort William Henry with whatever force he could muster, had to consider the possibility of a French inroad by way of South Bay. Webb had the choice of marching to the

Siege, Surrender and Massacre of Fort William Henry 15

relief of William Henry with what troops he could gather, or distributing his troops among the lower posts towards Albany, he chose the latter.

Opening his first parallel, Montcalm was soon ready to open an artillery barrage on the fort. This was returned with spirit for several days and the French continued their parallel until they had a battery erected within 250 yards of the fort. The position of the defenders was now deplorable. Over 300 had been killed and wounded; and smallpox was raging in the fort. Two sorties, one from the entrenched camp and the other from the fort, in which Rogers Rangers had fought courageously, had been repulsed with loss. All the large cannon and mortars of the fort had burst or were disabled by shot and only small pieces were left fit to fire. On August 9, the fort capitulated and it was agreed that the defenders should be escorted to Fort Edward by *French* troops and should not serve for eighteen months. One field-piece, the defenders were to retain in recognition of their brave defence.

The capitulation was broken by the allies of France when the bloodthirsty and scalp-hungry savages massacred 50 to 100 of the unarmed-prisoners when they were about to set out for Fort Edward. Having killed and scalped all the wounded in the fort, the Indians turned their attention to the throng of able prisoners preparing to be escorted to Fort Edward and some of these unfortunate victims suffered the same fate as their wounded comrades; a fate too often resulting from capitulation to an army composed in part, of savages. They were dragged from their ranks and tomahawked, in the sight of the Canadian officers, who were the only ones who understood the Indian dialects. Montcalm and his French Regular officers tried to stop the massacre and fortunately most of the prisoners were so dazed that they did not offer any resistance, which if they had, unarmed as they were, would have resulted in a general massacre. Lieutenant Noah Johnson with Rogers Rangers were near the New Hampshire Regiment in the rear of the column; and, though the New Hampshire Provincials suffered considerably, Rogers Rangers only lost one killed and two taken to Canada according to documents, although more might have been lost. Some of the Rangers like Private John Pollard, were warned in time by a solitary Indian leaping upon a log and giving a terrific war-whoop, the signal for the attack on the defenceless prisoners. Those that were attacked had their choice of leaping into the woods and try to reach Fort Edward or being cut down in cold blood or carried away by the Indians. Two of them seized a boy named Copp and were leading him away by the shirt sleeves. His cries caught the attention of big Mitchel, one of Rogers Rangers, better known as "Ben Richards", who, being a fearless giant of a man, rushed after them, and snatched away the boy, leaving his shirt sleeves in the savages hands.

All were not as fortunate, more than two hundred prisoners were carried away by the Indians and some of them were roasted and eaten by the Indians, who compelled the survivors to partake of the banquet also. The ferocious savages received their just reward when they dug up and scalped the smallpox corpses in the graveyard of Fort William Henry, Captain Richard Rogers being one of these. This time the ferocity of the savages cost them dearly, for they caught the disease, and it reaped great havoc among them. Returning to their country, the Indians carried the disease with them. The Pouteotame Nation, one of the bravest and most strongly attached to the French almost entirely perished from this epidemic.

The fate of some of Rogers Rangers who were dragged from the ranks and carried away by the Indians is revealed in documents of the time: John McKeen, a Ranger Private from Amoskeag, New Hampshire, was taken by the savages after a desperate struggle. A fellow captive who later escaped, relates that McKeen was not fortunate enough to be killed outright but was reserved by his captors for the excruciating refinements of the torture-pole. The night following the massacre, amid their triumphal dance, the savages maddened with excitement and liquor, brought forth the ill-fated McKeen. The Ranger was stripped of his garments and bound to a tree. In this position he stood as a mark for the keen edged knives and tomahawks of the infuriated warriors. When this primitive knife throwing act, in which the thrower always slipped and hit the target, was at an end, McKeen was gashed at every point. Fast becoming insensible to their inhumanity, his wounds were stuck with pitch-wood splints, and as a climax to their barbarity were set on fire, and the unfortunate but heroic Rogers Ranger became his own funeral pyre.

Other Rogers Rangers who were carried to Ticonderoga or Montreal by the Indians were bought by the humane French and their Priests. Private Elias Cummings was sent down the St. Lawrence to Halifax where he was exchanged, and sent to Boston. But Private James McLauchlan was bought from the Indians and sent prisoner to France. He was exchanged in February 1758 and returned to America on board the *Huzza*.

The bulk of Richard Rogers' Company, according to the terms of their capitulation, left the Corps when they were paid up on August 24th. Lieutenant Johnson remained with a few members of the Company. Even though they felt that the capitulation had been broken by the Indian Allies, still they did not actively serve, but remained on Rogers' Island the remainder of the campaign. Johnson hoped that by staying on he would be promoted to succeed Richard Rogers when, and if, the Company was ordered to be revived. He solicited Loudoun twice for the Captaincy, which his effective length of service entitled him. He was turned down at this time, and humiliated, because Loudoun did not even answer his petitions,[188] he left the service and did not return until 1759, when a new General held the reins.

* * * * *

Before leaving Halifax with Loudoun's army, "Major Rogers" had sent into New Hampshire and Massachusetts, Ranger officers to recruit, for the Rangers had lost considerable numbers from smallpox during their summer at Dartmouth and Lawrencetown. Rogers says he sent "several officers", while Loudoun states only one was sent besides an officer of Shepherd's Company.[189] This one was apparently James Rogers, who was only to glad to get away from the monotony of supervising hay-cutting parties. He was a very successful recruiter, for he rejoined Bulkeley's Company at Fort Edward in October with forty-one Privates for the Company. Among them was a Harvard University student, Issac Day.[190] Lieutenant Rogers' success as a recruiting officer was instrumental in his promotion to a Captain in a few months. Major Rogers always rotated the officers and sergeants he sent recruiting, so that all would have a chance at this form of *furlough*. This was the only *furlough* that Rogers could give his officers and sergeants (the Privates were predestined to remain at the *front* until they were discharged, this was one of the principal reasons why there was so much unrest among them, particularly the married Privates). They usually recruited in their home town or county and this gave them the opportunity to see their families.

After the disaster at William Henry, Fort Edward remained the only advanced stronghold to cover the northern frontiers of New York and the southern New England Colonies. Loudoun still feared for the safety of Fort Edward and points south. Consequently Rogers Rangers were rushed from Halifax in advance of the Regular Battalions. On August 7-10, they left Halifax, and to make sure they all embarked, the men were not paid until they were on board. Loudoun's fears for any of the Rangers wanting to remain were groundless, for they were disgusted with the abortivness of the *Louisbourg Expedition*,[191] and disgruntled at the enforced labor they had to do. Many grumbles were sounded that they had enlisted as Rangers to fight the "Frenchies" and not to cut hay. They contended that they could cut hay at home anytime.

When Rogers Rangers disembarked from their transports at New York, they carried with them all the provisions which were rationed to them on board. The average ration for every six officers or men, consisted of:-four pounds of bread, two pints of peas, four gallons of water and six gills of rum every day of the week. This was supplemented four days a week with four pounds of pork, or seven pounds of beef per day, and a half-a-pound of butter three days of the week.[192] Consequently Rogers Rangers were hungry when they landed in New York and when they disembarked with all the unconsumed provisions, the masters of the transports tried to stop them, saying that the provisions were supposed to be returned to the contractors. But the hungry Rangers laughed at them, and Lieutenant McCurdy told one of the sea Captains that the unconsumed food and rum was a *prerequisite* of theirs.[193]

During their week or more wait in New York, Rogers Rangers, with their 61 days pay burning their pockets, made up for their former restrictions and painted the town. With the barrels of rum from the transports to fortify them, the Rangers were in a glow when they begged, borrowed, or stole a boat to cross Long Island Sound to revel in the pastimes of the largest city in the Colonies.

By September 7, the sloops had been gathered at New York and they sailed up the Hudson, arriving in Albany on the night of the 14th, and marched for Fort Edward on the 17th.[194] During their two days stay at Albany, Rogers' famous Ranging School was formed. This *School* consisted of 55 British Volunteers who had been attached to the British Regular Regiments as Cadets. It was a fulfillment of Loudoun's and the Prime Minister's plan of imparting Rogers' tactics to these aspirants who were promised available commissions when they had learned the Rangers methods. Their commissions would be that of Ensigns (the equivalent of Second Lieutenants, in our present United States and British Armies). Consequently, they would personally lead the men in action, and British commanders had finally realized that Rogers' teaching of the future Ensigns was the most logical method of bringing Ranger tactics to the British soldier. Rogers formed these 55 Volunteers into a separate Company and took them directly under his wing. While under his command and inspection, Rogers was ordered to do everything in his power to teach them the ranging-discipline and methods of fighting, and to recommend those that showed the most adaptability. Loudoun's plan was to turn two Companies out of every Regiment of a thousand men into Ranging Companies, and to form a distinct Corps if necessary. Thus, Rogers Rangers, became the first school for the beginning of Light Infantry. For his pupils benefit and instruction Rogers put into writing his Ranging Rules, which he found by past experience to be of the utmost importance in the training and discipline of his Rangers. Rogers impressed on his pupils, that, although these were the basic rules to be observed in the Ranging service, there were however, a thousand and one circumstances that would make it necessary to deviate from them and use one's own judgement and common sense to fit the occasion. Rogers instructed his pupils, that above all, to "preserve a firmness and presence of mind on every occasion".[195] Of these fifty-five or more Light Infantry Students, twelve were commissioned in Rogers Rangers, and twenty-three in Regular Regiments before the close of 1758.[196]

Rogers' unique training school came into existance on September 14, when General Abercrombie officially issued certificates to all the British Volunteers who wished to serve with Rogers Rangers, and there were many, for it had been made known that all Volunteers would have to serve with Rogers before they could be elgible for a commission in the Regulars. The certificates gave the "Gentleman Cadet's" name and the Regiment that he had formerly been attached to and stated that "being desirous to go out with a Party of Rangers is hereby permitted to serve in that quality" and the next day the Volunteers were ordered to put themselves under "the command of Captain Rogers and to be ready to march with him at a minutes notice".[197] Although Rogers' Ranging School was now officially established, it had existed unofficially long before this. Practically from the beginning of the Corps appearance on the Lake George front, Rogers had trained various personages in the arts of hide and seek and kill or be killed, and other distinctions of Ranger warfare. The first Cadets were Israel Putnam and other Provincials of Johnson's army in 1755. The first English Cadet of noble birth was Ronald Chalmers, who had been serving under Rogers as a Volunteer since August of 1756.[198] In a memorial to Loudoun in April 1757, Chalmers mentions "Major Rogers" as being very kind to him.[199] Chalmers was probably the only nobleman to serve with Rogers for so long a time. Other Cadets who entered about the same time as Chalmers were Provincials William Stark, Robert Gibs, Francis Rolfe, Thomas Cunningham and Hugh Morrison. Needless to say, all of these Cadets were attached to Robert Rogers' own Company.[200]

No other Cadets entered until the official formation of Rogers' Cadet Company. These Gentlemen Cadets were mostly all young men, who, as Volunteers, had accompanied the British Army in no official capacity. Upon joining Rogers Rangers they were expected to perform whatever duties offered, or were assigned to them, whether Sergeants or Privates tasks in camp or scouting service with the Rangers. Since the rules of seniority did not apply to them, they were for the most part conscientious and enthusiastic in their efforts to acquire a knowledge of the Rangers' tactics. The majority of them aspired for commissions in the Regulars but there were a few who preferred to throw their lot with Rogers Rangers. Some of these were young eager warriors while others were seasoned soldiers of fortune who had been fighting in many of his Majesty's Wars. James Pottinger was one of these. He had served with King George in Flanders as a Volunteer. After the Battle of Val he obtained his Majesty's permission to go to Bergenopzoom, in which siege he served until it was taken by the French, after which, King George was pleased to give him an Ensigncy in the 44th. In 1752, Pottinger purchased a Lieutenantcy in the regiment. He knocked around Europe with his regiment until the Seven Years War broke out in North America, when his corps came across to serve in Braddock's fateful expedition. After

Braddock's Defeat, Jamey (as he was affectionately known by his friends) Pottinger's career started on the decline. Taking up with one of the inevitable camp women, she "led him into such a habit of drinking, that not only affected his understanding, but likewise his health, to such a degree, as to almost deprieve him of the use of his limbs. In such circumstances he was unable to do his duty as becomes an officer, and loaded besides with a debt, contracted to purchase his Lieutenantcy, he was obliged to leave the service". No longer an officer, his mistress left him flat, and with their baby in his arms. In spite of his former indiscretions, Jamey Pottinger was now aroused to his responsibilities, and he humbled himself so much as to throw himself on Loudoun's mercy by petitioning him, revealing all of his past follys and begging for a chance to regain "the character he once had in the army".

Three months before, Loudoun had wrote Cumberland that he had agreed to Lieutenant Pottinger "selling out" because he was "entirely a sot". But now with Pottinger strictly on the wagon, and apparently truly repentant, Loudoun changed his opinion. Any man who would reveal all of his indiscretions as Pottinger did in his petition to Loudoun, certaintly deserved another opportunity; and Loudoun gave it to him through Rogers Rangers. Jamey Pottinger entered the Corps as a *Rogers Rangers* Cadet,[201] a distinction from the other Cadets, for he, with five others, were destined to commissions in Rogers Rangers if they proved capable.[202]

Arriving at Fort Edward on September 21,[203] the Corps and Cadets re-encamped on Rogers' Island. The disaster at Fort William Henry did not retard the incursions of Rogers Rangers. General Webb still commanded the army at Fort Edward and by his orders the Corps were constantly employed in patrolling the woods between Fort Edward and Ticonderoga to frustrate the encroachments of the enemy, made bold by their victory at William Henry. Rogers always included several of his Cadets in these frequent scouts.[204] As usual, every time a party of Rangers launched forth they met with harrowing danger in one form or another.

On October 3, a hunting party of Rangers went out and were almost encircled by French Indians who were attracted by their shots. Rogers Rangers adhered to their chief's "Ranging Rules", and splitting up, every man took a different route to an appointed rendezvous and by this effective means eluded their pursuers. *The Hunting Scout 16*

Rogers had hurled scouts out in all directions to safeguard Webb's army. He concentrated mostly in the direction of Ticonderoga and Wood Creek but he did not overlook any possible route of approach. He sent Sergeant Martin Severance to scour the upper Hudson. It had been a long time since a patrol of Rogers Rangers had scouted in this direction. As usual, this theater was empty of approaching marauders, and Severance's patrol returned to Rogers' Island on October 4th. *Severance's Hudson River Scout 37*

McCurdy's Capture[38]

But not all of the Rangers' scouts were as uneventful. The same day, Lieutenant John McCurdy, Rogers' First Lieutenant, returned from a very successful coup near Ticonderoga. Immediately upon the Corps' arrival at Fort Edward, McCurdy had been sent to Ticonderoga to obtain a prisoner for information. Rogers' reliance in his First Lieutenant, and McCurdy's own initiative cohesed, for he returned to Rogers' Island on October 4, with a French prisoner which he had spirited away from the vicinity of the Second Narrows.

Rogers-Lord Howe Scout[39]

On the 9th, Rogers increased the number of his scouts and patrols. In one of these scouts Lord Howe accompanied Rogers and his men, to learn their method of marching, ambushing, retreating and the other unique tactics of Rogers Rangers. He returned full of praise of the abilities and methods of Rogers' Corps. Howe became an adept pupil of Rogers' tactics and instituted many reforms in the British army.

The Small-Pox Scout[40]

Joshua Phineas Goodenough, a Private of Stark's Company, tells in his own words of a gruesome scout that he and "Shanks" Shankland, a veteran Ranger, made at this time: "The Rangers were accustomed to scout in small parties to keep the Canada Indians from coming close to Fort Edward. I had been out with Shanks on minor occasions, but I must relate my first adventure. A party..(here the writing is lost).. was desirous of taking a captive or scalp. I misdoubted our going alone by ourselves, but he said we were as safe as with more. We went northwest slowly for two days, and though we saw many old trails we found none which were fresh. We had gone on until night when we lay bye near a small brook. I was awakened by Shanks in the night and heard a great howling of wolves at some distance off together with a gun-shot. We lay awake until daybreak and at intervals heard a gun fired all through the night. We decided that the firing could not come from a large party and so began to approach the sound slowly and with the greatest caution. We could not understand why the wolves should be so bold with the gun firing, but as we came nearer we smelled smoke and knew it was a camp-fire. There were a number of wolves running about in the underbrush from whose actions we located the camp. From a rise we could presently see it, and were surprised to find it contained five Indians all lying asleep in their blankets. The wolves would go right up to the camp and yet the Indians did not deign to give them any notice whatsoever, or even to move in the least when one wolf pulled at the blanket of a sleeper. We each selected a man when we had come near enough, and preparing to deliver our fire, when of a sudden one figure rose up slightly. We nevertheless fired and then rushed forward, reloading. To our astonishment none of the figures moved in the least but the wolves scurried off. We were advancing cautiously when Shanks caught me by the arm saying "we must run, that they had all died of the small-pox," and run we did lus-tilly for a good long distance. After this manner did many Indians die in the wilderness from that dreadful disease, and I have since supposed that the last living Indians had kept firing his gun at the wolves until he had no longer strength to reload his piece."

"After this Shanks and I had become great friends for he had liked the way I had conducted myself on this expedition. He was always arguing with me to cut off my ell-skin que which I wore after the fashion of the Dutch folks, saying that the Canada Indians would parade me for a Dutchman after that token was gone with my scalp."

The first part of November saw the disbandment of the Provincials and the slow withdrawal of the Regulars to Winter posts along the Hudson, and with them went most of Rogers' Cadet Company for it was officially disbanded on November 8, after a seven weeks existance.[205] However at least five of them remained on for James Pottinger, Samuel Stephens, Archibald Gregory McDonald, Caesar McCormick and Joseph Bolton were not attached to any Regular Regiment, instead they were designated as permanent Cadets of Rogers Rangers until fortunate enough to be granted commission.[206]

When the Provincials left Rogers' Island where they had been encamped during the fruitless campaign they had a tendency to take with them livestock, vegetables from the gardens and to destroy their huts. Strict orders were issued forbidding this waywardness, and "Majr.

Rogers" was ordered to post a guard of Rangers over the gardens to prevent further looting.[207]

Stark's Misbehavior Scout [17]

A few days later General Abercrombie's nephew and aide-de-camp, Captain James Abercrombie, decided that he wanted to do some "mischief to their enemy". As Rogers was sick with the scurvy and could not accompany him his second, John Stark, commanded the Rangers engaged. A "Grand scouting party" was formed consisting of Captain John Stark and 300 Rangers. Besides Captain Abercrombie there were two other British officers, Engineer Clark and Lieutenant Holland; and one of Rogers' Cadets, William Fraser. This was Stark's first opportunity to deliver a blow at the enemy since he had returned to the command of his Company. Although he had forgiven Lieutenant Brewer for confining him he was still touchy and being of a taciturn and independent nature he was in no mood for the bumptious and peremptory orders of Captain Abercrombie who superseded him in command. Consequently he did not try too hard to follow his abrupt orders. On the march to Ticonderoga all Abercrombie could do or say to the Ranger officers could not prevent the Rangers from firing at game. In a heavy fog during the morning of the sixth day they arrived at the hill on the southwest side of Ticonderoga. The fog not lifting by noon, they marched two miles further until it cleared then the British officers and ten Rangers left the main body to view the fort. At dusk they approached within 900 yards and saw twenty or

or thirty boats lying along the water side of
Ticonderoga. Returning to the main body of
Rangers a council of war was held. Abercrombie
was all for going that night and burning the
boats and attempt to take a prisoner. But "the
proposal was rejected by all the Ranging officers, and as we perceived the tracks of many
oxen and teams who had been drawing wood that
day, they proposed waylaying that road expecting that in the morning the teams would come
out with them, and we might easily destroy
them, accordingly I drew them up at a little
distance from the Road, and ordered that half
the party should remain under arms until 12
o'clock, and the other half to relieve them
at that hour, I gave orders to Captain" Stark
"for the posting of the Sentrys, not being able
myself to see it done having just before got
a severe fall which I imagined at first had
broke my thigh. Your Lordship I dare say will
be surprised to hear after such orders, that
neither officer or man but what was asleep
under his blanket. As I was not able to stir
I desired Mr. Clark" the Engineer "to go down
and make his remarks, which he did twice, the
last time Mr. Holland went with him. In the
morning, being able to walk a little. I placed
the whole party in Ambush along the Road, so
lay for two hours. At last six men came out
with their arms and hatchets and two of them
set to work within about 200 yards of us. We
lay looking at them for half an hour and more
at last seeing no prospect of any more coming

I ordered an officer and ten men to creep down and try to take some of them and gave the rest the stricest orders not to stir on any account. The party in creeping down to the men cutting wood were perceived by one of the six who set up a hollow and run, upon which Captain Stark who was with me set up the Indian hollow, upon that the whole party jumped up and yelled as if Hell had broke loose, and all fell a firing at a few men running away."

"In a few minutes they began to fire their cannon which silenced the whole party for a little, but no one being killed the officers called out to rejoice, then every one yelled and fired his piece in the air, calling out 'God save King George' and damned those in the Fort for a set of French rascals who durst not come out and fight them. On this the Enemy fired their cannon pretty quick, Eleven in all, which made our warriors sound the retreat, which they were most willing to perform, being afraid of a pursuit."

"I could not get any of them for the first few miles to form a rear-guard and to persuade them there was no danger in it. Mrss. Clark, Holland, and Fraser, a Volunteer in the Highlanders..made the rear guard, Altho our jaunt has not answered your Lordship's expectation, yet I am of opinion it has had this one good effect which is: that if your Lordship should increase the number of Rangers or even keep them up to their present numbers it will be necessary to put some Regular Officers among

them to introduce a great deal of subordination."
Abercrombie seems to forget that this was the Rangers' method of attack and retreat. In spite of the "misbehaviour" in this scout it did have its accomplishments for on December 28, Captain Abercrombie writes to Loudoun the information gleaned from a French deserter. He boastfully calls the scout "Mr. Clark's and mine" and states "that Mr. Clark's Scout and mine had a better effect than we imagined, for besides keeping the garrison three days under arms (the Indians having reported that we were bringing things over the carrying place) they, in firing their cannon at us killed one of their own men, and by frightening those away from the charcoal pit, it took fire and 3,000 Livres worth of charcoal was destroyed." Abercrombie relates the pathetic, but humorous excuse given by Bois, the deserter for deserting to the British: "This deserter's coat, waistcoat and hatt we brought off with us which he says was the reason of his deserting because his Captain would not give him another. Mr. Clark was present when I examined him and the fellow finding we knew something about his Cloaths modestly requisted we would get them for him..". Abercrombie adds the crowning touch of glory-hogging in his closing words: "I hope your Lordship will excuse the freedom the Secretary has taken, as it is a custom amongst warriors in this country to vaunt the mischief they do to their enemys..".
From Stark's actions in the scout it seems

that he had taken a particular dislike to young Abercrombie and determined to gall him by deliberately opposing him. On the return march to Fort Edward, Stark employed his dry humour in "pulling Abercrombie's leg" when he deliberately mistook South Bay twice for a *Beaver Pond*. Stark might have felt that he had a grievance because of Captain Abercrombie's curtness, still his attitude did not enhance the good fame of Rogers Rangers. When Stark allowed his men to fire at game on the march he was going contrary to Rogers' Ranging Rules. There were members of the Corps who would rather die than disobey the rules and endanger the whole party. Private Goodenough remembers on one occasion that he was standing by a tree in a snow storm, with his gun depressed under his frock the better to keep it dry. Chancing to glance quickly around he saw a large wolf just ready to spring upon him. He cautiously presented his fusee but did not dare to fire against the orders. Fortunately another Ranger came shortly into view and the wolf took himself off.[208]

Stark's cantankerous attitude was followed a week later by a piece of rugged individualism by certain members of Rogers Rangers which resulted in a Mutiny.

Probably no other Corps in the British or Provincial forces could boast with pride and then winch with shame at the varied collection of good, semi-good, and sordid individuals who comprised Rogers Rangers. The Corps had in it the constituents of the French Foreign Legion the Three Musketeers, Deerslayers, pious Puritans and an occasional Roman Catholic. Fortunately most of the Corps was composed of New Hampshire frontiersmen, either unmarried, or men who had families in the small bordertowns of the Connecticut River and Merrimack River valleys. Men who spent the Spring of every year beaver hunting. The rest of the time they had cared for their farms or fought off St. Francis Indian Raiders. There were several unmarried men like "Shanks" Shankland, who had spent most of their time in the woods hunting and exploring unsettled country. His type were the backbone of the Corps and such breed were most likely to adopt the adventurous life of Rogers Rangers and having no family ties would serve the duration without thinking of deserting to return home.

From such veterans the less experienced acquired the Ranging tactics and knowledge of woodcraft which Rogers was now unable to impart personally to each and every man due to the hundreds of men now under him. One of Shanks' *pupils* gives a vivid description of him:-"..I had got acquainted with a Hampshire borderer who had passed his life on the Canada frontier, where he had fought Indians and been captured by them..He was a slow man in his movements albeit he could move fast enough on occassion, and was a great hand to take note of things happening around him. No Indian was better able to discern a trail in the bush

than he, nor could one be found his equal at
making snow-shoes, carving a powder horn or
fashioning any knick-nack he was a mind to set
his hand to..I talked at great length with
this Shankland, or *Shanks* as he was called on
account of his name and his long legs, in
course of which he explained many useful points
to me concerning Ranger ways..".[209]

Then there were would-be-Rangers who brought
nothing but disfame an continually gave the
Corps a black eye. Some would enlist with the
sole purpose of obtaining the bounty money and
getting a few days view of the novelties of
camp-life. These *Bounty seekers* if not immediately discharged as being unfit, would soon
put themselves in that status by their drunken
carousels and refusal to go out on scouts.
Private Samuel Leech refused to go out on a
scout until he had his allowance of rum. He
received 500 lashes on the bare back with a
cat-and-nine-tails and was discharged as "being
unfit for service". Sad to say, Leech was not
a *Bounty seeker,* but had been one of Rogers'
Rangers since 1755.[210]

Although the bulk of Rogers Rangers were of
Scotch-Irish descent, there was a generous
sprinkling of plain Irish, English, German,
Dutch, and an occasional Half-Breed Indian,
Spaniard or Negro. Emanuel La Portegee was a
Spaniard. Robert Rogers had a negro servant
named Prince who enlisted in 1759. Prince was
a grave serious personality, and very pious. He
was well treated and considered himself free.[211]

The trades of the Rangers before entering the Corps were many and varied. Trappers, Traders, Farmers or Frontiersmen from New Hampshire, Massachusetts and New York. Shoemakers from Boston, Shipbuilders from Portsmouth, fugitives from justice from all points, and idle seamen from New York, Boston and Portsmouth. If Rogers had his choice he probably would have enlisted experienced woodsmen exclusively, but he could no longer personally recruit every member like he did when his Corps consisted of one Company. Instead, he had to turn most of this duty over to his new officers who, anxious to obtain their commissions had on occasion enlisted undesirables to fill up their Companies. Rogers was forced to accept them and gave them every chance to be disciplined into effective Rangers. Most of them "levelled" into good Rangers, but several (besides the Bounty seekers) did not. The worst of these were dismissed but those that showed a spark of promise were still carried.

It could well be said that Rogers Rangers represented the essence of the growing independent American spirit. Although there were doubtful characters, nevertheless, in the Corps were the best of American fighters. They were councious of their superior bush-fighting tactics and held the British Regulars pomp and parade in as much contempt as they held the Rangers loose but effective methods of march and battle.

Rogers Rangers, like any good organization,

needed activity, but since the Spring of the year they had not been given the opportunity of making any partisan strokes of consequence, although immense plans such as the taking of Louisbourg had been on the horizon. Now, on Rogers' Island, were thrown together 400 men to languish idly for the most part while alternate small bodies went out on comparitively uneventful scouts. It was in this stagnant atmosphere that the undesirables of Rogers Rangers manifestated themselves an promoted a rebellion against their own officers:-

When inactive certain Rangers were continually drunk and would go to any ends to obtain more than their allowance of Rum. Rogers could no longer cajole his men into obedience and since the undesirables did not care whether they went out on a scout or not his psychology of chastising them by leaving them behind no longer worked, an reluctantly he was forced to adopt the Regulars method of flogging with the cat-o'-nine-tails. The flogging of Samuel Leech for refusing to go on a scout until he had his allowance of rum was the first recorded instance of Rogers adopting these disciplarian tactics. Probably no one understood the independent nature of his men and their reluctance to harsh forms of discipline better than Rogers, and, though he knew some of his men would hate him for it, he employed the whip. He witheld the whip for awhile by dismissing the miscrepeants and sending them home but that was exactly what they wanted and he could not continue to do this for he would soon have no discipline, and worse, no Rangers. He had already discharged at least 24 Private men since October 24th.[212] The Rangers did not mind Rogers discharging the wayward members but they strongly resented Haviland, the post Commandant, doing so at the recommendation of Captain Abercrombie. Haviland discharged twelve Private men on November 24, as being "unfit for service".[213] These men were pointed out by Captain Abercrombie as the disobedient ones in the "Misbehaviour Scout".

The seeds of discontent sown they bore fruit the first part of December when Samuel Boyd and Henry Dawson were confined in the Rangers' Guard House on "Rogers' Island". Samuel Boyd had stolen rum from the British stores and Henry Dawson was implicated with him. Rogers' method of administering the whip was to pick a man from each of the four Companies of Rogers Rangers and have them alternately apply the lash. In this way he hoped to avoid any disturbance from the onlookers or create any qualms among the *Drummers*. His method was not unlike that of a firing squad. No man was directly responsible for delivering the lash. This disagreeable duty was repugnant to Rogers. Especially since the two Rangers were of his own Company; besides he was still ill and could not leave his hut. Accordingly, he transmitted the whipping orders to Captain Shepherd, his newest Ranger Captain. The assignment was equally abhorrent to Shepherd, but being the Junior Captain, he had no choice but to carry out his orders. Rogers Rangers getting wind of what was about to happen gathered in restless, noisy crowds and punctuating their remarks with strong terms, were heard to say "that they did not like the whipping post and if Boyd and Dawson were to be flogged there would be no more Rangers".

On December 5, Captain Shepherd carried out his assignment. Starting with the detail from Stark's Company the lashings started on the two Rangers. Then followed *Drummers* from Bulkeley's, Shepherd's and lastly, Robert Rogers' Company. How many lashes were applied was not recorded. Leech received 500 for refusing to go out on a scout. Whether Boyd and Dawson received the same is doubtful for Rangers were wielding the lash. General Abercrombie states that they received "a gentle correction".

The men of Stark's Company, like the rest of the Rangers, had no stomach for this crude business and resented the fact that they had to initiate the flogging. They contended that Rogers' Company, being the eldest, should have started the flogging. Several hours after the whipping, Shepherd, alarmed at the growing crowds of angry Rangers, determined to get at the bottom of Boyd and Dawson's case. Visiting the lacerated Rangers in their cell he tried to inveigle the truth from Boyd. At first Boyd stated that Charles Elder and Robert Clark, Privates of Rogers' own Company, had given him the money to buy the rum. But being pressed by Shepherd he finally admitted that Lieutenant Jonathan Brewer had given it to him in payment of work done. Boyd went on to state that he had endeavored to get more rum and had gone to Rogers direct. Rogers, still in bed sick, sent him to Lieutenant Burbank who signed an order for Boyd to obtain the rum. Boyd imprudently returned to Rogers with the order for his endorsement. Suffering from his illness and annoyed at Boyd's drunken persistence Rogers refused to sign the order. Consequently he and Dawson managed to steal the rum. Boyd naturally managed to omit in his story to Shepherd that it was because of his drunken condition that Rogers turned him down. Qualms of conscience must have struck the already dejected Shepherd as he looked at the Rangers lacerated backs and heard Boyd relate his incomplete story. There was already a strained relation of personalities between Shepherd and Rogers and now believing that he had been the administer of unwarranted punishment upon Boyd and Dawson, he was heard to say angrily "that Major or not Major, he would overhaul him and his men too".

In the meantime the undesirables of Rogers Rangers bolstered by Shepherd's careless remark, had fired to a white heat the men's hatred of the whipping post. The following evening, December 6th, a large body of them, under Abraham Parrot and Noah Porter, Privates in Rogers' Company, marched to the whipping-post on the island and one of their number,

Joshua Atwood, took an ax from another Ranger, and amidst the loud cheers of the others, chopped down the Whipping Post, which was to them the chief emblem of the discipline they detested. Turning to the Guard House nearby they surrounded it and clambered for the release of Boyd and Dawson. Being refused by the Rangers on guard, one of the mutineers climbed on the roof and pulled a board off in an effort to enter that way. About this time Captain Shepherd arrived on the scene. Because of his unmeaning remark about "overhauling the Major and his men too", the mutineers thought that he would join them. But to their surprise and annoyance Shepherd shouted to the men to break it up. Now a singular incident took place which did anything but enhance the fame of the Corps. Abraham Parrot leveled his firelock at Shepherd and told him not to interfere. Shepherd knocked the gun to one side with his sword and while Private McSterling of Stark's Company held Parrot, Shepherd wrenched the firelock from his grasp. Captain Bulkeley arrived at this time and ordered the men to disperse which they did immediately for the Parrot-Shepherd incident had considerably dampened their recklessness.

Unfortunately the Mutiny was not of a *quite* nature an Colonel Haviland, Commandant at Fort Edward, heard the riot from the fort and learning that it was a Mutiny he cleverly tricked Rogers into sending him the chief mutineers. He sent word to Rogers that he would like to

talk to the suspects. Rogers, thinking that
the men would be returned, sent them across
the river. No sooner had they entered Fort
Edward than Haviland clapped them into the
fort's Guard House, then ordered Rogers to
hold a Court of Inquiry on the Mutiny. Rogers
asked for the return of his men so that they
could be questioned at his Court of Inquiry
but Haviland flatly refused, replying that he
"would not trust them where there were so many
mutineers for fear of a rescue".

Rogers held his investigation from the 8th
through the 11th of December, on Rogers' Island. During the entire *Inquiry* all the Rangers questioned clung together and feigned ignorance of the cause of the Mutiny and those
engaged in it. Most of them stated that they
were some other place when the Mutiny took
place, either in their huts or "easing themselves on the River bank". Even Captain Shepherd would not divulge the identity of the man
who pointed the fire-lock at him, and it took
a Ranger Private to let it slip out that Parrot was the culprit. At least twenty Ranger
officers and men were examined and it is noteworthy of the Rangers loyalty to each other
and their Corps, besides their mutual hatred
of the Whipping Post, that not much could be
gleaned from them. Nothing could be more close
mouthed when he set his mind to it, than a
tight-lipped New England Rogers Ranger. Their
aversion to the Whipping Post is revealed in
memoirs of members of the Corps. One veteran

Private states that he "was in a mortal dread of the whippings which men were constantly receiving for breaches of the discipline. I felt that I could not survive the shame of being trussed up and lashed before men's eyes, but I did also have a great mind to fight the French which kept me along". Another Private Ranger gives an eye-witness account of one of these floggings: "Three men, for some trifling offence which I do not recollect, were tied up to be whipped. One of them was to receive 800 lashes, the others 500 apiece. By the time they had received three hundred lashes, the flesh appeared to be entirely whipped from their shoulders, and they hung as mute and motionless as though they had been long since deprived of life. But this was not enough. The doctor stood by with a vial of sharp stuff, which he would ever and anon apply to their noses, and finding, by the pain it gave them, that some signs of life remained, he would tell them, "dam you, you can bear it yet" and then the whipping would commence again. It was the most cruel punishment I ever saw inflicted, or had ever conceived of before, by far worse than death. I felt at the time as though I could have taken summary vengeance on those who were the authors of it, on the spot, had it been in my power to do it". A Rogers Ranger would have much more preferred the hazard of losing his scalp than suffer the humiliation of the whipping post.

Unfortunately, Rogers Rangers had an enemy

in Lieutenant-Colonel William Haviland, their Commandant at Fort Edward. Schooled in the popular belief that all soldiers were subject to their officers body and soul, without any individual opinions or independence, he could not bear the "rugged Americanism" which was continually cropping out in Rogers Rangers. Consequently he never overlooked an opportunity to chastise them; employing whenever he could the most humiliating methods. When Rogers submitted the proceedings of his Inquiry, Haviland sent them to General Abercrombie who in turn relayed them to the Commander-in-Chief Lord Loudoun. In his accompaning letter Haviland is full of scorn for Rogers Rangers, who in turn hated him for his trickery in confining the mutineers. He belittles the fact that they were continually practicing at shooting-at-marks to increase their marksmanship, and complains about the powder and ball they use. He forbade them to practice on their Island; but the feud was on; the Rangers retaliated by crossing over to the woods back of Fort Edward and made them fairly ring with their firing, this galled Haviland considerably. In regard to the Mutiny, Haviland would have hanged one of the mutineers as an example, and the others Court-Martialed and drummed out of the army, if he could have had the final word on their sentence. Haviland was afraid to order any execution on his own, but he implored Loudoun through General Abercrombie for his order to go ahead. Rogers, dejected and weary of the whole tragic affair, left his sick-bed in an effort to visit Haviland and patch things up. Haviland notes that this "was the first time of his coming abroad". Apparently they had not been on verbal speaking terms. Rogers informed Haviland that he was fearful least all the Rangers would desert if any of the suspected prisoners were hanged. But Haviland, uncompromising as ever, stated "that it would be better if they were all gone than to have such a riotous sort of people"; but if Rogers would produce the ring-leader of the mutiny he would have him hanged and release the others. Naturally Rogers refused. Haviland's letter to Abercrombie reveals that he feared the suspects would not receive a stiff enough sentence if the Court-Martial was composed entirely of Ranger officers. He urges Abercrombie to order Regular officers as well as Rangers to serve on the Court-Martial. By this means, Haviland hoped that the Regular officers would be permitted to outrank those of the Rangers and thus have the final word on the verdict. As a crowning touch of humility to the Corps, he recommends that the Regulars and Putnam's and Durkee's Connecticut Companies at Fort Edward administer the lash instead of men from Rogers' Corps.[214]

When Rogers saw that he could get no place by talking with Haviland he did not linger in camp now that he was well enough for active campaigning. While waiting for a decision from Loudoun he wisely set out the next day to

Rogers'
Xmas
Eve
Raid [18]

"distress the enemy at Carrillon", "in order to retrieve the character of the Rangers".[2][15]

This scout to re-establish the good name of Rogers Rangers resulted in an audacious attempt to take Ticonderoga itself. At two o'clock in the afternoon of December 17, Rogers marched from Fort Edward with 150 Rangers. They camped that night at Half-way-Brook in three inches of snow and during the night twelve inches more fell "which made" their lodging very "disagreeable". In the morning eight of the party "gave out" (actually, they were frost bitten) and Rogers sent them back to Fort Edward. Travelling by way of the charred ruins of Fort William Henry, Rogers party discovered a large quantity of cannon-balls and shells which had been hidden by the French after their capture of the fort. Making a mark so that they might find them again the Rangers proceeded on towards Ticonderoga. Due to the increasing snowfalls the going was slow and they averaged eight miles a day. The fifth day out, nineteen more Rangers "tired and fell sick" and they were also returned to Fort Edward, reducing Rogers force to 123 officers and men.

Arriving within 600 yards of Ticonderoga on December 24, Rogers Rangers lay in ambush and captured a French Sergeant of Marines who walked out of the fort directly into their hands. From him they learned that their were only 350 troops in garrison at Ticonderoga, and Rogers quickly conceived of the plausibility of capturing the fortress if he could induce the garrison to sally out so that his Rangers could get at them and cut in back Indian fashion and break through the gate. Rogers formed his Rangers for battle and seeing a hunter returning to Ticonderoga, Rogers ordered a party to pursue him to the edge of the cleared ground and capture him, firing a few guns to induce the garrison to sally out; while he remained in the woods with the bulk of his Rangers to attack the enemy Indian fashion, should they venture out to attack an insolent handful of Rangers who would have the audacity to pluck a Frenchman from the very gates of the fort. But all attempts along this line failed. The wary French suspecting a trap when they saw the buckskins of Rogers Rangers would not budge and Rogers turned to other means of harassing them. The keeper of the drove of oxen had let seventeen of them slip out and they were residing on the hoof just out of range of the cannon. The Rangers proceeded to butcher them under the eyes of the garrison, and set fire to five large stacks of firewood which had been laboriously cut and stacked by the French close to the fort. The angry garrison fired several cannon in the direction of the fires but did the Rangers no harm.

The Rangers *besieged* the garrison by firing pot-shots until eight o'clock that night when, finally despairing of inducing the enemy out of their stronghold, Rogers "left a receipt with the agent Victualler" for the oxen, and stuck the audacious note to the horns of one of the slain cattle, addressed to the Commandant of Ticonderoga, which read: "I am obliged to you sir, for the rest you have allowed me to take and the fresh meat you have sent me. I shall take good care of my prisoners. My compliments to the Marquis of Montcalm. Signed, Rogers, Commander of the Independent Companies". After composing this hectoring tidbit, Rogers and his Rangers returned to Fort Edward. The scout was considered a very successful one and the fact that Rogers even considered of attempting to take Ticonderoga with a garrison of three times the strength of his party did much "to retrieve the character of the Rangers".[216]

Arnoux's Defeat[19] About this same time the French received another buffing when a scouting party under Arnoux was completely defeated by Rogers Rangers (apparently a Ranger patrol from Fort Edward). Because of the lack of any Ranger or British accounts of this action, its actuality would be doubted if an authoritive French document had not so definitly described it. The French never admitted a defeat *unless it was a crushing one*.

CHAPTER IV

1758

A REGIMENT IS FORMED

Arriving at Fort Edward after his "Christmas Eve Siege of Ticonderoga", Rogers found a letter awaiting him with orders to wait on General Abercrombie at Albany (Abercrombie was second in command to Loudoun, who placed him in command of the New York outposts). Waiting on Abercrombie at Albany, Rogers softened him with details of his *siege*. Abercrombie was quite impressed and said as much when writing to Loudoun.[217]

Abercrombie had ordered Rogers down prior to his receiving news of the whipping post mutiny as Loudoun wanted to discuss with the Ranger Chieftan plans for augmenting the Rangers. But before Rogers had returned from his late scout, Haviland had wrote Abercrombie his unflattering thoughts of the Rangers and enclosed Rogers' proceedings of his Court of Inquiry on the Mutiny. This news, coupled with his nephew, James Abercrombie's account of their "Misbehaviour Scout", had not put his opinion of Rogers Rangers in a favourable light, and when Loudoun had asked him for his viewpoint on augmenting Rogers' Corps. Abercrombie wrote back on December 18, strongly recommending "the necessities of setting an officer over this Corps". He also suggests "intermixing some subaltern and non-commissioned officers from the Regulars in whom the superior officer can confide, especially, as you propose to add more Companies upon that same establishment..The present Rangers..might be reduced or brought down to reasonable terms" of pay if Gage's Light Infantry "Corps was established which I am confident would discharge all the functions of Rangers in a short time, better than those at present in your pay, so that in the end some such plan would be a great saving, and on the same footing the numbers might be augmented according to circumstances or turned into the Ranks until there should be a call for them..From anything I have said I would not be understood that I am for disbanding the present Rangers even if the Corps proposed by Gage as well as" Light Infantry "Companies from the Regiments should be constituted because I think you must continue them for this ensuing campaign under such regulations as your Lordship shall think proper..If anything further occurs upon talking with Rogers when he arrives I shall acquaint your Lordship who I conclude will speedily take your resolution" in deciding the fate of the mutineers "as this matter cannot admit of any longer delay".[218]

The fate of Rogers Rangers looked black indeed but thanks to the persuasive personality of their Chieftan they managed to continue to exist. Rogers' following bit of diplomacy is probably the most important conquest of his violent career. For if he had not exerted himself and maintained his Rangers the most important deeds of their existance would never have occurred. Rogers did not know the exact nature of the correspondence being carried on about him and his Rangers, but he must have had a good idea, for his three years campaigning with British officers had given him a good idea of their thoughts on undisciplined men and their indignation at the high pay Rogers Rangers were receiving. While their exploits in the field were admired still their carefree method of maintaining and living in camp exasperated the regimented British to no end. As long as the Rangers were performing incredible deeds their existance was assured. Unfortunately their activities since their return from Halifax had been stagnant and uneventful, and the only marked events had been a "misbehaviour scout" and a "mutiny" both unexcusable in the British doctrine. Fortunately Rogers had wrested himself from a sick bed to hurl his Rangers into one of their incredible scouts before he received word to talk with Loudoun about the continuance and expansion of Rangers and fate of mutineers. Rogers was fully aware of the effect of his daring one-day siege of Ticonderoga and he quickly capitilized on his invaluability as a partisan. Rogers' strategy is revealed in Abercrombie's letter to Loudoun, which he carried with him sealed when Abercrombie sent him off to New York. Abercrombie writes: "We have had a deal of

Conversation together, and consequently a good share of nonsense, he has got it into his head to be a Provincial Colonel, and has had offers already to be so employed, if he does not accept of that, he thinks his Service entitles him to a" Regular officer's "Rank in any Corps of Rangers raised, or to be raised, or at least to be Captain-Commandant of the present Rangers, for which Corps he is willing to raise from one to four or five hundred without any bounty money, at their present Establishment of Pay".[219]

Abercrombie had tried to inveigle a confirming statement from Rogers that his Rangers conduct was as serious as Haviland had written. But Rogers defended his men's conduct and warmly stated that the Corps was being prejudiced by Colonel Haviland. Abercrombie wrote Loudoun that "I am sorry to say, Rogers, has given me but little satisfaction, in Vindication of their past Conduct, or raised any expectations of reforming them. He desires that his men who are guilty of any Misdemeanours, may be tryed by their own officers, in the manner of Rigemental Court Martials, and their sentence to be first approved of by the Commanding officer of the Post where they are, and indeed, his or their only grievance is, that Colonel Haviland should have brought over from their island, the late Mutineers, and Confined them, for the more security, in Fort Edward, where they stay until your Lordship's pleasure is known. All this arose from two men of Rogers' own Company receiving a gentle correction on their own parade in the Island, by virtue of a Sentence from their own officers, upon which a Number of them gathered together and cut down the Whipping Post and afterwards attempted to rescue, from their own Guard, two Rangers..When your Lordship has leisure to look into the Court of Enquiry I sent you, you will see what senses, some of their officers have of discipline and punishment and how they have coloured that affair and prevented the greater parts coming to light, and by their bad conduct and folly, nine men from these four Companys have deserted since the last Return, and Rogers will tell your Lordship that a great many more will do so, and further that he will find it very difficult to raise more if they are to be punished as other Military delinquents. Upon the whole I desired him to consider, in his road to New York, what had passed between him and me and to lay before your Lordship only what was material and if your Lordship is for Augmenting that Corps, there are some officers and private men gone upon Furlow to that Country to be in readiness to Recruit."

With Regard to Rogers himself, I do think him so necessary and Usefull a Man, that I should be extremely Sorry to part with him, and rather than that, to give him some Encouragement to Continue diligent and hearty in the service. Without him these four Companys would be good for nothing, and therefore,

I suppose your Lordship will dispatch him as soon as possible with directions to repair here again as soon as he has regulated his affairs, and set his people to Work in the Recruiting way, because we can only depend upon him, for any sort of intelligence. He was talking of being absent two months, but I hope your Lordship will not give him half that time".[220]

Leaving Abercrombie, Rogers travelled to New York and saw Loudoun on January 9th. Here he met with the same reception that Abercrombie had given him and Loudoun "talked to him of the bad consequences of mutiny in particular and of the consequences of not keeping up discipline"; and Loudoun continues, to say: "that many things made me hesitate about augmenting the Rangers as much as I proposed".[221] After his little lecture, Loudoun listened to Rogers' side of the story and heard of how prejudiced Haviland was against him and his men. Fortunately for Rogers, Loudoun had no great love for the tactless Colonel who behind his back had derided Loudoun's defensive tactics in conducting the War. Looking at the weather-beaten and haggard countenance of his young Ranger Chieftan, one can easily imagine him reflecting for a moment on Rogers' latest daring scout, especially on the contents of his audacious "Thank You" note he left for the French Commandant, wrought all the more effective by the fact that Rogers had modestly omitted it in his written account. Loudoun, though he realized that Rogers imposed on his reputation, because it was great, like many of Rogers' superiors, secretly admired his popularity and exploits. He wrote Abercrombie that he suspected pains had been taken to make him discontented which was not helping the settling of the whipping post mutiny.[222] He wisely ordered Abercrombie to have Haviland restore the mutineers into Rogers' hands and Rogers dismissed them from the Corps without any further ado. So ended "The Whipping Post Mutiny", an incident, if it had not been handled so discreetly by Lord Loudoun may well have developed into a wholesale desertion of the Privates of the Corps and possibly the end of the spectacular Rogers Rangers. Had this tragedy occurred, the most brilliant chapters of the Corps' History could never have been written. Loudoun further surprised Rogers by telling him that he had been thinking over his advice of last October to augment his Corps to 1,000 Rangers, so that they would be on an equal footing with the increasing numbers of the enemies partisan forces.[223] Employing the right tact, Loudoun pacified Rogers and flattered him by asking him to recommend the officers for the new Companies and "Bid him make memorandums of all he had to propose".[224]

Loudoun would have liked to get Rogers Rangers on a cheaper establishment, but Rogers convinced him that none would enlist and those already in service would only be disatisfied. A uniform for the Corps was discussed to create a stronger *esprit de corps*. Loudoun was aware that the home office would not stand for the added expense of clothing Rogers Rangers so he told Rogers to have the uniforms made up and deduct their cost from the men's pay.[225] Rogers prepared a list of officers for twelve Ranging Companies (including the present four Companies), one of the new Companies was to be a Mohegan Indian Company with a white man for a Captain. He recommended for new Company commanders: John McCurdy, brother James Rogers, Jonathan Brewer, William Stark, Jonathan Burbank, John McDuffy, Thomas Lawrance, and Moses Brewer for the Captaincy of the Mohegan Company. Nine of the subalterns recommended had served in Rogers Cadet Company. The others were personal friends of Rogers from New Hampshire or Massachusetts.[226]

Rogers was careful not to mention to Loudoun that he was considering accepting a New Hampshire Provincial Colonelcy if he did not get a promotion, but he did "talk to Appy in this strain".[227] Appy was Loudoun's Secretary and Rogers hoped he would relay his threat to Loudoun. He did, as did Abercrombie in his letter delivered by Rogers, and since he was such "a necessary and useful man", Loudoun tried to satisfy Rogers by offering to increase his pay but rank was what he wanted and Loudoun found that "the hardest point to comply with",[228] as he was still reluctant to promote a Provincial to such an exalted position. However he promised Rogers that he would consider it, and

Rogers, ever hopeful, decided to make one more attempt. He would comply to the letter all of Loudoun's orders in raising the new Rangers and hoped that when the new Companies had been raised he would then be promoted.

Loudoun must have been somewhat flabbergasted at Rogers' proposal for twelve Companies. Rogers probably hoped that by proposing eight more Companies than he now had he would get at least four. He was almost right, Loudoun compromised and ordered him to raise five, and asked Rogers to decide which of the proposed eight Captains he wanted. Loudoun made only two recommendations in subalterns. He asked Rogers to make a place for James Pottinger and Archibald Campbell who had both served in Rogers Cadet Company.[229] Rogers returned the next day, January 11, with his revised list in which he recommends the senior and most deserving officers for Captaincys: the veteran and senior Lieutenants John McCurdy, James Rogers, the forceful Jonathan Brewer and John Stark's brother, William. Moses Brewer was still recommended for the Connecticut Mohegan Company. On this list Loudoun makes a few changes in the subalterns. He shuffles some of Rogers' recommended First Lieutenants to Second Lieutenants. He also added James White, Lawrence Smith and Henry Wendell (who was strongly recommended by General Abercrombie) and took off three men that Rogers was pushing.

As a result of all the proposed changes and promotions in the present four Companies and the recommended officers for the five new ones, it seems that Rogers recommendations prevailed except for the five subalterns preferred by Loudoun.[230]

While waiting for Loudoun to have the new commissions written up, Rogers' active mind was not idle. He penned a plan for taking Crown Point that winter with the 400 Rangers he had at Fort Edward. Rogers' daring plan was the ideal strategy for reducing not only the formidable and ancient Crown Point but Ticonderoga as well, thus clearing the way to Canada. Rogers knew from the information of his recent prisoners that the French tactics for garrisoning the two forts for the winter were to jam Ticonderoga with 350 or more troops besides alternate bodies of a hundred or more Indians who came from Canada to make raids. The French feared an attack at Ticonderoga if at all, since it was the closest fort to attack. While at Crown Point behind Ticonderoga the French posted only 150 men. Rogers shrewdly conceived a plan for taking Crown Point first, which would have cut off Ticonderoga and made succour to it almost impossible, and its eventual surrender by a siege inevitable.

The substance of his plan as presented by him to Loudoun on January 13, was to take Crown Point with 400 Rangers by travelling back of the mountains west of Lake George to Lake Champlain, there to intercept any party of sleighs travelling between St. Johns and Crown Point on the lake. Taking the drivers of the sleighs prisoners he planned to dress part of the men in their clothes, and with a few Rangers among them that could speak French, the sleighs were to proceed on to Crown Point. With this *Trojan Horse* to divert the attention of the Commandant and to open the gates; Rogers hoped to dash in with the rest of his Rangers before the Commandant had discovered the deceit. Of course Lake Champlain would have to freeze before French provision sleighs could be expected on it, but the way the weather was acting, this seemed very likely to happen, and soon.[231]

This daring plan was made to order for Rogers and his Rangers and the odds were even that Crown Point could have been taken by them and held until British reenforcements arrived. But jealousy frustrated Rogers' proposal. Loudoun had his own grand plan of making a formal winter siege of Ticonderoga and thus save face for the unagressive campaigns he had so far conducted. Knowing Rogers' latent capabilities, Loudoun feared he would succeed and thus minimize his own achievement of capturing Ticonderoga. He put Rogers off by telling him to talk his plan over with General Abercrombie, who would tell him when to make the attempt. Loudoun adds in his *Diary:* "I am bound to do this as he will break into my plan of taking Ticonderoga if the frost permits."[232] Rogers was so delighted in Loudoun's apparent trust in him by allowing him to pick his own officers and raise new Companies, not to mention putting one over on Colonel Haviland, that he did not doubt Loudoun meant what he said.

The next day, the 14, the commissions were ready and signed by Loudoun, and Rogers bid goodbye to New York.[233] At Albany, Rogers visited Forsey, the Clothier, and left him an order to make up the bulk of the uniforms for his Rangers. As Forsey did not have enough green cloth on hand, Rogers had to have the firms of Kennedy & Lyle and Peble & Wiles make up the balance.[234] Waiting on General Abercrombie on the 21st, Rogers expressed that he was "well satisfied with his reception from Lord" Loudoun "and the confidence he had reposed in him". Abercrombie sent orders to Colonel Haviland "*to restore the mutineers into Rogers own hands*" and to send down the new Ranger Captains.[235] As the new Captain, William Stark, was already on furlough in New Hampshire, Rogers wrote him, as well as his friends, who he had obtained Lieutenants and Ensigns commissions, telling them about their appointments and ordering them to recruit for their respective Companies; and Rogers, at his own expense, sent two of his Rangers to New Hampshire on horseback with these dispatches so that no time would be lost.[236]

While talking with General Abercrombie, Rogers naturally followed Loudoun's orders to talk over with him his proposal for taking Crown Point. Abercrombie and his erstwhile nephew absorbed attentively the Rangers' daring plan. The General told him he would let him know when to execute it and then went into a huddle with his young nephew and proceeded to give Rogers the double-cross. The very same night they penned their own proposal to Loudoun to take Crown Point and Rogers had no part in their scheme. This definitly killed any chance of Rogers being given the chance. Loudoun could not let Rogers try for fear of hurting General Abercrombie's feelings.[237] So ended an opportunity which might well have established undying fame for Rogers, not to mention preventing one of the bloodiest battles and worst defeats suffered by Rogers Rangers. Who can say but what gates of advancements might have been opened to Rogers if he had captured Crown Point. Rogers, trusting the apparent sincerity of the two Abercrombies, still believed that he would be given the opportunity when Lake Champlain froze. So he innocently waited and kept himself busy in making the arrangements for the raising of his new Companies and the recruiting for his old ones.

During Rogers' absence from Rogers' Island the Rangers had been having their troubles. Not by another Mutiny, or Battle with the enemy, but with the elements, in the nature of a flood. On January 3, the Hudson River rose to such a height that it flooded most of Rogers' Island and the Rangers were rudely awakened by being almost floated out of their huts. The water flooded some of the huts waist deep; and to top it all, the flood carried away the greater part of the fire-wood which the Rangers had so laboriously chopped and stacked. The Rangers crowded together in the unscathed huts on higher ground and remained there out of the pouring rain and cutting hail until the water subsided. The Rangers now turned Engineers and proceeded to repair the damages done by the flood. Besides repairing their own hut-village, they received orders from Haviland five days later, on the 8th, for 150 Rangers to clear the Saratoga road of fallen trees and repair the washed out bridges.[238]

The atmosphere now froze and the trees were loaded with ice, many of the limbs snapped and fell making a loud noise when cracking like guns going off. This happened in the woods opposite Fort Edward and frightened the Regular sentrys until the smiling Rangers *put them wise*.[239]

So passed the month of January for Rogers Rangers. Their monotonous and idle life was occasionally broken when the weather permitted by hunting in the woods. When the river finally froze, Colonel Haviland and the Regular officers could be seen skating on the ice and "made themselves much sport in sliding down the bank on a sleigh".[240] But none of the officers of Rogers Rangers were invited to share in the sport. Rogers had returned by this time and Haviland continued to snub him, particularly since Rogers had won out in deciding the fate of the mutineers. So Rogers remained on his Island and messed with his own officers and drank with them. There were five Volunteers of

Haviland's 27th Regiment who had served as Cadets in Rogers' training Company. They frequently came over to see their friend Rogers and break open a few bottles with him and his fellow officers. On one of these occasions two of the young Cadets deep in their cups were lamenting the misfortunes of their country, occasioned by her enormous debt. Rogers, with an expansive gesture, told them to give themselves no more uneasiness about the matter, as he would pay half the debt and a friend of his the other.[241]

Haviland was still inwardly boiling at the outcome of the Whipping Post Mutiny. The results had been anything but what he had hoped for. He continued to bait Rogers by shifting his tact. A recent fire at Fort Edward would have consumed the whole fort but for the efforts of Captain Israel Putnam, commanding one of the two Connecticut Provincial Ranging Companies stationed in Fort Edward and outlying blockhouses. Haviland took Putnam under his friendly wing and proceeded to shower attentions and favours on him that he had never done for Rogers. They went hunting together and Haviland, even recommended Putnam indirectly for the command of Rogers' Corps at the time of the Mutiny, when Haviland had visions of Rogers being relieved of his command because of the insubordination of his men.[242] Naturally Rogers got wind of all this and it did not increase his affection for the Colonel.

When Rogers returned to Rogers' Island from

228

Phillips' Ice Testing Scout[41]

Albany on January 25, he immediately sent out Lieutenant "Bill Phillips" to Lake George to see if it was frozen. The same day all the Rangers were mustered and Rogers computed the exact numbers necessary to fill up his present Companies.[243] Phillips and his party returned two days later, and he reported "..yt ye Lake is Froze Vary Strong.." Rogers was overjoyed, for this meant that Lake Champlain, the more northern lake, was also froze, making it possible to make his attempt on Crown Point.

On January 26, the day after Lieutenant Phillips set out, Lieutenant Fitch of the Connecticut Company records that in the morning another scout of Rogers' men went out. This party consisted of "Shanks" Shankland, Joshua Goodenough and two Mohegans (a few of the Connecticut Mohegans were already with Rogers Rangers). Their scout for a prisoner from Ticonderoga resulted in one of the most hardy and adventurous odysseys ever executed by a detatchment of Rogers Rangers. They ambushed and defeated a French patrol near Ticonderoga; met a strong French scout on their return and kept up a running fight with them back to Fort Edward. The two Mohegans having left them and Private Goodenough succombing to sheer exhaustion, Shankland held the enemy at bay while he kicked Goodenough into consciousness, so that they could outdistance their pursuers and reach Fort Edward *(See Appendice)*.

Shanks' Two Fights[20]

Meanwhile, excitement mounted high at Fort Edward, when the first suggestion of Loudoun's winter expedition on Ticonderoga became apparent. For, on January 28, a large convoy of sleighs arrived from Albany loaded with provisions and artillery shells.[244] Five days later, Rogers anxiously sent Captain Stark with a party to the First Narrows to determine if the lake was still frozen. While they were gone, Langy De Montegron, the most famous of the French Canadian partisan leaders on the Lake George front, and an able rival to Rogers for daring, managed, by taking the Wood Creek route, to slip by Stark and make a successful coup at Fort Edward.

Stark's Ice Testing Scout[42]

Langy's force of over 100 Indians, Canadians and Regulars arrived at the environs of Fort Edward on February 7, late in the afternoon, just as the customary wood-cutting party from Fort Edward was leaving the woods for the fort. Langy wisely withheld his men from attacking, for the English were fast marching within the protection of the outlying blockhouses of Fort Edward. Instead, he held back his grumbling savages and "Vieud ye Ground.. in order To Take all Possible Advantages" of the woodcutters when they returned the next day. The next morning, following the customary procedure of obtaining firewood, Sergeant Cooper and 24 Privates of the 27th Regiment issued out of Fort Edward at nine o'clock followed by a large party of unarmed Regulars and Connecticut Provincials with hand sleighs. They kept on a beaten path for none of them wore snowshoes. Langy, foreseeing this factor the day before, had cleverly deployed his men to drive the woodcutters into the waist deep snow on either side of the trail. He waited until the covering party were crossing a small gully on their way to the woods. Then while part of his detachment engaged the covering party in front, the rest of Langy's force surrounded the rear of the gully and drove the unarmed woodcutters like so many sheep or cattle. As soon as they were off the beaten path they were at the mercy of Langy's Indians who were on snowshoes and could slaughter at will the floundering English, hips deep in the snow. "..They Tomahawkd Kild and Scalped them or Carryd them away Prisoners as Best Gratifyd their Ungodly Heathenish Humors.." Fortunately not all of the unarmed woodcutters had descended the gully and they raced back to safety on the threaded path. The covering party, all of the 27th Regiment, suffered terribly; but it is a credit to that Corps' History that they behaved with unusual bravery and gave a good account of themselves before going down. Sergeant Cooper was able to fire three shots before he was overwhelmed, carried off and scalped. A Private was shot through both thighs, stood his ground and held the enemy at bay until the Captain of the pickets arrived with his men. The affair took place near a blockhouse where Putnam's Connecticut Company were lodged, but none of his, or Durkee's Provincial Rangers posted in adjacent blockhouses, could be induced by the Captain of the pickets

to put on their snowshoes and assist him. If
they had, they might have been able to save
some of Sergeant Cooper's unfortunate covering
party. Out of the 25 men in Cooper's covering
party, 13 were killed outright, 5 were carried
off, 4 were wounded, but with a Corporal and
two unarmed men, managed to escape. One of the
wounded privates was scalped alive, recovered,
and in relating his experience to his Regimental officers, whimsically pointed to his head
and said that he had lost his *night cap*. But
the Surgeon later found a concussion and the
poor fellow was four or five times out of his
head before he recovered. The Connecticut Provincial Woodcutters lost three men killed. Two
of these bodies were found ten days later. On
one of them was a letter addressed to Rogers. It
is not likely, but he could have been one of
Rogers Rangers, or a Provincial who had been
out with him on scouts. Outside of this possible member, none of Rogers Rangers participated in this massacre. As soon as the firing
started, Rogers, on his Island, attempted to
find out the strength of the attackers so that
he could organize a party on snowshoes strong
enough to engage them and to cover Stark's
scout who were still out. Due to the scattering about of the available snowshoes, it was
an hour-and-a-half before Rogers could fit out
a party of 140 Rangers of his Corps, and Putnam's and Durkee's who, now that they had obtained snowshoes, were willing to venture out.
Rogers saw by Langy's retiring tracks that the

Pursuit of Langy[43]

French were headed for the Wood Creek route to Ticonderoga. Hoping to cut them off by taking a short-cut. Rogers made a forced march to Lake George, met Captain Stark's scout at Half-Way Brook, and together they proceeded a few miles down the lake then crossed over to South Bay to waylay Langy, but found that he had already passed. Disgruntled, Rogers and Stark returned on February 10, to assist in Lord Howe's groundwork for his Ticonderoga Expedition.

Loudoun had originally planned to lead this expedition personally, but the exingencies of Provincial business compelled him to turn over to Abercrombie, his second, and Lord Howe, complete charge of the preparations and Howe was to be given the command. On February 2, Loudoun gave Howe his order to proceed when he was ready, and to destroy Crown Point and Ticonderoga. While ordinance and stores were being pushed up to Fort Edward as the weather and roads permitted;[245] Lieutenant Leslie, an Engineer, was sent up with some light sledges in order to test the road to the lake and survey the true state of Lake George. On the 11th of February he left Fort Edward with 30 light sledges. Captain Stark, two subalterns, and forty Rangers on snowshoes formed his escort. They went in advance to level a road for him with their snowshoes. It soon became apparent that forty Rangers were quite insufficient to break a path for men marching without snowshoes. Even though Rogers had proceeded Leslie

Leslie's Snow-Shoe Test[44]

the day before with more than 140 Rangers (returning from the pursuit of Langy) their snowshoe tracks would not bear Leslie's scout. The weather was so severe that even ten of the hardened Rangers awoke the next morning suffering from frostbite. They were sent back to Fort Edward and Leslie, leaving his sledges to follow, went on ahead with Captain Stark and ten Rangers to the lake. They arrived at 11:00 a.m and measured the depth of snow on either side, finding it four or five feet deep. The sledges arrived at 4:30 p.m and they were driven unto the lake which proved strong enough to hold them and the horses. Lieutenant Leslie returned to Albany on the 14th and made his report to Lord Howe and Abercrombie.

It was apparent that at least 300 to 400 pair of snowshoes would be needed to break the path for the Regulars and Artillery, and Rogers was blamed for not having that many pair ready. As early as November 1757, before Loudoun left Fort Edward, he had ordered Rogers to have every Ranger construct two pairs of snowshoes as he intended to double the number of Rangers by Spring. Since Rogers Rangers had dwindled somewhat due to desertion, sickness, and discharged men, it was estimated that he could build 700 pair. Rogers had other war contracts to fill. He had to construct *ice-creepers*, and *hand-sleys* for Howe's Expedition. On December 19, Colonel Williamson of the Royal Artillery wrote Loudoun from Albany that since Rogers had Loudoun's orders to make seven hundred pair of "ice creepers" at Fort Edward, he had directed that his Smith work with the Artillery Smith at Albany to facilitate production. Williamson stated that he would have enough "creepers" made for all the artillery-men and any number more that Loudoun cared to order.

 The Rangers also made 300 *Hand Sleys* and Rogers had his Rangers construct snowshoes, but the exingencies of constant scouting, sickness, and the effects of the Whipping Post Mutiny had slowed down production; not to mention the fact that not all of Rogers Rangers were experienced in constructing snowshoes. Due to these retarding factors, Rogers only had 200 pair ready when he saw Loudoun in January, and the wood bent for 400 more, which would be ready by the time that he returned to Rogers' Island. But they evidently were not, or if built, were washed away in the flood. There is no record of how many pair Rogers' men made and lost in the flood but there must have been several for Rogers had trouble in equiping scouts However there is reason to believe that Rogers Rangers at "Rogers' Island" must have had ready in February at least the minimum 300 pair needed to lay the path for Howe's unsnowshoed Regulars (who couldn't walk on them in any event) as Lieutenant Leslie stated in his report. It is more likely that 400 pair were ready for Rogers was aware that he needed that many if his own proposal to take Crown Point with 400 Rangers was granted.[246]

 No, the capture of Ticonderoga and Crown

Point in the dead of a violent Winter, called for something in the way of a *Commando Raid*[247] or: *Flying Party* (the term in vogue at that time for a fast moving partisan force) such as Rogers proposed against Crown Point. Loudoun, though a capable organizer, was continually making grand preparations at the wrong time and against the wrong place. It was apparent to every one that the depth of snow forbade the transportation of artillery, no matter how many men were employed on snowshoes. It should not have been expected that they could lay a path solid enough to bear even the lightest field pieces. If Loudoun, Abercrombie, or Howe, had any imagination they would have realized that *Rogers' plan* coupled with a surprise attack at the same time on Ticonderoga, by a larger body of troops, was the logical one.

In the meantime the French had gotten wind of something brewing from the prisoners that Langy took at Fort Edward, and they tried to find out mor by sending Captain Wolff and 16 men under a flag of truce with the pretext of discussing an exchange of prisoners. Wolff arrived at Fort Edward on February 17, but could not find out much for the newly arrived stores and ordinance were out of sight and Howe's invasion army had not yet arrived. Haviland did not allow Wolff to linger to long at Fort Edward; but while he was there, Rogers took the opportunity to rib Wolff about his recent "Xmas Eve Raid" and brief *Siege* of Ticonderoga. He "quizzed him on the fresh meat they let him eat at Carillon", but Wolff ominously answered him "to be careful of himself when he came again".[248] Rogers would not have smiled if he could have foreseen the result of his next visit to Ticonderoga, but like all militarists how was he to know and read the fortunes of war.

While supplies continued to arrive, 3,000 of the cream of the British Regulars were assembled at the lower posts on the Hudson.[249] Meanwhile the population of Rogers' Island was increasing daily as recruits for the old and new Companies arrived from New England. The new uniforms started to arrive also, and for the first time, most of the Corps were all dressed alike, presenting a more military bearing and greately increasing the *Esprit de Corps*.[250] While those experienced continued making snowshoes, the new recruits were initiated into the Corps by having Rogers' Ranging Rules drilled into them.

On the 19th of February a party were hunting in the woods and their gunfire could be heard by Haviland in Fort Edward "About which Colonel Haviland and Rogers had some Difference".[251] It appears that the feud would never end, and the new recruits came to dislike Haviland as much as the veteran Rangers.

The weather cleared on the 26th, and a party of Rogers Rangers on snowshoes were ordered to thread down the snow which had piled dangerously high on Fort Edward's glassess, making it easy for the enemy to escalade the fort.[252]

The next day, the fort received the "miserable news" that Howe's expedition was to be shelved and all the stores were to be sent back.²⁵³ Rogers hoped that he would now be given permission to make his proposed expedition against Crown Point, but to his amazement Haviland no sooner received the dispatch acquainting him of the abandoning of Howe's attempt, than the very same night he ordered his friend, Captain Israel Putnam, to command a large scouting party to Ticonderoga to take a prisoner. At the same time he gave out publicly that upon his return, Rogers would be sent on his proposed expedition with 400 Rangers. This was injudicious of Haviland for the fact was known to all the officers and men before Putnam's departure.²⁵⁴ The next morning was spent in hurriedly fitting out Putnam's scout. About one o'clock they marched out consisting of about 115 officers and men. Part of his force, Rogers notes, consisted of members of Rogers Rangers, but who their officer was has not been recorded. Rogers stood darkly by as Haviland's favorite filed out of the fort with the scout that should have been led by him. The Colonel had struck deep when he executed this bit of tact. Rogers had every reason to believe that the French were aware of his forthcoming expedition for on March 6, Putnam returned minus one of his men, John Robens, who had apparently got lost and was picked up by the French. Most everyone, including Rogers believed that he had deserted. If he had deserted, he would have informed the French of

Putnam's Ticonderoga Scout 45

ficers of Rogers' coming. However, the French were not aware of Rogers' advance until March 13, the day of his disastrous battle. French documents from "Carillon" before and after the battle do not mention Robens or Ranger Sutler Best's servant (who, on March 6, was taken by Langy's Indians) revealing any information about Rogers' movements. Consequently Rogers' statements that Haviland's ill-timed publicity of his scout had resulted in Robens and the servant informing the French of his coming, were wrong.

Sutler Best's servant was in a convoy of sleighs from Fort Edward to pick up supplies at Saratoga when they were attacked by 35 of Langy's Indians. The attack started about 10 a.m. Most of the sleighs managed to break free with the help of Lieutenant Belcher and a detatchment of the 27th Regiment who stayed behind and bravely covered their retreat to Fort Edward. Unfortunately Best's servant was captured in this affair. When the horse drawn sleighs galloped into Fort Edward, Rogers (in sharp contrast to his hour and a half delay in pursuing Langy) *immediately* pursued them with 100 Rangers. Observers at Fort Edward state that "he and a Number of his Men, with Snowshoes, arms and ammunition, most of them stripped to their shirts, were out of Sight of the Fort in less than a quarter of an hour, after the Alarm arrived there". Langy's Indians had a four mile lead on him and he could not catch up to them "notwithstanding he and his Party struggled hard until near 12 o'clock at night."

Pursuit of Langy's Indians[46]

Returning exhausted to Fort Edward that night they found Putnam returned from an unsuccessful scout to Ticonderoga. The next three days were busily spent by Rogers Rangers in preparing for their long heralded expedition.

They were interrupted on the 9th, with orders from Haviland to overtake Private Daniel Pratt of Durkee's Connecticut Company who had slung his pack after an alarm drill and marched homeward. Rogers sent a party after him who overtook him and Haviland confined him in the fort Guard House. He was courtmartialed and received 70 lashes, a light sentence compared to what Haviland tried to have Rogers inflict on his Rangers for the same offense. *March 9th Blood Hound Scout*[4]

On March 10, Rogers received "*positive*" orders from Haviland to make a scout to Ticonderoga "not with a party of 400 men, as at first given out, but of 180 men only, officers included". From these orders, Rogers knew that his project against Crown Point was now definitly stymied; for everything was against it. With or *without* Haviland's permission, he did not dare to attempt his *trojan horse* attack on Crown Point with only 180 men; besides, Rogers now believed that the element of surprise was gone. In his disappointment at Haviland's "*positive orders*", Rogers accumulated *differences* with Haviland came boiling to the surface and in his angry frustrated thoughts he definitly believed that Haviland was sending him into a trap. He states as much in his *Journals*: "I acknowledged I entered upon this service, and *The Battle of Rogers' Rock*[22] viewed this small detachment of brave men march out, with no little concern and uneasiness of mind; for as there was the greatest reason to suspect, that the French were, by the prisoner and deserter" (Best's servant and John Robens), "fully informed of the design of sending me out upon Putnam's return; *what could I think!* to see my party, instead of being strengthened and augmented, reduced to less than one-half of the number at first proposed. I must confess it appeared to me (ignorant and unskilled as I then was in the politics and arts of war) incomprehensible; but. my commander doubtless had his reasons, and is able to vindicate his own conduct." Whether Haviland was guilty of intending to send Rogers into a trap will probably never be known, for he would never put such incriminating thoughts down in writing. It is known that he had an intense dislike for Rogers and Rogers Rangers *and* had once stated that "it would be better they were all gone than have such a Riotous sort of people".[255] He also gave Rogers "*positive orders*" to scout towards Ticonderoga with 180 men instead of the originally planned 400. In spite of Rogers protests. Nevertheless, the French at Ticonderoga did not know of Rogers' forthcoming until the day of his arrival at Trout Brook. A factor in Haviland's favour was the presence of eight officers and men from his own 27th Regiment in Rogers' expedition. It does not seem likely that Haviland would allow three of his own officers, not to mention three Volunteers, a Sergeant and a Private, to go forth to their doom if he had any ulterior motive in launching Rogers on his ill-fated scout.

In spite of Rogers' uncustomary reluctance to be 'on party' he had a fine body of officers and men in his expedition. Though Haviland had cut his proposed party in half, he could still pick his own officers and men. Because of the *nature* of this scout Rogers allowed only veterans of his four old Companies to go. He did not want any raw recruits along that were unhardened to Winter marches on snowshoes. He could not afford to deplete his "180 men" after the first or second day out because of lameness or frostbite. However three of Rogers' five new Companies were represented by one officer from each Company. They were former Volunteers in Rogers' Cadet Company, namely: Ensign Andrew Ross (of Wm. Stark's); Lieutenant Archibald Campbell (of Jonathan Brewer's); both of these young Scots had originally carried arms as Volunteers in the 42d Highlanders (Black Watch); and Ensign Gregory McDonald (of James Rogers') who had originally carried arms as a Volunteer in Robert Rogers' own Company. All three of these fiery young Scots were to lose their lives in their first battle as commissioned officers of Rogers Rangers. Four other former Volunteers also formed the nucleous of the Ranger officers in the scout. They were First Lieutenant "Jamey" Pottinger whoes four months old child was soon to be an orphan. "Jamey", the veteran of many wars, was well liked by both officers and men. He was generous to a fault and it is said that he "lent a good many dollars to the Rangers before he went out on this his last Scout".[256] Ensign James White, one of the three subalterns *pushed* by Loudoun when the new Companies were commissioned in January. White, like Pottinger, was never to see his native England again. Lieutenant Edward Crofton, a personal friend of Sir John Whiteford was an Englishman of unusual daring and fighting ability, Crofton was to become one of the most famous officers in the Corps. He was one of four officers to survive this expedition. The seventh *new* officer in the scout was Ensign Joseph Waite, a personal friend of Rogers from Massachusetts (and later Alstead N.H.). Waite brought with him plenty of experience for he had served in the Militia Rangers guarding the home frontiers. Like Crofton he was fortunate enough to survive the forthcoming disaster.

The three veteran officers present (besides Rogers) were: Captain Charles Bulkeley who had missed serving at La Barbue Creek and the First Defense of William Henry. He was determined to serve in this scout. It would have been better if he had missed it for this excellent officer lost his life in his first *major* engagement with Rogers Rangers. The famous "Bill Phillips" was also present. He was the only Ranger officer to be taken alive. He managed to make one of the miraculous escapes that made his name a legend. Lieutenant Increase More a hero Sergeant of La Barbue Creek was present. This was More's last scout.

The Sergeants were well represented. There was James Tute who was to become a Captain in 1759. He was a close friend of Rogers besides being a very enterprising young warrior. Like many of Rogers Rangers he later worked his way up to a commission in the Regulars. When he did he added to his given name the resounding ones: *Marcus Anthony*. Other new Sergeants were the three Clarks: James, William and John. James Clark was one of Rogers original 1755 Rangers. A seasoned veteran, he was to be promoted, for his gallant conduct on March 13, to a Lieutenantcy, as were Tute and Francis Creed a British Volunteer in the 27th Regiment. James Faulkiner, a Sergeant in Bulkeley's, also "signalized" himself and jumped to a Lieutenant. Sergeant John Clark received an Ensign's berth after the Battle. Sergeants who did not survive were: Jacob Townsend, Moses Kelsey and Josiah Hale, all veteran Sergeants; and Robert Parnell and Philip Flanders who were seasoned Rangers but new Sergeants.

No one was *ordered* on this hazardous expedition. All members were accepted *volunteers*. An analysis of Rogers' complete force reveals that it consisted of 11 Ranger Officers, 11 Sergeants, and 150 Privates of Rogers Rangers; Corporal Sharmon of Putnam's Connecticut Company; Captain-Lieutenant Pringle, Lieutenant Roche, Ensign Bellfore, Volunteers Creed, Kent and Wrightson (all three had served in Rogers'

Cadet Company and were experienced Rangers), and Sergeant Humphreys and a Private of the 27th (Inniskilling) Regiment. In all, 184 officers and men.

On March 10, the detatchment filed out of Fort Edward with the apprehensive Rogers at their head. It was the middle of the afternoon and they marched only as far as the Half-Way Brook. The next day they reached the First Narrows and encamped on the east side of Lake George. Rogers seems to have had a premonition about this scout for he was more cautious than ever. After dark he sent "a party three miles further down the lake...to make discovery of any Enemies" coming towards the British Forts. They returned with a negative report. Rogers was taking no chances. He had parties walking on the lake and posted sentrys on the land during the night. The expedition was up and on their march by sunrise, marching in extended order on the lake with their snowshoes strapped to their backs. They kept close in against the east shore to prevent being observed from the hills. They had gone three miles when they spotted a dog running across the lake. Since dogs sometimes travelled with Indians, Rogers pulled his party into the fir trees along the shore and sent a detatchment to reconnoitre the islands "thinking the Indians might have laid in Ambush there". The dog undoubtedly belonged to a party of Indians but they were a good many miles southward. The Indians were a raiding party of 15 braves and at that very same hour were attacking the morning patrol of Rogers Rangers near Fort Edward. When Rogers scout "returned without discovering any further signs" of the enemy he did not take any chances of being spotted by lurking eyes on the hills but ordered his men to put on their snowshoes and they kept to the woods until they were opposite to Sabbath Day Point at 10 a.m. Here they remained the remainder of the day while parties kept a sharp vigil peering down the lake with "prospective Glasses". As soon as it was dark they continued on the lake. Phillips led the van, and men on ice skates went before him. Rogers kept the main body tight together to prevent separation in the dark. Ensign Ross flanked them on the west shore. They were within eight miles of the French advance guard at Coutre Coeur when Phillips reported that he had seen a fire on the east shore. Rogers marched to attack but could find no campfire and it was believed that Phillips and Ensign White who collaborated with him, had mistaken the fire for a patch of bleach snow or rotted wood which sometimes turned phosphorescent when damp; a common occurence which fooled the most veteran of scouts.

The Morning Patrol Fight[21]

Returning to where they had left their packs on the west shore they remained there the remainder of the night. The next morning, Monday March 13, (an unlucky number, as well as an unlucky day) Rogers held a council of war with his officers and it was agreed to put on their snowshoes and travel back of Bald Mountain

keeping it and adjoining ridges between them
and the French advanced posts on the end of
Lake George. They marched from 7 to 11 a.m and
halted on the back of the ridge, almost opposite Coutre Coeur. Here they ate a cold meal
and waited for the enemy's daily Trout Brook
patrol to return to Ticonderoga before they
proceeded on. Rogers judged that they should
have passed by three o'clock. At that hour the
Rangers resumed their march down the valley of
Trout Brook "thinking to lay an Ambush to Some
of their roads in ye Night, & meet with them
in the morning without being discovered". They
marched in two divisions: Captain Bulkeley at
the head of the first and Rogers the second.
Ensigns White and Waite "brought up the rear".
The other officers were distributed in each
division amongst the men. Frozen Trout Brook
was close on their left and Bald Mountain (Rogers' Rock) on their right. Rogers states: "We
kept close to the mountain, that the advanced
guard might better observe the rivulet, on the
ice of which I imagined" the enemy "would travel if out, as the snow was four feet deep,
and very bad travelling on snow shoes. In this
manner we marched a mile and a half, when our
advanced guard informed me of the enemy being
in their view; and soon after, that they had
ascertained their number to be 96 chiefly Indians. We immediately laid down our packs, and
prepared for battle, supposing these to be the
whole number or main body of the enemy, who
were marching on our left up the rivulet, upon

the ice, and would come within 15 Rods of My party by the Course they then Steered. I ordered Ensign McDonald to the command of the advance guard, which, as we faced to the left, made a flanking party to our right. We marched to within a few yards of the bank, which was higher than the ground we occupied; and observing the ground gradually to descend from the bank of the rivulet to the foot of the mountain, we extended our party along the bank far enough to command the whole of the enemies' at once; we waited until their front was nearly opposite to our left wing, when I fired a gun, as a signal for a general discharge upon them; whereupon we gave them the first fire, which killed above forty Indians, the rest retreated. My party pursued them & Scalped about forty Indians in about one quarter of an hour." If the Battle could have ended at this point the Rangers could have chalked up another great battle honour, but unfortunately it was only the beginning.

The French were aware of their approach. The day before Sieur La Durantaye, an Ensign en Second of the Colony Regulars, had arrived at Ticonderoga with 200 Iroquois and Nipissings from Sault St. Louis and the Lake of the Two Mountains. Durantaye also brought with him several ambitious Colonial Cadets, and 30 Canadians. They arrived in the evening of the 12th and the next morning the Indians applied to Captain De Hebecourt, Commandant at Ticonderoga, for provisions and brandy, stating that they wanted to rest a few days before starting against Fort Edward. Returning to their camp they broke open the brandy but one of their number, claiming to be a witch-doctor was soon consulting the spirits. Later he gathered his fellow warriors together, who were by this time well embedded with *liquid* spirits. He told them that he had been informed by the spirits that the English had a party out and that they could not be far distant. A scout of six Indians who had been scouting down the foot of the lake confirmed his belief when they came in excitedly with the news of seeing fresh tracks of 200 men (at the spot where Rogers' expedition left the lake). The Indians could not be contained after this seemingly miraculous fulfillment of their witch-doctor's prophecy. De Hebecourt was informed, and he was as delighted at getting rid of the Indians as he was of making a stroke against the English, for he had visions of the Indians hanging around Ticonderoga for days eating up his limited stores. Unfortunately for Rogers Rangers was the presence of the partisan Langy at Ticonderoga. Langy had been resting between raids against Fort Edward and he couldn't resist this call to action. Several Lieutenants and Sergeants of the garrison Regulars also volunteered besides several Regular Privates and Langy's own body of thirty odd Canadians (There is no mention of Langy's Indians being present. Evidently all but 15 had returned to their village. The 15 were on their way back from a scout to Fort Edward). In all, Langy mustered 50 Canadians and Regulars in Ticonderoga to join with Durantaye's 250 Indians and Canadians to make a total of 300 men sent against Rogers' 184. La Durantaye preceded Langy and the bulk of the column by starting out fifteen minutes earlier with 95 men, mostly Indians. They were the force that Rogers defeated at Trout Brook.

Returning to the scene of the conflict we find that half of Rogers Rangers tore themselves away from the profitable task of scalping their vanquished foe to pursue the 50 to 60 fleeing Indians. Rogers shouted to Ensign McDonald on the end of the line to "head them". McDonald was closely followed by Captain Bulkeley's "division" which included Lieutenants Moore, Pottinger, Campbell and Ensign White.

Meanwhile Langy, hearing the firing, threw his 205 men into bush-fighting formation and hurried forward. He received La Durantaye and his 55 survivors and the re-united force hurled themselves furiously against the pursuing Rangers who had pursued Durantaye right into Langy's musket fire. Up until this terrible awakening, the Rangers were unaware of Langy's force and they were caught completely by surprise. More than fifty fell from Langy's withering fire and savage attack. Captain Bulkeley and all the officers with him were killed instantly. Oddly enough, Ensign McDonald and Lieutenant Increase Moore who had preceded Bulkeley in the pursuit were not killed outright,

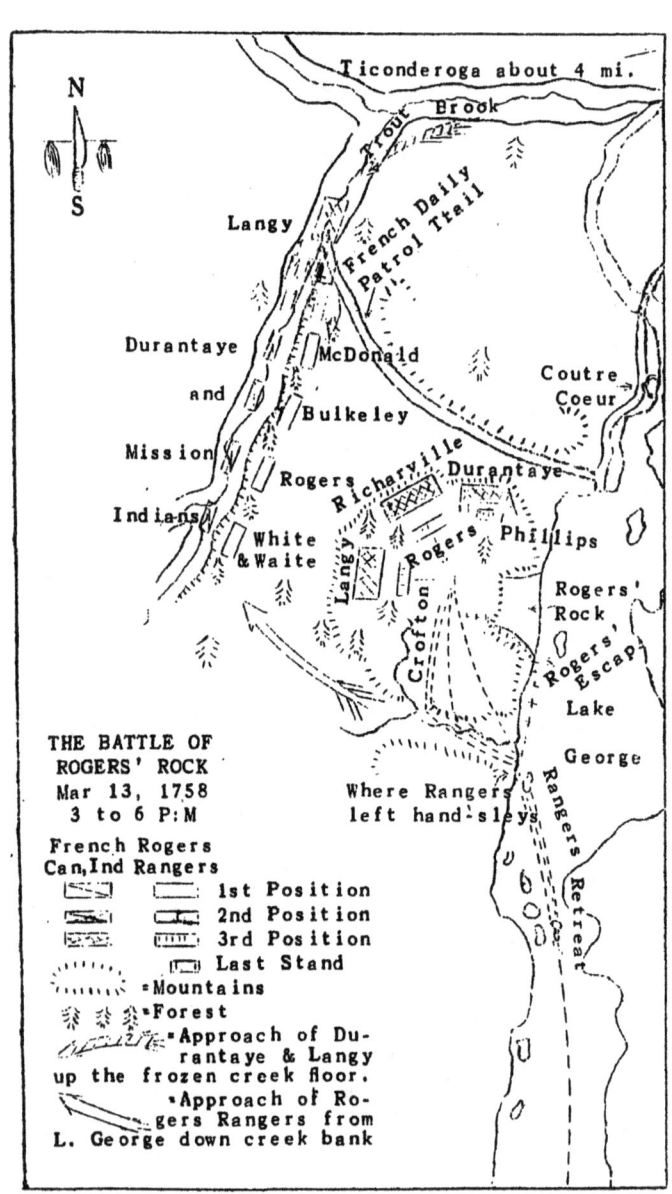

but mortally wounded. They managed to rally the survivors and get them back to Rogers "division" before they died. Rogers did not have time to form a front for Durantaye and Langy were upon his scattered force in an enveloping fury. Some of the Rangers were still scalping others were close behind Bulkeley's division in scattered pursuit of the beaten Indians. Rogers shouted the order to fall back to their original position on the slope of Bald Mountain (Rogers' Rock) which, Rogers states: "we gained at the expense of fifty men killed; the remainder I rallied, and drew up in pretty good order, where they fought with such intrepidity and bravery as obliged the enemy to retreat a second time; but we not being in a condition to pursue them, they rallied again, and recovered their ground, and warmly pushed us in front and both wings, while the mountain defended our rear". Rogers could not have presented a front of more than 120 men for he lost at least 50 in Bulkeley's and McDonald's detatchments and 10 more out of Ensign Waite's original rear guard of 12 men. The Indians, maddened by all the brandy they had consumed and the sight of their scalped comrades had rushed forward so rapidly that Waite's rearguard was cut off as Rogers fell back more to the right of his original attacking position. The rear-guard was practically wiped out when they tried to join Rogers. Ten were killed and one wounded "with whom" Wait and "the other Man made their Escape." Rogers would have had

Battle Of Rogers' Rock. From a painting of the Glens Falls Insurance Co.

a desperate battle if the odds were even, as it was he was outnumbered more than two to one by an infuriated savage foe who would be satisfied with nothing short of the complete defeat of Rogers Rangers. Rogers' ambuscade and the loss of so many scalped braves was like a cancerous sore that could not be stopped and they hurled themselves forward repeatedly to wipe Rogers out. Although they had lost one of their prominent war chiefs in Rogers' ambuscade (a factor which had angered them so) the Indians were well led by Durantaye and Langy who capitalized on the Indians intoxication and anger to hurl them forward unceasingly to break down Rogers' resistance.

Rogers states, that in their second attack "they were so warmly received, that their flanking parties soon retreated to their main body with considerable loss. This threw the whole again into disorder, and they retreated a third time". But the enemy marksmanship, particularly that of the Canadians, had also been deadly for Rogers notes that: "our number being now too far reduced to take advantage of their disorder, they rallied again, and made a fresh attack upon us." These two attacks had been so close together that only forty five minutes had elapsed. Durantaye and Langy now tried to envelop Rogers' flanks. They kept a thin body of skirmishers in their center and concentrated all the Indians on their left, with a similar bulk of Canadians on the right. The Indians on the left attacked first. Rogers wrote: "Lieu-

tenant Phillips informed me that about 200
Indians were going up ye hill on our right to
take possession of ye rising ground upon our
backs as he Supposed; whereupon I ordered him
with 18 Men to take possission of ye rising
Ground before the Enemy, & try to beat them
back, Accordingly he went, but I being Suspicious that ye Enemy would go round on our left
& take possession of the other part of the
hill, I sent Lieutenant Crofton with 15 Men
to take possession of the" rising "ground
there and soon after desired Captain Pringle
to go with a few more men & assist Crofton,
which he did with Lt. Roche & 8 Men. But the
Enemy pushed on So close in the front, that
the partys were not more than 20 yards apart &
oftentimes intermixed with each other." The
battle had been raging for an hour-and a-half
since Langy's first attack. Evening was near
and Langy and Durantaye wanted to finish Rogers
off before the forest darkened. They made a
final unrelenting attack from all three sides.
Rogers had lost more than 100 men and 8 officers of his total force of 181. Rogers only
had 31 men left to hold his center. Phillips
was on the right with 18; while Crofton and
Pringle held the left with 23 men. It was not
long before Phillips was completely surrounded
by the bulk of the Indians. Rogers and Ensign
Waite managed to hold the center until they
had lost ten more men. Rogers did not have
enough men left to hold his line and he was in
grave danger of being cut off for he was already

separated from Phillips. Rogers' center were almost engaging the enemy hand-to-hand when he wisely ordered his men to break and they ran up the hill to Crofton and Pringle's left wing whom they found fairly well intact but steadily being surrounded. At this same time Lieutenant Phillips was capitulating with Durantaye for himself and party. Rogers says that Phillips "Spoke to me & Said that he was incircled by 300 Indians" (actually 200) "who were within 10 rods of him & Said if they would give him & party good quarters he thought it best to surrender to them, otherwise that he would fight while he had one man left to fire a gun This officer and his whole party, after they surrendered, upon the strongest assurances of: good treatment from the enemy, were inhumanely tied up to trees", and most of them were slowly hacked to pieces while they still lived. The interventions of the French were of no avail for the discovery of several fresh Indian scalps inside the coats of slain Rangers had driven all thoughts of Christian humaness from their minds even though they were staunch Mission Indians. Phillips sometime later made one of his daring escapes. While the Indians were engrossed with other captives he got one hand loose, took a knife from his pocket, which he opened with his teeth, cut the deerskin cord that bound him and escaped.

Rogers writes that "Upon finding that Phillips & his party was obliged to Surrender, I thought it most prudent for me to retreat &

bring off as many of my people as I possibly could. Which I immediately did'. Captain-Lieutenant Pringle notes that "Captain Rogers with his party came to me, and said (as did all those with him) that a large body of Indians had ascended to our right; he likewise added, what was true, that the combat was very unequal, that I must retire, and he would give Mr. Roche and me a Sergeant to conduct us thru the mountain. No doubt prudence required us to accept his offer; but, besides one of my snowshoes being untied, I knew myself unable to march as fast as was requisite to avoid becoming a sacrifice to an enemy we could no longer oppose; I therefore begged of him to proceed, and then leaned against a rock in the path, determined to submit to a fate I thought unavoidable. Unfortunately for Mr. Roche, his snow-shoes were loosened likewise, which obliged him to determine with me, not to labour in a flight we were both unequal to." Rogers now put another "Ranging Rule" into effect and ordered his survivors to "disperse, and every one take a different route to the place of rendezvous" which in this instance was the place on Lake George where they had left their hand sleds. Fortunately darkness was in the ofting but until it descended several of the retreating Rangers were intercepted by the pursuing Indians. Like many of the Rangers, Rogers had thrown off his green jacket to facilitate his escape. In it were his March 24, 1756 commission from Shirley. When it was discovered by

the Indians and French it was believed that
Rogers was amongst the slain for they could
not imagine him leaving his treasured commission behind. One Iroquois boasted to Vaudreuil
that "he had himself killed him". Meanwhile
Rogers was making an escape that was to become
a legend and which resulted in this battle and
a mountain to be named after him. After giving
his last order of the battle to his survivors
Rogers made his escape by climbing up the west
slope of Bald Mountain. Arriving at the summit
he looked breathlessly down the precipitous
smooth wall of rock forming half of the eastern slope to the frozen surface of Lake George
more than a thousand feet below. Far behind
him he could hear his pursuers shouting exultantly as they picked up his trail in the
moon light. The dare-devil in the famous Ranger seemed to posses him for a moment as he
contemplated sliding down the dizzy cliff on
his snowshoes. Then his common sense got the
better of him and he conceived of the idea of
conveying the impression of this feat to his
pursuers. He quickly loosened the thongs that
bound his feet to his snowshoes, without removing them, he turned about face and laced
them on his feet the opposite of the way they
were made to be worn. Rogers then *back-tracked*
for some distance and swung himself by a convenient branch into a defile and followed it
down to the lake. Hardly had he reached the
lake than the exultant Indians reached the
summit and in the moonlight sighted Rogers ma-

king his way up the lake. They were awestruck at his apparent feat of sliding down the precipitous slide and firmly convinced that Rogers was *being watched over*, they gave up the chase.

It was about 8 p.m when Rogers landed on the lake. He had not gone far when he met other survivors and several wounded men. These they carried to their sleigh rendezvous at the southern end of Rogers' Rock. From here Rogers sent 3 Rangers on ice skates to Fort Edward for reenforcements for Rogers still expected a pursuit. Rogers had four badly wounded men with him and he laid them on four of the hand sleighs, and with two Rangers pulling each sleigh, he sent them off towards Fort Edward. Rogers with the remaining handful of survivors "tarried" at the rendezvous to cover any other survivors that might come in. They almost froze during the night for they had no blankets and they dared not light a fire. In the morning several more Rangers staggered wearily in. Some were wounded, and were helped in by comrades. Other wounded were not as fortunate and they had limped, crawled, or both around Rogers' Rock to the rendezvous. Rogers took them under his protective care and started out up the lake to Fort Edward.

Meanwhile Rogers' messengers sent for help had arrived at Fort Edward about noon on the 14th, to inform the astonished garrison that Rogers Rangers "Had a Hot Ingagment Such as Scarce Ever was Knowed in ye Country & Mostof His Party Distroyd". Haviland immediately sent Captains Stark, Shepard and Durkee with all the Rangers that "Could by any Means Be Spaird" to help in the survivors. They met Rogers at Sloop Island six miles from the head of Lake George. Rogers "tarried" there that night and sent to Fort Edward for three horse sleighs to carry in his wounded. They arrived the next morning and the Rangers started entering Fort Edward about 3 p.m in small bodies. Rogers himself came in about five o'clock bringing up the rear. Lieutenant Fitch at the Fort an eyewitness of this disheartening scene notes that it "was a Vast Cold & Tedious Day Espacially for ye Wounded Men". Rogers brought in 52 survivors, 8 of whom were badly wounded. He lost 124 on the field of battle and one more died of cold. He was Rogers' servant or orderly who had lost his reason from the horror of the battle. Captain Pringle and Lieutenant Roche, who had escaped from the field after darkness descended had made their way to the lake, where they met Rogers' orderly who guided them astray. On the sixth day he died of the cold but the two British officers on the 20th were in sight of Ticonderoga. They gave themselves up to the French officers who "ran violently" towards them to save them from the hands of the Indians who had also seen them.

It seems that Lieutenant Phillips and three others were the only Rangers captured who were not butchered. They were taken as "live letters" to the Indian village of Sault St. Louis near Montreal. Phillips managed to make his

escape. The fate of the other three is unknown.
None of the French accounts give a true statement of the actual numbers killed on their side. Hebecourt's official report to Montcalm in which he stated Durantaye's losses at 8 Indians killed, 17 wounded (2 of these later died), and 2 Colonial Cadets and 1 Canadian wounded; was adopted by all the other accounts. Rogers states that he killed and scalped 40 Indians in his Trout Brook Ambuscade and killed 60 more in the general engagement; and wounded 100. He probably killed at least 80 and wounded almost as many more. In any event it was a crushing defeat for Rogers Rangers in spite of their heroic stand against greater odds.

Rogers reluctantly dictated his official *Journal* of the battle on March 17, and the next day sent Lieutenant Crofton, one of the two officers who returned with Rogers, to Albany to convey the ill-tidings to General Howe who now commanded the New York front. In spite of the fact that Rogers had suffered a defeat, his ability to hurl the superior enemy back twice was "considerable proof of his bravery and conduct". The opinion of some of the Regulars is expressed by John Ogilvie the Chaplain of the Royal Americans at Albany. He notes that "envy, that arch fiend, will not allow him much merit". However the Provincial newspapers applauded his gallant stand and the dramatic battle enhanced his fame. The fact that Rogers Rangers had killed so many Indians set well with both the Provincials and British.

Upon the receipt of Rogers' *Journal*, Lord Howe immediately sent for the dejected Rogers. When Rogers arrived at Albany he notes that "I met with a very friendly reception from my Lord Howe, who advanced me cash to recruit the Rangers, and gave me leave to wait upon General Abercrombie at New York, who had now succeeded my Lord Loudoun". At Albany, Rogers learned much to his chagrin that four of the five new Companies on their way to Fort Edward had been re-routed to the Louisbourg front. Rogers says: "though I was at the whole expense of raising the 5 companies, I never got the least allowance for it".[257] It seems that all of Rogers plans had gone astray in the last two weeks. First, he had been refused to make his *trojan horse* attack on Crown Point. Secondly, he had suffered his first defeat as a consequence of this refusal. Now, it would seem, half of his Corps was being separated from him. Consequently Rogers was in a black mood when he saw Abercrombie in New York and he must have intimated that he wanted a Majority over his Independent Companies of Rangers or he would resign from the service. Abercrombie was no doubt perturbed at Rogers *attitude* for he expected him to be somewhat docile after his defeat at Rogers' Rock. He was also alarmed for he did not want to lose Rogers invaluable services. Pitt had been very explicit about maintaining the Rangers, and Abercrombie, new in command, wanted to follow his orders to the letter. Abercrombie personally, had the lowest regard for the Rangers whom he considered mutinous and cantankerous but in regard to Rogers he stated that "I do think him so necessary and Usefull a Man, that I should be extremely Sorry to part with him, and rather than that, to give him some Encouragement to Continue diligent and hearty in the service. Without him" the Rangers "would be good for Nothing".[258]

Before giving Rogers a reply, Abercrombie saw Loudoun and asked him if he had promised Rogers rank. Loudoun admitted that he had found it necessary to stall Rogers in January and he had promised to consider it as he did not want Rogers to "concur".[259] Abercrombie now realized that he would have to fulfill Loudoun's *promise* if he expected to maintain Rogers over the Rangers. Consequently Rogers long fight for *rank* was won and on April 6, 1758, Abercrombie commissioned Rogers "Major of the Rangers in his Majesty's service".[260]

Rogers' dream was fulfilled. He *now* had a battalion of Rangers. The first part of the Rangers History was behind them. The *'growing pains'* were over. Rogers Rangers came into their own when their leader received his long awaited Majority.

APPENDIX

I-ILLUSTRATIVE APPENDICES-

APPENDICE A

ROGERS' COUNTERFEITING TRIAL

(EXTRACTS FROM THE PROVINCIAL COURT FILES IN SECRETARY OF STATE'S OFFICE, CONCORD, N. H.)

1-WARRANT FOR ROGERS ARREST AND EXAMINATION:
Province of New Hampshire (to) the Sheriff of the Province of New Hampshire his under Sheriff or Deputy and to any and of every of the Constables-of the Province afore Said.- Greetings:
Whereas Information has been given to me the Subscriber one of his Majestys Justices of the Peace for the Province afore Said That there are many Bills passing Supposed to be Cour'erfeted - in Imitations of the forty Shilling Bills and of the Twenty Shilling Bills and of the Ten Shilling Bill and of the Six Shilling Bills of the Province afore Said.- and that there is Just Grounds to Suspect that there are many Persons Concerned in making and knowingly Passing such Bills. And in Particular that there is Reason to Suspect that
Samuel Duston of Haverhill, Essex Co., Mass., a Physician.
Timothy Sanders of Salem, New Hampshire.
Lacheriah Witney of Groton, Mass., Husbandman.
Ezekial Grale of Nottingham West, New Hampshire.
James Moor* of Merrimack, New Hampshire, Miller.
James McKnight of Merrimack, N.H., a Weaver.
James Matthews of Bedford, N. H., a Husbandman.
Joseph Winslow of Nottingham West, a Husbandman.
ROBERT ROGERS* of Starkstown, N.H., Husbandman.
RICHARD ROGERS* of Starkstown, N.H., Husbandman.
James Michael of Derryfield, N.H., Husbandman.
Nathaniel Martin of Goffstown, N.H., Husbandman.
William Walker of Rumford, N.H., a Husbandman.
William McAdams of Londonderry, N.H., Husbandman.
Benjamin Wilson of Nottingham West, Carpenter.
William Allard of Merrimac, N.H., Husbandman.
Lacheriah Ramsor of Merrimac, N.H., Husbandman.
Robert Gilson of Bedford, N. H., Husbandman.
Samuel Barnet of Merrimac, N.H., Husbandman.
Are concerned in making or knowingly passing such

*Became members of Rogers Rangers, however J. Moore did not enter until Mar 10, 1757. Any names asterisked in other pages likewise became Rangers.

Bills.-You are therefore in his Majesty's Name to Require you and every (one) of you forth with to make Diligent Search in all Suspected places within your Precinct for any such Counterfeit Bills and for any Plate or Places for making such Bills and for any tools or Instruments for making (or) Cutting Such plates and to Apprehend any Person or Persons in whose Custody Such Bills, Plate, or Tools, or Instruments shall be found or that there may be Just Grounds to Suspect are Concerned in making or knowingly passing any Such Bills and to bring them with the Bills, Plates or Instruments so found and also to apprehend (the above list of suspects) if they may be found in your Precinct and bring them before me or Some other of his Majesty's Justices of the Peace for the Province afore Said to be Examined....and dealt with as Law Directs here of. Fail not and make due Return. Dated at Portsmouth in said Province the 24th day of January in the 28th year of his Majesty's Reign, 1755. Signed *Mesheck Wear'*. *Wear sent the Warrant to Joseph Blanchard, his subordinate. Witnesses summoned were Thomas Hall of Goffstown, Robert MacKeen of Rumford, Moses Barret of Londonderry, Reuben Spaulding of Londonderry, Benjamin Win of Nottingham West, William Allen of Merrimac, and Stephen Spaulding.*

The next day, Jan. 25, John Chamberlain of Merrimac and James Walker of Bedford, New Hampshire were authorized to appear before Joseph Blanchard to be deputized. Chamberlain was sworn in on Jan 27th and Walker on Feb. 8th; so it is probable that Chamberlain arrested Rogers for he was picked up prior to Walker's deputization.-(Provincial Court Files, Case No. 27267-5 folios.).

2-*ROGERS' PRELIMINARY TRIAL AT RUMFORD, N.H:*
On February 7th Rogers was tried with fifteen others of the nineteen suspects before the Inferior Court at Rumford, N.H. In the following Examination Rogers' naive pose is revealed:
QUESTION: *Are you Guilty?*
ANSWER: *Not Guilty.*
QUESTION: *Do you know Sullivan?*
ANSWER: *I saw a man when I was Hunting in Goffs town near Martin's house, that called himself John McDaniel, and had some conversation with him, he wanted to buy a number of fat cattle and told me he would pay me as much as they would fetch in any market, and gave me my money (and told me) it*

would go through all the Laws in any of the Provinces, & maintain(ed that) his money (was) good.
QUESTION: What was the Occasion of his mentioning going through the law with his money?
ANSWER: I asked if his money was good.
QUESTION: Did you get and bring to any place appointed any oxen in consequence of your conversation with him at that time?
ANSWER: I got three pair and brought to Eben Martin's the place appointed in Goffstown, but the said McDaniel, otherwise Sullivan, was gone and I sold them to other people.
QUESTION: Did you know that McDaniel or Sullivan the man you saw there could make money or plates, or had so designed any such thing when you bought your oxen?
ANSWER: No, never. I saw him only that (one) time.
QUESTION: Did you ever propose to any body to become a Partner in Counterfeiting Bills?
ANSWER: Only to see if I could discover if they were concerned.
QUESTION: Who did you ask?
ANSWER: Joseph Blanchard. (This must have created a stir in the court-room for Captain Joseph Blanchard, Jr., was one of the four Justices of the Peace who conducted the examination.)
QUESTION: What did he say?
ANSWER: That he was not concerned nor never should be in such a devilish act and hoped' that men would be honest and strongly cautioned me against being concerned in any such thing.
QUESTION: Have you proposed it to any other person
ANSWER: Not that I rember now.
QUESTION: Who was at Martin's when you saw McDonald or Sullivan there?
ANSWER: James McNeil, Eben Martin, Samuel Martin and Nathaniel Martin.
QUESTION: Did Sullivan show you any bills?
ANSWER: Yes, he opened his book & showed me a handfull and said here is enough & gave me a 20 pd bill to pasture his horse he then had there at my place, and I was to bring him there agwin in two days. Which I did, when I brought the oxen, and Nathaniel Martin brought his brother Samuel for evidence that he had bought the horse of Sullivan & I then delivered the horse to Nathaniel Martin.
QUESTION: Did you meet McCurdy when you were carrying the horse to pasture?
ANSWER: Yes, to come out and go down to Capt Cum-

QUESTION: Whether he had any time seen any quantity of money on a table to the nature of a half a bushel full; or whether or not there was three men seen at his house one morning before day on a table counting money. Who answered there never had been.

THE EXAMINATION OF JOHN STARK:
Who says Robert Rogers some time last fall asked him if he (had) any oxen to sell. He answered yes, six oxen. Where are they? And he said they were at McCurdy's. And he asked Rogers what he was a going to do with them. Who said, a Gentleman from Boston wanted 3 yoke of oxen...Some time after he saw Rogers and asked him what he had done with his oxen, he said he sold em but not to the man he purposed them for, and said he was cheated for he intended the oxen for Sullivan and thought to have had a large quantity of Counterfeit money. But said he would not be concerned anymore in any such things.

THE JUSTICES MEMORANDUM ON THE RESULTS OF THEIR INVESTIGATION
Pursuant to a Warrant from the Honorable Mesheck Wear the following persons: Ezekial Grale, Benjamin Wilson, Joseph Winslow, James Moor, Samuel Barnet, Lachariah Stearns (a new suspect), William Ald, James Matthews, Robert Gilson, Wm. McAdams Nathaniel Martin, James McNeil of Deeryfield, Husbandman (a new suspect), ROBERT ROGERS of Starkstown, so called Husbandman, William Walker, all of New Hampshire; and Lacheriah Witney of Groton, Massachusetts on suspicion of their being concerned in making or knowingly passing Counterfeit bills...were brought before us the Subscribers: Joseph Blanchard, John Goffe, Matthew Thornton and Joseph Blanchard, Jr., four of his Majesty's Justices of the Peace of the Province of New Hampshire to be examined concerning the...aforesaid. All of which persons we have carefully examined, and also the following persons for Evidence: Thomas Hall, Moses Barrett, Robert Murdough, John Parker, John Marshall, Ebenezer Pollard, M Barron. Joseph Blanchard, Jr., four of his Majesty's Justices of the Peace of the Province of New Hampshire to be examined concerning the....aforesaid. All of which persons we have carefully examined, and also the following persons for evidence: Thomas Hall, Moses Barrett, Robert Murdough, John Parker, John Marshall, Ebenezer Pollard, Moses

Barron, John McCurdy*, Steven Spaulding, Phinias Underwood, John Marshall, John Stearns, Rodger Chase, Ezekiel Chase, Joseph Pollard, John Stark*, Samuel Page, Benjamin Smith, Jacob Hildreth, Reuben Greele, Robert Dorrah, James Blodget, Jeremiah Blodget, Ebenezer Blodget, Arthur Graham, Reuben Spaulding, Isaac Page, Thomas Murdough, John McQuigy, Abiel Lovejoy, Josiah Dutton*, Wm. Thornton James Wallace, Wm. Caldwell, Wm. Howard, John Snow Benjamin Marshall, John Whitten, Wm. Moore*, David McNight, John Burns, Robert Fletcher, James Blood, Samuel Clark* (Parker), Nehemiah Woods of Groton,- Samuel Rankins, Elizabeth Smith, Henry Dearing, Francis Diamond, Benjamin Hopkins, Annis and John Carson, James Caldwell, Samuel Patten, Matthew Thornton, Benjamin French, Archibald McCallister, Peter Russell, Jonathan Powers, Joseph Winslow, Lachiniah Stearns, Jr., and Robert Gilsen. And upon the Examination of the aforenamed respondents and the evidence aforesaid we adjudged that there is just grounds to suspect that the said E. Greele B. Wilson, James Moor, W. Alden, J. Matthews, Wm. McAdams, N. Martin, J. McNeil, ROBERT ROGERS, Z. Witney are concerned in making and knowingly passing the bills aforesaid, and accordingly have given (orders) for Benjamin Wilson, Wm. McAdams, James McNeill and Zacheriah Witney to be sent to his Majesty's Gaol in Portsmouth, there to be Received and Safely kept until they or others of them shall be from thence delivered by due course of law.

-And the said Ezekial Greele, William Ald, James Moor, James Matthews, Nathaniel Martin and ROBERT ROGERS to be admitted to Bail who recognised with sufficient suretys each for their appearance before his Majesty's Superior Court now held at Portsmouth on Wednesday next, the twelth of February, at ten of the Clock forenoon in the Sum of five hundred pounds lawful money each.

Wm. Walker, Samuel Barnard, Zachariah Stearns, Jr., Joseph Winslow and Robert Gilson on their Examination and the Examination of the evidences it did not appear that they had been concerned in the (Counterfeiting) therefor (they) were dismissed.

And upon the Examination of the evidences (witnesses) aforesaid, have thought it a necessety that Thomas Hall, John McCurdey, Wm. Moor, John Stark, Samuel Page, Ebenezer Blodget, Eben Pollard Ezekial Chase, Joseph Pollard, Jr., Robert Donah, Isaac Page, Benjamin Marshall, John Parker, Thomas

Murdough, John Marshall, Robert Murdough, Arthur
Graham and Phinias Underwood make their appearance
at his Majestys Superior Court now held at Portsmouth at the aforesaid (time)..and there to give
evidence of what they know concerning any persons
Counterfeiting or passing any Bills in imitation
of the bills of this Province or anything further
on his Majesty's behalf that shall then be required of them and not to depart without the leave of
the said Court and that they enter into Recognizance each in the Sum of one Hundred pounds lawful money, for performance (as witnesses). Thereof
which they did accordingly.
 The remainder of the Evidences on their Examination, appearing to us that they could say nothing
material in the business, were dismissed. The several examinations of the respondants as also that
of the (Witnesses) are hereunto annexed. '(Provin —
cial Court Files, Case No. 27267- 5 folios.)

3-ROBERT ROGERS' TRIAL AT PORTSMOUTH BEFORE THE SUPERIOR COURT ON FEBRUARY 12TH 1755:

Unfortunately there are no records preserved of
the minutes of his Superior Court trial. However
his extended liberty is revealed in a letter from
Major Frye to Wentworth in which he states that
Rogers had gone to Portsmouth to take the steps to
clear himself. (Frye to Wentworth, N.H. Province
Papers, VI, 364).

4-PROOF THAT ROGERS WAS PASSING COUNTERFEIT NOTES:

'The Examination of Carte Gilman* of Exeter..New
Hampshire taken before Samuel Gilman..Justice of
the Peace of said Province, taken this 24th Day of
April 1755: The Examenant Saith that he passed the
two 6 shiling bills in imitation of the six shilling bills of the Province aforesaid of Capt. Robert Rogers belonging to a place called Merimac in
said Province. And also he passed the Eight Pound
Bill..delivered to Phillip Celley his ken of the
same man (Rogers). And further the Examenant saith
that he has several more, the number he cant tell,
of six..pence and one shilling bills of said province of the said Robert Rogers, he declared it to
be stump money but as good as ever was. And that
the Examenant says he received part of said bill
of Robt. Rogers in pay for a wagon..which the Exammenant sold to said Rogers. Said Examenant confessed he had put off several of said bills and lately returned the rest to the said Robert Rogers.

The above taken on the day above mentioned before me Samuel Gilman Justice of Peace. (Provincial Ct. Files, Case No. 26954-1 folio)

5-SUSPECTS AND WITNESSES WHO SERVED IN ROGERS RANGERS:
   It has been generally set forth by historians in the past that Rogers and the other suspects who escaped punishment joined up with Rogers immediately and constituted the nucleous of Rogers Rangers. This did not happen for the only other two Rangers who were cleared were Dick Rogers and James Moor Richard was cleared in the preliminary trial at Rumford and Moor did not enter the Corps until 57' and then it was to serve in John Stark's Company. Probably the mistake was made due to the fact that Rogers turned over his 24 'Massachusetts' recruits to Wentworth at this time.
   It is interesting to note here that of the 19 suspects tried with Rogers only 3 of them entered his Corps; while 5 of the 62 witnesses also became Rogers Rangers. This does not include Garty Gilman who gave the most incriminating testimony against Rogers, and whom Rogers gladly signed up when Gilman came to Lake George; no doubt to keep him away from future examinations by curious New Hampshire Justices. When picked up as a suspect in April, Gilman was searched and two counterfeit notes and a letter from Rogers were found. The letter he had stuffed in his mouth partially eating it before: it could be recovered. The portion remaining served as exhibit B during his examination (see text p20 for Rogers' imploring letter to Gilman).

6-BIBLIOGRAPHICAL NOTE ON SOURCES FOR THE PROLOGUE AND APPENDICE ON ROGERS' COUNTERFEITING TRIAL:
   -Provincial Court Files (as cited) preserved in the Secretary of States Office, Concord, N.H.
   -Allan Nevins' 'Ponteach', pp 39-42.
   -Boston News-Letter, April 1, 1756.
   -N.H. Province Papers, Vol. VI., p. 364.
   -John Winslow's Journal, Mass.Hist.Soc.,I, p. 9.

APPENDICE B

ROGERS RANGERS UNIFORMS & EQUIPMENT 1755-83

There has been so much conjecture on the uniform that Rogers Rangers wore with no definite source being established that this writer made it his aim to turn up enough contemporary evidence to be able to set down an exact description before bringing this Volume to a close. This study will start with the first to the permanent uniform in 1758.

On January 25, 1756 Lord Loudoun in London summarizes a description of Robert Rogers' Winter Company that was given to him by Major John Rutherford who was Captain of a N.Y. Independent Company in 1755: He states that at the present they furnished their own clothing, were very ragged, and consequently caught colds easily. Rutherford, suggests that the Crown cloth them like the Canadians in blankets and Indian Stockings which came up middle thigh without britches and deerskin moccassins.-(LO 770). Evidently not all of Rogers' Company were clothed in the hunting shirt and Indian leggings at this time but rather in various garb. Some of which consisted of light weight linens suited for summer campaigning but not for winter scouts in sub-zero weather.

An effort was made to alay the dearth of heavy clothing for the winter garrisons of Forts William Henry and Edward by contributions from patriotic Provincials: General Johnson wrote Captain Blauvelt on January 12, 1756 acknowledging receipt of 55 coats from the inhabitants of Orange Town which he sent up to the two forts 'to the soldiers belonging to those garrisons, to whom they will be a very welcome and a well-timed benefaction.' Just how many of these coats Rogers Rangers received is not known.

Another 'benevolent intention' was received 'from the good Women of Suffolk County on Long Island'. 'Several large bags of Stockings and Mittens knitted by the above women were sent up the middle of January 1756.-(Boston News-Letter, Jan. 29, 1756).

Consequently Rogers' Company while on Wentworth's and Johnson's establishments in 1755 were dressed in whatever clothes they brought from home in Mar. and presents from benevolent Provincials.

However in April 1756 with the start of the Shirley establishment, Rogers' Company started to take on a more unified appearance in their clothing;

due to the 'Ten Spanish dollars allowed to each man towards providing cloathes, arms, and blankets.'-(Rogers' Journal, p. 14). Rogers maintained a certain uniformity of clothing and arms when he instructed his new recruits to purchase or bring from home the essentials described in this contemporary description of Rogers Rangers: 'These Light Troops have at present no particular uniform, only they wear their cloathes short [meaning the leather hunting shirt, or jacket coat, or both, and the Indian Leggings], and were armed with a firelock, tomahock, or small hatchet, and a scalping knife; a bullocks horn full of powder hung under their right arm, by a belt from the left shoulder; and a leathern or seal's-skin bag, buckled around their waist, which hangs down in front, this contains bullets, and a smaller shot the size of full grown peas: six or seven of which with a ball they generally load; and their officers usually carry a small compass fixed in the bottom of their powder-horns by which to direct them, when they happen to lose themselves in the woods'.-(Captain John Knox's Historical Journal, July 12/13, 1757, Vol. I, p. 34). A detailed description of each article of their clothing, arms and gear follows:-
HUNTING SHIRT: An Englishman describes a frontier 'Hunting Shirt': 'Their whole dress is very singular, and not very materially different from that of the Indians; being a hunting shirt, somewhat resembling a[n English] waggoners frock, ornamented with a great many fringes,[these leather shirts] they die in a variety of colours'.-(J.F.D.Smyth, Tour in the United States of America, London, 1784 in Mag. Amer. Hist., I, 387-88). Rogers had a definite Esprit de Corps and he must have realized the importance of having some part of the mens' clothing all the same colour. What would be more simpler and inexpensive than dyeing all the hunting shirts green, his favorite colour. This would give his two 1756 Companies a unified appearance for the summer campaigning when the men usually dispensed with their hunting jackets or coats because of the heat of the forests, and scouted in their more comfortable loose hunting shirts. There is no definite documentary evidence to this effect, but since Rogers in January 1758 clothed all his Companies in green hunting shirts and jackets there is reason to believe that he instigated this colour as early as 1756, at least in the two Rogers's Companies.

BREECHES: *Smyth describes breeches of Virginia Rangers which could also apply to Rogers Rangers:* 'Sometimes they wear leather breeches, made of Indian dressed elk, or deerskins, but more frequently thin trousers'. *These breeches wether buckskin or a coarse linen cloth made of flax and tow called Osnaburg or Duffle reached from the waist to the calf, fitting snugger at the calf similar to riding breeches. The estimated life of a pair of buckskin breeches was one year. They were much cheaper and lighter than breeches worn by the Regulars (they would outwear two pair of army breeches in a years time) and would protect the Ranger from the snow and cold in winter and the pesky fly in the summer.-(Major George Scott's* Proposal to Loudoun for Arming, Accoutring and Clothing the Rangers, LO 5573 and LO 6927).

LEGGINGS: *Indian Leggings, Boots, or Stockings are described as follows:* 'On their legs they have Indian boots or leggins, made of coarse woolen cloth that either are wrapped round loosely and tied with garters, or are laced upon the outside, and always come better than half way up the thigh; these are a great defence and preservative, not only against the bite of serpents and poisonous insects, but likewise against the scratches of thorns, briers, scrubby bushes, and underwood, with which this whole country is infested and over spread.'-(*Smyth's* Tours). *Knox adds several pertinent facts:* 'Leggers, Leggins, or Indian spatterdashes, are usually made of frieze or other coarse woolen cloth; they should be at least three quarters of a yard in length; each Leggin about 3 quarters wide (which is 3 by 3) then double it, and sew it together from end to end, within four, five, or six inches of the outside selvages, fitting this long narrow bag to the shape of the leg; the flaps to be on the outside, which serve to wrap over the skin, or fore-part of the leg, tied round under the knee, and above the ankle, with garters of the same colour; by which the legs are preserved from many fatal accidents, in marching thru /the woods/ The Indians generally ornament the flaps with beads of various colors, as they do their moggasen, for my part, I think them clumsy, and not at all military; yet I confess they are highly necessary in N. America; nevertheless, if they were made without the flap and to button the outside of the leg, in like manner as a spatterdash they would answer full as well: but this is a matter of opinion.'-

Knox, I, p. 286).

MOCCASINS: Were made of dressed deerskin. Their usefullness is described by the French Captain, Pouchot: 'Their shoes, although only a simple prepared skin, are very warm, and the snow is so dry that it does not wet. They wrap their feet with pieces of blanket (in the Winter) and the sides of the moccasins form a half boot which prevents the snow from getting in while their feet would freeze with European shoes, as many have unhappily proved.'-(Pouchot's Memoires, Vol. II., p. 215). On long scouts Rogers Rangers usually tucked an extra pair in their blanket roll or haversack.

HATS: The Privates of Rogers Rangers wore bearskin caps from 1755 to 1757. Their association with the 42nd Highlanders made them desirous of obtaining Scotch Bonnets which they admired very much. Their principal contractor notes that 'the Rangers who can get them wear nothing else when they go out' and writes his Employer to send a parcel of Scotch Bonnets as he believed they would sell well.-(John Macomb Letter Copy-Book, N.Y. State Lib., Macomb to Gregg & Cunningham, from Albany, Apr. 22, 1758.). However the Ranger officers invariably wore the cocked tri-cornered hat which gave them distinction from the men. Rogers distinguished himself by wearing a stiff jacked leather cap with a small metal plate in front (see illustration) which was intended to break the blow from a scalping ax or a musket ball. It is not known exactly when Rogers adopted this distinguishing cap but it was probably after he received his forehead wound at La Barbue Creek in Jan 1757. All Officers adopted this protective hat in 1758.

WEAPONS AND EQUIPMENT

MUSKETS: The Rangers brought their own muskets from home in 1755. However with the advent of the ten dollars bounty money in 1756 Rogers issued the following standing order: 'All Rangers to appear at roll-call every evening on their own parade, equipped, each with a fire-lock (musket) sixty rounds of powder and ball, and a hatchet, at which time an officer from each Company is to inspect the same, to see that they are in order, so as to be ready on any emergency to march at a minute's warning'.-(Rogers' Journal, p. 60). Consequently some of the Rangers who joined the Corps with unserviceable muskets had to purchase new ones. The Stockbridge and Mohegan Companies frequently entered the Corps with muskets that were virtually relics

and continually missed fire. However with this possible exception the firelocks of the Rangers were all true weapons, in spite of their varied appearance. Because the muskets were privately owned and of different manufacture, continual emphasis was stressed on their being tested for accuracy. Loudoun on January 11, 1758 when he authorized more Companies to be raised instructed Rogers that:
'Your men to find their own arms, which must be such as upon examination, shall be found fit, and be approved of.'-(Rogers' Journal, p. 77). A Ranger describing their arms for late 1757 notes that 'They were well armed'.-(Joshua Goodenough's:- Old Letter, in Harpers Monthly, Nov., 1897). The principal method of testing the firelocks was to shoot at marks, a custom much practiced in the Corps. This exercise of arms had the two-fold purpose of testing the weapon and increasing the Rangers accuracy. Goodenough notes that he tested his firelock by shooting 'it ten times on trial and it had not failed to discharge at each pull'. Rogers established the order for true firelocks but it was up to his Captains to see that they were kept that way or have the Rangers purchase new ones. Rogers in April 1758 began pricing short firelocks with bayonets that were being sold by Greg & Cunningham in New York through their agent John Macomb at Albany. Rogers' own Company was equipped with these in 1758 and the other Companies by February 1759. Rogers wrote Amherst's Adjutant on January 28, 17-59: 'The arms of the Rangers are in the hands of Mr. Cunningham at New York, which will be soon wanted at Fort Edward; I should therefore be glad they might be forwarded as soon as may be. I have wrote to Mr. Cunningham, to make application to you for convenient carriages for the same which I should be glad you would furnish him with.'-(Rogers' Journals, pp 122-123; Macomb Copy Letter Book, Macomb to Greg & Cunningham, Apr. 20, 1758).
Private Goodenough who reenlisted at this time bought one of these from Macomb in Albany. He says
'I bought me a new fire-lock at Albany which was provided with a bayonet. It was short, as is best fitted for the bush, and (shot) about 45 balls to the pound.' The scrupulous Amherst saw to the condition of Cunningham's firelocks by having them tested by the Artillery before sending them to Albany. His Adjutant writes Rogers 2/26/59: 'Your arms have been tried and proved by the artillery; they answer very well, and are ordered to be sent

to you as fast as possible'.-*(Rogers' Journals, p. 135)*. The barrel of these muskets were shorter than those of the Regulars and could be sighted quicker in the brush. The barrels were browned to conceal the metallic glitter which not only aided in camouglage but eliminated the glare of sunlight on the barrel when sighting it. The bayonets were also light and short, and in the form of a knife. and were used as such upon occasion. These effective bayonets were used in at least one Major engagement of Rogers Rangers for Amherst ordered Rogers to have his men carry fixed bayonets when they made their St. Johns expedition in 1760.-*(Rogers' Journals, p 174)*.

THE POWDER HORN: or Priming Horn was usually made of a bullocks horn. It was filled with a finer grain powder than that of the regulation cartridge, consequently the Ranger was not so likely to 'burn priming' or 'miss-firing' as he would by priming the touch-hole from a cartridge with coarser grain powder which did not get into the touch-hole and catch fire as quickly. Pouring from the horn also eliminated the spilling of more than half the powder which was common when using cartridges which had to be broken open and poured into the touchhole.-*(Scott's Proposal for Arming the Rangers, LO 6927)*. The Rangers usually carved their names and inscribed whimsical characters on their powder horns, and tallys of the enemy they killed.

THE TOMAHAWK: was a potent weapon. It was stated that one blow from a tomahawk or 'Scalping Axe' was equivalent to three from a broad sword. Rogers men captured a French ship in the Richelieu R in 1760 by swimming to it armed with tomahawks alone. It was also useful for chopping small wood for campfires and lean-toos. It was generally made of a steel head bound to a hardwood handle.-See A. Woodward's study of *Tomahawks* in Ft.Tic.Bull,VII,no3.

THE SCALPING KNIFE: was actually a long thin bladed hunting knife which removed the scalp of the vanquished foe by a circular incision. It was also used in close hand to hand fighting. Rogers in his printed Journals endeavoured to give the Scalping Knife the more delicate title of 'Cutlass'.

THE BULLET POUCH: was made of leather or sealskin containing 60 rounds of ammunition. Sixty rounds comprised 360 balls of buckshot the size of full grown peas and 60 bullets, for the Rangers loaded with six or seven balls and one bullet per round.-*(Knox, Vol. I, p 34; Rogers' Journals, p 60)*.

THE CANTEEN: was made of wood and held aproximately a quart of Rum. When entering on a scout the Rangers Sutler was authorized to advance the Ranger four days ration of Rum (4 gills) to fill his canteen which hung at his left side by a strap over his shoulder.

THE PACK OR HAVERSACK: of leather, carried on the Rangers back on the left side with a shoulder strap connected to the waist belt. It contained a staple supply of cornmeal and dried beef chips which were constantly in the pack whether the Ranger was at Rogers' Island or on party. This was to insure the Ranger at least an emergency ration if he was called out on an alarm before he had time to draw the customary field ration from the Sutler.

Other articles in the pack were a tin plate, a spoon and sometimes a horn mug. Occasionally a Ranger carried a small flask of poisoned rum tucked in his pack for the benefit of enemy Indians who might come in possession of it if he was captured or slain, or forced to leave his pack on the field of battle.

THE BLANKET: In 1755 and 1756 the two Rogers's Companies brought their own blankets from home or purchased them out of the ten dollars bounty money consequently they were varied in color. However in November 1756 Rogers prevailed on Abercrombie to obtain a quantity of Stroudes, a coarse blanket material, out of the King's stores at Albany.-(Thomas Saul to Loudoun, 'An Account of the Osnabrigs and Stroudes at Albany', Jan. 22, 1758, LO 5441). The color of these Stroudes is not stated, but it is a certainty that if there were any bolts of a green colour Rogers would have got them. At least the colour was uniform and the Rangers presented a more military appearance with blanket rolls of the same colour.-(LO 2196; LO 2225).

WINTER DRESS: The blanket became a hood and cape on Winter marches: 'The (Rangers) like the Indians fasten their blankets below with their belt and make them pass over the head like a monk's hood, arranging them so well that they only expose their nose and hands. They make mittens of skins or flannel, hung to their neck by a string (when not in use), which serves them better than gloves, because the separated fingers would be more liable to freeze.'-(Pouchot, Memoires, II, p 215). Rogers says 'we stripped off our blankets' before charging into a Winter battle.-(Rogers' Journals, p 131). Some of the Rangers added 'ruffs of black bearskin round their necks' for additional protection to the ears and face; and occasionally a bearskin was substituted in lieu of the blanket-coat, although Rogers favoured the latter.-(Entick, The General History of the Late War, III, p 227; F.P.Lawson's A History of The Uniforms of the British Army, II, p 47; Rogers' Journals, p 131; Goodenough's Old Letter). The blanket-coat offered the maximum in warmth and lightness of weight. Even Loudoun was aware of the indispensability of the blanket-coat, having received information on them before he left England and he was receptive to Rogers' request for blanket material in November 1756, and on January 11, 1758 he instructed Rogers to have new recruits 'provide themselves with good warm blankets'.-(Loudoun's Memorandum of a conversation with Major Rutherford relative to Rogers' Company, Jan. 25, 1756, LO 770; Loudoun's Instructions to Rogers for raising four New England and one Indian Company of Rangers, Jan. 11, 1758, in Rogers Journals).

Other winter dress consisted of beards grown by some of the Rangers. An observer says 'the beards of their upper lips some grown into whiskers, others not so, but all well smutted on that part'. -(Entick, III, p 227).

UNIFORMS OF HOBBS' (BULKELEY'S) AND SPEAKMAN'S (STARK'S) COMPANIES: Hobbs' and Speakman's Companies entered Rogers Rangers in January 1757 with the following Uniform and gear which was different from that of the two Rogers's Companies: The terms of their enlistments gave them a good Hunting Coat Vest and Breeches, a pair of Indian Leggings, Shoes; a Hatchet and a Firelock. All but the Firelock were to be delivered at Albany. However, 97½ yards of Osnaburg, a coarse linen cloth made of flax and tow, similar to duffle, was supplied to each Company by the contractor, John Erving, Jr., at Boston, by a verbal order from Shirley. The Captains had short hunting coats or jackets, vests and short breeches made up out of this cloth before they marched from Boston. The color of the cloth was grey for a private in Speakman's later Stark's speaks of being 'clad in skin and gray duffle hunting frocks'. The skins were adopted in 1757 when the duffle breeches were worn out. Erving also outfitted the Companies with a 32½ lb kegg of powder, 130 French Flints, 65 lbs of lead musket balls, 21 lbs of line and 12 lbs of twine per Company. One hundred muskets of the King's stores at Boston were cleaned by the Armourers and issued to

the two Companies; also 100 slings for the muskets and 100 cartridge boxes with straps and frogs. The muskets were standard army firelocks with steel rammer. They had a barrel of 3 feet 10 inches long a bore of .76 inches, and weighed complete, 12 lbs 4 ozs, and shot lead balls numbering 14½ to the pound. At Albany on September 17, 1756, the two Captains took an order from Abercrombie to Oliver Delancey an Agent of Baker & Kilby to supply them with 11 camp kettles and 62 canteens with ropes. The same day Delancey delivered Speakman 36 pair of shoes, and Hobbs 30 pair. These shoes were the regulation army shoes. Loudoun had superceded Shirley and he fulfilled his terms with the two new Companies except for the shoes. The men had to buy the shoes at a cost of 4 shillings 4½ pence sterling per pair. However they gained in the end for Loudoun supplied them with blankets purchased from Delancey. On the 17th Speakman received 38 striped blankets and Hobbs, 32. The colour was not specified. The new Companies were now completely equiped except for the hatchets, these were delivered by Delancey the next day: 35 hand hatchets with helves for Speakman's and 29 for Hobbs. According to the original terms the men were to furnish their own blankets out of their six dollars bounty money.-(Shirley to Winslow from N.Y., Apr. 30, 1756, LO 1090; Same to Same, same date, LO 1091; Shirley to Loudoun, from Boston, Sept. 22, 1756, Account of Sundrys supplied by John Erving Jr., for Captain Hobbs and Captain Speakman's Ranging Cos, Aug 24, 1756, LO 1566; Private Goodenough's Old Letter; James Furnis to Loudoun, Dec. 9, 1756, LO 23- 14; LO 6683; Abercrombie to Oliver Delancey, Albany, Sept. 17, 1756, LO 1832; Same to Same, Sept. 18, 1756, LO 1845; LO 3019; LO 2623; Thomas Saul to Loudoun, Jan. 22, 1758, Account of Christopher Kilby's order for shoes, LO 2623; Oliver Delancey to Loudoun, N.Y., Apr. 9, 1757, Account of Blankets received by Wm. Alexander and delivered by the order of the Earl of Loudoun, LO 5934; Loudoun's Warrant on A. Mortier to pay Delancey 15 pounds 8 shillings for Canteens, Camp Kettles and Hatchets, Apr. 20, 1757, LO 4565.).
THE COST OF CLOTHING AND EQUIPPING EACH MAN:
CLOTHING: 3¼ yards of Osnaburg - 4 s 9 d.
MUSKET: Valued at 1 pd. Turned in end of service.
   SLING: - 5 d.
CARTRIDGE (CARTOUCH) BOX: - 1 s 9 d.
   STRAPS: - 4 d.   FROGS: - 2 d.

FRENCH FLINTS: *four - 3 d.*
MUSKET BALLS: *two pounds - 1 s.*
LINE: *one half-pound - 9 d.*
TWINE: *one half-pound - 1 s 6 d.*
POWDER: *one pound - 2 s.*
CANTEEN WITH ROPE: *1 s 6 d.*
HAND HATCHET (WITH HANDLE): *2 s 6 d.*
BLANKET: *one - 15 s.*
SHOES: *one pair - 4 s 4½ d (Bought by Ranger).*
(The 11 Camp Kettles at 5 s each are not included; Scalping Knives, and skin caps provided by men) TOTAL: 2 pounds 16 shillings 3½ pence Sterling. (Based on the N.Y. Value of Exchange, Aug. 10, 1756, after the Declaration of War. LO 1463).

THE UNIFORM OF ROGERS RANGERS 1758: On Jan 11, 1758 Loudoun ordered Rogers to raise four more New England and one Indian Company of Rangers: 'Your men to find their own arms, which must be such as upon examination, shall be found fit, and be approved of. They are likewise to provide themselves with good warm cloathing, which *must be uniform in every company*, and likewise with good warm blankets. And the company of Indians to be dressed in all respects in the true Indian fashion'. Since it took better than a months pay of a Private to completely clothe, arm and equip himself, Loudoun insured the fulfillment of his orders by advancing Rogers a months pay for each of the new Companies which was to be deducted from their subsequent pay.-(*Rogers'* Journals, p 77). Now, Rogers could finally see all of his Companies in the same uniform. Heretofore the exact colour of the cloth has not been known (outside of the grey duffle for Hobbs' and Speakman's, now Bulkeley's and Stark's) but now for the first time in history an exact description can be given. The uniform that Rogers had made up for his new Companies as well as his old ones consisted of a short tailed jacket, and vest made of a low priced green frieze,- a rough heavy woolen fabric with a shaggy nap frequently referred to at that time as 'Bath Rug' cloth. The jackets were all lined with green serge which made the collar and cuffs the same color and material. The short green serge collar and cuffs offered enough contrast from the nappy frieze jacket or coatee to give it a distinct facing without detracting from the benefit of the overall green color so necessary for forest concealment. The officers and Sergeants were distinguished by white silver lace cord looping on the long button holes of the sleeves (See Plate I-pii) Both officers and men wore a double row of eight white metal buttons on the front of their jacket and four on each sleeve. Rogers and his officers were distinguished from the Sergeants and men by wearing black (Light-Infantrymen) hats with white silver lace bindings. They also were distinguished by wearing a broad Indian beaded shoulder strap in lieu of an officers customary waist-sash. There is no evidence of the officers wearing gorgets. The Sergeants and Privates wore green scotch bonnets of the same shape as those of the 42nd Highlanders. The Leggins were made of low priced brown or green ratten, a nubby woolen fabric similar to frieze. The buckskin breeches were still maintained.

The clothiers: Thomas and Benjamin Forseys at Albany, made up the greatest quantity of the new uniforms. They also re-uniformed the two former grey Companies of Stark and Bulkeley for the Account Books of these two Captains show accounts with this firm. The Captains of the old Companies, namely, Rogers, Stark, Bulkeley and Shepherd had to order the uniforms for their Companies on credit, for they were not advanced a months pay like the new Captains. John Stark alone, owed Forsey 100 pounds. The other clothiers who made up the uniforms were Kennedy and Lyle and Peble and Wiles of Albany. John Macomb, Greg and Cunninghams agent at Albany, wanted Rogers to place an order for a quantity of the uniforms with him although he 'apprehend(ed) it would be running a very great risque, the ordering a quantity of cloth without a certainty of gitting them disposed of' for all the Companies were equipped except the 125 replacements for the Rogers' Rock casualties. Rogers might have had trouble with some of his men when it came time to make the uniform cost deduction from their pay, for he informed Macomb on June 14, 1758 that he would 'not engage for any the clothing for his men (even though) he (was) satisfyd he would have them on better terms they coming from (Greg and Cunningham), than he had heretofore.' Rogers made an interesting excuse by telling Macomb that he expected to be removed into the Regulars soon. Macomb had been anxious to get Rogers order for uniforms to replace those that would be worn out at the end of the campaign, he wrote Greg and Cunningham on May 22, 1758 to this effect and added that there would be a great demand for clothing by the time the army returned to Winter quarters.

Brigadier Lawrence at Boston had been entrusted with the dispatching of four of the new Companies to Amherst's rendezvous at Halifax, and since he could not review them at Boston he was dubious as to the integrity of the Ranger officers in supplying their men with 'materials for clothing, with Arms, Blankets, etc., in according to their contract with Major Rogers'; and he wrote General Hopson at Halifax to have the Companies reviewed when they arrived and if any of their gear was lacking to have the Ranger officers provide it before any back wages were paid. However Entick, an observer at Halifax, states that Rogers' Companies were equipped with 'green jackets, with little round hats like several of our seamen (these were the scotch bonnets worn by the privates). Their arms were a fusil cartouche, box of balls and flints, and a powder horn flung over the shoulders'; so it was apparent that Rogers Rangers at Halifax were clothed and armed according to Rogers orders. Entick remarks that: 'The rangers are a body of irregulars, who have a more cut-throat savage appearance, which carries in it something of natural savages'. Even though Rogers Rangers were now in a definite uniform, it was still essentially the practical woodland uniform a little more dressed up. Their Indian Leggings and scalping knife and tomahawk in belt, not to mention their rakish-scotch-bonnets, gave them a hardy, if not somewhat sinister appearance.

There is evidence that Rogers Rangers in all theaters of action wore this same uniform during the remaining three years of the war. The continual use of the Indian Leggings, leather moccassins and breeches is established by the following notes Boston News-Letter for October 4, 1759: 'Last week the body of a Man was found in the River near Dunstable; it is thot it had been drowned sometime; the Body was naked, excepting a Pair of Indian Stockings on his Legs, and Moggasens on his feet: by which it is probable he was one of the men lately deserted from (Rogers) Rangers.' Lieutenant Montressor, who had an escort of Hazen's (formerly McCurdy) Company of Rogers Rangers at Quebec, notes on February 15, 1760, while crossing Maine, they were 'reduced to eat their leather Breeches'. In regard to the green jacket or coatee, Rogers was still wearing it in 1776 in London when he had his famous painting made. If his Rangers had a new uniform he would surely have worn it when he posed for his painting. There is a strong probability that the painting of Lord Howe in Benjamin West's 'Death of Wolfe' was posed by a model in the uniform of Rogers Rangers, for it is an exact replica of a back and side view of their uniform. It could not have been a portrayal of Howe's Light Infantry Regiment at Quebec for Knox describes their uniform and the coat does not conform with that in West's painting. Neither is it the uniform of the other provisional Light Inf. Battalion (Dalling's), for Knox describes their uniform as well as that of Goreham's and Dank's Companies of Rangers and none of his contemporary and accurate descriptions fit the painting. Wolfe's Light Infantry and Rangers at Quebec wore the Leggings but the cut and color of their coats were different from the painting of Howe. Gage's 80th Light Infantry Regiment with Amherst at Lake George wore the same sleeveless coat that Howe's and Dalling's Regiments. The only possible Corps left were Rogers Rangers in their green jacket or coatee which matched the one in West's painting perfectly. Rogers was in London when West did the painting and he could have borrowed a uniform from him for his model of Lord Howe. This is an important conclusion for it can now be said that there is a contemporary painting of the uniform of the famed Rogers Rangers in full color, and by the famous Benjamin West no less.

When Major Rogers revived his Rangers in the American Revolution as the Queen's Rangers he maintained the green coat with white metal buttons. However blue facings were added. The white bindings were continued on the hats, also the green waistcoats. When Simcoe took over the Corps in 1777 he stated that 'they were already clothed in green, and accoutred for concealment'. He also voiced Rogers' sentiments when he stated 'that green is without comparison the best color for light troops with dark accoutrements, and if put on in the spring, by autumn it nearly fades with the leaves, preserving its characteristics of being scarcely discernible at a distance'. A Ranger private in 1760 adds that: 'The forest always concealed a Ranger line, so that there might not have been a man within a hundred miles for all that could be seen.' Simcoe's statement that the green cloth faded to a brownish green by fall is interesting. This would suggest a variety of green

colors in the uniforms especially in the French
and Indian War when new recruits entered in the
Spring and Fall. Rogers might have overcome this
by having the veteran Rangers dye their uniforms
anew each Spring. It would be advantageous to wait
until Spring before re-dying them for a participant at Rogers' Rock on March 13, 1758, notes that
his comrade, a British Volunteer officer who was
wearing one of the new green jackets, 'laid aside
his green jacket in the field, which became a mark
to the enemy' against the white snow.

When Rogers revived his Rangers for the second
time in the American Revolution as a Loyalist body
called Rogers' King's Rangers they still maintained their green uniforms and moccasins, however
the coats were now faced with red. They wore black
tri-cornered hats. The history of Rogers' Queen's
and King's Rangers and more details of their uniforms will be portrayed in a subsequent volume.

SOURCES: for 'The Uniform of Rogers Rangers 1758'
-John Macomb to Greg & Cunningham, Albany, Apr 22,
1758, in Macomb Copy-Letter Book, unpublished MS in
N.Y. State Lib.: '..The close that Rogers had made
for his people are chiefly of Green Bath Rug & low
priced green cloths with white mettle buttons &
white silver lace Hats, some of them silver lace
cord or looping on their jackets, all lined with
green serge..'-*Courtesy of the N.Y. State Library.*
-Edna L. Jacobsen, Head, MSS and History Section,
N.Y. State Library, for her valuable research thru
the Macomb Copy Letter-Book, and Account Books of
similar date, for mention of clothing and costs.
-The Mezzotint of Rogers, first printed by T. Hart
October 1, 1776 in London. It is described in
Smith's British Mezzotint Portraits. Two other
Mezzotint's copied from the original except for
altered facial study were printed in France, and
in Germany entitled: Robert Rogers, Commandeur der
Americaner, *from Geschecte der Kriege in und aus-
ser Europa, Elfter Theil, Nurnberg, 1777.* The English and French prints are by far the best, with
the English print showing more of the uniform. A
re-print of it may be seen in Parkman's Conspiracy
of Pontiac. The French print is described in H.
MacFall's French Pastellists of the 18th Century,
and an excellent reprint may be seen in Kenneth
Roberts' Special Edition of Northwest Passage. A
re-print of the German edition may be seen in The
Bulletin of The Fort Ticonderoga Museum, Vol. VI,
January, 1941. All three of these with the back

and side view of Lord Howe in West's Death of
Wolfe served as the model for Helene S. Loescher's
excellent water color portrait of Major Robert
Rogers in the correct uniform color described for
the first time in the above study.
-J. Fortescue's The Empire and the Army. On pages
136-137 he gives a description of the distinguish-
ing marks of officers and sergts in the British army.
-Captain John Stark's Account Book. Extracts rela-
tive to his account with Forsey the Clothier at
Albany; kindly furnished by W.S.B.Hopkins, owner
of the unpublished Manuscript.
-Captain Charles Bulkeley's Account Book. Extracts
relative to his account with Thomas and Benjamin
Forsey the Clothiers, from the unprinted MS.
-John Macomb to Greg & Cunningham, June 14, 1758;
Ibid, May 22, 1758, relative to getting Rogers or-
der for more green uniforms, etc.
-Charles Lawrence to Abercrombie, from Boston, Apr
2, 1758, AB 99, relative to the Ranger officers
contract with Rogers to cloth and arm their men.
-Same to Same, April 5, 1758, AB 118.
-Entick's General History of the Late War, Vol III
p 227, confirming the new uniform.
-Boston News-Letter, October 4, 1759.
-John Montressor's 'Message to Amherst' Journal,
in N. Eng. Hist.Gen.Register, Jan 1882, pp 29-36.
-Marquess of Sligo's Key to the Figures depicted
in West's Death of Wolfe in Can.Hist.Rev.Sept, 1922
-See article by J.C.Webster in Trans.Royal Soc.Can,25
-Captain John Knox's Historical Journal, Vol. I,
pp 352-353, uniform descriptions of all provision-
al and established Battalions of Light Infantry in
Wolfe's and Amherst's armies; p 307, description
of Goreham's and Danks' Companies of Rangers.
-C.M.Lefferts' Uniforms of the American, British,
French and German in the War of the American Revo-
lution, N.Y. Hist. Soc., 1926,-note similarity of:
Queen's Rangers Light Inf. uniform with that of 1758.
-Colonel John Simcoe's Journal, p 20, etc.
-Ranger Joshua Goodenough's Old Letter, in Harpers
Monthly, November 1897.
-Captain-Lieutenant Henry Pringle to Haviland from
Carillon, March 28, 1758, in Rogers' Journal, p 94.
-Return of Cloathing issued out of the Quarter-
Master General's store to (Rogers' King's Rangers)
Sorel, 21st Feb, 1782-in Can. Arch, BM,21,849,p141.
-Francis Parkman's Transcripts, in the Mass. Hist.
Society, revealed nothing, but Parkman's Montcalm
and Wolfe, Vol. I, p 446, states that Rogers 'Ran-

gers wore a sort of woodland uniform, which varied in the different companies, and were armed with smooth-bore guns, loaded with buckshot, bullets or sometimes both.'
-*Allan Nevins, in his biography of Rogers in 'Ponteach', Caxton Club, Chicago, 1914, p 51, states:* 'They wore a uniform which varied slightly in the different companies, but which in all was only a: military variation of the ordinary garb of hunter and trapper.'
-*Queries to the following Historians brought some clues which proved most helpful:*
Cecil C. P. Lawson, London, England.
Kenneth Roberts, Kennebunkport, Maine.
S. H. P. Pell, Director, Fort Ticonderoga Museum.
Stanley M. Pargellis, Librarian, Newberry Library
Victor Hugo Paltsits, former Chief, American History Division, N.Y.Pub.Lib.
Frederick P. Todd, Secretary, American Military Institute, Washington, D. C.
H. Charles McBarron, Jr., Chicago, Illinois.
Robert W. Hill, Keeper of MSS, N.Y.Public Library
J.E.Jones, Editor, The Prospector, Chicago, Ill.
Detmar H. Finke, Washington, D. C.

UNIFORM OF ROGERS' INDIAN COMPANIES: See p435,n250
UNIFORM OF ROGERS' CADET COMPANY:
There is evidence that Rogers' Cadets may have worn the 'Green Uniform' during their short existance in the Fall of 1757. When the Cadet Company was disbanded, five of the Volunteers petitioned Loudoun in December 'for pay for their Cloaths', as Captain Rogers had directed them to purchase a Ranger uniform and the other necessities for that service, and had promised them that they would be reimbursed by Loudoun.-(*Eric Reinholdt, Charles Perry, George Wordemar* (name erased), *F. Bernard, Andreas Wacerberg and Engelbertus Horst:* Memorial to Loudoun, Dec 1757, LO 5172). This interesting Memorial establishes the possibility of Rogers' own Company being in 'uniform' in September 1757, for he would have ordered the Cadets to cloth themselves similar to his own Company and not the grey duffle of Stark's and Bulkeley's Companies. Since the 'Green Uniform' was the first definite uniform of Rogers' Own Company, it only seems natural that Rogers would order his Cadets to wear them.

Then again, Rogers may have just been contemplating clothing his Rangers in green at this time and decided to try it out on his Cadets who would have to have a bush-ranging uniform anyway.

APPENDICE C

ROBERT ROGERS' ORIGINAL AND "OWN" COMPANY AND THE SIX ESTABLISHMENTS OF THE RANGERS

Robert Rogers own Company formed the nucleous and hub of the Corps of His Majesty's Independent Companies of American Rangers. This Companies History began as early as January, 1755, when Rogers signed up 24 New Hampshire men for Major Frye's battalion of Shirley's Massachusetts Regiment.

These 24 original Rogers Rangers were:

Noah Johnson	Elisha Bennet	John Hartman
John McCurdey	Rowling Foster	James Morgan
Wm. Cunningham	James Grise	Isaac Colson
Wm. Wheeler	John Frost	Tim. Wodscan
James Mars	James Welch	Simon Tobey
James Henry	Matt Christopher	Ben Squanton
James Clark	James Simonds	Piller Simpion
Wm. McKeen	Charles Oudley	Piller Mahanter

These men formed the nucleous of Rogers' Ranging Company or the First Company of Blanchard's New Hampshire Regiment. They volunteered to remain on at Lake George with Rogers on October 6, 1755. On November 25, they, with the following adherents formed the first distinct Ranging Company of Rogers Rangers:(Listed in order of their enlistment date)

John (James) Michel Aug 15.	John Wadleigh Nov 26.
David Nutt Aug 15.	Stephen Young Nov 26.
Richard Rogers Oct 4.	Joshua Atwood Nov 26.
Jonathan Sillaway Oct 4.	Samuel Leech Nov 26.
John Kizer Oct 23.	John Brown Nov 28.
Nathaniel Smith Oct 23.	James Archibald Dec 13.
James McNeal Nov 5.	James Aldison Dec 13.
Nathaniel Johnson Nov 5.	William Akin Dec 13.
Philip Wells Nov 26.	John Leighton Dec 14.

All of these forty-two Rangers might be considered original Rogers Rangers for they all constituted the first distinct Company of the Corps from Nov. 25, 1755 to June 6, 1756.

As more Companies were added to Rogers' Corps the first Company was designated as Rogers' Own and took the place of honour in the Rangers' line when circumstances permitted. They also drew their rations and pay before the other Companies.

Rogers own Company was the only one of his Corps to remain in continual service throughout the French and Indian War, viz.: from January 1755 to January 1761. During this time they went thru the following six establishments, (other Companies of the Corps coming under these establishments are so mentioned):

FIRST (SHIRLEY'S) ESTABLISHMENT-Jan-Feb 11, 1755
The terms were the same as those of other members of Shirley's Massachusetts Provincial Regiment destined for the Beausjour Campaign in Nova Scotia.

SECOND (WENTWORTH'S) ESTABLISHMENT-Feb 11-Oct 6, 1755. The terms were the same as those for the other Companies of Blanchard's New Hampshire Provincial Regiment, namely: After receiving 5 pounds allowance for a blanket; 8, 10, or 12 pounds for a musket; and 13 pounds advanced wages (all money was New Hampshire Currency, old tenor); the Private or Sentinel (the designation for Privates in the Regiment) read, or had read to him, the following Enlistment Document, after which he signed his name: 'Province of N.H. We the under written Subscribers do hereby Severally Acknowledge to have Enlisted our Selves as Private Soldiers to serve his Majesty King George the Second in a Company of foot in a Regiment raised, or raising for an Expidition now Preparing for building a Fortress in his Majesties Dominions at the southerly End of Lake Irequois or Champlain near the Place called Crown Point or any other Places or Place within this Province - Cutting and Clearing roads, etc. to and from Such Places as Shall be ordered the Said regt to be under the Command of the Hon. Jos. Blanchard Esq.'-(Vol. I, folio 24, MSS Vols in the Adjutant General's Office, N.H.; printed in Hammond's State Papers, N.H., Vol XIV, I, p 19).

THIRD (JOHNSON'S) ESTABLISHMENT-Oct 6-Nov 25, 1755
At General Johnsons request, Rogers remained on at Lake George with 30 Volunteers from his & Symes disbanded Companys of Blanchard's Regiment. Evidently no provision was made for paying them.- (Johnson Papers, II, p 170; IX, p 247; Potter's Military History of N. H., pp 156-7; 142-3).

FOURTH (PROVINCIAL COMMISSIONERS) ESTABLISHMENT-Nov 25, 1755-June 6, 1756. On Nov 24, 1755 a Council of War was held at Albany by Johnson and Commissioners representing the New England Colonies. Although New Hampshire was not represented, it was 'adjudged, both by General Johnson and the Commissioners, that it would be of great use to have one Company of woodsmen or rangers under' Rogers 'command, to make excursions towards the enemy's forts during the winter.'-(Rogers' Journals, pp 9-10).

The Company was to consist of 91, but only 43 could be signed up. Both officers and men were promised that their pay should be continued until they were relieved in the summer of 1756. The pay consisted of 15 pounds (old tenor) Provincial Currency per month, and 15 pounds Bounty Money. Due to the tightness of the New Hampshire Council, not to mention the reluctance of the other Provincial Councils to pay since they had feed the New Hampshire troops during the 1755 campaign. Massachusetts no doubt added the fact that Rogers still owed them the enlistment money for the 24 men in his Company who he had originally signed up for the Massachusetts Regiment for Nova Scotia. Due to these difficulties Rogers had to pay the men out of his own pocket and spend the next seven years petitioning the various Provincial Governments and Commander-in-Chiefs for their pay. Evidently all the New England Provinces refused to pay and it remained for New Hampshire, who should have paid them anyways, to settle with Rogers on Feb 1, 1763 by paying him the 235 pounds, 11 shillings, 9½ pence Sterling due him.-(N.H.Province Papers, *VI*, pp 861, 865-866; Potter, Mil.Hist.N.H., pp 156-7).

FIFTH (SHIRLEY'S 'HIS MAJESTY'S INDEPENDENT COMPANY') ESTABLISHMENT-Mar 24, 1756-Feb 24, 1757.

Robert Rogers Company of Rangers was to consist of 50 Privates, at 3 shillings N.Y. Currency per day, 3 Sergeants at 4 shillings; an Ensign at 5 shillings, a Lieutenant at 7 shillings, and Rogers as Captain at 10 shillings per day. Ten Spanish dollars (each dollar worth 4 shillings 8 pence Sterling-LO 1224) were allowed to each man towards providing clothes, arms, and blankets. Rogers was 'to enlist none but such as were used to travelling and hunting, and in whose courage and fidelity he could confide, they were, moreover, to be subject to military discipline and the articles of war'. Shirley instructed Rogers that the principal aim of the Company was 'to distress the French and their allies, by sacking, burning, and destroying their houses, barns, barracks, canoes, battoes, etc., and by killing their cattle of every kind; and at all times to endeavour to way-lay, attack, and destroy their convoys of provisions by land and water, in any part of the country, where I could find them.'-(Rogers' Journals, pp 14-15).

Richard Rogers Company created on July 24, 1756, was on the same establishment.

SHIRLEY'S ESTABLISHMENT OF HOBBS' AND SPEAKMAN'S

COMPANIES-*May 27, 1756-Feb 24, 1757. Varied from the two Rogers's Companies (See text, pp 98-103).*
SIXTH (LOUDOUN'S) ESTABLISHMENT-*Feb 24, 1757-Jan 1761. Robert Rogers', Richard Rogers', Speakman's (Stark's), Hobbs' (Bulkeley's), and Shepherd's Companies came under this final establishment on Feb 24, 1757. The terms were:*
'Instructions from General Abercrombie for Captain Robert Rogers: His Excellency the Earl of Loudoun having given authority to me to augment the company of Rangers under your command, to 100 men each, viz. One Captain, Two Lieutenants, One Ensign upon English pay. Four Sergeants at 4s. each, N.Y. currency. 100 Private men at 2s. and 6d each per day, N.Y. Currency. And whereas there are some private men of your company serving at present upon higher pay than the above establishment, you are at liberty to discharge them, in case they refuse to serve at the said establishment, as soon as you have other men to replace them. If your men agree to remain with you and serve upon the above-establishment, you may assure them they will be taken notice of, and be first provided for; each man to be allowed ten dollars bounty-money, and to find their own clothes, arms and blankets, and to sign a paper subjecting themselves to the rules and articles of war, and to serve during the war. You are to enlist no vagrants, but such as you and your officers are acquainted with, and who are every way qualified for the duty of Rangers.'-*(Rogers' Journals, pp 49-50).*
On *Jan 11, 1758,* the 10 dollars bounty money to new recruits was deducted from their pay.-*(pp76-7)*

APPENDICE D

LOSSES IN ROGERS RANGERS 1755-Apr 1758:

Name of Company	Total en[1] listments	Killed[2] or Capt	Died of Smallpox	Dis[3] chrd	Unfit[4] for S	Deserted
Rt.Rogers-67*-	128	51	15	26	19	2
Rd.Rogers-51*-	124	20	3	12		
Speakmans-45*		4	3	15	10	15
(Starks)-	129	16	10		2	13
Hobbs- 23*		5	2	12	1	2
(Bulkeleys)-	127	50	12		4	9
Shepherds-64*	147	18	3		10	34
TOTAL 398:	723	164	48	65	46	75

EXPLANATORY NOTES FOR APPENDICE D:

[1] Total Enlistments in the Company from its beginning as one of Rogers' Independent Companies of His Majesty's American Rangers,-to after the Battle of Rogers' Rock, Mar 13, 1758.
[2] Killed in action, Lost or captured in the woods, or Captured in action and killed later by Indians, or died in captivity. None killed in 1755. Eight other captives were known to have escaped.
[3] Rangers already in service who refused to serve: on Sixth Establishment (Feb 24, 1757.).
[4] Found unfit for service after enlisted. Also cantankerous individuals who were discharged at Ft. Edward for Misbehaviour or Mutiny from 1756-1758.
*Original enlistment strength of the Company.

APPENDICE E

ROBERT ROGERS' FAMOUS RANGING RULES

This military treatise on the art of Ranger warfare and discipline is a unique and valuable work by Rogers 'The Father of American Rangers'. All of the '29 Rules' had been tried and tested by him and many of them were a result of lessons he had himself learned through encounters with the enemy.
These Rules of Rogers methods were crystalized on paper by him after the formation of his Cadet Company in 1757 at Loudouns request. When Loudoun had ordered the British Volunteers to serve under him he had asked Rogers to compose a treatise on his methods employed by his Rangers when scouting, fighting and in camp and Rogers sent him the original copy which is now among the Loudoun Papers in the Huntington Library. There must have been at least 60 copies printed up, for Rogers issued that many to members of his Cadet Company. The discovery of one of these pamphlets at this date would be a rare find indeed. Rogers sent Loudoun the original Copy on October 27, 1757. This Manuscript copy varies in text from the printed Rules in Rogers' Journals, and contains many additions. The Journals copy is here given with brief details of the additions in the Loudoun copy. Also a notice of the Battles and scouts where the rules were founded, or tested and proved......

I- All Rangers are to be subject to the rules and articles of war (and the General Orders in camp); to appear at roll-call every evening on their own parade, equipped, each with a fire-lock, sixty rounds of powder and ball, and a hatchet, at which time an officer from each company is to inspect the same, to see that they are in order, so as to be ready on any emergency to march at a minute's warning; and before they are dismissed the necessary guards are to be draughted, and scouts for the next day appointed.

II- Whenever you are ordered out to the enemies forts or frontiers for discoveries, if your number be small, march in a single file, keeping at such a distance from each other as to prevent one shot from killing two men, sending one man, or more, forward, and the like on each side, at the distance of twenty yards from the main body, if the ground you march over will admit of it, to give the signal to the officer of the approach of an enemy, and of their number, etc.

III- If you march over marshes or soft ground, change your position, and march abreast of each other, to prevent the enemy from tracking you, as they would do if you marched in a single file, until you get over such ground, and then resume your former order, and march till it is quite dark before you encamp, which do, if possible, on a piece of ground that may afford your sentries the advantage of seeing or hearing the enemy at some considerable distance, keeping one half of your whole party awake alternately through the night.

IV- Some time before you come to the place you would reconnotre, make a stand, and send one or two men, in whom you can confide, to look out the best ground for making your observations.

V- If you have the good fortune to take any prisoners, keep them separate, until they are examined, and in your return take a different route from that in which you went out, that you may the better discover any party in your rear, and have an opportunity, if their strength be superior to yours, to alter your course, or disperse, as circumstances may require.

VI- If you march in a large body of three or four hundred, with a design to attack the enemy, divide your party into three columns, each headed by a proper officer (viz., the senior officer in the center, the next senior officer on the right, and the third officer on the left), and let these columns march in single files, the columns to the right and left keeping at 20 yards distance or more from that of the center, if the ground will admit, and let proper guards be kept in the front and rear (these guards to be composed of 10 or 12 men placed 30 yards before each column, with two scouts preceding them at the same distance. The rear guard to consist of a Sergeant and 8 men), with orders to halt on all eminences, to take a view of the surrounding ground, to prevent your being ambuscaded, and to notify the approach or retreat of the enemy, that proper dispositions may be made for attacking, defending, etc. And if the enemy approach in your front on level ground, form a front of your 3 columns or main body with the advanced guard, keeping out your flanking parties, as if you were marching under the command of trusty officers, to prevent the enemy from pressing hard on either of your wings, or surrounding you, which is the usual method of the savages, if their number will admit of it, and be careful likewise to support and strengthen your rear-guard.

VII- If you are obliged to receive the enemy's fire, fall, or squat down, until it is over, then rise and discharge at them. If their main body is equal to yours, extend yourself occasionally; but if superior, be careful to support and strengthen your flanking parties, to make them equal with theirs, that if possible you may repulse them to their main body, in which case push upon them with the greatest resolution, with equal force in each flank and in the center, observing to keep at a due distance from each other, and advance from tree to tree, with one half of the party before the other ten or twelve yards. If the enemy push upon you, let your front fire and fall down, and then let your rear advance thru them and do the like, by which time those who before were in front will be ready to discharge again, and repeat the same alternately, as occasion shall require; by this means you will keep up such a constant fire, that the enemy will not be able easily to break your order, or gain your ground.

VIII- If you oblige the enemy to retreat, be careful, in your pursuit of them, to keep out your flanking parties, and prevent them from gaining eminences, or rising grounds, in which case they would perhaps be able to rally and repulse you in their turn.

IX- If you are obliged to retreat, let the front of your whole party fire and fall back, until the rear has done the same, making for the best ground you can; by this means you will oblige the enemy to pursue you, if they do it at all, in the face of a constant fire.

X- If the enemy is so superior that you are in danger of being surrounded by them, let the whole body disperse, and every one take a different road to the place of rendezvous appointed for that evening, which must every morning be altered and fixed for the evening ensuing, in order to bring the whole party, or as many of them as possible, together, after any separation that may happen in the day; but if you should happen to be actually surrounded, form yourselves into a square, or if in the woods, a circle is best, and, if possible, make a stand till darkness of the night favours your escape.

XI- If your rear is attacked, the main body and flankers must face about to the right or left, as occasion shall require, and form themselves to oppose the enemy, as before directed; and the same method must be observed, if attacked in either of your flanks, by which means you will always make a rear of one of your flank-guards.

XII- If you determine to rally after a retreat, in order to make a fresh stand against the enemy, by all means endeavour to do it on the most rising ground you can come at, which will give you greatly the advantage in point of situation, and enable you to repulse superior numbers.

XIII- In general, when pushed upon by the enemy, reserve your fire until they approach very near, which will then put them into the greater surprise and consternation, and give you an opportunity of rushing upon them with your hatchets and cutlasses to the better advantage.

XIV- When you encamp at night, fix your sentries in such a manner as not to be relieved from the main body until morning, profound secrecy and silence being often of the last importance in these cases. Each sentry therefore, should consist of six men, two of whom must be constantly alert, and relieved every two hours until all six have stood guard; when relieved by their fellows it should be done without noise; and in case those on duty see, or hear anything which alarms them, they are not to speak, but one of them is silently to retreat and acquaint the commanding officer thereof, that proper dispositions may be made; and all ocasional sentries should be fixed in like manner. (Rogers had originally instructed only 1 of the 6 sentries to remain awake an hour but after the 'Misbehavior Scout' in November 1757, when Captain Abercrombie found all the sentrys asleep, Rogers changed the regulation and ordered two sentrys to stay awake for two hours. By this means one could catch the other if he started to doze.).

XV- At the first dawn of day, awake your whole detachment; that being the time when the savages choose to fall upon their enemies, you should by all means be in readiness to receive them.

XVI- If the enemy should be discovered by your detachments in the morning, and their numbers are superior to yours, and a victory doubtful, you should not attack them till the evening as then they will not know your numbers, and if you are repulsed, your retreat will be favoured by the darkness of the night.

XVII- Before you leave your encampment, send out small parties round it, to see if there be any appearance or track of an enemy that might have been near you during the night.

XVIII- When you stop for refreshment, choose some spring or rivulet if you can, and dispose your party so as not to be surprised, posting proper guards and sentries at a due distance, and let a small party waylay the path you came in, least the enemy should be pursuing.

XIX- If, in your return, you have to cross rivers, avoid the usual fords as much as possible, least the enemy should have discovered, and be there expecting you.

XX- If you have to pass by lakes, keep at some distance from the edge of the water, lest, in case of an ambuscade, or an attack from the enemy, when in that situation, your retreat should be cut off.

XXI- If the enemy pursue your rear, take a circle until you come to your own tracks, and there form an ambush to receive them, and give them the first fire.

XXII- When you return from a scout, and come near our Forts, avoid the usual roads, and avenues thereto, lest the enemy should have headed you, and lay in ambush to receive you, when almost exhausted with fatigues.

XXIII- When you pursue any party that has been near our forts or encampments, follow not directly in their tracks, least you should be discovered by their rear-guards, who, at such a time, would be most alert; but endeavour, by a different route, to head and meet them in some narrow pass, or lay in ambush to receive them when and where they least expect it.

XXIV- If you are to embark in canoes, battoes, or otherwise, by water, choose the evening for the time of your embarkation, as you will then have : - the whole night before you, to pass undiscovered by any parties of the enemy on hills, or other-places, which command a prospect of the lake or river you are upon.

XXV- In padling or rowing, give orders that the boat or canoe next the sternmost, wait for her, and the third for the second, and the fourth for the third, and so on, to prevent separation, and that you may be ready to assist each other on any emergency.

XXVI- Appoint one man in each boat to look out for fires on the adjacent shores, from the numbers and size of which you may form some judgement of the number that kindled them and whether you are able to attack them or not.

XXVII- If you find the enemy encamped near the banks of a river, or lake, which you imagine they will attempt to cross for their security upon being attacked, leave a detachment of your party on the opposite shore to receive them, having them between you and the lake or river.

XXVIII- If you cannot satisfy yourself as to the enemy's number and strength, from their fire, etc. conceal your boats at some distance, and ascertain their number by a reconoitring party, when they embark, or march in the morning marking the course they steer, etc. when you may pursue, ambush (by marching ahead of them to a narrow place in the river and extend along the bank so as to cover all their boats with the first fire), and attack them, or let them pass, as prudence shall direct you. In general, however, that you may not be discovered by the enemy on the lakes and rivers at a great distance, it is safest to lay by, with your boats and party concealed all day, without noise or show and to pursue your intended route by night; and whether you go by land or water give out parole and countersigns, in order to know one another in the dark, and likewise appoint a station for every man to repair to, in case of any accident that may separate you.

(XXIX- If you are attacked in flat rough ground, retreat in a scattering method and let the enemy believe you are routed until you come to an advantageous spot, then allow the enemy to come close

and deliver a volley, and immediately after, my
men nearest to them to rush upon them with hatchets, and the rest to surround their flanks in
their confusion.).-(Rogers' Journals, pp 59-70;
Rogers to Loudoun, from Ft. Edward, Oct. 25, 1757,
LO 4701; Same to Same, Oct. 27, 1757, LO 4707).

The value of these Ranging Regulations is evi-
dent even today for when the First United States
Ranger Battalion was training with the Commandos,
the American Commanding Officer, Lieutenant Colonel
William Darby, U.S.A., issued copies of Rogers'
Ranging Rules to his men.-(Ft.Tic.Mus.Bull,VI,no6)

APPENDICE F

ROBERT ROGERS' CADET COMPANY

Listed alphabetically with sketch of their petitions; and subsequent promotions in Rogers Rangers
or British Regiments:

BERNARD, FRANCIS: Petitioned Loudoun in Dec 1757
that he was returning to Germany and would like to
be reimbursed for the Ranger uniform he had to
purchase while serving as one of Rogers' Cadets.-
(LO 5172). He had been a Volunteer in the Fourth
Battalion of Royal Americans. Not commissioned.

BOUJOUR, JOHN: A Swiss Volunteer from the 4th
Battalion of Royal Americans. Not commissioned.

BOYCE, RICHARD: A British Volunteer from the
48th Regiment. Not commissioned.

BRIDGE, BENJAMIN: A Ranger Private from Bulkeley's Company of Rogers Rangers. He had entered
the Company on March 12, 1757. Not commissioned.

CAMPBELL, ARCHIBALD: A Scotch Volunteer from the
42nd Highlanders. Brother of Captain-Lieutenant
John Campbell of the same Regiment. He had served
as a soldier of fortune in the Dutch army for four
years. Petitioned Loudoun Nov 23, 1757 for a commission.-(LO 4888). Pushed by Loudoun for a Lieutenantcy in Rogers Rangers which he gave him on
Jan 14, 1758, in Jonathan Brewer's Company. Killed
March 13, 1758 at Rogers' Rock.

CAMPBELL, ARCHIBALD, JR.: A Scotch Volunteer from

the 42nd Highlanders. Son to the above Archibald.
Ensign in the 42nd, July 21, 1758; Lieutenant, Feb
14, 1760. See footnote 247.

CARRUTHERS, FRANCIS: A British Volunteer from the
44th. Commissioned Ensign in James Rogers' Company
Mar 30, 1758, to replace Gregory McDonald, killed
at Rogers' Rock.

CHALMERS, RONALD: A British Volunteer unattached
to any Regiment. Served with Rogers from Aug 1756
to Apr 1757. Petitioned Loudoun Apr 5, 1757, from
Albany.-(LO 3287). Not Commissioned in America.

CHRISTOPHER, JOHN: A British Volunteer from the
55th. Ensign in the 17th Regiment, March 21, 1758;
Lieutenant, Sept 18, 1760.

CLARKE, JOHN: A British Volunteer from the 44th
Regiment. Commissioned Ensign in Burbank's Company
Apr 7, 1758, to replace James White killed Mar 13.

CROTTY, ANDREW: A British Volunteer from the
22nd. He had served as Quartermaster, Ensign, and
Lieutenant, in the East India Service.-(Pargellis,
Loudoun in N. America, p 312). On Nov 19, 1757 he
petitioned Loudoun for an Ensigncy in any Regular
Regiment.-(LO 4861). Ens, 44th 9/15/58; Lt,8/16/60

CREED, FRANCIS: A British Volunteer from the 27th.
A Nephew to Lord Blakney. Petitioned Loudoun Jan
1, 1758.-(LO 6325). Commissioned Lieutenant in Rogers Rangers, Apr 6, 1758, to replace Lieutenant
Gilman, who resigned from John Shepherd's Company.
He had served with distinction at Rogers Rock, Mar
13, 1758. Left the Corps for the Regulars to replace Ensign Balfour of the 27th Regiment.-(AB 96)
His Ensigncy was dated Mar 27, 1758; promoted to a
Lieutenant in the 34th Regiment, July 27, 1762.

CROFTON, EDWARD: A British Volunteer who had served as a Volunteer in his friend, Sir John Whiteford's Regiment in England. Hoping for quicker advancement he arrived in North America in 1757 as a
free-lance Volunteer not attatched to any Corps.
He involved himself in a serious quarrel with Major Darby and petitioned Loudoun to allow him to
engage in a duel with him.-(LO 5992; 4816). Loudoun instead attatched Crofton to Rogers Rangers
as a Volunteer when the Cadet Company was formed

Rogers liked his fearless personality and quick adaptwbility to Ranging methods and he recommended him to Loudoun for a Lieutenantcy in his own Company on January 10, 1758. Crofton was notified of his appointment but he wrote Loudoun politely refusing because it would not give him rank, and asked that he might be placed in some Regiment as a Volunteer or be allowed to return to England and Whiteford's Regiment. Crofton was evidently prevailed upon to accept the commission for he was commissioned a Lieutenant in John Stark's Company on January 14, 1758, and served with distinction at Rogers' Rock by commanding Rogers' left flank. He was one of the two officers to return with Rogers. Soon after a First Lieutenant's vacancy occurred in Wm. Stark's Company and he was promoted and transferred to it. He accompanied the Company to Louisbourg the same year and besides other outstanding service he defeated a body of Louisbourg Indians and drove them back into the fortress. He was transferred to Jonathan Brewer's Company in the Spring of 1759 and served with Wolfe at Quebec Wolfe realized his valuable talents and Crofton was chosen to perform a difficult assignment prior to the Battle of the Plains. On September 25, 1759, Crofton received a Second Lieutenant's berth in the 45th Regiment where he served until February, 1761, when he was killed in a pistol duel with a fellow officer over a question of rank. His commanding officer, Lieutenant-Colonel Montagu Wilmot of the 45th, clearly indicates his own sympathy when he reported the affair to General Amherst on Feb. 8, 1761: 'I have the honour to acquaint Your Excellency with an unfortunate accident that happen'd in the 45th Regt..Lieutenant Crofton (who had been put into the Regiment by General Wolf over all the Ensigns from being an officer of Rangers.) having as I am informed treated Lieutenant Burns with very opprobrious Language in Public, laid that unhappy Gentleman under a sort of fatal necessity of acting in opposition to his Duty by seeking a revenge in a manner contrary to the articles of war, the result of which was, that Lieutenant Crofton received a Pistol shot, of which he died the Day after.'-(W.O.34, Vol. 84, ff 87, 177; Wolfe to Monckton from Montmorency, Aug. 4, 1759, in Northcliffe Coll., Vol. XXII, p 149).

CROFTON, WALTER: *A British Volunteer from the 4th King's Own Regiment. Ensign 46th Regt. July*

24, 1758; Lieutenant, Oct 19, 1762.

DEKEFAR, LUHAINSANS: A Swiss Volunteer from the 4th Battalion of Royal Americans. Not Commissioned

DROUGHT, THOMAS: A British Volunteer from the 44th. Ensign in the 80th Regiment (Gage's) Dec 25, 1757; Lieutenant, July 28, 1758.

ELRINGTON, RICHARD: A British Volunteer from the 22nd Regiment. Ensign 22nd Regiment July 5, 1758.

FRASER, WILLIAM: A Scotch Volunteer from the 42nd Highlanders. Gazetted for an Ensigncy in Gage's 80th Regiment by Barrington, Sept 11, 1757. After serving in Rogers' Cadet Company he entered Gage's as a Volunteer-(AB 857). Served until Dec 27, 1757 when he was commissioned Ensign; Lieutenant, Sept 25, 1760.

FRASER, WILLIAM, JR.: Son of William Sr., a Volunteer in the 42nd. Ensign, 44th, Mar 23, 1758.

FRISBOROUGH, : A British Volunteer from the 2nd Battalion of Royal Americans. Not commissioned*

GRAHAM, JOHN: A Scotch Volunteer from the 42nd. Ensign 42nd Highlanders July 25, 1758; Lieutenant July 31, 1760; Captain-Lieutenant Aug 15, 1762.

GRANT, ALLEN: A British Volunteer from the 2nd Battalion of Royal Americans. Served as a Volunteer for two years before he petitioned Loudoun on Feb 3, 1758.-(LO 5532). Commissioned Ensign in the 60th on July 28, 1758; Lieutenant, Oct 7, 1763.

HAMILTON, JOHN: A British Volunteer from the 55th. Ensign in the 55th July 26, 1758; Lieutenant Sept 7, 1761.

HILL, JAMES: A British Volunteer from the 3rd Battalion of Royal Americans. Ensign in the 60th Aug 23, 1758; Lieutenant Sept 15, 1760; Lieutenant in the 64th, Dec 25, 1770.

HORST, ENGELBERTUS: A Swiss Volunteer from the 4th Battalion Royal Americans. Petitioned Loudoun with five others in Dec 1757 that he was returning home and would like to be paid the cost of his Ranger uniform while one of Rogers' Cadets.-(LO-

5172). On Jan 10, 1758, he was recommended by Rogers for an Ensigncy in a new Ranger Company. He was not commissioned.

HUMBLE, CHARLES: *A British Volunteer from the 22nd Regiment. Ensign in the 48th, Dec 18, 1757 Lieutenant, Aug 18, 1759.*

IRWIN, WILLIAM: *A British Volunteer from the 44th Regiment. Ensign in the 80th Light Infantry Dec 26, 1757; Lieutenant, Dec 3, 1759.*

KENT, MICHAEL: *A British Volunteer from the 27th Regiment. Killed at Rogers' Rock, Mar 13, 1758.*

LYSAUGHT, CORNELIUS: *A British Volunteer from the 4th Regiment. Ensign 35th, Jan 24, 1758; Lieutenant, June 11, 1760.*

McBEAN, DONALD: *From the 4th Battalion of Royal Americans. Not commissioned.*

McDOUGAL, JOHN: *From the Second Battalion of Royal Americans. Petitioned Loudoun Jan 5, 1758.-(LO 6000). Ens., 60th, Feb 24, 1760; Lt, Apr 29, 1761.*

McDONALD, GREGORY: *Entered Rogers' own Company May 25, 1757 as a Volunteer. Recommended by Rogers on Jan 10, 1758, for the Ensigncy of James Rogers new Company. Commissioned Jan 14, 1758. Killed at Rogers' Rock, March 13, 1758.*

MENZIES, CHARLES: *A Scotch Volunteer from the 42nd. Commissioned Ensign in the 42nd July 28, 1758; Lieutenant, Oct 8, 1761.*

MILLET, THOMAS: *A British Volunteer from the 22nd. Ensign in that Regiment Mar 11, 1759.*

MONFEL, : *From the 27th. Not commissioned.*

NICHOLSON, WILLIAM: *From the 48th. Ensign July 20, 1758 in the 48th Regiment.*

OLIVER, ROBERT: *Entered Mar 15, 1757, as a Cadet in J. Stark's Company. Sick in November and not in service in April 1758.*

PATTERSON, WALTER: *From the 48th Regiment. After Rogers' Cadet Company served as a Volunteer in the*

80th (Gage's) until Dec 29, 1757 when commissioned Ensign; Lieutenant, Oct 4, 1760.

PERRY, CHARLES: From the 48th. Petitioned Loudoun Dec 1757 for pay for Ranger uniform he had to purchase while attatched to Rogers' Corps.-(LO 5172). Not commissioned. Returned home.

POTTINGER, JAMES: See sketch in text, pp 187-8. Commissioned Lieutenant of Charles Bulkeley's Company Jan 14, 1758. Killed Mar 13, 1758.

REINHAULT, ERICKE: From the 4th Battalion Royal Americans. Petitioned Loudoun Dec 1757 for cost of Rogers Ranger uniform while a Cadet. Not commissioned. Returned home.

ROBERTS, BENJAMIN: From the 4th Regiment. Commissioned Ensign in the 46th, July 23, 1758; Lieutenant, Sept 12, 1762. Commissary at Michilimackinac in 1767 when he quarreled with Commandant Rogers & accussed him of treason after being put in irons.

ROBERTSON, JOHN: From the 42nd Highlanders. Lieutenant in that Regiment July 21, 1758.

ROSS, ANDREW: A Scotch Volunteer from the 42nd. Recommended by Rogers Jan 10, 1758, for an Ensigncy in a new Company of Rangers. Commissioned Ensign in Wm. Stark's new Company Jan 14, 1758. Killed Mar 13, 1758, at Rogers' Rock.

SCHLOSSER, JOHN CHARLES: A German Volunteer from the 4th Battalion of Royal Americans. Recommended by Rogers on Jan 11, 1758 for the Ensigncy of McCurdy's new Company. He was crossed out by Loudoun but was finally commissioned as an Ensign in the 60th on Oct 31, 1760. In 1762 he was in command of Ft. St. Joseph's near the head of Lake Michigan and fell prey to Pontiac's hordes on May 25, 1763. He was taken to Detroit and exchanged.

STEPHENS, SIMON: A Provincial Volunteer Cadet in Rogers Rangers. Entered Rogers Company on Mar 20, 1757, as a Cadet. Recommended by Rogers on Nov 10, 1757 for a Lieutenantcy in John Stark's Company. Continued as a Cadet. Again recommended by Rogers on Jan 10, 1758 for the same Lieutenantcy. Commissioned by Loudoun the Senior Lieutenant of John Stark's Company on Jan 11, 1758. Of Deerfield, Mass.

STERLING, HUGH: *The Clerk of Rogers' own Company Apr-Oct 6, 1755. Re-entered Mar 15, 1757 as a Cadet. Recommended by Rogers Nov 10, 1757 as First Lieutenant of Bulkeley's. On Jan 10, 1758, at N. Y., Rogers recommended him as Ensign of William Stark's new Company, but he was not commissioned. He evidently left the service soon after.*

STILL, : *From the 55th. Not commissioned.*

VEN BEBBER, HENRY: *From the 4th Battalion - Royal Americans. Not commissioned.*

WACKERBERG, ANDREW: *Ibid. Petitioned Loudoun - Dec 1758 for cost of Ranger uniform while a Cadet Returned home.-(LO 5172).*

WARD NICHOLAS: *From the 3rd Battalion of Royal-Americans. After Rogers' Cadet Company served as: a Volunteer in Gage's 80th until Dec 28, 1757. On that date commissioned Ensign in the Regiment. On June 15, 1761, promoted to a Lieutenant.*

WARDOMAN, GEORGE: *From the 4th Battalion of Royal Americans. Not commissioned. Petitioned Loudoun in Dec 1758 for cost of Ranger uniform while he was with Rogers. Returned home.-(LO 5172).*

WILCOX, JOHN: *From the 27th. Ensign July 21, 1758.*

WRIGHTSON, JOHN: *From the 27th. Captured at Battle of Rogers' Rock, Mar 13, 1758. Later exchanged. Purchased Captaincy in the 27th on Dec 16, 1762.*

WRIESBERG, DANIEL: *A German Volunteer in the 2nd Battalion of Royal Americans. Left his native Hanover about January 1756. Recommended by Colonel Haldimand. Petitioned Loudoun Jan 30, 1758.-(LO-5493). Lt, 60th, July 1761; Lt, Dec 25, 1770.*

YOUNG, WALTER: *From the 55th. Ensign in the 55th, July 26, 1758; Lieutenant, Jan 31, 1761.*

The above sketchs compiled from Ford's British Officers in North America; The various Petitions of the Cadets to Loudoun in the Huntington Library soliciting him for a commission, usually stating their length of service as a Volunteer. Rogers correspondence with Loudoun recommending certain Cadets for commissions. Rogers, Journals, provided the bulk of the names of Volunteers in his Cadet Company but several were discovered who were not on his list. Only Volunteers who served during the official existance of the Company from Sept 14, to November 8, 1757, are in the above list (with the exception of Ronald Chalmers who served earlier).

APPENDICE G

TABLE OF VARIOUS PAY ESTABLISHMENTS

	2nd Estab. Wentworths	3rd Est. Johnsons	Commis- sioners	5th Est. Shirleys	Spkms Hobbs	6th Est. Loudoun
Priv:	13 pds per mo.	- None		- 15 pds per mo.	- 3s, N.Y.C.	- 10¼d, - 2s 6d NYC Ster 1 1s 5½d Stg
Corp		- None		-		- 11d Stg
Sergt:		- None		-		- 4s, N.Y.C. 12½d, - 4s N.Y.C. Ster 1 2s 4d Stg
Surgeon						- 5s Stg.
Adjutant						- 4s Stg.
Ensign		- None				- 5s, N.Y.C - 3s, 8d - 3s, 8d Ster 1 Ster 1
Lieutenant		- None				- 7s, N.Y.C - 4s, 8d - 4s, 8d Ster 1 - Ster 1
1st & 2nd Captain		- None				- 10s, NYC - 10s, - 10s, Ster 1 - Ster 1
Major						-

CODE: pds: Pounds.   N.Y.C: New York Currency.
s: Shillings.   Ster 1 or Stg: English-
d: Pence.   Sterling.

Unless otherwhise stated the above table is for pay per day. Spaces left blank indicate that that-position did not exist at that time, or, that the exact pay is not known.

APPENDICE H

THE WHIPPING POST MUTINY

Due to the kind permission of the officials of the Huntington Library the following official documents concerning the Rangers' Mutiny are printed for the first time:

'The Court of Inquiry held by order of Lieutenant Colonel Haviland to examine into a Mutiny entered into on the Evening of the Sixth Instant. Captain Rogers, President. Island near Fort Edward, December 8-11, 1757:-

'..To examine into a Mutiny etc...for which the undernamed Person, Private in a Company of Rangers in his Majesty's Service, commanded by Captain Robert Rogers, Viz: Corneilus Culliner, Noah Porter, Abraham Parrot, Thomas Thomson, and James Akin were suspected and Confined the Said Evening by Captain Shepherd and also Joshua Atwood, private in the aforesaid Company was Confined at the said time by Lieutenant Burbank's Order on The Said-Suspicion.

Captain Robert Rogers-President.
Captain Charles Bulkeley-Member.
Lieutenant Jonathan Brewer-Member.
Lieutenant James Neale-Member.
Ensign Francis Rolfe-Member.

Persons Examined, Viz:

Captain Shepherd being called informed the Court that he transiently over heard people say as he was passing and repassing in Camp since the Confinment of the above prisoners that the cause of the above disorder was occasioned by two of Captain Rogers Company being punished at the Whipping Post but cannot recollect nor does not know the person or persons that uttered the Said words and further Says that he does not know the person from whom he wrested a firelock but supposes him to be endeavoring to propagate mutiny at that time.

Lieutenant Gilman appear'd & Said he was Ignorant of the Cause of the above disturbance and knows nothing of it.

Lieutenant Moore being Called Says that he heard two of Captain Stark's Men say a day or two before the disorder that Captain Shepherd had Expressed himself thus That Stark's Company began first with flogging, his own Company next, that Captain Bulkeley followed and that Captain Rogers came last who ought to have been first.

Lieutenant Burbank declares before the Court what Lieutenant Moor has said concerning Captain Shepherd's Expression above Mentioned.

Lieutenant Phillips being Called says he knows nothing Concerning the cause of the Above disorder

Edward Adams private of Captain Stark's Company says to the Court that he is ignorant of the persons Suspected to be concerned in the Mutiny of

their being at the Guard house at the time of the
disorder & does not know Who was Guilty and that
he a day or two before it happened hear'd Captain
Shepherd Express himself at Mr. Lotridge's Hutt in
the following words, Viz: That he had a flogging
all round it began in Captain Stark's Company,
next in Captain Bulkeley's then in his own and afterwards in Captain Rogers but thought to have begun with the latter.

Ebenezer Cadwell private in Captain Stark's Company bieng called says that he does not know the
person or persons concerned in the Mutiny. That
the Evening before the disorder at the Guard house
he went into Mr. Lottridges house where he heard
Captain Shepherd express himself in these Words,
Viz: by rounds there had been a general flogging it
began with Captain Stark's, then his own, next
Captain Bulkeley's, & afterwards Captain Rogers
which he said he thought ought to have begun first
in the latter because it was the Eldest Company.

Mr. Robert Lotridge being called Says he heard:-
Captain Shepherd say in his house Something concerning Whipping but cannot particularise the
Words; That he also heard several Rangers say they
did not like the Whipping Post and if the Rangers
were to be flogged their wou'd be no more Rangers.

Robert Rood, private of Captain Rogers Company
being called says he knows not that the prisoners
confined for the Mutiny were Concerned in it or if
any other persons being so That he heard Captain
Shepherd say to a Gentleman as they passed him
that he had two flogged for one which happened Just
after two of Captain Rogers' Company had been punished. That he heard Captain Shepherd call turn
out Rangers turn out, and that Captain Bulkeley
called turn out Rangers; at which time he kept his
tent till Serj. Wilson Came to him & ordered him
to turn out, which was a quarter of an hour afterwards & was the sixth instant early in the Evening
& before he went to the Parade with Serjt. Wilson
heard an uproar in the Camp.

Aaron Burt private in Captain Rogers Company
being called Said he knew nothing of any person
either of the prisoners Confined or any other that
was concerned in the Mutiny of the sixth instant
in the Evening. At the time that disorder began he
was easing himself upon the Bank near the River &-
heard Captain Shepard call turn out my people
and shoot the first man that touches the Guardhouse
on which I thought there was a Mutiny in the Camp

and immediately went over to my tent and Staid there in a surprise, not knowing how to turn till I was called by Lieutenant Moore to turn out which I did.

Charles Elder or Elden private in Captain Rogers Company says that being upon guard the day Samuel Boyd & Henry Dawson were Confined, Captain Shephard came to the guard house and asked Boyd where he got his Rum who answered with my money and afterwards said he had it of Lieutenant Brewer for whom he said he had been to work, then the Captain asked him if he had got anymore, who answered again. that he had been to the Major for an order to get some & was sent by him to Lieutenant Burbank who signed an order for some but that he then said Boyd I could not get it, answered on which, Captain Shepard turned about and said Major or not Major I'll over haul him and his Men, so That he said Elden did not know of any person Whatever that was concerned in the said Mutiny nor anything of it or the Cause till he heard the Noise Occasioned by the Said Disturbance but did not turn out till Call'd by Serjt. Wilson by reason of being disposed.

David Keer private in Captain Rogers' Company, says he is entirely ignorant of the persons that were in the mutiny on the 6th instant and knew nothing about it till he heard the General Cry for the Rangers to turn out & when the Major's Company was ordered to do it he took his Arms with him & went to the Guard house to be paraded, he knows nothing of the Cause of the said Mutiny excepting that the Major's Company was in General uneasy & thought themselves ill used but Cannot particularise any person that was so and thinks their unesiness arose from some of the Men being punished at the Whipping Post and from Captain Shepard saying He would over haul the Major and his Company.

Robert Clark private in Captain Rogers' Company being called said he was on Guard the day the Mutiny happened and knew Nothing of the Cause of Said Mutiny or of any person concerned in stirring it up. That the day Samuel Boyd and Henry Dawson were Confined he was also on Guard When Captain Shepherd Came to the Guard House and asked Boyd where he got his rum who answered with my money & afterward said he had it of Lieutenant Brewer for whom he said he had been to work, that the Captain asked him if he had got any more, who answered again that he had been to the Major for an order to get some and was sent by him to Lieutenant Burbank who signed an order for some but that the said Boyd could not get it, answered on which Captain Shepherd turned about and Said Major or Not Major I'll over haul him and his men too.

Daniel McKenney private in Captain Rogers Company being called Says that the Gun Wrested by Captain Shepherd out of one of the Mutineers hands on the Evening of the sixth instant, he thinks belongs to Abraham Parrot one of the prisoners confined on suspicion of being concerned in said Mutiny.

Thomas Beverly private in Captain Rogers Company being called says he supposes the gun taken from one of the mutineers on the sixth instant by Captain Shepherd belongs to Abraham Parrot a prisoner confined on suspicion of being in the Mutiny; and that he is ignorant of any person that was in the Said Mutiny.

Examination on the 9th of December, 1757:-
John McMahan private in Captain Shepherd's Company being called says that being near Mr. Canes Door on the evening of the 6th inst. he saw a number of men round the Whipping post and knew no one but Joshua Atwood Whom he saw take an ax from an other man & cut at the said post & soon afterwards saw it fall. He knows no other person concerned in the said Mutiny nor of any intentional design so perpetrated.

Serjt. Moor of Captain Rogers Company being called Said he heard Noah Porter say the 6th in a poking way he thought the Whipping post would not last long but did not at that time think the said Porter had any intention to do any such thing as happened afterwards he further says he is entirely ignorant of any Person or Persons concerned in Mutiny that Evening.

McSterling of Captain Stark's Company being called says that on the evening of the 6th instant and on hearing the Noise in Camp he went toward the Guard house and near it he meet a mutiny and Abraham Perry and took hold of him when Captain Shepherd came up and Wrested a Firelock out of his Hands.

Isaac Baldwin private in Captain Stark's Company being called says that he saw Captain Shepherd wrest a firelock out of a mans hand on the evening of the 6th instant when the Mutiny happened Which man he believes to be Abraham Parrot.

Examination of the 11th December, 1757:-
Serjt. Severance of Captain Rogers Company says that being Serjt. of the Guard the 6th instant in the evening he was in the Guard house when he was alarmed with the Noise and Cry of Rangers turn out which he did immediately with his Guard and found several Armed Men round the house Some of whom Demanded the Prisoners Confined there whilst one man laid hold of one of the boards of the Roof and pulled it off he saw a man present a firelock at Captain Shepherd which the Captain put by with a stick or Sword he had in his hand and thinks it was Noah Porter at which time Captain Bulkeley came up and spoke to the People who immediately Dispersed. A Number of other persons were called before the Court & Examined but their being nothing final relating either to the Cause of or persons concerned in the Mutiny of the Sixth instant, and in their Examinations we think it immaterial to rehearse what passed thereon and as we have done our endeavours to find out all and every Circumstance that could give any light into the cause of the intended execution of the foregoing Mutiny. We Submit our proceedings to Colonel Haviland Commandant at Fort Edward, at 10 O'Clock A.M. the 11th December, 1757. Signed Robert Rogers, President'.-(LO 4969).

Colonel Haviland sent Rogers' Proceedings of the Inquiry to General Abercrombie on December 16, 1757 with the following letter:
'..I think it appears by the said Court that some of those now Confined deserves to be brought to a Court Martial and severly punished for unless they are got the better of it is better to be without them, than have them, by what I can learn the Mutiny was much greater than they are willing to own, Captain Rogers was with me this Day, which was the first time of his coming abroad, and told me he hoped I would soon put an end to this Affair for it had given him great uneasiness. I answered I would not take another step till had your order. I believe he and most of his officers would now be glad that I had not heard of it and suppose they would have patched it up for fear of their Men, Captain Rogers likewise told me that he apprehends most of his men will desert, I answered it would be better they were all gone than have such a Riotous sort of people, but if he could catch me one that attempted it, I would endeavour to have him

hanged as an Example. When you have Perused this and the inclosed Proceedings, I must beg your Orders how to act, If you think a General Court Martial is necessary for them, Captain Archibald Gordon of the Inniskilling Regiment who is here, has often acted as a Judge Advocate if he is appointed it will save the trouble of sending one. If you think another Court Martial sufficient I think it would be of service to have it composed of officers in the Garrison as well as Rangers, to prevent these Mutinous fellows escaping a punishment suitable to their Crime. I believe it would be necessary to have your Order, for trying those Rangers with the like Court Martials, when guilty of neglect of duty or any other great crimes and as they have not Drumers, to have them punished by ours, and the Connecticuts, If you approve of this method of Court Martials, I must beg to know how the officers of the Rangers are to Rank with the Regulars. I believe if I had not told the officer that first informed me of the Mutiny, that I wanted to talk to some of those Men, they suspected to be concerned, and desired that Captain Rogers would send them to me, I would have had a Battle upon the Island before they could be taken, as soon as I got them into the Fort I secured them, Captain Rogers wanted them back at the time of the Court of Enquiry. I sent him for answer that I would not trust them where there were so many Mutineers for fear of a rescue.

If you don't chuse to try the Mutineers by a general Court Martial I would be glad to know whether you would desire to see the sentence before it is put in Execution.

I this day got a return of the quantity of ammunition that four Companys of Rangers wants to compleat to their usual quantity of 60 rounds, and find it to be 80 one pounds and half of Powder and 6,484 Balls, a great quantity indeed, considering what they got when going on the last scout which Captain Abercrombie knows, I told Captain Rogers this day that no stores could support their extravagance in Amunition, and that I would acquaint you with it, and that they ought to pay for every Ball wanted, he said his people could not do without practicing at marks. I answered if you allowed them to fire at Marks now and then for practice, Amunition ought to be given to him for that purpose, and not to break in upon that intended for service.

I got the better of their constant firing upon the Island but no sooner that they got into the Woods, they make them ring, they fired yesterday above 100 shots in hearing of the Garrison, therefore I hope you'll give me some direction upon this head.
N.B. I believe it will be necessary to return the Proceedings of the court of enquiry (of Rogers that I am enclosing).'-(LO 6859).

General Abercrombie was reluctant to commit himself in regard to settling the fate of the Mutineers and he passed Rogers' Proceedings along to Loudoun on Dec 18, with a copy of Haviland's letter and his own views in the following letter:
'..I find it difficult to reconect myself to any opinion I have endeavored to form in regard to' increasing the 'body of Rangers, not the less so by a letter received yesterday from Colonel Haviland, duplicate of which together with the examinations at a court of inquiry I herewith transmit to your Lord that I might receive your orders thereupon..who I conclude will speedily take your resolution as this matter cannot admit of any longer delay..'-(LO 5038). See text pp 213-219 for other documents relative to the Mutiny.

The closing lines of the documents relative to the Mutiny were written by Abercrombie to Loudoun on Jan 22, 1758, after Rogers had returned from his profitable conference with Loudoun:
'..as I conclude your Lordships willingness to grant an Indemnity for past offenses I shall write to Colonel Haviland to restore the mutineers into Rogers own hands..'

A glimpse at the length of service of the six Mutineers who were confined by Haviland reveals that four of them were comparitive new Rangers: James Akin and Thomas Thompson entered Rogers Company on February 24, 1757. While Corneilus Culliner and Noah Porter entered May 25, 1757. Only two Joshua Atwood and Abraham Parrot were old timers. They both had been Rangers since June 1, 1756. These two veterans and Noah Porter were the chief instigators. Atwood cut down the Whipping Post and Parrot or Porter threatened Captain Shepherd with a firelock. All six were dismissed from the Corps, but oddly enough, Rogers slipped Noah Porter back in on Jan 14, 1758, as the First Lieutenant of his new Ranger Company of Connecticut Mohegans.

II-SELECTIVE DOCUMENTS ON THE ACTIONS & AMBUSCADES OF ROGERS RANGERS SEPT 29, 1755-MAR 13, 1758

1.-ROGERS AMBUSCADE NEAR ISLE AU MOUTON 9/29/55

ROGERS OFFICIAL REPORT TO COLONEL BLANCHARD:
'A Journal of the N. H. Scout of 5 men sent from the Encampment at Lake George to recoin. the encampment of the French and Indians at Toronduroque Sept 27, P.M. Set forward in a Birch Canoe. Past that night Sundry Fires (their Spyes) by the sides of the Lake. Put ashore about 7 miles from the Carrying place, left 3 with the Canoe- 2 went forward. Early on the 28th about 10 in the morning came in view of an Encampment at the lower end of the L. at the Carrying Place, of about 1,000 Fr. & Inds.- We Crawled thro' their Guards to within about 30 or 40 Rods of the Encampment. There was no Fort nor Artillery there. We retired & went about 1 Mile & a half further, & discovered their Grand Encampment.- Crept thro' their Guards to within about 60 rods, found a Ft. building there- discouver'd a No. of Cannon Mounted- We had a Convenient Situation for a View, which we kept till toward night & by the appearance of the Tents & Troops, Fr. & Inds we Judged likely to be about 3,000.
Their Situation Comands the passage at the Carrying place & (we tho't) the passage down Champlain from Wood Creek to Crown Pt. Began our return the 29th, in which we found that the enemy had a large advanced guard at the north-end of the Lake, where the river issues out of it into Lake Champlain. Returned to our Canoes & found a Large Indian Canoe had passed up the Lake with one Frenchman, & Nine Indians, who on their return we waylayed on a point of the Lake - they came in reach of our small arms, at whom we fired about Forty Gun loads. Disabled or killed six of them, & Chased the remaining four, but at their Schrieks three Indian Canoes came to their relief which Prevented our bringing them in. Returned to our Camp that night etc..'-(Doc. Hist. N.Y., IV, 170).

ROGERS' JOURNALS 'ACCOUNT':
The details of the scout are the same but he includes more details of the ambuscade:
'While we were viewing' the advanced guard, 'I observed a bark-canoe..up the lake. We kept sight

of them till they passed the point of land, where
our canoe and men were left, where, when we arrived, we had information from our people that the
above..had landed on an island five miles to the
south of us, near the middle of the lake. In a
short time after, we saw them put off from the island, steer directly towards us; upon which we put
ourselves in readiness to receive them in the best
manner we could, and gave them a salute at about
100 yards distance, which reduced their number to
four. We then took boat and pursued them down the
lake, till they were relieved by two canoes, which
obliged us to retreat towards our encampment at
Lake George..'-(Rogers' Journals, pp 3-4).

SETH POMEROY' ACCOUNT:
'..Plac'd themselves in a narrow Place on a
Point of Land to wt there return ye Battoes that
went up to an Island ye men Laned Staid a little
while & then Cambe back So Came by Capt. Rogers &
his 4 men within gun Shot they fired upon ye Battoe
which had 9 Inds & a franch man in it they K 2 ye
first Shot So Continud firing till they had Shot 4
or 5 times apace kill'd or So Disabled Six of em
yt they ware not abled to Paddle ye Battoe only 4
yt cou'd work they Put In there Canoe & jumpt into
it Persued em till they had all moust Come up with
em Drawing So near ye Franch Army they Sent out a
no. of there Battoes after them So our People were
oblig'd to turn & make ye best of there way off but
they all arrv'd Safe with out any harm from ye E
nemy & a bold adventure It was.'-(Seth Pomeroy's
Provincial Journal, pp 120-121).

2.-BATTLE OF THE ISLE OF MUTTON, Nov 2, 1755

PRIMARY REASONS FOR THE EXPEDITION:
As early as Oct 5, Governor Hardy of New York
proposed the expedition in a letter to Johnson:
'..I would also recommend to you in the meantime
to send strong Scouting Parties on the Lake, to
drive the enemy from any Lodgments they may have
on any of the Islands where they resort, I suppose
only to observe your motions, this will have the
appearance of doing something, and indeed may have
usefull Consequences, by keeping your Men in Action, and may put a Prisoner into your hands, from
whom you may get a more perfect intelligence of
the Enemy's motions.'-(Johnson Papers, II, p 143).

As a consequence of this letter Johnson ordered Rogers on his abortive 'Decoy Scout' on Oct 7th. The Oct 29th Expedition was a renewal of that attempt. Johnson notifys Governor Hardy on Oct 31, that: '..Captain Rodgers the most active officer in this Army is gone down the Lake with about 28 or 30 picked Men in Battoes in order to intercept one or more Canoes wich Blanchard the French Deserter tells me, are daily sent about 12 or 15 Miles this way in order to make Discoveries. I gave him particular Directions & if the Enemy comes in his way, I hope he will do something..'- (Johnson Papers, II, p 258).

JOHNSON'S ORDERS TO ROGERS, Oct 29, 1755: 'You are to embark in the Battoes with the party under your command & make the best of your way down the lake to within about 6 Miles of the Advanced guard of the Enemy, & make the best Disposition wich circumstances will permit to intercept any Scouting parties of the Enemy who may be sent on this Lake for Discovery & take as many Prisoners as you possibly can.'-(Johnson Papers, IX,288)

JOHNSON'S INSTRUCTIONS TO ROGERS AFTER RECEIVING HIS MESSAGE FOR REENFORCEMENTS: 'Camp at Lake George, Nov 2, 1755: Agreable to Your Message & Desire I send You a Reinforcement of 80 Men under the Command of Capt. Billings who with the Men are to put themselves under your Command. I would recommend to you to act with silent Caution & so to post your Men as to cut off their retreat to Tionderogo. It appears to me most adviseable to begin the Attack from the Water securing their Canoes & that at break of Day. You will consult with the Officers upon your proceedings but the Stroke must be struck without delay. If there are any Works & time will permit destroy them, do your Business as soon as possible & dont delay one Moment when you have done the best you can suffer no Men to delay time by looking after Plunder, for if you are dilatory the Enemy from Tionderoga may come upon you & be too powerful for you to make a safe Retreat.'-(Johnson Papers, II, pp 268-269).

JOHNSON'S ORDERS TO CAPTAIN BILLINGS: 'Camp at Lake George, 2nd Nov, 1755: You are to imbark with the party under your Command in order to join Capt. Rodgers. You are to keep the Men orderly and Silent upon pain of Death & not scatter the Battoes out of sight of each other. Your self or the next officer in Commwnd to be in the last Battoe in order to bring up the Rear regularly, on your joining Capt. Rodgers you are to be under his Command & deliver him my Letter herewith. I have directed him to consult with the Officers when Occasion requires Your Success depends upon Secrecy & Silence let that be your principal care & Attention. Take Connor in the Battoe with you as a Pilot. And Let the Officer who brings up the Rear, have the Indian who came from Capt. Rodgers in his Battoe.'-(Johnson Papers, II, p 263).

ROGERS' OFFICIAL REPORT TO JOHNSON:
'Novr 3d 1755, Camp at Lake George, Report of Capt Rodgers & Co. Of Their Skirmish With The Enemys Advanced Guard: May it Please your Honour.
Pursuant to your Orders of ye 29th of October Last I set off with ye Party to me Ordered and Went Down ye Lake and ye 31st made a Discovy of a number of fires By night Situated on a Point of Land on ye West side of ye Lake, upon Which we Landed and Secured our Battoes upon ye Same Side of ye Lake about a mile & half Distance from their Encampment, Next morning Sent out Spies for further Discovery, in ye Evening Capt Fletcher one of ye Spies return'd Leaving 2 of ye Spies there, and made Report yt there was four Tents and Sundry Small fires on Sd Point, and upon yt after Consultation it was Concluded advisable to acquaint your Honour of our Discovery and reinforce us if you thought advisable in order to Proceed further and Make a Push upon our Enemy, accordingly Capt Fletcher was Dispatchd to you with Six men in ye Battoe and Six being return'd as Invaleeds Leving me with nineteen men only, but being un Easie with the Report, I took a Battoe with 5 men and went Down within 25 Rods of their Fires Discovered a Small Fort with Several Small Log Camps within ye Fort which I judged to Contain about ¼ of an acre Said Fort being open towards ye Water The rest Picketted. Made no further Discovery there and Returnd to My Party, found all well except Capt Putnam and ye Spie with him, who was not returned, The next Morning about 10 o the Clock Capt Putnam return'd and ye Spie with him who Gave much the Same acct as above Saving yt ye Enemies Centrys was sett 20 Rods from their Fires and for a more Crittical examination of ye Enemies Proceedings he went forward till he Came so nigh yt he was fired

upon by one of ye Centeries within a Rod of him, But unfortunately upon Preparing to Fire upon him fell into a Clay Pit and wett his Gun made ye Best retreat he was able, hearing ye Enemy Close to their Hells, they made a Tack & Luckely escapd Safe to our Party, Soon after there was a Discovery made of two Frenchmen upon a Hill a Small Distance, who Called to us, said Hill overlooked our ambush, in a few minutes they retreated, and Two Canoes appeared and went by us & Lay in ye middle of ye Lake about 40 Rods Distance from Each other, Finding by yt Behaviour, there was a Party Coming by Land yt we must inevitably be between 2 Fires.

Upon Which I ordered Two Battoes into ye Water Leut Grant with 6 men, and I went into ye other with 6 more & Put on Board Each a Wall peice and Went out towards ye Canoes, who seemed to Ly upon their Paddles as tho' they had a Design to Decoy us into some mischief by their Party yt was Designed to Surround our People on Shore and then attack us by keeping us between ym and their Land party findg there Design we attacked them first put ym to ye Rout and surprised so yt they made to ye shore Where Capt Putnam with ye rest of our Party Lay, but unhappy to ym he was Prepared for ym shot and kill'd their Cockson; and by our Wall Peices &c; kill'd Divers of ym Butt upon his fireing upon yr Canoe, Immeadiatly ye Enemy Upon that was upon his Back fired upon and had but just time to Shove his Battoe into ye Water, and Gett into Before ye Enemy appeared upon ye Waters Edge and Made a Brisk fire upon him Shot Thro' his Blanket in Divers Places, and thro' ye Battoe, and then made to our Battoes for refuge, upon his Escape we pursued ye Cannoes with a constant fire upon them till we came within Eighty Rods of yr fires, Discovered a nomber of men upon Each Side of ye shore within about 40 Rods of us Gave ym Each a Broad side which put ym to ye Bush, and Gave us a Clear Passage Homewards and after we Got fairly into ye Lake Lay upon Our Oars and Inquired after the Circomstances of ye Party. Found none killed, but one Wounded which Gave Joy to all of us after so Long an Engagement which I Judge was near 2 Hours &c.

And Then we made ye Best of our Way to our Head quarters about half Way, We met With ye Reinforcemt- But upon Consultation, Thought Best to report What happend Without further proceeding, and accordingly arrived here to ye Encampmt ye 3rd Instant- All which is Hum Submitted by your Dutyfull

Servts. Robert Rodgers, Israel Putnam, Noah Grant'.
-(Doc. Hist. N.Y., IV, pp 272-273).

ROGERS' 'JOURNALS' ACCOUNT:
Rogers' printed account in his 'Journals' varies considerably in details, names and dates:
'November 4, 1755: Agreeable to orders from General Johnson this day, I embarked for the enemy's advanced guard before mentioned, with a party of thirty men, in four battoes, mounted with two wall pieces each. The next morning, a little before day light, we arrived within half a mile of them where we landed, and concealed our boats; I then sent four men as spies, who returned the next evening, and informed me, that the enemy had no works round them, but lay entirely open to an assault; which advice I dispatched immediately to the General, desiring a sufficient force to attack them which, notwithstanding the General's earnestness and activity in the affair, did not arrive till we were obliged to retreat. On our return, however, were met by a reinforcement, sent by the General, whereupon I returned again towards the enemy, and the next evening sent two men to see if the enemy's sentries were alert, who approached so near as to be discovered and fired at by them, and were so closely pursued in their retreat, that unhappily our whole party was discovered. The first notice I had of this being the case was from two canoes with thirty men in them, which I concluded came out with another party by land, in order to force us between two fires; to prevent which, I with Lt. McCurdy, and fourteen men, embarked in two boats, leaving the remainder of the party on shore, under the command of Captain Putnam.-In order to decoy the enemy within the reach of our wall-pieces, we steered as if we intended to pass by them, which luckily answered our expectations; for they boldly headed us till within about a hundred yards, when we discharged the pieces, which killed several of them, and put the rest to flight, in which we drove them so near where our land party lay, that they were again galled by them; several of the enemy were tumbled into the water and their canoes rendered very leaky. At this time I discovered their party by land, and gave our people notice of it, who thereupon embarked likewise, without receiving any considerable injury from the enemy's fire, notwithstanding it was for some time very brisk upon them. We warmly pursued the enemy,

and again got an opportunity to discharge our wall pieces upon them, which confused them much, and obliged them to disperse.- We pursued them down the Lake to their landing, where they were received and covered by 100 men, upon whom we again discharged our wall-pieces, and obliged them to retire; but finding their number vastly superior to our's we judged it most prudent to return to our encampment at Lake George, where we safely arrived on the 8th of November.'-(Rogers' Journals, p 6-8)

CAPTAIN ROGER BILLINGS' REPORT:
'Lake George, Novr. ye 2, 1755: I ye subscriber, Beeing ordered With a number of men to Go Near ye Narrows to Join Capt Rogers and his men but on my way their I met Capt Rogers Returning home he Being Discouer'd by a party of the Enemy & attacked & thought Best to Return to ye Camp & I also Returned Back With him by his Desire.'-(Doc. Hist. of N.Y., IV, p 274).

PROVINCIAL JOURNAL ACCOUNTS:
Of the many contemporary Journals and Diaries studied for additional facts on the Action, only three offer weather notes and conflicting details. It seems not all the Army was aware of Rogers goal CAPTAIN NATH DWIGHT'S JOURNAL: 'Cct 29, Wed, hazey in the morning. Looks like Snow tho the wind prety much north as it Generally is. Hear Capt Rogers went off with 25 men for Crown Point.
Nov 2, Sunday, before night Came in a party of:- Capt. Rogers men which went off Wed., bring news from him that he has found an advance party on this side Tianterogo building a Small fort & he thinks with 100 men he can Drive them off there. About 150 men in battows meet Capt. Rogers returning...found there was no agreement to send for them, but one Capt. Fletcher came off unadvisedly for them..'-(In N.Y.Gen.&Biog.Rec,1902,p3-9,65-70)
PRIVATE JAMES HILL'S DIARY: 'Oct 29, Capt. Rogers Went to tianderroger. Pleasant Weather but Praty Cold.'
Nov 2, Sonday, fin Pleasant Weather, & they sant Capt Rogers 80 more men but he was discovered & was obliged to fit His way thru & Com Hom, & the Hol with him. They fit tham with thair Walpeasses & with Blonder Boses and thay vary narerly escaped with thair Lives. They Wonded one of our men & it is thought that they Kiled Six or Eight of tham..'
-(In New England Quarterly, V, pp 602-618.).

DR. THOMAS WILLIAMS DIARY-LETTER TO HIS WIFE:
Lake George, Nov 2, 1755: 'About 200 Men are
gone this day to the Narrows to give the enemy's
advanced party a salutation, who by Capt Rogers'
acct from them are about 100 in number. He was
sent with about 30 men 3 days since, & this morning sent a man back for the 200 with which he
thinks he can do the job..'-(In Hist.Mag,Apr,1870)

CASUALTIES: The consensus of opinion is that the
French and Indians lost 6 or 8 killed besides several wounded. Rogers' force suffered no casualties among his Rangers but Lieutenant Durkee of
the Connecticut Provincials was shot in the thigh.

3. -MASSACRE OF SERGT ARCHIBALD'S SQUAD 4/12/56
Principal Sources are Capt. Jeduthan Baldwin's
Diary, Apr 11-12, 1756 entries.-(In Jrn of the Military Service Inst., XXXIX, 1906, pp 121-130).
-Boston News-Letter, Apr 30, 1756; Oct 12, 1758:
States that Private John Mitchel 'Died on board..
his passage to France' before Feb 16, 1758. The
fate of Sillaway, the other captive, is unknown.
-Declaration of James Archibald, A Serjt. in Capt.
Robert Rogers' Company of Rangers, to Loudoun from
Ft. Edward, Oct 6, 1756,-after his escape.-LO 1978
-Archibald's escape is mentioned by Loudoun to Fox
Oct 8, 1756-LO 1986; Winslow to Loudoun in LO 1982

4. -THE RETALIATION SCOUT, May 22, 1756:
Rogers must have sent an official report to Shirley but its whereabouts are not known.

ROGERS' JOURNALS ACCOUNT:
'May 20, 1756: Agreeable to orders from the General, I set out with a party of 11 men to reconnoitre the French advanced guards. The next day
from the top of a mountain, we had a view of them,
and judged their number to be about 300; they were
busy in fortifying themselves with palisades. From
the other side of the mountain we had a prospect
of Ticonderoga Fort, and, from the ground their
encampment took up, I judged it to consist of about 1000 men. This night we lodged on the mountain, and next morning marched to the Indian carrying-path, that leads from Lake George to Lake
Champlain and formed an ambuscade between the
French guards and Ticonderoga Fort. About six o'-

clock 118 Frenchmen passed by with out discovering us; in a few minutes after, 22 more came on the same road, upon whom we fired, killed six, and took one a prisoner; but the large party returning, obliged us to retire in haste, and we arrived safe, with our prisoner, at Fort William Henry on the 23rd.'-(Rogers' Journals, pp 17-18).

CAPTAIN DE LERY'S FRENCH ACCOUNT:

'May 22: At 9 o'c. of the morning there arrived 13 men of the Canadian Militia, who escaped from the portage where they were attacked by some 15 English as they say. It is true that M. de Beaujeu had ordered M. de Fontenay, Cadet, to go there with 20 armed men, each one with an axe, to work on the portage trail. They left their arms at one end of the said portage with a sentry to guard them, and came to the other end to work there. This portage is ¾ of a league across. The English killed one man & scalped him, after which they left more promptly than they had come, without taking the trouble to follow the fleeing men; they could have captured those 20 men without firing a shot if they had wanted, as they were all sitting in a circle smoking their pipe (calumet). There is still missing from this detail only the Sieur Fontenay and we are very anxious as to his fate. At 10 o'clock, we had a cannon shot fired, which is the signal to pursue the Enemy; a picket of La Reine and of Languedoc, another of the Marine, and a third of Canadian Militia, have set out from our camp. At 4:30 our pickets returned without having found anything.'-(De Lery's Diary, Courtesy of the N. Y. Historical Society). In retaliation for Rogers ambuscade Captain Colombiere and 403 troops de la Marine, Canadians and Indians erupted from Ticonderoga on the 21st to raid Fort Edward, they returned on the 29th, with 4 prisoners and 3 scalps.

5.-THE OTTER CREEK MOUTH AMBUSCADE, 7/7/56:

ROGERS' OFFICIAL REPORT:

'Journal of a Scout From Fort Wm Henry down into Lake Champlain pursuant to an order from his Excellency Major-General Shirley, as followeth:

June ye 28th 1756 Set out with a party of fifty men in five Whale Boats & Proceeded at abt twenty miles to an island in Lake George were we encamped ye next day went five miles farther Down ye Lake and there landed, halled out our Boats ashore and carried them over a Mountain about six miles to South Bay where we arrived ye 3d July in the afternoon and ye Same evening went down ye Lake at about six miles Distance from ye Forts.

July ye 4th towards morning we halled up ye Boats on the East side of the Lake & Concealed them & lay by untill Evening, then set Out again & Passed by Tiantiroga & found we were not Discovered by being so near ye Enemy as to hear ye Sentery Watch word. We judged from the number of their fires they had a body of about two thousand men, & yt ye Lake in this Place to be about Seventy Rods- Continued on till Day light about five miles from ye Fort. Then halled up ye Boats & Concealed all day on ye Same Shore and discovered Sundry Battoes Loaded and unloaded which ware Comeing & going upon ye Lake - in ye Evening of ye fifth Day Put of again & attempted to Pass by Crownpoint But thought it imprudent to Pursue this Intention by Reason of the Clearness & light of the Night, so halled up ye Boats again & Lay concealed all Day being of 6th Currant. this day near one hundred Boats passed us Seaven of Which Came very near us and asked to land at the Point Where we lay but their officer went farther on & Landed about 25 Rods from us Where they Dined in our View But did not think it advisable to Attack them in the Situation we were in - About 9 in ye Evening Set 'out again Passed ye fort at Crownpoint & went ten mile from it Down ye Lake & halled up ye Boats about brake of Day.

July 7th about 10 in ye Morn. 30 Boats Passed towards Canda also a Light Schooner of about 35 or 40 tuns- Set out again in ye Evening & went 15 miles farther Down and went ashore about 1 o'clock a:m upon a Point on ye East Side of & immediately Sent a party farther Down the Lake for Discovery. who Saw a Schooner at Anchor Some Distance from ye Shore about a mile from us and upon this Intelligence lightned our Boats & prepared to Board them but were prevented about 3 of ye Clock by two Lighters Coming up the Lake who we found intended to land in ye Place were we Were, which Vessels we fired upon immediately and afterwards hailled them and offered them Quarters if they would Come ashore which they said they would Comply with but Instead thereof put off in their Boats to ye opposit Shore but we followed them in our Boats & Intercepted them & taking them found twelve men three of which were killed & two wounded one of wounded Could not March therefore put an end to him to Prevent Discovery- As soon as ye prisners were Secure we employed our Selves in Destroying & Sinking Vessels and Cargoes- Which was Chiefly Wheat & flour Rice Wine & Brandy excepting Some few Casks of Brandy & Wine which we hid in very secure Places with our Whale boats at Some Distance on ye opposite Shore the Prisoners informed yt about five hundred men of which they were formemost, were on their Passage at about two Legs Distance which occasioned us to set forward on our Return ye Mirning of the 8th Currant & persued our March till ye 12th Where we arrived on the West Side of Lake George about 25 miles from Fort Wilm Henry & Sent Lieut Rogers to Said fort for Battoes & Provisions to Carry us by water the 14th in ye evening ye Lieut Returned to us with thirty men and ten Battoes & ye 15th at two of the Clock we arrived safe With all my Party & Prisners at Fort Wilm Henry.'-(Doc.Hist.N.Y.,IV, pp 285-287). Rogers gave his report to Johnson for Shirley had been superceded by Abercrombie.

ROGERS' JOURNALS ACCOUNT: (pp 19-22)
The dates and facts are the same except that Rogers supresses the fact that they killed and scalped the Frenchman who was mortally wounded.
In both accounts Rogers states that they went 25 miles up Lake George then hauled their boats 'over a Mountain about six miles to South Bay'. Actually they only went as far as Sabbath-Day-Point and crossed over (See map-p 339). For security reasons Rogers kept his actual route a secret. On Aug 20, 1758 Prevost reveals it in a proposal to Abercrombie to re-attack Ticonderoga: He suggests that 'Major Rogers to be sent by night opposite to Sabbath-Day-Point, from thence to proceed, carrying his boats to Wood Creek as he did before.'-(AB 548)

ROGERS' LAST REPORT TO SHIRLEY:
On June 24, 1757, Rogers wrote Shirley from Wm. Henry that he expected to start out on the 27th with 55 Rangers and if he took a prisoner on the way he would return him with a detail of Rangers so that he could quiz him before he returned. Rogers also mentions that he is leaving a reliable Ser't with the rest of his Company at Wm. Henry in case scouts were needed in his absence.-(LO 1245).

PROVINCIAL AND NEWSPAPER ACCOUNTS:
Evidently one of Rogers Rangers missed his boat

before one of the night trips for the Boston News-Letter on July 29, 1756, reports that from the 'Extract of a Letter from Albany, June 10,: The brave Capt. Rogers is gone out with a Party of 55 Men on a very bold and daring Enterprise and by the Accounts I have had since is likely to succeed When I was at Ft. Wm. Henry (which was the 2nd Instant) it was thought he had got safe past the French army at Crown Pt. Fort & got undiscovered into Lake Champlain. Since I came from the Ft. 1 of Rogers's Party is returned who says, he lost himself; and the Acct he gives is, That they got over Lake George, cut a Road thru the Bushes, first carried their Packs & then their Whale-Boats on their Shoulders, to L. Champlain. Tis said Rogers designs to strike a Blow in the Heart of Canada, or burn the French Brig on L. Champlain.'

The same Copy reports that: 'Camp at Ft. Hardy (28 Miles beyond Half-Moon) On our arrival Heard an agreeable piece of News, That Capt. Rogers being out on a scouting Party got 4 Leagues beyond Crown Pt., where he met with 2 Scowes, laden with Flour, Pork, Wine, Brandy and some Money, 6 Men in each, they killed 4 and took 8; one of the former a Lt; They also found 30 or 40 Letters, with Intelligence greately to our Satisfaction. Rogers & his prisoners are on the road coming to Albany.'

The eight prisoners were kept in the upper part of the Albany Town Hall.-(LO 1402).

In Shirley's letter to Henry Fox from N.Y., July 26, 1756, he states that: 'Capt. Rogers....whom I sent five Weeks ago, with five Whale boats to try to intercept the Enemy's Convoy of Provisions and Stores upon Lake Champlain and to make Discovery of their Strength and Motions..Besides the other good effects of his Success some reasonable intelligence may be got from the Prisoners..'-(Correspondence of Wm. Shirley with Fox, II, p 491).

FRENCH ACCOUNTS:

The following account printed in Documents Relative to the Colonial History of N.Y.,X, p 482,- sounds like one of Vaudreuil's distortions of the true facts. Nevertheless it is interesting and establishes the exact spot of the ambuscade:

'An English party at Otter Creek, six leagues this side of Fort St. Frederic, has destroyed on us two armed bateaux, having six men each, whom they have surprised. Though these were destitute of powder and ball, the English were in such haste

that they abandoned their own provisions, and did not lay a finger on the cargoes of these two batteaux, which consisted of cats, bran and meal. All the letters were found in a bag, and the appearance was, that only one man had been killed. We have learned from some English prisoners that 8 prisoners had been carried to Orange (Albany).'
The two batteaus were evidently discovered soon after the ambuscade for Private Thomas St. Leau a French deserter in an examination on July 25, revealed the following: 'Question: Had you any Acct. at the Ft. at Carilong before you came away of any French being taken in Lake Champlain? Answer: Yes, 11 or 12 missing, 1 was found killed in a Battoe, the others they supposed to be taken Prisoners; & further says, that the French are generally surprised to think how a Party of English could get into that Lake.'-(Boston News-Letter, Aug 5, 1756)
Rogers was able to obtain knowledge of the consequences of his raid by questioning subsequent prisoners he obtained. A prisoner examined on September 2, 1756 informed him: 'that since the two shallops or lighters were taken, they had augmented the number of men on board the large schooner in Lake Champlain from 12 to 30.'-(Journals, p 30)
On Oct 31, 1756 another captive revealed: 'that the French had taken four of Captain Roger's whale boats in Lake Champlain.'-(Journals, p 36). Evidently the fifth boat was never discovered.

6.-LIEUTENANT JACOB'S AMBUSCADE, Aug 10, 1756:
Jacob's official report is in the Loudoun Papers dated Aug 13, 1756.-(LO 1480).
William Hervey's Journal, p 34, Aug 9, and 11th entries record the scout.
Jacob took two scalps but 2 Stockbridges and 1 Provincial were captured or lost their way.

7.-CAPTAIN JACOB'S SCALP SCOUT, Sept 2-8, 1756:
Rogers' Journals, pp 30-31; Hervey's Journals, Aug 30, Sept 2, 8, entries. He states Jacob had 22 Stockbridges with him and one of the scalps he took was an officers.

8.-THE BATTLE OF LA BARBUE CREEK, Jan 21, 1757:
ROGERS' OFFICIAL REPORT TO ABERCROMBIE:

January 15, 1757[1], Marched from Fort Edward with Lieutenant Stark of my Company and Ensign Page of Captain Richard Rogers's and fifty Men from the said Companies, and the same Evening arrived at Fort William Henry,[2] and there remained till the 17th when being joined by Capt. Spikeman, Lieut. Kennedy, Ensign Brewer and fourteen of Capt. Spikeman's Company, together with Ensign Rogers, and fourteen of Capt. Hobb's Company, and Mr. Baker a Voluntier in His Majesty's 44th Regiment of Foot, I set out[3] and at Night encamped at the first Narrows on the East Side of the Lake. As some of the Detatchment had hurt themselves on the Ice, and could not proceed on the Scout, I sent so many back as reduced my Party to seventy four Men Officers included.

The 18th, marched twelve Miles down Lake, and camped on the West Side.

The 19th, marched three Miles farther down the Lake, then took to the Land on our Snow Shoes, and marched N. by W. and encamped about[4] eight Miles from the Lake.

The 20th, continued our Course[5] till Night and encamped opposite to Lake Champlain about three Miles westward from it.

The 21st, marched East till we came on Lake Champlain about midway betwixt Crown Point and Ticonderoga. As soon as we came to the Lake discovered a Slay going from Tionderoga to Crown Point, on which I dispatched Lieut. Stark with a party of twenty Men towards Crown Point to head the Slay, at the same Time I set out with another Party towards Tionderoga, leaving Capt. Spikeman with a Party in the Center. Lieut. Stark's Order was to march as far down as he could, while the Slay came against the Center Party, then push on the Ice to head em, whilst I with my Party designed to do the same on the Lake to prevent the Slays returning to Tionderoga, I soon after discovered about ten[6] Slays more coming down the Lake, and immediately dispatched two Men to tell Lieut. Stark not to discover himself and let the first Slay pass, but before the Men could overtake him he had got on the Lake and was seen by the People in the Slays who turned and fled for Tionderoga. We pursued them and took three Slays seven Prisoners and six Horses; the others made their Escape to Tionderoga. We immediately examined the Prisoners separately, and they informed us that two Hundred Canadiens, and forty five Indians just arrived at Tionderoga, who were to be joined that Evening or the next Morning by fifty Indians more from Crown Point, and that there were three Hundred and fifty regular Troops at Tionderoga, and six Hundred at Crown Point, that they expected in a short Time at Tionderoga a Number of Troops to attack our Forts in the Spring and had large Magazines of Provisions, and that their Canadiens and Indians were well equiped and ready to march at a Moments Warning, from which Circumstance[7] I concluded they would turn out and pursue us. I then gave Orders if we were attacked, those that had the Care of the Prisoners should kill them, and as the Day was wet [8] we returned with all possible Expedition to our Fires at our last Encampment in Order to dry our Guns which we did effectually, and then marched keeping a good rear Guard. I with Lieut. Kennedy took the Front, Capt. Spikeman the Center, and Lieut Stark the Rear. Ensign Page and Rogers were between the Front and Rear, the Rear Guard being under the Command of Serjt. Walter. In this Manner we[9] proceeded and in crossing a Valley betwixt two very Steep Hills, which was about fifteen Rods wide, when the Front to the Number of ten or twelve had raised the Summit of the western Side a Volley of two Hundred Shot or there about was fired upon us from the Enemy who had formed themselves into a half Moon to intercept and surround us which killed Lt. Kennedy and Mr. Gardiner a Voluntier, and wounded several of our Party and myself Slightly on the Head, which Fire we returned after killing our Prisoners and then I ordered the whole to retreat to the opposite Ridge, where Lieut. Stark and Ensign Brewer had with about forty Men made a Stand. The Enemy pursued us so close thro the Valley that they took some Prisoners, and killed Capt. Spikeman and several of our Men; but were beaten back again from the Brisk Fire of Lieut. Stark's Party, that covered and secured our Retreat![10] They then sent out a flanking Party on our Right which Lieut. Stark discovered, and called out to me to acquaint me of upon which I ordered out a Party under Serjt Phillips to head, and prevent 'em, which he accordingly did by having the first Fire at, and killing several of them, the Rest retreating to their main Body. The Enemy soon after made an Attempt to push up to us, but having the Advantage of the Ground and good Shelter from Trees we obliged them a second Time to retreat as they could not stand our continual Fire upon them. They then sent out another Party to flank us, which I perceived and sent Ensign Rogers with twelve Men who repulsed and forced them back again to their own Ground, and afterwards ordered the same Party into the Rear to prevent any further Designs of this Kind from the Enemy; then formed ourselves for the Battle, taking my Station on the Right, Ensign Brewer on the Left, and Lieut Stark and Mr. Baker in the Center, the latter of which I desired to go into the Rear to assist Ensign Rogers, but he did not incline to leave his Post and soon after was killed. We continued a constant Fire on both Sides till Sunset[11], the French often calling to us, and desiring us to accept of Quarters, promising that we should be treated with Humanity and used kindly, and at the same Time called to me by Name and threatened us that if we did not embrace their Offers as soon as the Party joined them from the Fort, which they expected every Moment, they would cut us to Pieces but we absolutely refused to receive their proffered Mercy and I told them that we had Men sufficient to repell any Force that could come against us, and that we should have it in our Power to cut them to Pieces and scalp them. About Sun setting I received a slanting Wound in my Hand thro my Wrist which disabled me from loading my Gun, on which I sent a Man to the Rest of my Officers desiring them not to be discouraged but maintain their Ground, which they did very gallantly till Daylight ceased when both Sides left of Firing, upon which I consulted all my Officers who unanimously were of Opinion, that it was more prudent to carry off the wounded of our Party and take the Advantage of the Night to return Homeward, least the Enemy should send out a fresh Party upon us in the Morning, and then our Ammunition being almost expended we were obliged to pursue this Resolution, so travelled all Night, and the next Morning[12] dispatched Lieut. Stark with two Men to Fort William Henry to get Slays to carry the wounded Men thither, and about seven O'Clock the same Evening he got in, and[13] in the Morning was met by a Party and one Slay at the first Narrows, and in the Evening got into Fort William Henry with forty five Effectives and nine wounded Men.[14] We imagined the Enemy consisted of two Hundred and Fifty French and Indians, of which Number we suppose forty were killed[15] besides the Prisoners we had taken, and that we wounded many of them.'-(From the printed account in the Boston News-Letter, Feb 10, 1757-No 2849, The original is *in the* Loudoun Papers, Huntington Library, LO 2704 A&B. *Loudoun's copy to Prime Minister Fox is in the British* Colonial Office, 5: 48, pp 194, 197, 197-204. *Exact copies were printed in the Provincial Newspapers.*).

FOOTNOTES FOR THE ABOVE ACCOUNT:*Consist of the additions found in the Rogers' Journals Account:*
1'Agreeable to orders from the commanding officer at Fort Edward,'
2'where we were employed in providing provisions, snowshoes, etc.'
3'on the ice down Lake George'.
4'8 miles from our landing, and 3 from the lake, where we encamped.'
5'north by east the whole day'
6'eight or ten sleds'
7'From this account of things, and knowing that those who escaped would give early notice of us at Ticonderoga, I concluded it best to return'
8'it being a rainy day'
9'advanced half a mile, or thereabouts, over broken ground,'
10'which gave us an opportunity to ascend, and post ourselves to advantage.' *Rogers states in his Journals that he formed his line of battle at this time, but in the original report he states that he did not form his line until after all the major attacks had been beaten back. Continuing his printed 'Journals' account he states that:* 'After which I ordered Lt. Stark and Mr. Baker in the center, with Ensign Rogers; Sergeants Walter and Phillips with a party, being a reserve, to prevent our being flanked, and watch the motions of the enemy. Soon after we had thus formed ourselves for battle, the enemy attempted to flank us on the right but the above reserve bravely attacked them'
11'till the darkness prevented our seeing each other,'
12'arrived at Lake George, about six miles south of the French advance guard,'
13'the next morning we were met by a party of 15 men and a sled, under the command of Lt. Bulkeley of Hobb's Company of Rangers'
14'48 effective, and six wounded men, arrived... being the 23rd of January, 1757.'
15'we afterwards had an account from the enemy, that their loss in this action, of those killed, and who afterwards died of their wounds, amounted to 116 men. *Rogers adds the following tribute:*

329

'Both the officers and soldiers I had the honour
to command, who survived the first onset, behaved
with the most undaunted bravery and resolution,
and seemed to vie with each other in their respective
stations who should excel.'

LOSSES OF ROGERS' FORCE:

*Compiled from a digest of both of Rogers' Accounts
and the various other Ranger and French Accounts:*

ROGERS' OWN COMPANY

Captain Robert Rogers Wounded in head and hand.
Sergt James Henry Captured, later escaped.
Sergt (Priv) Wm. Morris Captured, later escaped.
Private Hugh Morrison Wounded 11 times, Captured.
Private Thomas Stinson Killed.
Private Thomas Burnside Wounded in hand.

RICHARD ROGERS' COMPANY

Ensign Caleb Page Killed.
Private Joseph Stephens Killed.
Private Benjamin Woodall Captured, joined French.
Private David Kimble Captured, joined the French.
Private Joshua Martin Wounded in stomach and hip.
Private David Page Wounded in the side.
Private Nathaniel Merril Wounded in the forehead.
Private John Shute Wounded in the head.

HOBBS' COMPANY

Sergt Jonathan Howard Killed.
Corporal John Edmunds Killed.
Private Phineas Kemp Killed.
Private Thomas Farmer Killed.
Private Emanuel Lapertagee Killed.
Corporal Ebenezer Perry Wounded-shot in shoulder.

SPEAKMAN'S COMPANY

Capt Thomas Speakman Wounded, Scalped alive, beheaded
Lieutenant Samuel Kennedy Killed.
Corporal Samuel Fisk Killed.
Private Robert Avery Killed.
Private Thomas Brown Wounded, Captured, Exchanged.
Sergt Increase Moore Wounded slightly in the arm.
Private Jonathan Cahill Wounded in the mouth.
Private Michael Connelly Wounded on Jan 24, roll.
Private John Carrole Wounded on Jan 24, roll.

VOLUNTEERS

Andrew Gardiner of Rogers' own Company, Killed.
Robert Baker of the 44th Regt. Wounded & Captured.

TOTAL LOSSES:
KILLED: *13* CAPTURED: *7 (3 escaped)* WOUNDED: *11* who returned with Rogers. Two of these received minor wounds. One of the men captured may be added to those killed for he died as a consequence of the 11 wounds he received in the battle. Two others taken were also wounded bringing the total to 13.
 The fate of all the seven captives has been discovered. They are listed in the order of their death or escape.
-*Private Hugh Morrison* Died the middle of February of his eleven battle wounds.
-*Private Benjamin Woodall* Sold out to Rigaud and was killed in March or May by his Indian captors.
-*Private David Kimble* Sold out to Rigaud to guide him to Wm. Henry. Killed in Mar or May by Indians.
-*Sergt Wm Morris* Escaped from Montreal May 7, 1757
-*Sergt James Henry* Escaped from Montreal June 1757
-*Private Thomas Brown* Exchanged Nov 19, 1758.-
-*Volunteer Robert Baker* Reported alive and recovering from his wounds. Not known if exchanged.

ACCOUNTS OF THE THREE RANGERS WHO ESCAPED:
SERGT WILLIAM MORRIS'S ACCOUNT: *In the Boston News-Letter, June 16, 1757, re-printed from a N.Y. Newspaper, June 6, 1757:* 'Since our last, came to town, one, Wm. Morris, a Ranger, who was taken prisoner by the French, in the Engagement near Ticonderoga on the 21st of Jan last, with Capt Rogers (now promoted to the Rank of Major) & informs us, That immediately on his being captivated, he was carried with 6 more of his companions to Ticonderoga (one of which died 3 weeks after, having received 11 shot in his Body) where there was then only 40 Men left in Garrison; 200 Regulars, 45 Indians and 36 Canadians, having sallied out to attack Major Rogers whose Party only consisted of 75 Men; when 30 of the Enemy were killed on the spot, and 32 more died soon after they reached the Fort. Having remained a Month at Ticonderoga he was sent to Crown Point where he halted 1 night, being carried from thence by some of the Ottaway Indians, whose Prisoner he was, and who proposed to carry him to their Country and adopt him for one of their Children; but the Severity of the Weather obliging them to remain some time at Montreal, he found an opportunity when the Indians were gone upon a Scout, to make his Escape, with 3 more, and left Montreal May 7th with about 4 days Provisions and Gun and some Powder and Ball which he took out of the Indian Hut. They all arrived safe at Ft. Wm

Henry May 18, much fatigued'.
SERGEANT JAMES HENRY'S ACCOUNT: *In Boston. News-Letter, July 1, 1757, reprint from a N.Y. paper:*
   'Our Accounts from Albany since our last, are, that on June 8th, one other of Rogers' Rangers who was taken in the Battle Rogers had last Winter, came in there from the Enemy and gave out, that in that Battle there were 23 Whites and 9 Indians killed outright on the side of the French; that 39 were dangerously wounded, insomuch that they all died with their wounds, save 5; and that when he made his Escape, one of them was dying. That he, together with the other of his Brother-Prisoners, were carried to Ticonderoga, where there were not above 30 men posted (all invalids), that he was carried from thence to Montreal, where he was employed in cutting and raising Timber from the West Side of Lake Champlain, from thence he made his Escape. That the French and Indians at Ticonderoga when they returned from Rogers' Battle and afterwards from Ft. Wm. Henry, came in scattered and much dejected, Numbers being killed and many perished in the Woods returning.'
PRIVATE THOMAS BROWN'S ACCOUNT: *Excerpts from Brown's 'Narrative' printed in Boston, 1760, by Fowle and Draper. Outside of Rogers' report, this is the best account of the action by a Ranger participant. Due to the sufferings that Brown experienced as a consequence of the battle he was somewhat prejudiced against Rogers because he was unfortunate enough to be one of the few wounded Rangers that were overlooked in the darkness.-*
   'On the 18th of Jan. 1757, we march'd on a Scout from Fort William Henry; Major Rogers himself headed us. All were Voluntiers that went on this Scout. We came to the Road leading from Tionderoga to Crown Point, and on Lake Champlain (which was froze over) we saw about 50 Sleys; the Major thought proper to attack them and ordered us all, about 60 in Number, to lay in Ambush, and when they were near enough we were order'd to pursue them. I happened to be near the Major when he took the first Prisoner, a Frenchman. I singled out one and follow'd him. They fled some one Way and some another, but soon I came up with him and took him. We took seven in all, the rest Escaping, some to Crown Point, and some return'd to Tionderoga. When we had brought the Prisoners to Land the Major examined them, and they inform'd him that there were 35 Indians and 500 Regulars at Tionderoga. It be-

ing a rainy Day we made a Fire and dry'd our Guns. The Major tho't best to return to Fort William Henry in the same Path we came, the Snow being very deep; we march'd in an Indian File and kept the Prisoners in the Rear, lest we should be attack'd. We proceeded in this Order about a Mile and a half, and as we were ascending a Hill, and the Centre of our Men were at the Top, the French, to the Number of 400 besides 30 or 40 Indians, fired on us before we discovered them. The Major ordered us to advance. I receiv'd a Wound from the Enemy (the First shot they made on us) thro' the Body, upon which I retir'd into the Rear, to the Prisoner I had taken on the Lake, knock'd him on the Head and killed him, lest he should Escape and give information to the Enemy; and as I was going to place myself behind a large Rock, there started up an Indian from the other Side; I threw myself backward into the Snow, and it being very deep, sunk so low that I broke my Snowshoes (I had Time to pull 'em off, but was obliged to let my Shoes go with them) one Indian threw his Tomahawk at me, and another was just upon seizing me; but I happily escaped and got to the Centre of our Men, and fix'd myself behind a large Pine, where I loaded and fir'd every Opportunity; after I had discharged 6 or 7 times, there came a Ball and cut off my Gun just at the Lock. About half an Hour after, I receiv'd a Shot in my Knee; I crawled again into the Rear, and as I was turning about receiv'd a Shot in my Shoulder. The Engagement held, as near as I could guess, 5½ Hours, and as I learnt after I was taken, we Killed more of the Enemy than we were in Number. By this Time it grew dark and the Firing ceased on both Sides, and as we were so few the Major took the Advantage of the Night and escaped with the well Men, without informing the wounded of his Design, lest they should inform the Enemy and they should pursue him before he had got out of their Reach.'-See text, pp 136-137............

'..As I was travelling as well as I could, or rather creeping along, I found one of our People dead; I pull'd off his Stockings (he had no shoes) and put them on my own Legs.

'By this Time the Body of the Enemy had made a Fire, and had a large number of Centries out on our Path, so that I was obliged to creep quite around them before I could get into the Path; but just before I came to it I saw a Frenchman behind a Tree, within two Rods of me, but the Fire shining right on him prevented his seeing me. They cried out about every Quarter of an Hour in French All is Well! And while he that was so near me was speaking, I took the Opportunity to creep away, that he might not hear me, and by this Means got clear of him and got into our Path. But the Snow and Cold put my Feet into such Pain, as I had no Shoes, that I could not go on. I therefore sat down by a Brook, and wrapt my Feet in my Blanket. But my Body being cold by sitting still, I got up, and crawl'd along in this miserable Condition the Remainder of the Night.

'The next Day, about 11 o'clock, I heard the Shouts of Indians behind me, and I suppos'd they saw me; within a few Minutes four came down a Mountain, running towards me. I threw off my Blanket, and Fear and Dread quickened my Pace for a while; but, by Reason of the Loss of so much Blood from my Wounds, I soon fail'd When they were within: a few Rods of me they cock'd their Guns, and told me to stop; but I refus'd hoping they would fire and kill me on the Spot; which I chose, rather than the dreadful Death Capt. Spikeman died of. They soon came up with me, took me by the Neck and Kiss'd me. On searching my Pockets they found some money, which they were so fond of, that in trying who could get most, they had like to have Kill'd me. They took some dry leaves and put them into my Wounds, and then turn'd about and ordered me to follow them.

'When we came near the main Body of the Enemy, the Indians made a Live-Shout, as they call it when they bring in a Prisoner alive (different from the Shout they make when they bring in Scalps, which they call a Dead-Shout). The Indians ran to meet us, and one of them struck me with a Cutlass across the Side; he cut thro' my Cloaths, but did not touch my Flesh; others ran against me with their Heads. I asked if there was no Interpreter, upon which a Frenchman cry'd, I am one. I ask'd him, if this was the way they treated their Prisoners, to let them be cut and beat to Pieces by the Indians? He desired me to come to him; but the Indians would not let me, holding me one by one Arm and another by the other. But there arising a Difference between the four Indians that took me, they fell to fighting, which their commanding Officer seeing, he came and took me away and carry'd me to the Interpreter; who drew his sword, and pointing it to my Breast, charged me to tell the

Truth, or he would run me through. He then ask'd
me what Number of Scout consisted of? - I told
him 50. He ask'd where they were gone? I told him,
I supposed as they were so numerous they could
best tell. He said I told him wrong; for he Knew
of more than 100 that were Slain; I told him we
had lost but 19 in all. He said there were as many
Officers. On which he led me to Lieut. Kennedy. I
saw he was much Tomahawk'd by the Indians. He as-
k'd me if he was an Officer. I told him, he was a
Lieutenant. And then he took me to another; who, I
told him, was an Ensign. From thence he carried me
to Captain Spikeman, who was laying in the Place I
left him; they had cut off his Head, and fix'd it-
on a Pole.

'I beg'd for a Pair of Shoes, and something to
Eat; the Interpreter told me, I should have Relief
when I came to Tionderoga, which was but one Mile
and a ¼ off, and then delivered me to the 4 Indians
that took me. The Indians gave me a Piece of Bread
and put a Pair of Shoes on my Feet.

'About this Time Robert Baker, mentioned above,
was brought where I was; we were extremely glad to
see each other, tho' we were in such a distress'd
Condition. He told me of five Men that were taken.
We were ordered to march on toward Tionderoga. But
Baker replied, he could not walk. An Indian then -
pushed him forward; but he could not go, and there
fore sat down and cried; whereupon an Indian took
him by the Hair, and was going to kill him with
his Tomahawk. I was moved with Pity for him, and,
weak as I was, I took his Arms over my Shoulders, and was enabled to get him to the Fort.

'We were immediately sent to the Guard House,
and about half an Hour after, brought before the
Commanding-Officer, who, by his Interpreter, examined us separately; after which he again sent us
to the Guard-House. The Interpreter came and told
us, that we were to be hang'd the next Day, because we had kill'd the 7 Prisoners we had taken
on the Lake; but was afterwards so kind as to tell
us, this was done only to terrify us. About an
Hour after came a Doctor, and his Mate, and dressed our Wounds; and the Commanding-Officer sent us
a Quart of Claret. We lay all Night on the Boards,
without Blankets. The next Day I was put into the
Hospital, (the other Prisoners were carried another Way) here I tarried till the 19th of Feb. and
the Indians insisted on having me, to carry to
their Homes, and broke into the Hospital; but the

Centinel call'd the Guard and turn'd them out; after which the commanding Officer prevailed with them to let me stay 'till the 1st of March, by which Time I was able to walk about the Fort.

'As I was one Day in the Interpreter's Lodging, there came in 10 or 12 Indians, with the Scalps they had taken, in order to have a War Dance. They set me on the Floor, and put 7 of the Scalps on my Head while they danc'd; when it was over, they lifted me up in triumph. But as I went and stood by the Door, two Indians began to dance a Live-Dance, and one of them threw a Tomahawk at me, to kill me, but I wathc'd his Motion and dodg'd the Weapon.... See text, pp 157-158.

'..Soon after this I was taken out of Irons, and went to live with the Interpreter till the 27th of March, at which Time the Indians took me with them in order to go Montreal and set me to draw a large Sled with Provisions, my Arms being tied with a Rope. By the Time we got to Crown Point, I was so lame that I could not walk. The Indians went ashore and built a Fire, and then told me I must dance; to which I complied rather than be kill'd. When we set off again I knew not how to get rid of my Sled, and I knew I was not able to draw it, but this Fancy came into my Head. I took three Squaws on my Sled, and pleasantly told them I wish'd I was able to draw 'em. All this took with the Indians; they freed me of the Sled, and gave it to other Prisoners. They stripp'd off all my Cloaths, and gave me a Blanket. And the next Morning they cut off my Hair and painted me, and with Needles and Indian ink prick'd on the back of my Hand the Form of one of the ScalingLadders which the French made to carry to Fort William Henry. I understood they were vex'd with the French for the Disappointment.

'We travelled about nine Miles on Lake Champlain and when the Sun was two Hours high we stop'd; they made a Fire, and took one of the Prisoners that had not been wounded, and were going to cut off his Hair, as they had done mine. He foolishly resisted them, upon which they prepar'd to burn him; but the Commanding Officer prevented it at this Time. But the next Night they made a Fire, stripp'd and ty'd him to a Stake,' (apparently this was either Woodall or Kimble who had sold out to Rigaud, for all the other captives have been-accounted for) 'and the Squaws cut Pieces of Pine, like Skewers, and thrust them into his Flesh, and

set them on Fire, and then fell to pow wowing and
dancing round him; and ordered me to do the same.
Love of Life obliged me to comply, for I could expect no better Treatment if I refus'd. With a bit-
ter and heavy Heart I feigned myself merry. They
cut the poor man's Cords, and made him run backwards and forwards. I heard the poor Man's Cries
to Heaven for Mercy; and at length, thro' extreme
Anguish and Pain, he pitched himself into the
flames and expired.
'From thence we travelled, without any Thing
worthy of Notice happening, 'till we came to an
Indian Town, about 20 Miles from Montreal. When we
were about a Gun's shot from the Town, the Indians
made as many Shouts as they had Prisoners, and as
many dead Ones as they had Scalps. The Men and Women came out to meet us, and stripp'd me naked;
after which they pointed to a Wigwam and told me
to run to it, pursuing me all the Way with Sticks
and Stones.
'Next Day we went to Montreal, where I was carried before Governor Vaudreuill and examined. Afterwards I was taken into a French Merchant's
House, and there I lived three Days. The third
Night two of the Indians that took me came in
drunk and asked for me; upon which the Lady called
me into the Room, and as I went and stood by the
Door, one of them began to dance the War-Dance
about me, disigning to kill me; but as he lifted
up his hand to stab me, I catch'd hold of it with
one of mine, and with the other knock'd him down,
and then ran up Garret and hid. The Lady sent for
some Neighbours to clear the House of her Guests
which they did. It was a very cold Night, and one
of the Indians being excessive drunk, fell down
near the House and was found in the morning froze
to death. The Indians came to the House, and finding their Brother dead, said I had kill'd him; and
gathering a number together with their Guns, beset
the House and demanded me of the Lady, saying I
should die the most cruel Death. The Lady told me
of it, and advis'd me to hide myself in the Cellar
under the Pipes of Wine; which I did. They searched the House and even came down Cellar, but could
not find me. The Lady desired a Frenchman to tell
the Indians That he saw me without the City, running away. They soon took after me, every Way. The
Merchant pitying my condition, covered me with a
Blanket and carried me in his Conveyance about five
Miles, to a Village where his Wife's Father lived,

in order to keep me out of the Way of the Indians.
When the Indians that pursued me had returned, and
could not find me, they concluded that I was concealed by the Merchant; and applied to the Governor that I might be delivered to them in order
that they might kill me for killing their Brother;
adding, by way of threatening, that if I was not
delivered up to them they would turn and be against the French. The Governor told them he had
examined into the Matter, and found that I did not
kill the Indian nor know any Thing about it; but
that he froze to Death. On this they said they
would not kill me, but would have me to live with
them. The Governor then informed them where I was,
and they came and took me with them to Montreal
again, and dressed me in their Habit.
'On the 1st of May we set off to go to the Mississipi, where my Indian Master belonged, and two
other English Prisoners with them. For several
Days the Indians treated me very ill; but it wore
off. We went in Bark Canoes, 'till we came to Lake
Sacrement, the first Carrying Place. We continued
our Journey till we came to the Ohio, where General Braddock was defeated. Here they took one of
the Prisoners,' (Apparently this was either Woodall or Kimble who had sold out to Rigaud, for all
the other captives have been accounted for) 'and
with a Knife ript open his Belly, took one End of
his Guts and tied it to a tree, and then whipt the
miserable Man round and round till he expired; obliging me to dance, while they made their Game at
the dying Man. From hence we set off to go to an
Indian Town about 200 Miles from the Ohio, where
we arrived in 15 Days, and tarried three. The
third Night one of the Indians had a mind to Kill
me; as I was standing by the Fire he ran against
me to push me into the Flames, but I jumped over,
and Escaped being burnt; he followed me round and
round, and struck me several Times with his Head
and Fist; which so provoked me that as he was Coming at me again I struck him and knock'd him backwards. The other Indians laugh'd, and said I was a
good Fellow.
'The next day we set off for the Mississippi,
where we arrived the 23d of August, having passed
over thirty-two Carrying-Places from our leaving
Montreal. When we came here I was ordered to live
with a Squaw, who was to be my Mother. I liv'd
with her during the Winter, and was employed in
Hunting, dressing Leather, &c., being cloath'd af-

ter the Indian Fashion.

'In the Spring a French Merchant came a Trading in Bark Canoes, and on his Return wanted Hands to help him; he prevailed with my Mistress to let me go with him to Montreal. When we came there, and the Canoes were unloaded, I went into the Country and liv'd with his Wife's Father, and worked at the Farming Business for my Victuals and Cloathing I fared no better than a Slave. The Family often endeavoured to persuade me to be of their Religion making many fair Promises if I would. Wanting to see what Alteration this would make in their Conduct towards me, one Sunday Morning I came to my Mistress, and said, Mother, will you give me good Cloaths, if I will go to Mass? She answered Yes, Son, as good as any in the House. She did so, and I rode to Church with two of her Daughters; in giving me Directions how to behave they told me I must do as they did. When we came Home I sat at the Table and ate with the Family, and Every Night and Morning was taught my Prayers.

'Thus I lived 'till the next Spring, when my Master's Son-in-law, that bro't me from the Mississippi, came for me to return with him, as he again there to trade. I refus'd to go, and applied to the Governor. I was then put into Gaol, where I tarried 5 weeks, living on Bread and Water and Horse-Beef. When some Prisoners were going to be sent to Quebeck, in order to be trwnsported to Old France, I went with them. Here we laid in Gaol 6 Weeks. But happening to see one of my Master's Sons, he prevailed with me to go back with him and work as formerly; I consented, and tarried with him till the 8th of September.

'There was at the next House an English Lad, a Prisoner; we agreed to run away together, through the Woods, that so, if possible, we might get home to our Friends. But how to get Provisions for the Way, we Knew not; till I was allowed a Gun to kill Pigeons, which were very plenty here. I shot a number, split and dried them, and concealed in the Woods. We agreed to set off on a Sunday Morning, and were to meet at an appointed Place, which we did, and began our Journey towards Crown-Point. After we had travelled 22 Days, 15 of which we had no Provisions except Roots, worms and such like, we were so weak and faint that we could scarce walk. My Companion gave out, and could go no further; he desired me to leave him, but I would not. I went and found three Frogs, and divided them between us. The next Morning he died. I sat down by him, and at first concluded to make a Fire, as I had my Gun, and eat his Flesh, and if no Relief came, to die with him; but finally came to this Resolution: to cut off of his Bones as much Flesh as I could and tie it up in a Handkerchief, and so proceed as well as I could. Accordingly I did so, and buried my Companion on the Day I left him. I got three Frogs more the next Day. Being weak and tired, about 9 o'clock I sat down, but could not eat my Friend's Flesh. I expected soon to die myself; and while I was commending my Soul to God I saw a Partridge light just by me, which I thought was sent by Providence. I was so weak that I could not hold out my Gun; but by resting, I brought my Piece to bear, so that I kill'd the Partridge. While I was eating of it, there came two Pigeons, so near, that I kill'd em both. As I fired two Guns I heard a Gun at a Distance. I fired again and was answered twice. This roused me; I got up and travelled as fast as I could towards the Report of the Guns; and about half a Mile off, I saw three Canadians. I went to 'em, and pretended to be a Dutchman, one of their own Regulars, that was lost in the Woods. They brought me to Crown Point; upon which I desired to see the Commanding Officer. He knew me again, and asked me how I came there. I told him my story and what difficulties I had met with. He ordered me to the Guard-House, and to be put in irons. About an hour after he sent me a Bowl of Rice. After I had been at Crown Point ten or twelve Days, the Commanding Officer sent me back under a Guard of 12 Soldiers to Montreal,- in a Battoe, and wrote a Letter (as I afterwards understood) to my Master not to hurt me.

'When I came to the House, one of his Daughters met me at the Door, and pushed me back, and want and called her Father. At this House there was a French Captain, of the Regulars, billeted; he was a Protestant. He hearing my Voice, called me to him and asked me where I had been. Upon my telling him he called me a Fool, for attempting a thing so impossible. My Master coming in, took me by the Shoulder, and threatened to kill me for stealing his Gun when I ran away. But the good Captain prevented him from using any Violence. The Captain asked me if I had been before the Governor; I told him I had not; and he then advis'd my Master to send his Son with me (who was an Ensign among the Canadians). When he came to a small Ferry, which we were to pass, I refus'd to go any further; and after a great deal of do, he went without me. On his Return, he said he had got leave of the Governor, that I should go back to his Father and work as formerly. Accordingly I lived with him 'till the 19th of November; and when Col. Schuyler was coming away, I came with him to Albany...' Brown joined Gage's Light Infantry and was re-captured in Sept 1759; lived again with the Farmer until Nov 25, 1759 when he was exchanged. Except for certain errors in his description of the Battle, Brown's 'Narrative' is an excellent account of the fate of captured Rangers. It is to bad that more Rangers were not as prolific in recording their experiences.

CAPTAIN JOHN STARK'S ACCOUNT: Stark bagged his first Indian in this Battle for he: '...stated in after life that he was never conscious of taking the life of an individual except in this action. While the Rangers were defending their position on the crest of the hill he observed that several balls struck near him from a certain direction. In a moment afterward he discovered an Indian stretched at full length upon a rock, behind a tree. His gun was soon ready and he shot the Indian through the head as he was about to fire again and the Indian rolled off the rock into the snow which was four feet deep on the level ground'.- (Caleb Stark, Memoir and Corr. of John Stark, p 19)

PRIVATES JOHN SHUTE'S & SAMUEL EASTMAN'S ACCOUNT: These two veterans of Rogers Rangers, both from Concord, N.H., collaborated and agreed in their statements on the Battle: '..Shute says that after taking the sleds, a council of war advised to return by a different route from that by which the party came, which was the usual practice of the Rangers, and on this occasion would have enabled them to escape the hazards of a battle. Rogers however, said in regard to the enemy, that they would not dare to pursue him, and took the same route back. The first notice the Rangers had of the enemy was the noise in cocking their guns, which Shute supposed was one of the Rangers preparing to kill a partridge. He was himself struck senseless by a shot which ploughed the top of his head. On coming to himself, the first sight which meet his eyes, was one of the Rangers cutting off Rogers' cue to stop the hole in his wrist, through which a shot

had passed.'-(Caleb Stark's 'Reminiscenses of the
French War', Concord, N.H., 1861).

BRITISH ACCOUNTS:
Three of the following 7 accounts trace British
opinion from Maj. Eyre at Wm. Henry to Loudoun in
Boston. The other four are here printed because
they a. so portray interesting and newly discovered
reference to the Battle:
MAJOR EYRE'S ACCOUNT TO GENERAL ABERCROMBIE:
Jan 28, 1757-: 'I am sorry to acquaint you that
Captain Rogers has failed in his Scout towards the
Enemy. This afternoon he returned with 54 men out
of 73 he took from hence. It is imagined that 4 or
5 are taken prisoners. Last Fryday About 10 or 11
o'clock, when he no sooner arrived than he saw a
Slay on the ice going towards Crown Point, he immediately sent a few men to head the Sley, which
was no sooner done than some more appeared behind;
the foremost Slay being stoped, those in the rear
discover'd it, so they immediately turns about to
get back as fast as they could to Ticonderoga; how
ever he took 7 Prisoners and 2 or 3 horses.....
Capt. Rogers got to the river between Crown
Point and Tyconderoga.........By all accounts
they behaved gallantly and I apprehend did
a good deal of execution; their prisoners they
knocked in the head as soon as they were attacked.
Each party was drawn up upon the side of rising
ground with a small valley between and by what I
can learn we were most advantageously posted. The
Regulars exposed themselves much so as to afford as
fair shots to our people as they could wish. The
Indions were the only marksmen that did execution;
by their accts this savage race behaved well.
By what I can learn Capt. Rogers thought it not
prudent to remain any longer then, as the enemy
were so superior and within hearing of the garris-
son of Ticonderoga, so left the enemy then about
half an hour after the firing ceased and made the
best of his way to this Place. From here he sets
out tomorrow for Fort Edward. He is shot thro his
left hand and grazed on the head by a ball. He
brought in four men hurt, viz., very much and two
others slightly. Our Rangers here have lost by
this Accident two of the best Officers, and eight
or nine chosen men, and though I have two companies here they are by no means equal in goodness
to those at Fort Edward; for several of them are
very young and I am amprehensive they are not able

to bear much hardship. You are the best judge what
should be done in this case.
This affair may likely (provock)...some of our
neighbors (at) the other end of the Lake to return
the Visit; I shall do my (endeavor) to prevent any
accident from happening. I have not yet been able
to get the Rangers Picketed quite sound the Ground
being so exceptionally hard, besides the moving of
the huts into one Place for that purpose Have
greately increased the work.
The Lake is quite frozen over from here to the
Falls which procures the Enemy easy access to this
place. By any means that I can think of I shall
not be wanting to have all things in Readiness to
do our best. P.S: There are two or three wounded
more than I mentioned'.-(LO 2718. Courtesy of the
Huntington Library, San Marino, California.)

GENERAL ABERCROMBIE'S ACCOUNT TO LOUDOUN: From
Albany, Jan 27, 1757: '...Captain Robert Rogers...
behaviour upon this late Occasion intitles him to
marks of your Lordship's favour and Countenance.
His relation by way of journal is very modest; for
besides the French and Canadians which dropt, I am
told that about 15 Indians shared the same fate;
and if they had not been this roughly handled they
would have certainly pursued him, and at least
prevented his carrying off his wounded men. The
prisoners Rogers took informed him that this party
of Canadians and Indians were intended to set out
the next day to attempt the cutting off our convoys
between the two forts, which luckily are very well
supplied, for a much larger number than what these
Garrissons consist of..'-(LO 2716. Courtesy of the
Huntington Library).

LOUDOUN'S ACCOUNT TO PRIME MINISTER FOX: From
Boston, Feb 8, 1757, Loudoun sends a copy of Rogers' original report accompanied by his letter in
which he notes that '..Abercrombie Acquaints me
that Rogers thinks, there were fourteen of the
french Indians amongst those killed, if that is
true, it will carry all the others home, and they
will find it very difficult to bring them out again'.
-(Colonial Office, 5: 48, pp 194, 197-204).

CAPT. JAMES ABERCROMBIE TO ROGERS: From Albany,
Feb 6, 1757, 'The General received your letter
that was sent by Major Sparks, and returns you and
your men thanks for their behaviour, and has re-

commended both you and them strongly to my Lord
Loudoun, as also that they have payment for the
prisoners' (scalps) 'they took. Upon receiving an
account of your skirmish we sent an express to
Boston, and, by the said opportunity recommended,
for Spikeman's company, your brother James Rogers
for a Lt. We expect the express back in a day or
two, by whom, I dare say, we shall have my Lord's
approbation of the Rangers. Please to send me the
names of the officers you would recommend for your
own company, and also to fill up the vacancies in
the others; as I am certain you have the good of
the service at heart, your recommendation will be
paid great regard to. I yesterday received your's
of the 30th of January. You cannot imagine how all
ranks of people here are pleased with your conduct
and your mens behaviour; for my part it is no more
than I expected. I was so pleased with their appearance when I was out with them, that I took it
for granted they would behave well whenever they
met the enemy. When I returned I reported them as
such, & am glad they have answered my expectation.

'I am heartily sorry for Spikeman and Kennedy,
who I imagined would have turned out well, as likewise for the men you have lost; but it is impossible to play at bowls without meeting with rubs. We
must try to revenge the loss of them. There is few
people that will believe it; but, upon honour, I
could be glad to have been with you, that I might
have learned the manner of fighting in this country. The chance of being shot is all stuff, and
King William's principle is much the best for a
soldier, viz. 'that every bullet has its billet,'
and that 'It is allotted how every man shall die;'
so that I am certain that every one will agree,
that it is better to die with the reputation of a
brave man, fighting for his country in a good cause
than either shamefully running away to preserve
one's life, or lingering out an old age and dying
in one's bed, without having done his country or
his King any service. The histories of this country, particularly, are full of the unheard of
cruelties committed by the French, and the Indians
by their instigation which I think every brave man
ought to do his 'utmost to humble that haughty nation, or reduce their bounds of conquest in this
country to a narrow limit. As soon as General Abercrombie receives my Lord's instructions in regard to the Rangers I shall send you notice of it.
In the meantime I hope you will get the better

of your wound. If I can be of any service to you
of your men as long as they continue to behave so
well, you may command. Your most humble servant,
James Abercrombie, Aid-de-Campe'-(Rogers, Jrn,47)

COLONEL RALPH BURTON TO LOUDOUN: from Albany,
Feb 2, 1757, '..Rogers and his people by all the
accounts, I have, had behaved extremely well, are
not dejected from their loss, on the contrary are
elated from being convinced they behaved well and
killed above twice the number of the enemy that
they themselves lost. It's certainly right encouraging them in this believe.'-(LO 2753. Courtesy of
the Huntington Library.).

NEWS OF, AND RECOMMENDATION FOR ROBERT BAKER: On
April 28, 1757, the Boston News-Letter printed an
Extract of a letter from N.Y., dated April 11, giving details gleaned from a recent French prisoner
'..Baker who was supposed to be killed in Rogers'
Affair some time since, is yet alive, a Prisoner
with the French, and is thought will recover of
his Wounds. Rogers killed at that time 28 of the
Enemy on the Spot, of which 15 were Indians and 28
more died afterwards of their wounds..'
On Aug 8, 1757, Major Massey Eyre, at Halifax,
strongly recommended Baker to Loudoun for an Ensign's berth, stating that although Baker was
still a prisoner, he had behaved exceptionally
well under Wm Eyre's command at Ft. Wm. Henry and
while with Rogers at La Barbue Creek..-(LO 4147).
Baker is the only one of the 7 prisoners who has
not been definitly accounted for. Eyre evidently
expected Baker to be exchanged soon but his name
does not appear on any exchange lists and his name
does not appear in Ford's British Officers who
Served in North America. The only logical answer:
is that Baker either died in prison or was shipped
to France and exchanged there directly to England.

MATRON CHARLOTTE BROWN'S ACCOUNT: Even the Matron
of the General Hospital with the English forces in
North America found time while stationed at Albany
to pen a few lines in her Journal about the Battle: 'Jan 27: News came from the Lake that Capt.
Rogers had ingaged with a Party of French and was
much wounded and had lost 20 of his Men but he had
taken 7 Prisoners and killed them all and retreated.'-(In Colonial Captivities, Marches and Journeys
by Isabel M. Calder, N.Y., 1935). She might have

received more information from Rogers himself for he was a patient at her hospital for some time.

PROVINCIAL ACCOUNTS:
Are many but their principal source is the newspaper account of Rogers official report. There were no Provincial troops at the two Forts where the Rangers were stationed consequently no additional details were found in their Diaries. However the scope of Rogers Rangers' public is revealed in the fact that the Virginia Gazette, No 328, Mar 30, 1757, print: '..We are credibly informed..that the French in the late Action with the brave Captain Rogers, had not less than 50 Men killed & wounded'.

While Provincial Robert Eastburn, a prisoner at Montreal records a first hand account from Sergeant Henry: '..I was informed by Serjeant Henry, who was brought in Prisoner, being taken in a Battle, when gallant, indefatigable Captain Rogers, made a brave Stand, against more than twice his Number..' (Robert Eastburn's Narrative, 1758, pp 60-61).

FRENCH ACCOUNTS:
French accounts are many and they differ in losses sustained by both sides and other details of the fight and aftermath. In regard to Rogers' ambuscade at Five Mile Point the French and Rangers accounts agree. The principal French source is De-Lusignan's official report to Governor Vaudreuil and General Montcalm.-(In Quebec Documents, IV, 91)

MONTCALM'S ACCOUNT: Montcalm copied Lusignan's report almost verbatim in his Journal.-(Printed by the Abbe Casgrain in Vol VII, pp 147-149 of 'Collection des Manuscripts du Marechal Levis'). Montcalm copied from this for the following accounts to France:

Montcalm to M. de Paulmy, Minister of the Navy Board (the affairs of New France were conducted through his department), dated Montreal, Apr 24, 1757: '..A detachment of 60 picked men of the English troops, with 10 sergeants and 7 officers, consisting in all of 77 men, set out to take some prisoners near our forts; captured 7 of our soldiers on the 21st January, between Fort Carillon and St. Frederic. On receipt of the news, M. de Lusignan, a Colonial Captain, commanding at Fort Carillon, detached 100 men under the orders of Messrs de Basserode and de Grandville, Captains in the regiments of Languedoc and La Reine, with some

Indians and Canadians. This detatchment came up with that of the enemy at three o'clock in the afternoon, and fell on their van-guard with fixed bayonets. As we had neglected to occupy a small hill near the road, the English retired thither, and the firing continued until nightfall. The enemy took advantage of the obscurity to retire, leaving on the field of battle 42 dead, 3 of whom were officers. We took 8 prisoners and recovered our men. It has since been ascertained that, of the 77 men composing this detatchment, only three reentered Fort George, the others having perished of cold and hunger, and perhaps of their wounds. We have had 9 men killed and 18 wounded, some of whom have died of their wounds. Captain de Basserode, who commanded, has been dangerously wounded. I cannot too highly praise the manner our officers and soldiers behaved in this engagement, which has been preety sharp, and devolved almost solely on the troops of the Line, as there was only one solitary Colonial Ensign and some Indians in it.'-(Documents Relative to the Colonial Hist of N.Y.,*X*,554)

On the same date Montcalm strongly recommended Captain Basserode to Count d'Argenson: 'I flatter myself that if you have not this year found sufficient seniority of service in M. De Basserode to entitle him to the Cross of St. Louis, his action and wound will procure it for him next year. I shall have the honor to write to you on the subject at the end of the campaign, when submitting to you favors for our battalions.-(Ibid, X, p 548)

Basserode was again wounded at the Battle of Ticonderoga, in July 1758.

A new Minister of the Navy Board was in office when Montcalm's and Vaudreuil's reports reached France, and he (M. de Moras) sent a congratulatory letter stating that the King was satisfied with the conduct of the land officers and troops; 'he has seen in it a proof of the zeal and emulation that exists in the various corps of the colony'.-(Canadian Archives, Orders of the King and Dispatches, Series B, Volume 105, Folio 28, 1 page).

The following anonymous account sent to France is identical with that of Montcalm in his Journal except for different statements of losses:

'Jan. 21, 1757: At 9 o'clock in the morning, Mon de Rouilly an officer of the Colony, acting as:-Major at Fort Carillon, received orders from M. De Lusignan, the Commandant to proceed to Ft. St Frederic and have some brandy and forage loaded there on eight sleighs, having 8 horses harnessed to each, under an escort of 15 soldiers and one sergeant, Messrs de Liebot, an officer of the Royal Rousillon, Varennes, a Colonial officer, two sleighs, with ten men had gone ahead; being at Presqu'isle, M. de Rouilly discovered the enemy issuing from the wood to the number of 70 or 80 men, who captured there two sleighs, and seven out of the ten men who were in charge of them were taken prisoners. The other three escaped on horseback. The enemy, to the number of 120, then advanced at great speed, detached the swiftest runners among their men to cut off our people but in vain. Under these circumstances M. de Rouilly sent off a man on horseback to the Commandant at Carillon, with news of what occurred. The latter, not wishing to have anything to reproach himself with, forthwith dispatched a detatchment of 100 men, including Indians, soldiers and Canadian Volunteers to intercept them, under the command of Captains de Basserode, of the Languedoc, La Granville of La Reine, Lieutenants Dastrel of the Languedoc, and Langlade a Colonial officer, with 5 Cadets; half an hour afterwards ten men were sent off to convey to our detatchment, provisions and ammunition, which it required.

About 3 o'clock in the afternoon this party halted and waited for the English, within 3 leagues of Fort Carillon, and seeing them come singing, allowed them to approach to within musket-shot, then saluted them with one-half of our musketry, the other having missed on account of the rain. This ceasing, the firing became brisk on both sides until nightfall, when the enemy, after retreating some time posted themselves very advantageously. In this interval two Canadians went to notify the fort that the ammunition was exhausted; the Commandant immediately ordered off a detachment of 25 men, under the command of M. Le Borgne, a Colonial officer, to carry some to them.

In the course of the night the enemy abandoned the field of battle, in order to retire, which they effected, leaving their provisions, ammunition and the arms of the wounded.

The English have lost 34 men who remained on the field; of these, three were officers. On our side we lost two soldiers of La Reine, two of the Royal Rousillon, two of Languedoc, and one Colonial.

We have taken 6 prisoners, who report that the English in the two forts of Lake St Sacrement num-

ber 1,000 men and that Governor-General Loudoun is to send a considerable army to attack Fort St. Frederic. It is calculated that we have lost, on this occassion, 11 soldiers in all, including Regulars and Colonists and one Sauteur Indian, and that we have had 27 wounded, among whom are Captain Basserode, of the Languedoc regiment and M. Clapier.'-(Docs.Rel.Col.Hist.N.Y.,X, pp 569-70).
This excellent impartial account is the best one of the Battle. Unlike Montcalm's or Vaudreuil's accounts, it does not hog the glory for the Regular or Colonial troops.

GOVERNOR-GENERAL VAUDREUIL'S ACCOUNT: to the Minister on April 19, 1757, emphasisis the part the Colonial troops played in the action due to the fact that Captain de Lusignan, the Commandant at Ticonderoga who launched the expedition, was a Colonial officer; and also Ensign Charles Langlade,: the veteran partisan of Braddock's Defeat fame. Although Vaudreuil's letter is full of his customary gasconade, it established the total number of men sent against Rogers. Ensign Langlade arrived at Ticonderoga the end of December with 90 Canadians and Ottawa Indians. They were making preparations for a raid south to the British forts when Rogers interrupted them and they sallied out against him accompanied by 89 Regulars, making a total of 179 men sent against Rogers' 74. Vaudreuil does not mention if Le Borgne's reenforcement of 25 men is included in this figure. If not, it would make 204, or almost three to one against Rogers.

FRENCH LOSSES: All French reports including De Lusignan's official report underestimate the true French losses. None but Montcalm would admit that any of the 27 or more wounded died. The two Ranger Sergeants who were captured and escaped state that 32 to 39 were wounded and all but four died. Considering that most of the wounded died probably De Lusignan's report is accurate enough, viz, 19 killed on the field of battle (including Rogers' 7 prisoners) and 27 wounded, of whom all but four died, making a total of 42 killed. Rogers' estimate in his report and printed 'Journals' of 40 killed and 76 wounded, who all died, is way out of line. Montcalm in his Journal states that only 8 were killed and 21 wounded. However he gives an interesting list of the losses of each Corps engaged and the names of the officers wounded:

CORPS	KILLED	WOUNDED	TOTAL
La Reine	2	4	6
Royal Roussillon	1	1	2
Languedoc	2	5	7
Troupes de la Colonie	1	5	6
Canadians	0	1	1
Indians	1	2	3
Officers, Cadets &	0	3	3
Storehouse Clerk*	1	0	1
TOTALS:	8	21	29

*The commander, Captain De Basserode was the Officer wounded. Senior Cadets De Mauran and De Clapier were wounded; while Sieur Sanguinet, was the brave Storehouse Clerk of Ticonderoga who died of his wounds.

BOUGAINVILLE'S ACCOUNT: of Sanguinet's distinguished part in the action is described in his Journal: 'Cinq commis des magasins qui avaient voulu aller a l'action s'y sont conduits a merveille; l'un d'eux a recu un coup de fusil a la gorge, dont il est mort le lendemain. En Canada, tout soldat n'est pas egalement brave'.

LOCATION AND DESCRIPTION OF THE BATTLEFIELD: The Battlefield is located by Mr. Watson in his History of Essex County, page 64, as near the residence of M.B.Townsend in the present town of Crown Point

The French Engineer, Captain Pouchot, gives a contemporary description of the Riviere a la Barbue (called Putnam's Creek by the English, and shortened at the present time to Put's Creek by local inhabitants): 'It has a sandy bottom and four feet of water at lowest, or at least seven in the spring. Its bed is all covered with rushes, and very thickly bordered by willows. It has no very plain channel as we can find. The breadth of the stream is a gun shot. The bank from St. Frederic is about forty feet above the water and very uniform, and the woods thin and very open. In going a league up this river, on the same side, we meet a very high and steep mountain. The course of this river is entirely among these mountains, and quite impassible for an army. Its length is seven, or eight leagues.'-(Pouchot's Memoires, II, p 68).

FATE OF THE SEVEN SLEIGHMEN CAPTURED BY ROGERS:
Rogers in his printed Journals, suppresses the fact that his men carried out his orders and disposed of the seven sleighmen taken at Five Mile Point, by knocking them on the head, for that

would not set well with his reading public. However he mentions this unsavory episode in his original report to Abercrombie so that he might collect the 35 pounds sterling to divide amongst himself and his men (according to the terms of their enlistment, Rogers Rangers were to be paid 5 pounds sterling for every scalp or prisoner brought in). It is not known how many of the prisoners were scalped, if any, for the Rangers did not have any time to spare, and there is no mention of any scalps being taken. There is French evidence in an anonymous document that three of the seven prisoners survived from being 'knocked on the head'.-(An Account of What Occurred this year in Canada, in Docs. Rel. Col. Hist. of N. Y., X, p 646).

9.-FIRST DEFENSE OF FT WILLIAM HENRY, Mar 19-23:
10.-STARK'S MARCH 21ST SORTIE:
11.-MARCH 22ND RUM SORTIE:
-Stark, Caleb: Memoir & Correspondence of J. Stark, p 22, for his efforts in keeping the Rangers sober and vigilant. However, Caleb Stark overemphasis is the Rangers part in saving the fort. Eyre's Regulars were not drunk when Rigaud appeared, but they were suffering from a bad hangover. An idea of the Provincials admiration of Stark's part in saving the fort is expressed in the following award they presented him with: "Some time after this affair, a few gentlemen from Nantucket, stranger to him, presented Captain Stark with a cane, made from the bone of a whale, headed with ivory, as token of their admiration of his conduct in the defense..the cane is still in the possession:- of the family'.-(Stark, Memoir, p 23).

THE UNPUBLISHED OFFICIAL BRITISH DOCUMENTS IN THE LOUDOUN PAPERS, HUNTINGTON LIBRARY:
-LO 3107: Major Eyre to the Commanding officer at Albany (Loudoun had gone to Philadelphia and Abercrombie, his second, had left Albany for N.Y., to command in his absence; while Gage, due to Webb's illness, took over at Albany), March 20, 1757, his first report of Rigaud's attack.
-LO 3109: Chevalier Mercier's message to Eyre as written by Gov. Vaudreuil, received by Eyre, March 20, from Camp devant Le Ft. George (Ft. Wm. Henry).
-LO 3126: March 21, 1757, Gage forwards Eyre's first report to Abercromby with a letter.
-LO 3137 A&B: March 22, Abercrombie at N.Y., an-

swers Gage, notifying him that he is on his way.
-*LO 3138*: March 23, 1757, N.Y., Abercrombie writes
Loudoun and forwards Eyre's first report.
-*LO 3146*: March 23, at Ft. Wm. Henry, after Rigaud
retired down the lake, two wounded prisoners, Privates Guillaume Chasse and John Victor, were examined and among other things they revealed the fact
that two of Rogers Rangers had undertaken to guide
Rigaud for 1,000 Crowns each (which they were to
receive if the attack was successful) thus confirming Ranger Thomas Brown's story. However, the
French prisoners state that one of the Ranger betrayers was a Sergeant and the other one a Private
They must be in error though, for both the Ranger
Sergeants taken at La Barbue Creek later escaped
and were honourably received by the English.
-*LO 3151 A&B*: March 24, 1757, Eyre to Gage, mentions burning of Rangers' huts and storehouse.
-*LO 3157 A&B*: March 24, 1757, Lt.Colonel Monro to
Gage, from Ft. Edward, encloses above letter.
-*LO 3176*: The prisoners were examined again by Eyre on March 25, and their Declaration sent to Loudoun with LO 3179: Eyre's official report of the complete-Siege on March 26th. This is a combination of all of Eyre's first reports.
-Other Documents relative to the Siege are:
LO 3299: Gage to Abercrombie, March 28th; LO 3299:
Eyre to Webb, from Albany, Apr 6th; LO 2242: Nov
19, 1756, Nathan Whiting to Loudoun, 'Return of
the Sloops and Boats left at Ft. Wm. Henry'; LO-
4521: Robert Leake to Loudoun, Apr 15, 1757, State
of the British Stores Destroyed. The closing item
in the Loudoun Papers is Loudoun's report to Pitt,
in which he pays the garrison and Rangers a fitting
tribute: '..I cannot enough on this occasion Commend every officer, who had either the Defense of
the Fort or the Command of the Regts., for the alertness and activity with which each behaved in
their different Stations as well as the behaviour
of the men; Those in the Fort determined to defend
it to the last, and the Sick crawled out to the
Ramparts..'-(LO 3467, April 25, 1757).
-Gruesome reminders of the Siege were turned up 10
days later proving that Stark's sorties had been
effective. Eyre writes Johnson from Albany on April
3rd: '..The Morning I left Fort Wm. Henry there
was two dead Men found in the Pile of Chord Wood,
and an Indian that had been scalped and covered
with snow; besides which some more were discovered
in a hole made in the Ice close to where the

Stream runs into the Lake. Its imagined a good many will be found of the Enemy when the Snow disappers and the Ice melts..'-(Johnson Papers,II,p696) Provincial Newspaper 'Reporters' got authentic first hand accounts at Albany, N. Y. which were printed in The Boston Gazette, No. 106; Boston Evening Post, No. 1,128; An Abstract of Letters from Albany, in Boston News-Letter, No. 2,860. But strangely enough the Virginia Gazette, No. 328, Apr 22, 1757, printed the best account for their informant had penetrated as far up as Fort William Henry and obtained 'an Eye-Witness' account.
FRENCH ACCOUNTS are many: Relation de Campagne sur le Lac St. Sacrement pendant L'Hiver, 1757, is the best. It is in the Collection Moreau St. Mery, Canadian Archives, Vol XIII, F, Folio 25 (States that 17 of the Rangers huts were burned). Other accounts are in: Bougainville's Journal; Malartics Journal; Montcalm to the Minister, Apr 23, 1757; Montreuil to the Minister, Apr 23, 1757.

12.-RD. ROGERS' ATTACK ON COUTRE COEUR, 6/6/57:

The best accounts are in: The Boston News-Letter July 1, 1757; Loudoun to Pitt, June 17, 1757 -LO-3845 (also in Corr. of Pitt, Kimball, Edit.); Luke Gridley's Provincial Diary, June 8, 1757, entry.
COUTRE-COEUR: Pouchot in his Memoires brings to light the name of the most important French advanced post: '..The camp of observation at the entrance upon Lake Sacrement was called the camp of Coutre-Coeur. It was not well located, because it could be turned by the Arbres Mataches (Rogers' Rock) and by the lake'.-(II, p 72). Robert Rogers describes the post in 1755 as '..a Small Fort with Several Small Log Camps within ye Fort which I Judged to Contain about ¼ of an acre. Said Fort being open to-wards ye Water, The rest Picketted.' This key post was abandoned before July 1758.

13.-JULY 1ST AMBUSCADE, 1757: Gridley's Diary

July 10, 1757: '18 of Captain Rogers men killed & taken near Crown Pint'. However, a return shows only 7 men lost on July 1st: Privates John Glinns, Robert Paterson, Matthew Read, William Kennedy, Joseph McCartney, Joseph Steward & Ephraim Smith, all new recruits with only 3 months service-AB4867
FRENCH ACCOUNT of Vaudreuil to Bourlamaque, Montreal, July 15, 1757: '...The last party of our sav-

ages have well executed the two scouts and the 12 prisoners that they have taken have slackened the arrogance and confidence of Rogers to make such frequent scouts near our camps.'-(Bourlamaque Collection-Vol II, Lettres Vaudreuil, pp 129-132).

The only answer to the disparity of the losses stated in these 3 accounts is, that Ogden's Rangers must have also served in this action and suffered the remaining 11 that were captured or killed.

14.-AMBUSCADE AT ISLE LA BARQUE, July 16, 1757:

The French pen 3 skillfully worded accounts which literally turned St. Ours's defeat into a victory: ANONYMOUS ACCOUNT: While Montcalm was preparing to advance on William Henry, M. Sieur Rigaud de Vaudreuil having established himself at the head of the portage of Lake George with a corps of Colonial troops, Canadians and Indians sent out 3 scouting parties.-'The first, which consisted of only ten men, was attacked on Lake Saint Sacrament by several canoes containing one hundred and twenty to one hundred and thirty Englishmen. Although Lieutenant de St. Ours of the Colonials, who commanded the party, was wounded at the first volley, he defended himself with so much firmness as to oblige his enemies to retire.'-(Docs. Rel. Col. Hist. of New York, Vol X, p 647).

DORIEL'S ACCOUNT: 'A small body of men under the orders of Lieut. de Saint-Ours, of the Colonial troops, fell a fortnight ago into an ambush of 120 Englishmen. He cut his way through them, killed some of their people and returned to the camp with 4 men wounded, 2 of whom are dead. M. de St. Ours himself received a gun-shot in the hand. This action entitles him to the highest praise. It bears no resemblance to those of the English.'-(Doriel to Paulmy, Que., Jul 31, 1757-Doc. Rel. C. H. N. Y.,X, p 594)

JOURNAL OF THE EXPEDITION AGAINST FT. WM. HENRY:
'July 21st, Learned at 3 o'clock in the afternoon that M. de St. Ours, who was scouting at Isle a la Barque' (now, Harbour Island, south of Sabbath-Day-Point) 'with 10 men, had been attacked by five English barges, each carrying 15 men, and 100 men who were firing on shore; that he had made so vigorous a defence as to force the English to retreat; to allow him to embark in a barge and quietly to regain his camp whither he returned with his ten men, one of whom, a Cadet was mortally, and three Canadians, slightly wounded.'-(Docs. Rel.

Colonial History of New York, *Vol X, p 599)*.

15.-SIEGE, SURRENDER & MASSACRE OF FT WM HENRY August 2-9, 1757:

SOURCES: *A MSS Journal of the Siege of Fort William Henry, evidently kept by a British Officer, is in W.O.34, 101/73ff. It mentions the Sorties of the Provincials and Rangers.* Parkman's Montcalm and Wolfe, II, pp 509-523. Pargellis's Lord Loudoun in N. America *gives the best account of the Siege based on the original Loudoun Papers. Ranger Richard's heroic feat is from Stark,* Reminiscences, *p44*

LOSSES OF ROGERS RANGERS: *Richard Rogers' Company had a strength of 101 Officers and Men at the time of the Siege-(AB 4867-5). Of these, at least five were carried off by Indians and four survived to be bought by French Priests or Officers. They were:*
Private Elias Cummings.-(Boston, Mass, Nov 4, 1757 Return of Men Belonging to Different Corps which had been taken by the Enemy and sent from Halifax to Boston. Mustered in Nantasket Road with 51 others by Henry Liddel, Commissary. *LO 4758).*
Private John Staynes.-('Ranger of Lt. Johnson's in Rogers Corps'. Sent by Vaudreuil to Halifax. List of New England Forces in the Capitulation of Ft. Wm. Henry- arrived at Halifax and put on board Capt Nichols's Schooner bound to Boston. Boston, Nov 7, 1757. *LO 4778).*
Private James McLauchlan.-('Ranger..entered on board *H.M.S. Huzza* after his exchange and arrival in England..Feb 1758'.-Bost. News-Letter, Oct 12, 58'
Private Jacob Ames.-('Died on board passage to France'.-List of Persons who died in Quebec and France to the 16th of Feb 1758, by Israel Calkins, Serjt. in the 13th Company of Lyman's Conn. Regt., in Boston News-Letter, Oct 12, 1758).
   Captive Rogers Rangers and English and Provincial prisoners had a strong champion in the Jesuit Priest, Father Pierre Roubaud, who served as Chaplain to Montcalm's Indian forces. He purchased from the Indians, at an outlay of 6,800 Livres out of his private purse, the lives of 103 prisoners. Some of whom he bought from the torture pole. Unfortunately, Ranger McKeen was not among these. Mc Keen was the only Ranger reported to have been thus killed as a result of the fall of Wm. Henry.
C.E. Potter's History of Manchester, N. H., p 315-

316, relates his torture and death. Father Robaud at the risk of his life, snatched from an Indian an English child, who was about to be tossed into a large kettle to be boiled alive.-(Northcliffe Collection, Vol XXXV, p 283). Robaud relates: 'My tent had been placed in the middle of the encampment of the Outanoucs. The first object which presented itself to my eyes on arriving there was a large fire, while the wooden spits fixed in the earth gave signs of a feast. There was indeed one taking place. But, O Heaven! What a feast! The remains of the body of an Englishman was there, the skin stripped off, and more than one-half of the flesh gone. A moment after I perceived these human beings eat with famishing avidity of this flesh; I saw them taking up this detestable broth in large spoons, and apparently without being able to satisfy themselves with it. They informed me that they had prepared themselves for this feast by drinking from skulls filled with human blood, while their smeared faces and stained lips gave evidence of the truth of the story.'-(Kips, Jesuit Missions p 155.)

16.-THE HUNTING SCOUT, Oct 3, 1757: Metcalf's Diary, Oct 3, 1757 entry, is the principal source.

17.-STARK'S MISBEHAVIOUR SCOUT, Nov 17-28, 1757:
Captain James Abercrombie's account to Loudoun, from Albany, Nov 29, 1757.-(LO 4915); and General Abercrombie to Loudoun, from Albany, Dec 30, 1757. -(LO 5159) are the critical British accounts. In this letter, Abercrombie states that his nephew omitted stating one circumstance of the Rangers' ignorance: '..in twice taking South Bay for a beaver Pond, which mistake he had secrued by a sketch he had of these parts..'
Captain Abercrombie's letter to Loudoun vaunting the mischief he did at Ticonderoga is LO 5132.

FRENCH ACCOUNT: Adjutant Malartic describes the Rangers' Attack in his Journal under the Nov 22, 1757 entry: 'M. de Bleury, who arrives at Montreal from Carillon says, the English showed themselves there to the number of 300, intending to burn the outer posts; that they have not been able to force a guard of one Sergeant and 15 men who were in a little intrenchmen.. they opened the vent of the charcoal pit, after which they retired, and that one soldier of the Bearn Regiment has been killed.'-(Docs. Rel. Col. Hist. N. Y., Vol X, p 836).

Rogers in his printed Journals makes no comment on the Scout. He simply states that his Rangers '..were sent out on various scouts, in which my ill state of health at this time eould not permit me to accompany them..'-(Journals, p 71). Captain Abercrombie bemoans Rogers abscence when he writes to Loudoun: '..I wish with all my heart some officers of more experience had been with us to have given your Lordship a better account of the places.'

18.-ROGERS' XMAS EVE RAID ON TICONDEROGA, Dec 24, 1757: Rogers dictated his official report to Loudoun from Albany, Jan 1, 1758, LO 5314. It contains items of interest about the march that are left out of his printed account in his Journals. However, the accounts of the Siege are the same:

'The 24th marched six more miles and halted within in 600 yards of Carillon Fort. Near the mills we discovered five Indian's tracks, that had marched that way the day before, as we supposed, on a hunting party. On my march this day between the advanced guard and the fort, I appointed three places of rendezvous to repair to, in case of being broke in an action, and acquainted every officer and soldier that I should rally the party at the nearest post to the fort, and if broke there to retreat to the second, and at the third to make a stand till the darkness of the night would give us an opportunity to get off. Soon after I halted, I formed an ambush on a road leading from the fort to the woods with an advanced party of 20 men, and a rear guard of 15. About 11 o'clock a Sergeant of Marines came from the fort up the road to my advanced party, who let him pass to the main body, where I made him prisoner. Upon examination he reported etc..About noon, a Frenchman, who had been hunting, came near my party in his return when I ordered a party to pursue him to the edge of the cleared ground, and take him prisoner, with this caution, to shoot off a gun or two, and then retreat to the main body, in order to intice the enemy from their fort; which orders were punctually obeyed, but not one of them ventured out. When I found the French would not come out of the fort, we went about killing their cattle, and destroyed 17 head, and at night set fire to the wood, which

they had collected for the use of the garrison and
consumed five large piles; the French shot off some
cannon at the fires, but did us no harm. At eight
o'clock at night I began my march homewards, and
arrived at Fort Edward at 2 o'clock in the afternoon on the 27th..'-(Rogers' Journals, pp 73-74).

ROGERS' 'THANK YOU NOTE': These few lines hastily
scrawled on a scrap of paper won as many gasps of
admiration on the British side as it wrung gasps
of shocked amazement from the French. Abercrombie
in writing to Loudoun from Albany on Jan 1, 1758,
states that Rogers arrived, weary from a hard but
successful excursion against the enemy; and that
he modestly omitted in his official Journal that:-
after killing all but three oxen he left a receipt
for the Commandant as a Voucher to pass his accounts with 'the Agent Victualler' and stuck it in
a stick into the ground. By the French deserters
he learned that Commandant Hebecourt '..was much
provoked at it..'-(LO 5311).

M. Doreil to Marshall de Belle Isle, Que, Apr 30
1758, describes the raid and note: '..Captain Robert Rogers, a great partisan, came roving in the
neighborhood of Carillon with a detachment of 70
men. The artillery of the fort drove him away
pretty quick. In his retreat he burnt a pile of
timber and charcoal, took a woodcutter prisoner...
and killed 18 oxen or cows, which he could not remove; they were found in the woods and have served
to subsist the garrison. He had caused to be at
tached to the head of one of the oxen a letter addressed to the commandant of the fort, the contents whereof were an ill-timed and very low piece
of braggadocio.'-(Docs.Rel.Col.Hist.N.Y., X, p 703)

Montcalm to Levis from Que, Jan 26, 1758 writes:
'..The billet of Captain Rogers is some of this
partisans customary gasconnade. Perhaps we can
dampen his spirit..'-(Casgrain, Levis MSS, VI, 122)

Malartic's Journal, Jan 2, entry: 'A Courier
from Carillon reports, that the English showed
themselves there on Christmas eve to the number of
150, with the design of setting fire to the houses
under the curtain of the fort; that the cannon
prevented them doing so; that they killed some 15
beeves, to the horns of one of which the commander
had affixed a letter couched in these words;' See
text, p 212. (Docs.Rel.Col.Hist.N.Y., X, p 837).

This audacious affair of Rogers contributed lar-
gely to there being a superiority of numbers at

the unfortunate battle of Rogers' Rock on Mar 13, 1758, for we note in the testimony of an escaped Irish settler being reviewed by Johnson on Mar 24, 1758, that: '..He saw three of the Prisoners who were taken this Winter at Fort Edward, a little before he left, and that he heard it was on acct of the Cattle killed this Winter at Ticonderoga, and Wood burnt by our People there, and a Store House, the Governor prevailed on a body of Indians to Join some French to go & revenge it..'-(Johnson Papers, II, p 787).

COMMANDANT HEBECOURT'S ACCOUNT: to Bourlamaque from Carillon, Jan 6, 1758: '..I will take the liberty to give you an account not very exact as the one that I am going to give but as I am the protector of Carrilon it is my duty to give you these annoying details. On the 20th last, I sent a courier to tell M. de Vaudreuil and Levy of this action. The 24th, at 7 o'clock in the evening, the fire caught a cord of wood and two bundles on the top of the rampart.

'The next morning I sent one Sergeant and ten men to search, and M Wolff with 20 men, as much to review the damage as to look for the deserter in case the tracks of the enemy were not so many as was said. They saw that the English had occupied during the night the breastworks and a little bit farther found 13 skeletons of oxen fron the Hospital killed. The Keeper had let slip out against my order 3 oxen belonging to different people and they found the oxen so thin that they did not take anything but their tungs. Except the cow of the soldier that had some flesh on it. Altogether they only weighed 1,550 lbs, they will serve to feed the Hospital during the Winter. Anyway they would have died later and we would not have profitted. M Wolff estimated, by the place where the bodies were found, that there had been 150 men, and came back with a letter of thanks from Robert Rogers that I am sending to M. de Vaudreuil with a bullet. The Sergeant found many bullets in the ramparts and some packages of matches. So, it is to be supposed that M. Rogers had no other idea than to burn the wood but having learned by the Sergeant of the Marine who left at 2 in the afternoon that the Canteen was closed; that there was to be no Midnight Mass; and that the garrison were doubling the watch,-All of this might have changed his plans.

'Another thing to be noticed is that all the bodies that have come here have passed by the portage and oven without having made the least damage. The old Light Infantryman of the Hospital who left on the 21st did not come back. It could be him and the Sergeant that Captain Rogers took prisoners, because of what he said in his letter.' (Evidently Rogers 'Thank You Note' was lengthier than Malartic's resume of it)-Bourlamaque Collecttion, Can. Arch, Vol IV, Lettres Variarum, pp281-4

ACCOUNT OF COURCEL (AN OFFICER AT CARILLON): to Bourlamaque, Jan 6, 1758: '..Please let me give you a little detail of the last surprise that the enemy attempted on the night of the 24th of December who appeared while I was making my watch. The sentinel told me that he saw a fire where we kept the wood. After having seen it myself, I gave an account to M. de Hebecourt and some officers came up on the parapet where they saw the fire and even the powder burned. Then M. de Hebecourt decided to fire the cannon which succeded very well so that they were prevented from coming back and finishing what they had started, which was probably to put on fire the lower part of the city and the Hospital, since they had brought with them many fire bombs, if we can judge by the fragments that we have discovered the next day at the door..'-(Bourlamaque Coll, IV-Lettres Variarum, pp 325-8 trans)

DESERTER JEAN BOIS' ACCOUNT: Upon being questioned by Capt Abercrombie at Albany on Dec 28, 1757, Bois stated that: The Rangers had only burned two Cord of wood, having been in such a hurry that several of the fire-balls were found whole.-(LO 5132)

THE BOSTON NEWS-LETTER ACCOUNT: of Jan 19, 1758 states that: '..In an Excursion he lately made..to Ticonderoga he set fire to, and destroyed, sundry of their Wood-Piles, out houses etc., and would also have destroyed their Battoes had they not secured them in places improper for the Major to attempt. He gave them a fair opening to come to battle, which was not accepted; and at last brought off 18 head of cattle and 2 French prisoners. There were also two German Deserters that he brought down to Fort Edward, they having followed the Major's tracks a considerable way from Ticonderoga before they overtook him.'

RANGER GOODENOUGH'S ACCOUNT: '..I was one of 150

Rangers who marched with Captain Rogers against
the Enemy at Carrillion. The snow was not deep at
sterting but it continued to snow until it was
heavy footing and many of the men gave out and returned to Fort Edward, but notwithstanding my exhaustion I continued on, for six days until we were
come to within 600 yards of Carrillion Fort. The
Captain had made us a speech in which he told us
the points where we were to rendevoux if we were
broke in the fight, for further resistance until
night came on, when we could take ourselves off as
best we might. I was with the advance guard. We
lay in ambush in some fallen timber quite close to
a road, from which we could see the smoke from the
chimneys of the Fort and the centries walking their beats. A French soldier came down the road from
the Fort..We lay perfectly still not daring to
breath, and though he saw nothing he stopped once
and seemed undecided as to going on, but suspecting nothing he continued and was captured by our
people below..A man taken was threatened with Death if he did not tell the whole truth, which under the circumstances he mostly did to save his
life. The French did not come out of the Fort after us, though Rogers tried to entice them by firing guns and showing small parties of men which
feigned to retreat. We were ordered to destroy
what we could of the supplies, so Shanks and I
killed a small cow which we found in the edge of
the clearing and took off some fresh beef of which
we were sadly in need, for on these scouts the
Rangers were not permitted to fire guns at game
though it was found in their path, as it often was
in fact..We burned some large wood piles, which no
doubt made winter work for to keep some Frenchers
at home. They only fired some cannon at us, which
beyond a great deal of noise did no harm. We then
marched back to Fort Edward and were glad enough
to get there, since it was time for snow-shoes,
which we had not with us'.-(Goodenough's Old-Letter)

ROGERS' TWO PRISONERS: It seems that they were
actually deserting from Ticonderoga when they were
captured by the Rangers. Hebecourt in his letter
to Bourlamaque states: '..I have taken every method for apprehending all the desertions. But with
out Savages I cannot prevent it. The fifth, a Sergeant of the Marine; the sixth four of La Point;
the 13th, a servant of M. Noagaine; and the 24th,
a Sergt of the Marine, and a man of confidence who

was keeping the duty of huntsman and after spending the money of the workmen of whom he was in charge he was forced to flee and has taken with him the hat and coat of his friend; and then the 26th, two of the picket. From this time I have called roll four times a day..The discontent of this garrison..is because their equipment is not the same as of the previous year..'

19.-*ARNOUX'S DEFEAT*, Dec 1757: The only definite document turned up relative to this action is that of Courcel (an Officer at Carillon) to Bourlamaque dated Jan 6, 1758 (mentioned on p 359): '..M Wolffe told us of the battle between Robert Rogers, the.. commander of the English party, and the soldiers of Arnoux. The latter has been utterly destroyed', without paying me one-tenth of what was due me having taken all the money with him.
  Rogers notes in his report of his Xmas Eve Raid, that: '..On the 24th..Near the mills we discovered five Indian's tracks, that had marched that way the day before, as we supposed, on a hunting party..'
  This might have been Arnoux's party, but they were not attacked by Rogers. They could have been attacked farther south by a patrol of the Rangers.

20.-*SHANKS' AMBUSCADE AT LITTLE MARY R.*, Feb 2, 1758: Fitch's Jrn, Jan 26. Abercrombie to Loudoun, Feb 14:-mentions a Ft.Anne Scout on Feb 8-LO 5594.
  RANGER JOSHUA GOODENOUGH'S ACCOUNT: 'The Canada indians were coming down to our Forts and even behind them to intercept our convoys or any parties out on the road, so that the Rangers were kept out to head them when they could, or get knowledge of their whereabouts. Shanks and I went out with two Mohegon Indians on a scout. It was exceedingly stormy weather and very heavy travelling except on the River. I had got a bearskin blanket from the indians which is necessary to keep out the cold at this season. We had ten days of bread, pork and rum with a little salt with us, and followed the indians in a direction North-and-bye-East toward the lower end of Lake Champlain, always keeping to the high-ground with the falling snow to fill our tracks behind us. For four days we travelled, when we were well up the west side. We had crossed numbers of trails but they were all full of old snow and not worth regarding-still we were so far from

our post that in event of encountering any numbers
of the Enemy we had but small hope of a safe return and had therefore to observe the greatest
caution. As we were making our way an immense panther - so menaced us that we were forced to fire our
guns to dispatch him. He was found to be very old,
his teeth almost gone, and was in the last stages
of starvation. We were much alarmed at this misadventure, fearing the Enemy might hear us or see
the ravens gathering above, so we crossed the Lake
that night on some new ice to blind our trail,
where I broke through in one place and was only
saved by Shanks, who got hold of my eel-skin que,
thereby having something to pull me out with. We
got into a deep gully and striking flint made a fire
to dry me and I did not suffer much inconvenience.

The day following we took a long circle and
came out on the lower end of the Lake, there laying two days in ambush, watching the Lake for any
parties coming or going. Before dark a Mohigon
came in from watch saying that men were coming
down the Lake. We gathered at the point and saw
seven of the Enemy come slowly on. There were 3
indians two Canadians and a French officer. Seeing
they would shortly pass under our point of land we
made ready to fire, and did deliver one fire as they
came nigh, but the guns of our Mohigons failed to
explode, they being old and well nigh useless, so
that all the damage we did was to kill one indian
and wound a Canadian, who was taken in hand by his
companions who made off down the shore and went into the bush. We tried to head them unsuccessfully,
and after examining the guns of our indians we feared they were so disabled that we gave up and retreated down the Lake, travelling all night. Near
morning we saw a small fire which we spied out only
to find a large party of the Enemy, whereat we were
much disturbed, for our travelling had exhausted
us and we feared the pursuit of a fresh enemy as
soon as morning should come to show them our trail
We then made our way as fast as possible until
late that night when we laid down for refreshment.

We built no fire but could not sleep for fear of
the Enemy for it was a bright moonlight, and sure
enough we had been there but a couple of hours
when we saw the Enemy coming on our track. We here
abandoned our bearskins with what provisions we
had left and ran back on our trail toward the advancing party. It was dark in the forest and we
hoped they might not discover our back track for

some time, thus giving us a longer start. This ruse was successful. After some hours travel I became so exhausted that I stopped to rest, whereat the Mohegans left us, but Shanks bided with me, though urging me to move forward. After a time I got strength to move on. Shanks and the Canadians would come up with us if we did not make fast going of it, and that they would disembowel us or tie us to a tree and burn us as was their usual way, for we could in no wise hope to make head against so large a party. Thus we walked steadily till high noon, when my wretched strength gave out so that I fell down saying I had as leave die there as elsewhere. Shanks followed back on our trail, while I fell into a drouse but was so sore I could not sleep. After a time I heard a shot and shortly two more when Shanks came running back to me. He had killed an advancing indian and stopped them for a moment. He kicked me vigorously, telling me to come on, as the indians would soon come on again. I got up, and though I could scarcely move I was minded diligently to persevere after Shanks. Thus we staggered on until near night time when we again stopped and I fell into a deep sleep but the enemy did not again come up. On the following day we got into Fort Edward, where I was taken with a distemper, was seized with very grevious pains in the head and back and a fever. They let blood and gave me a physic, but I did not get well around for some time. For this sickness I have always been thankful otherwise I should have been with Major Rogers in his unfortunate battle.'

21.-THE MORNING PATROL FIGHT, March 12, 1758: JABEZ FITCH'S JOURNAL ACCOUNT: 'Mar 12, 1758, Sunday..In the Morning Before I was Up There was a Larem ye Morning Scout of the Rangers (which Consisted of only 6 Men) was attacted on ye Top of ye Hill Toard Ft. Wm. Henry and tho ye Indions Had ye First Shot & their Party soposd To Be about 15 Yet our Men all Escapd without any Hurt- our People Persued them about an Hour But Did not over Take them- & so Returned- After our People was Returnd we was Alarmd Again By Som Shots yt Som of ye Rangers Said they Heard Down ye River &c- our Two Companies all yt was able was Emmediately Sent Down ye River. To Se what was ye Matter- But they Returned Befor Night & Made No Discovery Neither.' (Courtesy of the Mass. Society of Mayflower Desc..)

22.-THE BATTLE OF ROGERS' ROCK, March 13, 1758:

An interesting item has come to light in regard to the antecedents of the Battle. General Abercrombie at Albany, in writing to Loudoun on Feb 21 1758, states that a Captain Ezra Clap of Westfield had wrote a letter to Rogers offering to join him with 500 Provincials in a Winter campaign against the enemy. The letter was entrusted with a New Englander named Furnis who was enroute to Albany. Furnis made it a point to broadcast the contents of the letter on his way to Albany, and the offer reached Abercrombie's ears by the time Furnis arrived. Since the offer had been so publicized Abercrombie was afraid there would be a clamour if he rejected the proposal and he told Furnis that he would approve the offer and sent him back to Westfield with a letter to Clap stating as much.

But this was the last that Abercrombie ever heard of Clap's offer. It smacks very much of a feeler instigated by Rogers through his recruiting officers to see if Abercrombie was receptive to a Winter Expedition unhampered by Regular troops.

ROGERS' OFFICIAL REPORT: Abercrombie sent Rogers' official Journal to Pitt with this prefext: 'April 28, 1758..After the Departure of the Packet, with my last Dispatches, I received an Account of a Skirmish, between Capt. Rogers, and a Superior party of the Enemy, on the 13th of last Month, within five Miles of Tienderoga, in which the Captain and his Command, distinguished themselves, but for a more particular Detail thereof, I must beg leave to refer you to His own Journal. Since that Affair, all has been pretty quiet in that Quarter..'-(This prefext is printed in Kimball's Pitt Correspondence, I, 232, but not the Journal).

The following Journal is from an exact duplicate of the original, printed in the Boston News-Letter April 7, 1758 copy, which was probably issued to the press by Abercrombie. The News-Letter prefext their account: 'Copy of a letter from N.Y: N.Y., March 27, Fry Night last the Albany Post came to Town, and brought us the following particular Account of a Battle between the famous ROGERS, and the Enemy on the 13th of March..' Rogers' original copy sent by Abercrombie to Pitt, is in the Colonial Office, 5: 50, pp 57-65.

'Journal of a Scout of Captn. Robt. Rogers. Mar. 10th 1758: This Day Set out On a Scout to march to the Neighbourhood of Carilong, in Company with Captn Pringle, Lieut. Rouch, Ensn. Bellfore, three Voluntiers Vizt. Messrs. Creed, Kent, & Rightson, one Serjt & one private all of His Majesty's twenty seventh Regiment: and a Detachment from His Majesty's four Companies of Rangers quartered in the Island near Fort Edward Vizt. Captn. Bulkley, Lt. Phillips, Lt. Moors, Lieut. Crafton, Lieut. Campbell, Lt. Pottinger, Ensigns Ross, Wait, McDonald, and White, and one hundred and Sixty four Men, Marched to the half Way Brook on the Road towards Lake George & encamped there that Night.

11th We proceeded as far as the first Narrows on Lake George, & encamped on the East Side of the Lake, & after dark Sent out a party three Miles further down to make discovery of any Enemies that Might be coming towards our Forts, the party returned Without any Discovery, kept parties on the Lake walking all night besides Centrys at all necessary places on the Land.

12th Began our March at Sun-rise & when we had distanced our Encampment three Miles, We Saw a dog run across the Lake, Whereupon I sent a Detatchment of the party to reconnoitre the Islands, thinking that the Indians might have laid an Ambush there for us, but they returned without discovering any further signs, upon which I thought it expedient to put to shore and lay by till night, to prevent any partys of the Enemy that Might be on the Hills or other places from discovering us, which I accordingly did, & halted the party at a place called Sabbath Day point, on the West Side of the Lake about 10 oClock, & kept them from going on the Lake the remaining part of the day, & sent parties out by land, to look down the lake with prospective Glasses which I had for that purpose. As soon as 'twas dark proceeded down the Lake, Sent Lt. Phillips with 15 Men as an advance Guard Some of whom went on Scates before him, Ensn Ross with a party flanked us on our left under the West Shore, The Main Body I marched as Close as possible to prevent Seperation, in this Manner continued our March till within eight Miles of the french Advance Guard, when Lt. Phillips sent a Man on Scates to desire Me to Halt, upon which I ordered my Men to Squat on the Ice, Lt. Phillips Soon came to Me himself, leaving his party to look out, & Said that he imagined he had discovered a fire on the East Shore, but was not Certain, upon which I sent him with Ensign Waite to go nearer and make a discretional Discovery thereof, & to return as Soon as they had effected the Same, in about an hour they returned, & Said they were persuaded, that a party of the Enemy were encamped there, I called in the Advance Guard, & put into the West Shore & there hid our packs & Slays in a Thicket, leaving three Men with them, & marched the remainder to attack ye Enemy's Encampment if there, but when I came near the place, there were no fires to be Seen, which made us conclude that it was some bleak patches of Snow, or pieces of Rotten Wood (Which in ye Night resemble fire at a distance) thereupon We returned to our packs & there lay the remainder of ye Night without any fire.

13th in the Morning I had a Consultation with my officers how to proceed, who were of opinion that it was best to put on our Snow Shoes and go by land, least We should be discovered if we went farther on the Ice. We began our March about seven o Clock continued on the West Side of the Lake, keeping back of the Mountains that overlook ye french Advance Guards. I halted my party at 11 o Clock, two Miles West from the Advance Guard to refresh themselves & tarried there till 3 o Clock, that the Day Scouts from the forts might be returning home, before I went nearer, thinking to lay an Ambush to Some of their roads in ye Night, & meet with them in the morning without being discovered, then marched in two divisions, Captn Bulkley at the head of one, Myself at the head of ye other, Ensign White & Wait brought up the rear, ye other officers were fixed in each Division amongst the Men, in this Manner we marched on, one Mile & a half, when our Advance parties discovered the Enemy, & immediately sent one back to inform me thereof, I sent the Messenger back again to See if they could ascertain the Number of Enemy, or near it, then ordered my People to throw off their packs & prepare for the Enemy, which they immediately did, Some of ye Advance party by this time came & acquainted me that they believed their Number was one hundd, & were going on our left & would come within 15 Rods of My party by the Course they then Steered. I ordered Ensn. McDonnald to ye Comand of the Advance Guards, Which as we face to the left made a flanking part to our Right, we gave the Enemy the first fire, upon which they retreated. My party pursued them & Scalped about forty Indians in about one quarter of an hour. We imagining the Enemy had been beat, Ensn McDonald with his Advanced

Party Strove to head them that none might escape, but we soon found that the party we had engaged were only the Advance Guards of the Enemy, their Main body coming up in great numbers & joining them occasioned my People retreating to their own Ground, where they stood & fought with ye greatest Intrepidity & bravery imaginable, in So much that in a very Short time, the Enemy were forced to retreat a second time, but being reinforced recovered their Ground & a party of them having got round upon our Rear were in possession of both our flanks as well as the Front but upon encouragg my Men they soon beat off both the flanking parties and cause them to retreat to their Main body with Considerable loss. When we had fought them in this Manner about three quarters of an hour, Lt. Phillips informed me that about 200 Indians were going up ye hill on our right to take possession of ye raising Ground upon our backs as he Supposed; whereupon I ordered him with 18 Men to take possession of the raising Ground before the Enemy, & try to beat them back, Accordingly he went, but I being Suspicious that ye Enemy would go round on our Left & take possession of the other part of the hill, I send Lt. Crafton with 15 Men to take possession of the Raising Ground there, & soon after desired Capt. Pringle to go with a few more men & assist Crafton, which he did with Lt. Roch & 8 Men. But the Enemy pushed on So close in the front, that the partys were not more than 20 yards apart & oftentimes intermixed with each other. The fire continued very hot for one hour & a half from the beginning of the Attack, in which time I lost 8 Officers & about 100 Men from the Detachment killed on the Spot, the Enemy being So numerous that My party broke & about 20 of them run up the Hill to Phillips & Crafton where we Stopt & fired a Volley upon the Indians who were eagerly pursuing them, Seeing that I had not numbers sufficient to withstand them, Lieutenant Phillips was at this time capitulating with them for himself & party on the other part of the hill, Who Spoke to me & Said that he was incircled by 300 Indians who were within 10 rods of him & Said if they would give him & party good quarters would Surrender to them, otherwhise would fight whilst one Man was left to fire a gun. Upon finding that Phillips & his party was obliged to Surrender, I thought it ye most prudent for me to retreat & bring off as many of my people as I possibly could. Which I immediately did, the

Indians pursuing us at ye Same time & took Several of them prisoners. I came to Lake George in the evening about 8 o Clock, & found there Several Wounded Men, which I took with me to the place where we left the Slays, from whence I sent an express to fort Edward desiring Col. Haviland to Send out A party to meet us, & detached eight Men to draw the wounded on Slays homewards. I with the party tarried there the remainder of the Night without either blanketts or fire, in the Morning found several wounded Men which came up to us with Some other of the party, whom I took under my care, &-
In the Morning proceeded up the Lake, & Met with Captn. Starks at Sloop Island six Miles North from fort Wm. Henry, tarried there that Night and-
The 15th in the evening we arrived at fort Edward. The Number of the Enemy with whom we engaged according to the best Computation I was able to make amounted at least to 700 Men of whom 600 were Indians. My party Officers included consisted of 183 all of whom both Officers & Men behaved with ye utmost bravery & Coolness & in particular Lt Moore & Ens. McDonald (whom I cant forbear mentiong here) altho mortally wounded in ye beginning of ye Action, yet kept up their fire, and encouraged the Men so long as they lived. Capn. Bulkley, Lieuts. Campbell & Pottinger & Ensn. White were killed in the beginning of the fight, tho it did not in the least dampn the Spirit of any of the party. Serjeants Toot, Falkinner, Willm Clark, John Clark, & James Clark signalized themselves by their good behaviour during the Whole Action; Ensn: Wait who was in the Rear Guard with 12 Men before the Action Commenced, attempted to join the Main body untill ten of his Men were killed on the Spot, & 1 wounded with whom he & the other Man made their Escape. Lt. Crafton got off with me in my party as also did Mr. Creed the Volunteer, both of whom behaved exceedingly well. I believe the Number of the Indians killed was about one hundred, & the Number Wounded about the Same. here follows a List of the Killed & Missing of the Detachmt. (See next note) The foregoing is as true an Account as I am able to recollect: Island near Fort Edward March 17th, 1758. To Col. Haviland (signed) Robt Rogers'

(The above report varies from Rogers' account in his published 'Journals'. The varying statements are included in the text of this History:-See pp 239-259).

ROGERS' LOSSES & SURVIVORS: Compiled from both of Rogers' Accounts and various Musters and Returns of prisoners in Newspapers and French Accounts:
ROGERS' OWN COMPANY
Lieutenant Increase Moore Wounded-Died fighting.
Sergt Robert Parnell Killed.
Private Joshua Conkey Captured-Exact fate unknown.
Private Jacob Bacon Captured-Exact fate unknown.
Private John Hunter Jr. Captured-fate unknown.
Private John Stewart Captured-fate unknown.
Private Robert Nae Captured-fate unknown.
Private Matthew Spencer Captured-fate unknown.
30 Privates Killed.
Captain Robert Rogers, Ensign Joseph Waite, Sergeants James Tute, James Clark, John Clark, William Clark; and 16 Privates Escaped.
JOHN STARK'S COMPANY
Sergt Jacob Townsend Killed.
Sergt Philip Flanders Killed.
Private Edward Adams Killed.
Private Cloud Crain Killed.
Private Nathaniel Clark Killed.
Private Jonathan Watson Killed.
Private John Ryan Killed.
Private James McDugle Killed.
Private Daniel Kennedy Killed.
Private Alexander Robeson Killed.
and Privates:
David McCracken
John Welch
Gideon Hedgcok
Davison Dudley
Nathaniel Fuller
Jeremiah Eastman
William Munn
John Munn
Samuel McFarling
Lieutenant Edward Crofton and 4 Privates Escaped.
CHARLES BULKELEY'S COMPANY
Captain Charles Bulkeley Killed.
Lieutenant James Pottinger Killed.
Lieut Wm Phillips Surrendered-Escaped by Apr 7, '58
Ensign James White Killed.
Private Aaron Smith, Jr. Captured-fate unknown.
Private Boaz Brown Captured-Exact fate unknown.
Private William Prentice Captured-fate unknown.
Private David Wallace Captured-fate unknown.
Private William Willson Captured-fate unknown.
Private Samuel Clark Captured-fate unknown.
Private Leonard Taylor Captured-fate unknown.
Private Charles McCoy Captured-fate unknown.
Private Andrew Lovejoy Captured-fate unknown.
38 Privates Killed.
Sergt James Faulkiner and 16 Privates Escaped.
JOHN SHEPHERD'S COMPANY
Sergt Moses Kelsey Killed.
Sergt Josiah Hale Killed.
Sergt Abal Ferror Wounded-Died Apr 9, at Ft. Ed.
Private John Stansel Killed.
Private Simeon Cole Killed.

Private John Black Killed.
Private Robert Simpson Killed.
Private Joshua Cate Killed.
Private Nathaniel Mann Killed.
Private Ephraim Molton Killed.
Private Phineas Wheeler Captured-Fate unknown.
Private David Wiswell Wounded-Died Apr 9, at Ft.Ed.
Private Benjamin Evans Wounded-Died Apr 9 at Ft.Ed.
Private Joseph Cragen Wounded-Died Apr 9, at Ft.Ed.
-Sergt Abal Ferror and Seven Privates Escaped.
JAMES ROGERS' COMPANY
Ensign Gregory McDonald Wounded-Died fighting.
JONATHAN BREWER'S COMPANY
Lieutenant Archibald Campbell Killed.
WILLIAM STARK'S COMPANY
Ensign Andrew Ross Killed.

 The above compilation furnishes the names of all Officers and men of Rogers Rangers (hitherto unknown) who were killed or died of their wounds.

 The names of all the Officers and Sergeants who escaped are also given. The names of 40 of the 43 Ranger Privates who returned with Rogers are unknown. Most of the 17 Rangers mentioned as being captured were in Lieutenant Phillips party that surrendered. The French credit the Indians with bringing in 12 prisoners, 2 of whom were officers. If this is true it means that only five were butchered by the Indians. However there is no record of them being exchanged and Lieutenant Phillips was the only one who managed to escape.

TOTAL RECAPITULATION OF ROGERS RANGERS ENGAGED: 172 (11 Officers-11 Sergts-150 Privates) engaged. 104 (7 Officers-5 Sergts-92 Privates) Killed on the field of Battle. 4 (1 Sergt-3 Privates) mortally wounded and died at Ft.Edward. 16 Privates captured and undoubtedly killed. TOTAL DEAD: 124 (7 Officers-6 Sergts-111 Privates).

SURVIVORS: 52 (3 Officers-6 Sergts-43 Privates)-escaped from the field of battle. 1 Officer escaped from captivity. Of these 53 survivors, 4 (1 Sergt-3 Privates) died of their wounds at Ft. Edward.

ACTUAL SURVIVORS: 49 (4 Officers-5 Sergts-40 Priv)

LOSSES OF THE 27TH REGT. AND PUTNAM'S COMPANY:
27TH REGIMENT
Captain-Lieutenant Henry Pringle Surrendered-Exchg
Lieutenant Boyle Roche Surrendered-Exchanged.
Ensign Bellfore (or Balfour) Killed.
Volunteer Francis Creed Escaped.
Volunteer Michael Kent Killed.

Volunteer John Wrightson Captured-later exchanged.
Sergeant Humphreys Killed.
Private............Killed.
ISRAEL PUTNAM'S CONNECTICUT COMPANY
Corporal Sharmon Killed.

RECAPITULATION OF ROGERS COMPLETE FORCE: *129 Dead: (8 Officers-1 Volunteer-7 Sergts-1 Corporal-112 Privates). 4 Captured:(3 Officers-1 Volunteer) who survived to escape or be exchanged. There were at least 4 wounded who survived. They are included in the* 53 TOTAL ACTUAL SURVIVORS: *(6 Officers-2 Volunteers-5 Sergts-40 Privates) out of 181 engaged:(14 Officers-3 Volunteers-12 Sergeants-1 Corporal-151 Privates).*

FATE OF PHILLIPS' DETAIL AND OTHER CAPTIVES TAKEN:
As stated on the preceding page Phillips is the only known survivor of Rogers' Rangers captured.
It was generally believed at first that 'they Gave (Rogers') People Vary Good Quarter..'-(Fitch, Journal, Mar 15, 1758). Rogers compiled a list of the 16 men who he thought were in Phillips original party of 18 men who he had ordered to defend his flank-(M.C. Rogers' Battle on Snowshoes); and their names were carried on the rolls until April 24, 1758. Eleven days later Rogers learned from prisoners he took at Crown Point that Phillips and 'his whole party, after they surrendered, upon the strongest assurances of good treatment from the enemy, were inhumanely tied up to trees, and hewn to pieces in a most barbarous and shocking manner' -Rogers' Journals, p 87). The Boston News-Letter: add the following facts on the Rangers fate in the May 25, 1758 copy: '..that some of the Prisoners inform that above 30 of the English which the French and Indians took in the Skirmish they had with Major Rogers some Time ago, were killed and cut to pieces after they had capitulated. The Indians being enraged at finding a Number of Scalps in an Officers' Pocket which they took.' The French (as can be seen in their accounts) state from 3 to 12 Rangers including 2 officers were brought in but they were evidently not sold to the French. Source for Phillips escape is Boutoun's Hist. of Concord.

LIEUTENANT EDWARD CROFTON'S ACCOUNT: *as given to John Macomb, Contractor to the Rangers, adds a few facts omitted by Rogers: He states that they pursued Durantaye's advance column of Indians for '50*

yards' before they ran into Langy's horde. After
the third attack 'as many as could, fought their
way and made the most speed to Sabbath Day Point
from whence ye Major dispatched 2 men to Ft.Edward
for reinforcements. There were about 100 killed on
the spot & abt 50 taken prisoners (as is hop'd)
only the Major with 40 returning, 8 of whom are
dangerously wounded. They think they kill'd about
200 of the enemy, whose number they thought to be
from 700 to 1000 composed chiefly of Canadians &
Indians..This acct is genuin, as I have it from Lt
Crofton, the only officer save one that returned,
and who was sent here yesterday by the Major with
ye acct to the Commanding officer.' -(Macomb to Gregg
& Cunningham, from Albany, Mar 19, 1758, in Macomb
Copy Letter-Book, N.Y. State Library).

JABEZ FITCH'S ACCOUNT: Gives an eyewitness record
of the arrival of Rogers' messengers and survivors
into Ft. Edward (See text-pp 258-9); and the folo-
wing facts omitted by Rogers: 'Mar. 14, 1758 About
Noon Som of Maj. Rogerss Scout Came in..This after
noon Som other Cam in & Inform Much Like ye Former
Mar.15: About 40 Returned 5 of Which were Wounded.
The Battle..Begun at 3 o Clock..& Lasted Till Sun-
set-ye Majr Drove ye Enimy of from ye Ground 3 Times & Got a number of Scalps..In ye Majrs Last Re-
treet He Lost all His Scalps Except one'-(Courtesy
of the Mass. Society of Mayflower Descendants).

ROGERS' ESCAPE DOWN ROGERS' ROCK: Is not recorded
in either of his reports for the simple reason
that he was trying to convey the impression that
his detatchment was not completely broken; which
impression might be formed if he stated that he
had ordered his men to separate into small parties
to elude pursuit. This Ranger tactic coupled with
approaching darkness and the rum found in the dead
Rangers packs, slowed the pursuers down and allowed 52 of Rogers' force to escape. Whereas, if 52
men had tried to retire in a body they would have
offered a central target of attack which might have
dragged the action on throughout the moonlight.
  Rogers was able to retire in a body at La Barbue
Creek because the action had ceased before he retired from a strong position which he was in possession of; not so, the Battle of Rogers' Rock,
this action was a desperate fight for survival.
  Rogers states that Lt. Crofton and Volunteer
Creed were in his retreating party. Rogers could

have ordered Crofton to the lake with the party while he detracted their pursuers with his illusion of sliding down Rogers' Rock (as related in the text). Rogers must have related to Crofton and other Rangers of his fox-paise, and like all incredulous deeds, it was often told until someone with a little imagination stated that Rogers actually descended the Slide, and this plausible story spread throughout New England. By the time of the Revolutionary War, the story was going something like Lt. Hadden's account in his Journal for July 27, 1777: '..We passed Rogers's Rock famous for his descending a part of it with his Detatchment (during the last War) where it appears almost perpendicular. This was his only alternative to escape falling into a superior Corps of Savages..It happen'd during the Winter which no doubt facilitated his descent by flakes of Snow etc collected on the Rock as in its present state one would doubt the fact if not so well authenticated.'-p104

S. R. Stoddard, in his 'Lake George Illustrated' gives a version of Rogers escape: 'Pursued by the savages, he made for the summit of what was then called Bald Mountain, possibly with the object of putting in practice the ruse which his dare-devil nature may have suggested. Arriving at the brow of the precipice, he threw his knapsack down over the cliff, and loosening the thongs that bound his feet to his snowshoes, without moving the latter, turned about face and laced them on his feet the reverse of the way they were made to be worn, and on them 'made Tracks' down a ravine at the southwest to the lake, thence to the foot of the slide where he regained his luggage and proceeded on his way.

'The Indians following to the edge of the precipice found where apparently two wearers of snowshoes had come together -for the toes of each pair pointed to the same direction. They saw also in the track made by the falling bundle down the cliff evidence that the two, whoever they were, had gone that way to a certain death. And when they saw the man they had been pursuing making off on the ice, seemingly unhurt, it took the form of a miracle, and they, feeling that he must be under the protection of the Great Spirit, with reverence for their deity desisted from further pursuit.'

Mary Cochrane Rogers, Great-Great-Granddaughter of Robert Rogers states that: 'The Indians have a superstition, that the witches or evil spirits of bad Indians, on their way to the happy hunting grounds, slide down the precipitous cliff with them into the lake where they are drowned. Atalapose is their word for a sliding place.-(A Battle Fought on Snowshoes, p 6) This author and others claim that Rogers actually did slide down the Rock, but it is an unsupported tradition and it is more than likely that Rogers made his way down to the lake by the defile.

DESCRIPTION OF THE FIELD OF ACTION: 'Trout Brook was called by the French Bernetz Riviere. The action took place on the grounds of what is now the Ticonderoga Golf Club'.-(S.H.P.Pell) Rogers' Rock, at the time of the battle, was called Bald Mountain by the English and les Arbres Mataches by the French. The French bivouacked on the battlefield.

CAPTAIN-LIEUTENANT PRINGLE'S ACCOUNT: to Colonel Haviland at Ft. Edward: 'Carillon, March 28, 1758- Dear Sir, As a flag of truce is daily expected here with an answer to Monsieur Vaudreuil, I sit down to write the moment I am able, in order to have a letter ready, as no doubt you and our friends at Fort Edward are anxious to be informed about Mr. Roche and me, whom probably you have reckoned amongst the slain in our unfortunate encounter of the 13th, concerning which at present I shall not be particular; only to do this justice to those who lost their lives there, and to those who have escaped, to assure you Sir, that such dispositions were formed by the enemy, (who discovered us long enough before) it was impossible for a party so weak as ours to hope for even a retreat. Towards the conclusion of the affair, it was cried from a rising ground on our right, to retire there; where after scrambling with difficulty, as I was unaccustomed to snow-shoes, I found Capt Rogers, and told him, that I saw to retire further was impossible, therefore earnestly begged we might collect all the men left, and make a stand there. Mr. Roche, who was with him, was of my opinion, and Capt. Rogers also; who therefore desired me to maintain one side of the hill, whilst he defended the other our parties did not exceed above ten or twelve in each, and mine was shifting towards the mountain, leaving me unable to defend my post, or to labour with them up the hill. In the meantime Capt Rogers with his party came to me, and said (as did all those with him) that a large body of Indians had ascended to our right; he likewise added, what was

true that the combat was very unequal, that I must
retire, and he would give Mr. Roche and me a Sergt
to conduct us thru the mountain. No doubt prudence
required us to accept his offer; but besides one,
of my snow-shoes being untied, I knew myself unable to march as fast as was requisite to avoid
becoming a sacrifice to an enemy we could no longer
oppose; I therefore begged of him to proceed, and
then leaned against a rock in the path, determined
to submit to a fate I thought unavoidable. Unfortunately for Mr Roche, his snowshoes were loosened
likewise, which obliged him to determine with me,
not to labour in a flight we were both unequal to.
Every instant we expected the savages; but what
induced them to quit this path, in which we actually saw them, we are ignorant of, unless they
changed it for a shorter, to intercept those who
had just left us. By their noise and making a fire,
we imagined they had got the rum in the Rangers
packs. This thought, with the approach of night,
gave us the first hopes of retiring; and when the
moon arose we marched to the southward along the
mountains about 3 hours, which brought us to ice,
and gave us reason to hope our difficulties were
almost past; but we knew not we had enemies yet to
combat with, more cruel than the savages we had
escaped. We marched all night, and on the morning
of the 14th found ourselves entirely unacquainted
with the ice. Here we saw a man, who came towards
us; he was the servant of Capt. Rogers, with whom
he had been oftentimes all over the country, and,
without the least hesitation whatsoever, he informed us we were upon South-Bay; that Wood Creek
was just before us; that he knew the way to Fort
Anne extremely well, and would take us to Fort Edward the next day. Notwithstanding we were disappointed in our hopes of being upon Lake George, we
thought ourselves fortunate in meeting such a guide, to whom we gave entire confidence, and which
he in fact confirmed, by bringing us to a creek,
where he showed the tracks of Indians, and the
path he said they had taken to Fort Anne. After
struggling thru the snow some hours, we were obliged to halt to make snowshoes, and Mr. Roche and
the guide had left theirs at arriving upon the ice
Here we remained all night, without any blankets,
no coat, and but a single waistcoat each, for I
gave one of mine to Mr. Roche, who had laid aside
his green jacket in the field, as I did likewise my
furred cap, which became a mark to the enemy, and

probably was the cause of a slight wound in my face; so that I had but a silk handkerchief on my head, and our fire could not be large, as we had nothing to cut wood with. Before morning we contrived, with forked sticks and strings of leather, a sort of snowshoes, to prevent sinking entirely; and, on the 15th, followed our guide west all day, but he did not fulfill his promise; however the next day it was impossible to fail, but even then, the 16th, he was unsuccesful; yet still we were patient, because he seemed well acquainted with the way, for he gave every mountain a name, and showed us several places, where he said his master had either killed deer or encamped. The ground, or rather the want of sunshine, made us incline to the southward, from whence by accident we saw ice, at several miles distance to the south east. I was very certain that, after marching two days west of South Bay, Lake George could not lie south east from us, and therefore concluded this to be the upper end of the bay we had left. For this reason, together with the assurances of our guide, I advised continuing our course to the west, which must shortly strike Fort Anne, or some other place that we knew. But Mr. Roche, wished to be upon ice at any rate; he was unable to continue in the snow, for the difficulties of our march had overcome him. And really Sir, was I to be minute in those we had experienced already and afterwards, they would almost be as tiresome to you to read, as they were to us to suffer.

'Our snow shoes, breaking, and sinking to our middle every fifty paces, the scrambling up mountains, and across fallen timber, our nights without sleep or covering, and but little fire, gathered with great fatigue, our sustenance mostly water and the bark and berries of trees; for all our provisions from the beginning were only a small Bologna sausage and a little ginger, I happened to have, and which even now was very much decreased; so that I knew not how to oppose Mr. Roche's entreaties; but as our guide still persisted Fort Anne was near, we concluded to search a little longer and if we made no discovery to proceed next day towards the ice; but we sought in vain, as did our guide the next morning, though he returned, confidently asserting he had discovered fresh proof that the Fort could not be far off. I confess I was still inclined to follow him for I was almost certain the best we could hope from descending upon

this ice to our left, was to throw ourselves into
the hands of the French, and perhaps not be able
to effect even that; but, from the circumstances I
have mentioned, it was a point I must yield to,
which I did with great reluctancy. The whole day
of the 17th we marched a dreadful road, between
the mountains, with but one good snowshoe each,
the other of our own making being almost useless.
The 18th brought us to the ice, which though we
longed to arrive at, yet I still dread the consequence, and with reason, for the first sight informed us it was the very place we had left five
days before. Here I must own my resolution almost
failed me; when fatigue, cold, hunger, and even
the prospect of perishing in the woods, attended us
I still had hopes, and still gave encouragement,
but now I wanted it myself; we had no resource but
to throw ourselves into the enemy's hands, or perish. We had nothing to eat, our slender stock had
been equally shared amongst us three, and we were
not so fortunate as ever to see either bird or beast to shoot at. When our first thoughts were a
little calmed, we conceived hopes, that, if we appeared before the French Fort, with a white flag,
the commanding officer would relieve and return us
to Fort Edward. This served to palliate our nearest approach to despair, and determined a resolution, where in fact, we had no choice. I knew Carillon had an extensive view up South Bay, therefore we concluded to halt during the evening and
march in the night, that we might approach it in
the morning, besides the wind pierced us like a
sword; but instead of its abating it increased,
together with a freezing rain, that incrusted us
intirely with ice, and obliged us to remain until
morning, the 19th, when we fortunately got some
juniper berries, which revived, gave us spirit,
and I thought strength. We were both so firmly of
that opinion, that we proposed taking the advantage of its being a dark snowy day, to approach
Carillon, to pass it in the night, and get upon
Lake George. With difficulty we persuaded the guide
to be of our opinion, we promised large rewards in
vain, until I assured him of provisions hid upon
the lake; but we little considered how much nature
was exhausted, and how unequal we were to the task
however, a few miles convinced us we were soon mid
way up our legs in the newly fallen snow; it drove
full in our faces, and was as dark as the frogs u-
pon the banks of New Foundland. Our strength and

our hopes sunk together, nay, even those of reaching Carillon were doubtful, but we must proceed or perish. As it cleared up a little, we laboured to see the Fort, which at every turn we expected, until we came to where the ice was gone, and the water narrow. This did not agree with my idea of South Bay, but it was no time for reflection; we quitted the ice to the left, and after marching 2 miles, our guide assured us we ought to be on the other side of the water. This was a very distressing circumstance, yet we returned to the ice and passed to the right, where, after struggling thru the snow, about four miles, and breaking in every second step, as we had no snow-shoes we were stopped by a large water fall. Here I was again astonished with appearances, but nothing now was to be thought of only reaching the fort before night; yet to pass this place seemed impracticable; however, I attempted to ford it a little higher, and almost gained the opposite shore, where the depth of the water, which was up to my breast, and the rapidity of the stream, hurried me off the slippery rocks, and plunged me entirely in the waters. I was obliged to quit my fuzee, and with great difficulty escaped being carried down the fall. Mr. Roche who followed me, and the guide, though they held by one another, suffered the same fate; but the hopes of soon reaching a fire made us think lightly of this; as night approached, we laboured excessively through the snow; we were certain the Fort was not far from us, but our guide confessed, for the first time, that he was at a loss. Here we plainly observed that his brain was affected; he saw Indians all around him and though we have since learned we had every thing to fear from them yet it was a danger we did not now attend to; nay we shouted aloud several times to give information we were there; but we could neither hear nor see any body to lead us right, or more likely to destroy us, and if we halted a minute we became pillars of ice; so that we resolved, as it froze so hard, to make a fire, although the danger was apparent. Accidently we had one dry cartridge, and in trying with my pistol if it would dash a little of the powder, Mr. Roche unfortunately held the cartridge too near, by which it took fire, blew up in our faces, almost blinded him, and gave excessive pain. This indeed promised to be the last stroke of fortune, as our hopes of a fire were now no more but although we were not anxious about life, we

knew it was more becoming to oppose than yield to
this last misfortune. We made a path around a tree
and there exercised all the night, although scarcely able to stand, or prevent each other from
sleeping. Our guide, notwithstanding repeated cau-
tions, straggled from us, where he sat down and
died immediately. On the morning of the 20th, we
saw the fort, which we approached with a white flag
the officers ran violently towards us, and saved us
from a danger we did not then apprehend; for we
are informed, that if the Indians who were close
after them, had seized us first, it would not have
been in the power of the French to have prevented
our being hurried to their camp, and perhaps to
Montreal the next day, or killed for not being able to march. M. de Hebecourt and all his officers
treat us with humanity and politeness, and are solicitous in our recovery, which returns slowly, as
you may imagine, from all these difficulties; and
though I have omitted many, yet I am afraid you
will think me too prolix; but we wish, Sir, to
persuade you of a truth, that nothing but the situation I have faithfully described could determine us in a resolution which appeared only one
degree preferable to perishing in the woods.
'I shall make no comments upon these distresses;
the malicious perhaps will say, which is very true
we brought them upon ourselves; but let them not
wantonly add, we deserved them because we were unsuccesful. They must allow we could not be led a-
broad, at such a season of snow and ice, for amuse
ment, or by an idle curiosity. I gave you, Sir, my
reasons for asking leave, which you were pleased
to approve, and I hope will defend them; and the
same would make me again, as a volunteer, experience the chance of war tomorrow, had I an opportunity. These are Mr. Roche's sentiments as well as
mine; and we both know you, Sir, too well, to harbour the least doubt of receiving justice with regard to our conduct in this affair or our promotion
in the regiment; the prospect of not joining
that as soon as we flattered ourselves has depressed our spirits to the lowest degree, so that we
earnestly beg you will be solicitous with the General to have us restored as soon as possible, or
at least to prevent our being sent to France, and
separated from you, perhaps during the war. I have
but one thing more to add, which we learned here,
and which perhaps you have already observed from
what I have said, that we were upon no other ice

than that of Lake George; but by the day overtaking us, the morning of the 14th, in the very place we had, in coming, marched during the night, we were entirely unacquainted with it, and obliged to put a confidence in this guide, whose head must have been astray from the first or he could not so grossly have mistaken a place where he had so often been. This information but added to our distress, until we reflected that our not being entirely lost was the more wonderful. That we had parted from South Bay on the 14, was a point with us beyond all doubt, and about which we never once hesitated, so that we acted entirely contrary to what we had established as a truth; for if, according to that, we had continued our course to the west, we must inevitably have perished; but the hand of Providence led us back contrary to our judgment; and though even then, and often afterwards, we thought it severe, yet in the end it — saved us, and obliged us to rest satisfied that we construed many things unfortunate, which tended to our preservation.'-(Rogers' Journals, pp 90-102).

Haviland forwarded this letter to Abercrombie who wrote Vaudreuil from N.Y. on Apr 24, 1758:

'Sir, Having learned by a letter written to Col. Haviland that Captain H. Pringle and Mr. Roche of his Majesty's 27th Regiment of Infantry, who, it was supposed, were killed at the late action between Major Rogers and a detachment of His Most Catholic Majesty's troops, were living and prisoners in Canada; as they will be in want of money to support themselves whilst prisoners, I request your Excellency to be so good as to have the enclosed letter forwarded to them, which, as you will observe, is nothing more than a letter of credit for their money to the amount of their pay; I flatter myself that you will be pleased to assist them to have it paid, which I shall regard as a particular favor on your part, and be always ready to: acknowledge under similiar circumstances.'-(Doc. Rel. Col. Hist. N.Y., X, pp 713-714).

On May 14, 1758, Abercrombie wrote Cornelius Cuyler, a merchant, that he would vouch for his loan of 100 pounds which Haviland stated Pringle & Roche neede to subsist while prisoners.-(AB 908).

Pringle and Roche were exchanged Nov 15, 1759.

A study of the Army Lists reveals that Henry Pringle was appointed Captain-Lieutenant of the 27th, or Inniskillings, on Feb 2, 1757. He was commissioned a full Captain on July 21, 1758 while still a prisoner; Appointed Major in the 56th Foot Sept 11, 1765; Lt-Colonel of the 51st, on Aug 16, 1770; went to Minorca with the 51st in 1772; became Brevet-Colonel in 1779; and Major General Nov 20, 1782, when the 51st returned to England. Retired from the command of the 51st in 1790, and died senior Major-General in 1800.-(Army Lists; Docs. Rel. Col. Hist. N.Y.. X, p 714).

Boyle Roche was commissioned Lieutenant in the 27th on Dec 10, 1755; Captain-Lieutenant on Aug 25 1762; Captain May 8, 1767; exchanged into the 28th on Dec 4, 1767, and left the army in July, 1770, after repeatedly petitioning General Gage for a transfer to some post in his native Ireland. On March 2, 1775 he petitioned Lord Dartmouth, related his past 24 years service; refers to Amherst Monckton, Howe and General Keppel for his military character; desires appointment to some post.-(Correspondence of Gage, Carter, Ed; Dartmouth MSS; Docs. Rel. Col. Hist. N.Y., X, p 714).

ABERCROMBIE'S APPEAL TO GOVERNOR FITCH OF CONN:
As a result of the heavy loss of Rangers at Rogers Rock, Putnam's & Durkee's Connecticut Companies were forced to stay on at Ft. Edward longer than their enlistments called for. Abercrombie wrote Fitch on Mar 20, 1758: 'P.S. Just after I had closed my letter, I received by Express from Albany an Account of a smart Skirmish..between..Rogers..& a Much Superior Body of the Enemy's Indians & Canadians..by which..we suffered greately..but as Rogers was not come in when this Account came away, I cannot with Certainty give you the Particulars; but be they what they will they confirm me the stronger in my opinion that your Rangers ought to continue where they are, lest the Enemy, who certainly must have information of their moving, when ever they do, take the Advantage of it.'-(AB 58)

THE VARYING EFFECT OF FRENCH PRISONERS ACCOUNTS:
Loudoun in his Diary for Apr 8, 1758, conveys the impression that Rogers was greately outnumbered, for by all the accounts he heard, the French lost 100 out of 700 engaged. However his friend, Dr. Huck-Saunders, writing to Loudoun from Albany, on May 29, 1758, revealed how the French insistance that they only had 150 Indians and Canadians commanded by a mere Cadet engaged, was undermining Rogers' report of 700 against him (actually, there were 300); the prisoners insistance that only 12

were killed, did not help matters. Dr. Huck-Saunders adds: that '..Rogers since this intelligence begins to fall into Disrepute. My high opinion of him is wavering. There are reasons to doubt his veracity. The return of Pringle and Roche, may make us better judges of his courage and conduct'. -(LO 5837. Courtesy of the Huntington Library).
 This wavering 'high opinion' of Rogers was not felt by all the Regulars though: Chaplain John Ogilvie of the Royal American battalion at Albany in writing to Johnson on Mar 28, 1758, says- 'The late affair of Rogers was gallant and bloody, and a considerable proof of his bravery and conduct, but envy, that arch fiend, will not allow him much merit'.-(Johnson Papers, Vol II, p 801).
 Captain Thomas Mante of the Highlanders states: that '..both the Major and those under him did everything that could be expected from good officers and soldiers..'-(Mante, Late War in America, p 111)
 Pringle's account of the uneven odds in the battle in his letter to Haviland did much to clear up the doubters minds, and was the principal reason why Rogers printed the letter in his published Journals in 1765.

FRENCH ACCOUNTS :

French accounts are many and several repetitious only those that offer different facts will be given. None of them present a true picture. They all minimize Rogers' ambuscade of Durantaye at Trout Brook; and it took Levis to establish the actual numbers of the French force engaged. It is interesting to note that the accounts penned down in the French private Journals came close to the truth, but when they were drawn from to send official reports to the Minister they spilled all out of proportion:-

VAUDREUIL'S ACCOUNT: to Marshal Duke de Noailles, from Montreal, Aug 6, 1758, employs his usual gasconade and tries to horde all the credit: '...I shall confine myself, my Lord, to that detatchment, on whose return the enemy's army was to put itself in motion. 'Twas a detatchment d'elite commanded by Major Robert Rogers, the most celebrated English partisan. He had orders from his officer to break up the ice, to lay down the route the army was to follow. But that detachment was entirely defeated by a party of soldiers of the Marine, Ca-

nadians and Indians, the command of which I confided to a few simple cadets belonging to our troops.
'In this way, my Lord, I protected the colony, during the winter, from the menaces of our enemies.'-(Docs. Rel. Col. Hist. N.Y., X, pp 808-809).

DURANTAYE & RICHERVILLE RECOMMENDED FOR PROMOTION:
Vaudreuil to M. de Massaic, dated Montreal, Sept 28, 1758: 'Nothing less, my Lord, than the success of the detatchment I had confided to Sieur de La Durantaye, was necessary to make our enemies renounce their projects and preparations for scaling Carillon in winter. Messrs La Durantaye and de Richerville having been included in the promotion of 1757, as Ensigns en Second, I employ them in the propositions I have the honor to submit to you this year, as Ensigns on full pay..I have anticipated his Majesty's favorable disposition towards them, by making them participate in the 6,000 livres he has granted on his list of 1757 to those who have distinguished themselves the most. I gave each at first 200 livres. You will perceive, my Lord, by one of my letters, that I have not as yet received that sum. Our officers are generally penetrated by the attention with which his Majesty has honored their services and the rewards he has been disposed to grant them. I lost no time in informing them thereof..'-(Doc. Rel. Col. Hist. N Y., X9 24

MINISTER'S CONGRATULATIONS TO VAUDREUIL:
Minister of the Navy Board to Vaudreuil, Paris, June 24, 1758: '..The Expedition of the Sieur de La Durantaye shows..that he neglects nothing that is calculated to destroy the enemy and to maintain the advantages continually gained by him (Vaudreuil) up to the present. The King desires to testify by some favour his satisfaction with the Sieur de La Durantaye for the bravery and ability he displayed in deceiving Robert Rogers and leading him to leave his advantageous position that he occupied on the mountain. Will do the same for the Sieurs de Richarville and de la Chevotiere, who formed part of the expedition. The loss the English sustained by the defeat of Robert Rogers must have been considerable, since, in the account they have given of this expedition they claim he escaped after losing many of his officers. They have no others with the Indians except Colonel Johnson.'-(Can.Arch: Orders of the King & Dispatches,-Series B, Vol 105, Folio 42, 3 pages).

MONTCALM'S ACCOUNT to the Minister, M. de Paulmy from Montreal, Apr 10, 1758: 'Captain D'Hebecourt, of the regiment of La Reine, who commands at Carillon, having been informed, on the 13th of March, that the enemy had a detatchment in the field which was estimated by the trail to number about 200 men sent a like detachment of our domicilated Indians, Iroquois and Nepissings, belonging to the Sault St Louis and the Lake of the Two Mountains, who had arrived on the preceding evening, with some 30 Canadians and several cadets of the Colonial troops, under the command of Sieur de la Durantaye, of the same troops; Sieur de Langy, one of the officers of the colony, who understands petty war the best of any man, joined the party with some of the Lieutenants of our battalion, who are detached at Carillon. The English detachment consisted of 200 picked men, under the command of Major Rogers, their most famous partisan, and 12 officers. He has been utterly defeated; our Indians would not give any quarter; they have brought back 146 scalps; they retained only three prisoners to furnish live letters to their father. About four or five days after, two officers and five English surrendered themselves prisoners, because they were wandering in the woods, dying of hunger. I am fully persuaded that the small number who escaped the fury of the Indians, will perish of want, and have not returned to Fort Lydius. We have had two Colonial Cadets and one Canadian slightly wounded, but the Indians who are not accustomed to lose, have had eight killed and seventeen wounded, two of whom are in danger of dying.'-(Docs. R. C. H. N. Y, X, pp 693, 697)

ADJUTANT MALARTIC'S ACCOUNT:

'A Cadet, detached from Carillon, came to inform the General that M. La Durantaye's party had arrived the 12th, on which day an old sorcerer had assured them that they would see the English before long; on the morning of the 13th 5 or 6 Indian scouts came to say that they had discovered fresh tracks of 200 men, whereupon the chiefs raised the musterwhoop and set out immediately with their warriors, some soldiers and Canadians, who traveled nearly 3 leagues without meeting any one; suspecting that the English had taken the Falls road they took the same course; M. Durantaye, who had joined them at the Bald Mountain, was with the van guard; he received the enemy's first fire, which made him fall back a little, and gave them time to scalp two Indians whom they had killed; meanwhile, M. De Langy, having turned them with a strong party of Indians, and having fallen on them when they felt sure of victory, had entirely defeated them; the Indians having discovered a chief's scalp in the breast of an officer's jacket, refused all quarter, and took 114 scalps; the opinion is, that only 12 or 15 men escaped, and that this detachment was composed of 170 or 180, commanded by Captain Rogers, who is supposed to be among the killed.'-(Docs.Rel.Col.Hist.N.Y., X, pp 837-838).

ROGERS' 'DEATH': The reason for this belief in Rogers' death is mentioned in a letter from Vaudreuil to M. de Massiac: 'Mr. Robert Rogers, who was at the head of the detatchment defeated by our cadets, had the knack to escape when he saw his ruin imminent; he left on the field of battle, his coat, and even the order he received from his General, which gave me every reason to believe that he had been killed, the rather as an Indian assured me he had himself killed him.'-(Ibid, X, p 924)

A French officer expressed the jubilance they felt at the report of Rogers' death: 'Saint-Saveur says his favorite phrase is-'Rogers is killed completely, clothes, coat and breeches!...'-(Bourlamaque to Levis, 1758,-Vol V, p 267, Coll. de Levis)

Their joy ceased when Rogers started raiding again in May. Malartic pens in his Journal on May 27, 1758 that 'M. de Hebecourt sends word that... Captain Rogers is not dead; that 'twas he who took the 4 men belonging to the garrison of Ft. Frederic..'-(Malartic's Journal, Paris, 1890).

Montcalm's Journal on the same date records: 'Robert Rogers is moving again since the action of March 13..'-(Montcalm's Jrn, p 356, Casgrain, Ed.)

DOREIL'S ACCOUNT: to Marshall de Belle Isle, from Que, Apr 30, 1758, sheds light on prisoners who survived the Indian's fury: 'The Indians brought back 144 scalps and some prisoners; among the latter were two officers. There were twelve in the party. Robert escaped almost naked, with some fifteen men and two officers. There is reason to presume that he will have perished of cold and hunger in the woods, inasmuch as three days subsequently, the two officers, after having wandered in a vain effort to escape, came to surrender themselves prisoners at Carillon, having left two men dead of fatigue and hunger within 2 leagues of that place.

This action has been brisk, and our detachments
have performed wonders in it. We have had two Cadets dangerously wounded, 4 Indians killed and 16
wounded.'-(Docs. Rel. Col. Hist. N.Y., X, p 703)

VAUDREUIL REWARDS THE INDIANS: From the 'Bulletin
of the Most important Operations during the Winter
of 1757-8', dated Montreal, Apr 18, 1758: '..We
have lost 8 Indians, and have had 17 wounded; also
two Cadets of the Colony and one Canadian. The dead have been covered with great ceremony; presents
have been made to the families in the name of the
King (the Great Ononthio). The Governor-General
will reward the bravery of our Iroquois by a promotion and presentation of some gorgets and medals
to those who have distinguished themselves; they
will be thereby more encouraged to revenge the
loss they have suffered.'-(Docs.R.C.H.N.Y., X, p 697)

Malartic's Journal records the return of the Indians and their grief over their losses:
March 27, 1758- 'Some Indians arrived (at Montreal) from Carillon. March 28,- All the Indians
arrived at Sault St. Louis; La Durantaye came to
report to the General the action of the 13th. Mar.
29,- The Governor-General sent some Surgeons to
Sault St. Louis for the wounded Indians who had
arrived there. March 30,- Some Indians came to see
Ononthio. March 31,- The grand chief of the Sault
with several warriors, have asked a talk with his
father, to set before him the loss his village has
suffered. Ononthio has opened his ears, cleansed
his throat, wiped away his tears and covered the
loss of his dead with some large presents.'-(Docs.
Rel.Col.Hist.N.Y., X, p 838) Apparently 'Ononthio'-
the King, was represented by Governor Vaudreuil.

Pouchot, in his Memoires, Vol. I, pp 100-102,
states that::'This was one of the most vigorous
actions of the Indians. They afterwards formed a
select detachment of volunteers under the name of
Decouvreurs (to go and discover)'.

HEBECOURT'S ACCOUNT TO BOURLAMACQUE Mar 15:
On March 19, 1758, Bourlamacque at Montreal sent
Levis the following extract from Hebecourt's
letter-'Following a savage trick, the English were
at the door of Carillon, M. de Hebecourt sent from
that place about twenty men to investigate and
they returned as fast as they could to warn us
that they had found very important fresh tracks.

The savages and the Canadians did not delay in deciding what to do. Just time enough to get the powder, bullets, their guns and provisions, and they left immediately, between two and three hours. M. de Langy left also with some savages and it may be said that all those who were there did marvels, having been forced to receive the first fire of the enemy who discovered us first [Rogers' Ambuscade — at-Trout-Brook]. The Sieur Rogers was saved, with about twenty men and an officer, as reported by two prisoners taken yesterday morning, 14th. The savages have forty-four scalps and seven prisoners, with two others who surrendered on the 14th in the morning. The enemy were from 170 to 180, comprising 10 or 12 officers. We had a wonderful result but it cost us dearly through the loss which we suffered [Hebecourt is the only French authority to admit a large loss, and if he admitted such, his statement could be relied upon for he was in a position to know the true state of losses]
    The affair took place oonthe 13th in the evening, at about the same place as that of January 21st last year. They were going between the Pointe and Carillon to take prisoners. Those whom we captured report that they were very determined to come to Carillon, this winter, if it had not been for the great quantity of snow which is at fort Lydius [Edward];...that Sieur Rogers was expecting five companies of 100 men each, to increase his troops and to be used as scouts, here and also around their fort..[The Commissions]of Capt. Robert Rogers, March 4, 1756; of Ensign [Bellfore] in the 27th Regt; of Lieutenant [Increase Moore]; of Ensign [Gregory McDonald were taken from their bodies except Rogers, whoe's commission was recovered from his green jacket which was left on the battle field]...The particular order given to Captain Rogers to command the party was also found [the discovery of this document would be a valuable find!]; The fact that 200 men were there is specified; so there is no doubt that Captain Rogers has been killed, in spite of what the prisoners are saying. ...I hope you will be kind enough to communicate this detail to M. de Doreil.'-(Coll MSS.Levis, V, Lettres Bourlamaque au Levis, pp 213-15 translated)

OTHER REFERENCES: Pouchot gives two repetitious Accounts in his Memoires (Vol I, pp 100-102; II, pp 228-9). He seems to have confused the action with that of Jan 21, 1757, at La Barbue Creek. He des-

cribes the Indian Sorcerer's prophecy of Rogers'
approach and adds that 'The Commandant although
astonished at this idea, was quite willing to get
rid of them'. According to Levis the French force
consisted of 250 Indians and Canadians; and a number of officers, Cadets and soldiers from Ticonderoga.-(Levis Journal, in Coll.de Levis-Casgrain)
The 'Journal of the Expedition in America, Commencing on the 15th of March, 1756', p 317, in the
Rapport of the Quebec Archives, 1923-24,-describes
the action. Casgrain's Montcalm et Levis, pp 353-
357 gives an excellent secondary account. John Jennings' Novel, Next to Valour, Chapter 16, 'Battle
in the Snow', pp 568-619, gives a dramatic and
accurate portrayal of the Battle.

389

III-SOURCES AND NOTES FOR EVERY RECORDED SCOUT, EXPEDITION, AND INDIVIDUAL FIGHT, 1755-Mar 1758

1.-(p 25) CONSTRUCTION OF FORT WENTWORTH, May -June 1755: Potter, Military Hist. N.H., pp 143-4.

2.-(p 26) ROGERS' FIRST RECONNOITRES, Aug 26 Sept 1755: See Footnote 9; Rogers' Journals, Intro

3.-(p 27) ROGERS' HUDSON RIVER SCOUT, Sept-Sept 9, 1755: Rogers' Journals, Introduction.

4.-(p 27) CONSTRUCTION OF FORT LYMAN (EDWARD), Aug 26-Sept 8, 1755: Johnson Papers, II, 24, 39, 55, 61 ; See Burk, Hawley, W. Hill Diaries in Bibliography

5.-(pp 27-29) THE GOPHER SCOUT, Sept 14-23, 1755 Rogers Jrns, 1; Original Jrn, Doc.Hist.N.Y,IV, 259.

6.-(pp 33-34) THE DECOY SCOUT, Oct 7-12, 1755: Rogers' original report was destroyed by fire, but fortunately it had been printed in the Doc. Hist. N.Y., IV, pp 262-63. Rogers sent Captains Putnam and Hunt, and Ensign Putnam forward to scout. Their reports to Rogers are on pp 264-266. Rogers' force consisted of 'about 50 men'. About 7 a.m. on the 10th, 3 canoes carrying 23 men '..Came by ye East Shore..within 70 Rods of ye Point where we were weel ambushed for them. They lay on their oars for ye Best Part of an hour, then sent out our burtch Canoe to Decoy them up by the Point, our Cannoe went Parilled with them within 30 Rods then turned and Padeled Back up by ye Point But they Did not folow them but turnd Down ye Lake half a mile and bore over to the west shore & their landed'. Rogers' scouts now came in and informed him that there were Indians behind him, finding their numbers to many, Rogers force returned 15 miles to an island, and the 12th, entered camp.
Johnson's Order to Rogers in the Johnson Papers, IX, p 250. Rogers' Journals, pp 4-5.

7.-(pp 34-35) ROGERS' SCALP SCOUT, Oct 14-21, 1755: Original Report in Doc.Hist.N.Y, IV, p 175. Rogers' Journals, p 5. Rev. Chandler's Diary and Nath Dwight's Jrn for Oct 13th state that Captain Butterfield and John Alexander were two of Rogers' party. Johnson to Phips, Oct 13: '..Capt Rogers..a Gallant honest Man..I send to Crn Pt'- Jhn MS, II, 192

8.-(p 45) SIXTH FRENCH FORT SCOUT, Nov 5-11, 1755: *Rogers'* Journals, *p 8. Dwight's Jrn,Nov 5,11 Rogers returned on the 11, not the 19, as he says.*

9.-(p 45) NOVEMBER 11-15 ALARM: *Dwight's & Hill's Jrns Nov 11-15. Johnson to Shirley Nov 12, regarding Rogers and the Indians veracity: '..If my opinion leans any way it is in favour of Capt. Rodgers..'*-Johnson Papers,*II,295.* Doc.H.N.Y,*IV,279-80*

10.-(p 46) RICHARD ROGERS' SCOUT, Nov 16-25, 1755: *Johnson's orders to Lieut Rogers, and official report of Lieuts Rogers and Claus to Johnson, are in* Doc.Hist.N.Y., *IV, pp 281-83. Also: Daniel Claus'* 'Narrative of his Relations with Sir Wm. Johnson', *Soc. of Colonial Wars in N.Y., 1904.*

11.-(pp 48-50) THE FISHERMEN SCOUT, Dec 19-24, 1755: *Rogers' official Report is in the* Colonial Office *5:17, pp 251, 261-263, sent to Sir Thomas Robinson by Governor Hardy. In his* 'Journals' *account, pp 9-10, Rogers adds: The first day 'we discovered a fire upon an island. This obliged us to lie by and act like fishermen, the better to deceive them, till night came on, when we proceeded'*

12.-(pp 51-52) ROGERS' RAID AT FIVE MILE POINT, *Jan 14-19, 1756: Rogers' official report to Johnson is in* Johnson Papers, *II, pp 416-17. His* Journals Account *on pp 10-11.* Boston-News Letter, *Feb 12th. Baldwin's Journal: 'Jan 19, 1756-..In the morning about 6:30 we were alarmed by Capt Rogers firing as he came in on the Lake from ye L. Champlain, where he took 2 pris & brot them with him. It rained.'*

13.-(pp 52-3) A RANGER'S ODYSSEY, Jan 20, 1756 *Nathan Whiting to Johnson from Ft. Edward, Jan 24, 1756, in* Johnson Papers, *II, pp 423-4.* Boston News Letter, *Feb 12, 1756, gives an interesting but partly inaccurate account. Baldwin's Journal: 'Jan 20,-A wet day. A scout chased by the Indians at S. Bay, W. from Ft. Edward. Jan 21,-Cold & cloudy. Capt Rogers lost a man yt went into Ft. Edward.'*

14.-(pp 53-4) ROGERS' FIRST CROWN POINT VILLAGE RAID, *Jan 29-Feb 6, 1756: Gleasier's orders to Rogers and Rogers' official report are in* Doc.Hist.N.Y., *IV, pp 283-5. He states he killed 50 Cattle, Horses and Hogs. In* 'Journals' *account pp 11-12 he says '50 cattle'. The* Boston News-Letter *Feb 26th*

Copy describes the raid then adds a 'P.S. *Just now
I further hear that..Capt Rogers stayed but 1 Day
in the Fort and then went out again with a fresh
party of men.'* It was actually 3 weeks before he
scouted again, but it was rumours like this along
with actual accounts of his prowess that impressed
his reading public and enhanced his fame. Baldwins
Journal, Jan 30, says two of Rogers men returned
in the evening.

15.-(pp 55-60) SECOND CROWN POINT VILLAGE RAID,
Feb 29-Mar 14, 1756; Rogers' Journals, pp 12-13.
Best account is Captain Baldwin's Journal, Feb 29-
Mar 14, 1756 entries. Boston News-Letter, Mar 25,
and Apr 1st copies. An idea of the number of barns
near Crown Point is revealed in the Swedish Naturalist Kalm's Journal for 1751: *'14 farms were occupied in the vicinity of Crown Pt., and great encouragement given by the King for that purpose',*
and that *'other colonists were approaching'*.

16.-(pp 71-3) THE THREE WEEK ALARM, Apr 12-
May 3, 1756: Baldwin's Journal Apr 12-May 3, 1756.
Boston News-Letter, May 20, copy.

17.-(p 72) AKIN'S NIGHT SCOUT, Apr 12-13, 1756
Baldwin's Journal, Apr 13, 1756 entry.

18.-(p 72) AKIN'S UPPER ISLAND SCOUT, Apr 22,
1756: Baldwin's Journal, Apr 22, 1756 entry.

19.-(pp 66-7) THE CATTLE TONGUE SCOUT, Apr 28-
May 11, 1756: Rogers' official report to Shirley, a
copy is in the Loudoun Papers-LO 1088. This is a
more complete account than that in Rogers' Journ—
nals, pp 15-17.

20.-(p 73) RICHARD ROGERS' WOOD CREEK PATROL,
May 9-12, 1756: Rogers' Journals, p 17.

21.-(p 74) ROGERS' WOOD CREEK HUNT: May 24-30,
1756: Rogers' Journals, p 18. Hervey's Journal,
June 1,: *'..Rogers did not meet with 'em, going to
S. Bay he perceived that they had just returned in
their batteaus..'* David Humphrey's in his 'Contemporary Life of Putnam', pp 209-210: gives an interesting, but entirely exagerrated account, in
which he describes 2 battles being fought.

22.-(pp 74-5) THE DISCIPLINE SCOUT, June 13-18,

1756: Rogers' Official Account to Shirley, a copy
is in the Loudoun Papers, *LO 1219.* This account is
more complete than that in Rogers' Journals, pp 18
19. Boston News-Letter, *July 1, 1756 Copy.*

23.-*(p 84)* ROGERS' HORSE RAID, Aug 2-10, 1756
Rogers' Official Report to Loudoun, *LO 1469,* gives
more details than Rogers' Journals account, pp 23-
25. This was Rogers first 'Report of a Scout' sent
direct to Loudoun. Wm. Corry to Johnson, from Albany, Aug. 6, 1756: describes the French deserter-
betrayer.-(Johnson Papers, II, pp 530-31). Captain
Ebenezer Learned (who accompanied Rogers as far as
Ticonderoga) sends his report of the scout to Loudoun, on Aug 7th.-*LO 1447.*

24.-*(pp 85-87)* ROGERS' CANADA RAID, Aug 16-
Sept 2, 1756: *Rogers' to Loudoun, Aug 11, 1756:*
His proposal to go into Canada to distress the en-
emy-*LO 1467.* Same to Same, Aug 16, 1756: His pro-
posal to go into Canada to Scalp-*LO 1501.* Rogers'
Official Report, Sept 3, 1756,-*LO 1689.* Rogers to
Loudoun, Sept 3, 1756: Copy of the Examination of
the Prisoners-*LO 1690.* Winslow to Loudoun, from Ft
Wm. Henry, Sept 5, 1756-*LO 1710.* Colonel Ralph
Burton to Loudoun, from Saratoga, Sept 16th: He
states he in enclosing a report of Rogers scout
and a map of Ticonderoga by Rogers-*LO 1818.* Rogers
Jrn., 26-30. Loudoun to Abercrombie, Nov 11-*LO2196*

25.-*(p 90)* PUTNAM'S POND BLOODHOUND SCOUT,
Sept 18-23, 1756: Rogers' Official Report to Burton
Sept 23, 1756, at Saratoga-*LO 1882.* Captain John
Stark's report to Burton, from Ft. Edward, Sept 21
1756 (Rogers had sent Stark to Ft. Edward with his
prisoners)-*LO 1866.* Burton to Loudoun, from Sara-
toga, Sept 16, 1756-*LO 1818.* Loudoun to Cumberland
Oct 3, 1756-*LO 1968.* Rogers' Journals, p 30.

26.-*(p 93)* ROGERS' SEPT 7-13TH SCOUT, 1756:
Rogers' official report to Loudoun-*LO 1776.* Rogers'
Journals, pp 31-33.

27.-*(pp 93-4)* WOOD CREEK-SOUTH BAY PATROLS,
Sept 24-Nov 19, 1756: Rogers' Journals, pp 33, 37.

28.-*(p 94)* QUI ETES VOUS SCOUT, Oct 22-31,
1756: *Rogers'* Journals, pp 34-37. Rogers' prisoner
was *La Verdure,* a Grenadier Private of the Languedoc Regiment-*LO 2129.* Loudoun to Fox, *LO 2263 A&B.*

29.-(p 24) SECOND BLOODHOUND SCOUT, Nov 16, 1756: Hervey's Journals, Nov 16, 1756 entry.

30.-(pp 94-5) ROGERS-ABERCROMBIE SCOUT, Nov 19-25, 1756: Rogers' Journals, p 37. General Abercrombie to Loudoun, Nov 27, 1756, from Ft. Edward-LO 2285 Received the 28th. Same to Same, from Albany, Kan 17, 1757: Recommending Dunbar for an Ensigncy in the 44th; states that he was the only Volunteer who offered to serve in this scout-LO2675

31.-(p 166) CAPT. STARK'S APRIL SCOUT, 1757: Gage to Loudoun, from Albany, Apr 16, 1757-LO 3367 Loudoun to Webb, N.Y., May 26, 1757-LO 3722.

32.-(p 166) MC CURDY'S SHORT SCOUT, May 1757: Webb to Loudoun, Albany, May 9, 1757-LO 3590. Gage to Loudoun, Apr 16, 1757-LO 3367.

33.-(p 166) SCOUT OF BULKELEY'S COMPANY, May 11, 1757: Bulkeley to Loudoun, Halifax, July 27, 1757-LO 6645-1.

34.-(p 167) RELIEF OF NUMBER FOUR, Mar 18-24, See p 423, footnote 165.

35.-(p 172) LAWRENCETOWN BLOODHOUND SCOUT, July 5- , 1757: Loudoun's Diary, July 5, 1757 entry: also adds that the Governor had also sent a party after the deserters, in a whaleboat. Rogers' Journals, p 54.

36.-(p 172) NORTHWEST NOVA SCOTIA BLOODHOUND SCOUT, July 13-28, 1757: Surgeon Cutter's Journal, July 13, 1757 entry. Rogers' Journals, p 54. Loudoun's Diary, Aug 1, 1757 entry.

37.-(p 189) SEVERANCE'S HUDSON RIVER SCOUT, Oct 2-4, 1757: Rufus Putnam, Jr's Journal, Oct 2-4 entries. Putnam accompanied Sergt. Martin Severance.

38.-(p 190) MC CURDY'S CAPTURE, Oct 1-4, 1757: Rufus Putnam Jr's Journal, Oct 4, 1757 entry.

39.-(p 190) ROGERS-LORD HOWE SCOUT, Oct 1757: Rogers' Journals, p 56.

40.-(p 190) THE SMALLPOX SCOUT, Oct 1757: Joshua Goodenough's Old Letter.

41.-(p 228) PHILLIP'S ICE TESTING SCOUT, Jan 25-27, 1758: *Jabez Fitch's* Journal, *Jan 25, 27th.*

42.-(p 229) STARK'S ICE TESTING SCOUT, Feb 5-10, 1758: *Jabez Fitch's* Journal, *Feb 5, 10th.*

43.-(pp 231-32) PURSUIT OF LANGY, Feb 8-10, 1758: *Eyre to Colonel Forbes, from Albany, Feb 14, 1758-LO 5596. Abercrombie to Loudoun, Feb 14, 1758 LO 5594. Jabez Fitch's* Journal, *Feb 8, 10, 18th. Pouchot's* Memoir, *I, pp 99-100.*

44.-(pp 232-33) LESLIE'S SNOWSHOE TEST, Feb 11-12, 1758: *Abercrombie to Loudoun, Feb 8, 1758-LO 5561. Report of Lt. Leslie, Feb 11, 1758-LO5553*

45.-(p 237) PUTNAM'S TICONDEROGA SCOUT, Feb 28-Mar 6, 1758: *Rogers'* Journals, *p 79: '..he had ventured within eight miles of..Ticonderoga; and that a party he had sent to make discoveries had reported to him, that there were near 600 Indians not far from the enemy's quarters.' This number is exagerrated. Only a few of Langy's Indians were there. Jabez Fitch's* Journal: *Feb 27, 28, 'Mar 2,- This Day Som of Capt Putnams Scout Returnd..Mar 5, -This Evening I Understand Som of Ct. Putnam's Scout Came In for a Slay in order to Bring a Sick Man on. They Say They Left Him at ye Plais where ye French Did Keep their Advanced Guard..Mar 6,-.. Toard Night Capt Putnam Returnd with His Scout all Safe Except John Robens who He (one or more words seem to have been omitted) In a Vary StrangManner' Lt. Fitch says he compiled a Journal of Putnam's scout for him, but it is not in the Loudoun or Abercrombie Papers.*

46.-(pp 238-39) PURSUIT OF LANGY'S INDIANS, March 6, 1758: *Jabez Fitch's* Journal, *Mar 6th. N. Y. Gazette, Mar 27, 1758 copy. Doreil to Belle Isle, Que, Apr 30, 1758- in* Doc.Rel.C.H.N.Y,X,F703.

47.-(p 239) MARCH 9TH BLOODHOUND SCOUT: *Jabez Fitch's* Journal, *March 9, 11, 13th entries.*

BIBLIOGRAPHY OF PRINCIPAL SOURCES
(With Key Word by which cited in Notes)
See: pp 284-286, for Uniform Sources.

PRINCIPAL MANUSCRIPTS

Key
LO   LOUDOUN PAPERS, *Huntington Library, San Marino, California*. All of the 10,000 items have been consulted. This exhaustive collection was the principal source for this volume.
AB   ABERCROMBIE PAPERS, *Huntington Library*. An invaluable source. All items were consulted.

MANUSCRIPT AND PRINTED DIARIES, JOURNALS, NARRATIVES, LETTER-BOOKS, ORDERLY-BOOKS, ACCOUNT BOOKS, LETTERS AND SECONDARY SOURCES

Abercrombie   Capt. James Abercrombie; *Orderly Book:* July 25,-Aug 12, 1757, LO 3993-A
Appy   John Appy; *Account Book in North America;* MS. in N.Y.Hist.Society.
Bacon   Capt. William Bacon; *Journal: Ft. Wm. Henry, 1756;* Walpole, Mass., 1901
Baldwin   Capt. Jeduthan Baldwin; *Journal: Ft. Wm. Henry, 1755-6;* Journal Mil.Ser. Institute, XXXIX, July-Aug, 1906.
Barrows   Priv. Abner Barrows; *Diary: 1756-7 at Fts.Wm.Henry & Edward;* Mayflower Soc Boston News-Letter: 1755-1758.
Bougainville   Rene de Kerallain; *Les Francais au Canada. La Jeunesse de Bougainville et la Guerre de SeptAns;* Paris, 1896
Bourlamaque   *Bourlamaque Collection;* Vol IV, Lettres Variarum; Canadian Archives.
Bouton   Nathaniel Bouton; *History of Concord, New Hampshire;* Concord, N.H., 1856.
Brown   Priv. Thomas Brown; *Narrativ;* Mag. of Hist With Notes & Queries, Extra No, 1908
Bulkeley   Capt. Charles Bulkeley; *Account Book;* Photostat Copy in Mass. State House.
Burk   Private John Burk; *Diary: Ft. Lyman, 1755;* Photostat Copy Mass. Hist. Soc.
Butler   B. C. Butler; *Lakes George and Champlain*
Casgrain   Abbe H. R. Casgrain; *Guerre du Canada, 1756-60, Montcalm et Levis;* Que, 1891
Chandler   Rev. Samuel Chandler; *Diary: Ft. Wm., Henry, 1755-6;* N E. Hist. Gen. Reg, 1863
Chapin   Clerk Edward Chapin; *Diary: L. George, 1755;* Palmer, Annals of Chicopee St.

Church	John Church; *Journal: Fort Edward, 1757;* Mass.Hist.Soc., Israel Williams MSS, II
Claus	Daniel Claus; *Narrative of His Relations with..Wm. Johnson;* NY, Soc.Col.Wars, 1904
C.O.	Colonial Office, *V:* 17; 48; 50. London. Collection de Manuscrits contenant documents historiques relatifs a la Nouvelle France. 4 Vols; Quebec, 1885.
Cutter	Surgeon Ammi Ruhamah Cutter, Jr.; *Journal, Ft. Edward, 1756; Falifax, 1757;* B.Cutter, *Hist. Cutter Family,* Bost, 1871
De Lery	Capt. Gaspard De Lery; *Diary kept at Carrillon May-July 1756;* Tic.Mus.Bul, VI, 4
Deshon	Maj. Moses Deshon; *Orderly Book: 1756, Ft Edward;* MS in Boston Atheneum, Unpub.
Dussieux	Louis-Etienne Dussieux; *Le Canada sous la domination francaise, d'apres les archives de la marine et de la guerre* Paris, 1862.
Dwight	Capt. Nathaniel Dwight; *Diary: 1755, Ft. Wm. Henry;* N.Y, Gen &Biog. Register, 1902
Eastburn	Robert Eastburn; *Narrative: 1756-7 while prisoner;* J. Spears, Ed, Cleaveland, 1904
Entick	J. Entick; *The General History of the Late War, Vol 3;* London, 1763-1764.
Everett	E. Everett; *John Stark,* Spark's American Biography, Vol 5; N.Y., 1902.
Fitch	Lt. Jabez Fitch; *Journal: 1757-8, Ft. Edward;* Vols 8-13 Mayflower Descendant.
Frederici	G. Frederici; *Scalping in America;* Smithsonian Institute Reports, 1906, p 437.
French	Rev. Jonathan French; *Diary: 1757 at Ft. Edward; Memoir..,* T. Alden, Ed, N.Y, 1810.
Frye	Col. Joseph Frye; *Journal: Siege of Fort Wm. Henry 1757;* Copy in Lib. of Cong.
Gabriel	Charles Nicolas Gabriel; *Guerre du Canada, 1755-60;* Verdun, France, 1887.-
Ford	W.C.Ford, Ed; *General Orders of 1757 issued by Loudoun (Webb) and Lyman (at Ft.Edward);* Webb Series, No. 1, N.Y, 1899. Gentlemen's Magazine; March, 1758, Lond.
Godfrey	Capt. Richard Godfrey; *Diary: 1755, Lake George; Hist. of Taunton, Mass,* 419-424.
Goodenough	Private Joshua Goodenough; *Old Letter(-Narrative); 1757-8, 1760;* Frederic Remington, Ed, Harpers' Monthly, Nov, 1897.
Graham	Rev. John Graham; *Diary: Fort Wm. Henry, 1756;* Mag.Amer.Hist, 8, Mar, 1882, 206-13.
Gridley	Private Luke Gridley; *Diary: Ft. Edward, 1757;* Acorn Club, pub no X, 1906, Hartford

Hall	Edward Hagaman Hall; *Major Robert Rogers Indian Fighter*; Amer. Scenic and Hist. Preserv, Soc., 10th Annual Rep., 1905, p 215
Hawley E	Lt. Elisha Hawley; *Diary: Ft. Lyman 1755* J.R.Trumbull, Hist. of Northampton, II.
Hawley G	Rev. Gideon Hawley; *Diary: Fort Edward, 1756;* Congregational Library, Boston.
Hayward	Capt. Benjamin Hayward; *journals: 1757-8 Fort Edward;* MS Conn. Hist. Society.
Hill	Private James Hill; *Diary: L.George 1755* N.Eng.Quart,V,602-18, Edna V. Moffett, Ed
Hervey	Capt. Wm. Hervey; *Journals: 1756-8 Lake-George front;* Suffolk Green Books, 14, V. 16
Hill	Wm.S.Hill; *Old Ft. Edward;* 1929, Ft. Ed.,N.Y.
Hough	F. B. Hough, Ed; *Journals of Maj. Robert Rogers..;* Albany, 1883.
Humphreys	David Humphreys; *An Essay on the Life of the Hon..Israel Putnam;* Boston, 1818.
James	A.F.James; *Writings of..John Forbes;* 1938
Jennings	John Jennings; *Next to Valour;* N.Y, 1939
Jesuit Relations	R.G.Thwaites, Ed; *Jesuit Relations;* Volumes 40-60; Cleaveland, 1896-1901.
Johnson Papers	General Wm. Johnson; *The Papers of Sir Wm. Johnson;* Vols I-IX; N.Y.State
Kalm	Peter Kalm; *Diary;* Munsell, Annals of Albany
Kelsey	Moses Kelsey; *Journal: Lake George front 1757-8;* Granite State Mag., II, Aug,1895
Knox	Capt. John Knox; *An Historical Journal of the Campaigns in..America..1757-60,* 3 Vols, A. G. Doughty, Ed; Toronto, 1914
Levis	Chevalier de Levis; *Journal: 1756-60;* Vol I, Coll. MSS, Levis, Casgrain, Ed; Que, 1889
Livermore	Private Samuel Livermore; *Diary: Gilman's N.H.Regt, L.George, 1755;* N.E. Hist. Gen. S.
Livingston	W.F.Livingston;..*Israel Putnam;* N.Y, 1901 *London Magazine;* September, 1756. *London Monthly Review;* XXXIV, pp 9, 22, 242
Loudoun	John, IV, Earl of Loudoun; *Diary: Jan 1, 1756-July 15, 1758;* 5 Vols; & 11 Vols of Indices & Memorandum Books; MSS in Huntington Library, HM 1717 (call no)
Macomb	John Macomb; *Letter-Copy Book;* NY. State Lib
Malartic	Adjutant Joseph Malartic; *Journal des Campagnes au Canada, 1755-60;* Paris 1890
Merritt	Clerk Daniel Merritt; *Diary and Orderly Book: Ft.Wm.Henry 1756;* Maine Hist. Soc.
Metcalf	Private Seth Metcalf; *Diary: Ft. Edward, 1757;* Hist.Rec.Survey, Bost, 1939, 12pp.
Mante	Capt. Thomas Mante; *History of the Late War in North America;* London, 1762.

Mass Arch	Massachusetts Archives; *Letters*, Vol 4, 38A, 55, 109; *Military*, Vol 75.
	Memoire du Canada; Rapport Que. Arch, 1924
	Memoire sur le Canada depuis 1749 jusqu a 1760; Lit. & Hist.Soc.Que,1st Series I
Moore	Farmer Moore's; *Historical Collections;* I
Montcalm	Marquis de Montcalm; *Journal..en Canada 1756-59;* Vol VII, of Collections MSS Levis, Casgrain, Ed; Quebec, 1889-95
	New Hampshire Province Papers, VI.
	N.H. Historical Society Collections, X.
	State Papers of N.H., XIV; Hammond, Ed.
	New York Gazette; 1755-58.
	New York Weekly Post Boy; 1755-58.
Nevins	Allan Nevins; *Biography of Robert Rogers;* Introduction to Ponteach, Caxton Club, Chicago, 175 Copies, 1914.
O'Callaghan	E.B.O'Callaghan, Ed; *Documentary History of the State of N.Y.*, IV; 1849-50
O'Callaghan	E.B.O'Callaghan, Ed; *Documents relative to the Colonial History of the S. of New York procured in Holland, England & France*, Vol 8, 10; 1858.
O'Conor	N.J.O'Conor; *John Appy..in America;* 1938
Palmer	Palmer; *Lake Champlain.*
Pargellis	S. M. Pargellis;: *Lord Loudoun in North America;* Yale Univ. Press, 1933.
Pargellis	S. M. Pargellis, Ed; *Military Affairs in North America, 1748-65;* Selected Documents from Cumberland Papers in Windsor Castle; N. Y., London, 1936
Parkman	Francis Parkman; *Montcalm and Wolfe*, 2 Vols; Boston, Little, Brown, 1907.
Pell	S.H.P.Pell, Ed; *The Bulletin of The Ft. Ticonderoga Museum*, VI, 1, Jan, 1941
Pitt Correspondence	G.S. Kimball, Ed; *Correspondence of Wm. Pitt when Secretary of State with Colonial Governors and Military, Naval Commanders*, 2 Vols; N.Y, 1906
Pomeroy	Seth Pomeroy; *Journal: L. George, 1755;* Soc. of Col. Wars, N.Y., 1926; Forest, Ed.
Potter C E	C.E.Potter; *History of Manchester, N.H.*
Potter	Col. C.E.Potter; *Military History of N.H*
Pouchot	Capt. M. Pouchot; *Memoir upon the Late... War in..America..*, 2 Vols; F.B.Hough Ed; Roxbury, Mass., 1866.
Pound	Arthur Pound; *Robert Rogers;* in 'Native Stock', pp 109-148; 1931.
Powers	Reverend G. Powers; *Historical Sketches of Coos County, New Hampshire.*

Putnam R	Rufus Putnam; *Journal; 1757-60 L. George front;* E. C. Dawes, Ed; Albany, 1886
Que Arch	Quebec Archives *Rapport* for 1923-24. Report of the Adjutant General of N.H., for 1866, Vol II.
Roberts	Kenneth Roberts; *Northwest Passage,-* Special Limited Edition in 2 Vols, Vol II, comprising the Documentary Appendix to this classic Novel; 1936
Rogers M	Mary Cochrane Rogers; *A Battle Fought on Snowshoes;* Published by the Author at Derry, N.H., 1917. 66 pp, ill.
Rogers	Major Robert Rogers; *Journals: 1755-Feb 14, 1761;* First Edit: 1765, J. Millan Bookseller near Whitehall, London; reprinted at Dublin, Ireland, by R. Acheson, at Horace's-Head, William-St, for J. Milliken, no. 10 in Skinner-row in 1769; 2nd reprint by J. Potts, at Swift's Head in Dame St., in 1770; 3 more reprints in America.
Shirley Corr	Wm. Shirley; *Correspondence,* 2 Vols; C.H. Lincoln, Ed; N.Y., 1912.
Stark, Memoir	Caleb Stark; *Memoir and Correspondence of John Stark..;* G. Lyon, Concord, 1860.
Stark, Reminiscences	Caleb Stark; *Reminiscenses of the French War;* Concord, 831
Stark	Caleb Stark; *History of Dunbarton, Merrimack County, N. H.;* Lyon, Concord, 1860
Stark	Capt. John Stark; *Account Book: 1757-60 L. George front;* MS owned by W.S.B. Hopkins, Worcester, Mass.
Stoddard	S. R. Stoddard; *Lake George Illustrated.*
Thomas	Dr. John Thomas; *Diary: 1755 Nova Scotia* N.E.Hist.Gen.Reg., Oct., 1879, 383-398. Truscott's Rangers; Newsweek, Aug 31, 1942 *Virginia Gazette, 1755-1758.*
Watson	Watson; *History of Essex County, N.Y.*
Wells	Capt. Edmund Wells; *Diary: 1756-57 Lake George front;* Conn. State Library.
Willard	Abijah Willard; *Journal-Orderly Book. 1755-6 Nova Scotia;* MS Huntington Lib.
Williams	Dr. Thomas Williams; *Letter-Diary: to his Wife 1755-6 from L. George front* Historical Magazine, April, 1870.
Winslow	John Winslow; *Journal: 1755-6 Nova Scotia;* Nova Scotia Hist. Soc. Coll., 3-4. *Letter-Book: 1756 Lake George front,* etc; MS in Mass. Hist. Society.
W.O.34	War Office Class 34: *Amherst Papers,* V 76

HISTORICAL NOTES

To avoid repeating the full title of a source citation most citations have been made by the use of key-words, usually the names of the writers or editors of the works cited, such as 'Rogers', for Robert Rogers' 'Journals'. All key-words appear in the 'Bibliography of Principal Sources' preceding these notes on pp 395-399.

CHAPTER ONE (pp 23-50)

p-23 [1]Wentworth, besides receiving a substantial fee on each land petition granted, was empowered to set aside a reservation of 500 acres of the choisest land for himself. The safer he could make his frontier, the easier it would be to insure the growth of his towns and personal estates-*N.H.P.P.*

p-24 [2]*F. Moore*, III, 326. Due to the absence of preserved muster rolls of Rogers' First Company of Blanchard's N.H. Regiment the names of the officers have never been known up to this time. Now at last the names of Rogers' first officers are known. Moore gives his source for the roster of officers: '*From a Journal kept by an officer in Blanchard's-N.H. Regiment in 1755*'. This newly discovered information destroys the popular belief that Rogers' brother Richard was the First Lieutenant. Richard Rogers was a Sergeant in Captain Wm. Simes' 10th Company of Blanchard's N.H. Regiment from April 24 to Oct 4, 1755; and did not enter Rogers Rangers until Oct 4, and did not officially become Rogers' First Lieut. until Nov 28, 1755-*Potter*, 142, 156.

p-24 [3]'Coo' was the Indian for pine tree and 'Cooash', the plural of 'Coo', meant pine trees; hence the Indian word 'Cooash-auke', as applied to the country on the Connecticut R., at Haverhill and Lancaster, meaning literally 'the pine-tree's place', and hence our words 'Coos', 'Cohos', and 'Cohosuck'. The 'Great', or 'Lower Coos', was at Haverhill, and Upper Coos at Lancaster-*Potter*, 365

p-25 [4]Wentworth, in excusing himself to General Johnson, for not ordering the N.H. Regiment to march directly to the army's rendezvous at Albany, states: '*The Money Granted for Carrying on this*

Expedition being paper, it has no Currency either
in the Massachusetts or in New York Governments,
for which reason I have been obliged to March the
regiment by Land to Connecticut River, from thence
to march over to Crown point to Joyn the main body
of the Troops under your Command.'-Wentworth to
Johnson, June 17, 1755: *Johnson Papers*, I, 606-7.

p-25 [5]Potter, *Military History of N.H.*, 143-4.

p-26 [6]See Appendice B: *Uniforms and Equipment*, p271
Besides food, one gill of Rum constituted the
daily ration for Rogers' men as well as other Provincial troops. It seems that some members of
Johnson's Army were receiving more than their
share of Rum while rendezvouing at Albany for
Johnson had to issue the following General Order
on July 28th: '..That no more than one *Gill of Rum*
per day for each Man be issued by any *Regiment* or
Company and half of that in the morning and half
in the Evening. And whoever presumes to make any
Disturbance in consequence of this Order be immed
iately put in Confinement, and if tending to mutiny
or Desertion to be tried by a General Court Martial..'-*Johnson Papers*, I, 787.

p-26 [7]Rogers' Introduction to his *Journals*.

p-26 [8]*Ibid*. On Aug 18, Johnson, then at the site
of Fort Edward, ordered the tardy Colonel Blanchard to convoy a Massachusetts and Connecticut
provision train to 'The Great Carrying Place' (Ft.
Edward), and hopes that his Regiment: '..will be..
marching at that time and all your obsticles remo
ved..'-*Johnson Papers*, I, 859. But Blanchard's ob-
stacles were not removed, for he could not march
without a provision train for his own Regiment.
Wentworth could not induce his Assembly to outfit a
wagon train unless the Regiment were reduced from
500 to 250 men. Johnson received Blanchard's disquieting packet on Aug 22, and immediately called
a Council of War. It was decided to 'retain' the
N.H. Regiment and feed them out of the provisions
sent by the other Colonies for their Regiments-*Po-
und*, 194; *Johnson Papers*, I, 871; Blanchard to
Wentworth, Aug 28, 1755, in *N.H.P.P.*, VI, 429.

Blanchard had trouble in obtaining these provisions though, and it was not until Sept 27, when
Johnson called another meeting on the matter, that
the following proportions were set: Massachusetts

to supply 4/9, Connecticut 2/9, N.Y. 2/9, R.I. 1/9 Johnson Papers, II, 123). While waiting for Johnson's answer, Blanchard ordered Rogers on Aug 20, with his Company and one other to convoy the Massachusetts and Connecticut provision train to Fort Edward. Rogers says he left Albany on Aug 26, but he is in error, for he could not have met Johnson at Fort Edward if he left on that date for that was the day Johnson himself left Fort Edward for Lake George. All of Rogers' accounts for 1755 in his published *Journals* are usually from five to ten days ahead of his original accounts, due to the fact that the Old Style Calendar then lately adopted in England and the English Colonies, had not, as yet, come entirely into vogue when the actual events were taking place. Figuring that a fast packet took two days from Fort Edward to Albany, Blanchard must have received Johnson's Aug 18, letter on the 20, and due to it's urgent contents he undoubtedly sent the provision train off the same day under the protection of Rogers convoy of 100 men. This would just about give Rogers time to arrive at Ft Edward before Johnson left on the 26.

p-26 [9]Rogers' Introduction to his *Journals*. On Aug 26, the day he left Fort Edward for Lake George, Johnson left the following orders to General Lyman (commanding the construction of Ft. Lyman (Edward) until the arrival of Blanchard with the rest of the N.H. Regiment): '*That a Scouting Party be sent every day for 2 or 3 Miles round*' Ft. Edward-Johnson Papers, I, 887. Since Rogers was so well recommended for this service he no doubt had more than his share of these routine scouts or patrols.

p-27 [10]Much to the chagrin of Rogers he had no part in the Battle of Lake George or the actions preceding or after on the same day. Lieutenant John Stark commanded the bulk of his Company which remained behind at Fort Edward while Rogers with the remainder were scouting up the Hudson on Sept 8, the day of the battle. Although no N.H. men were with Johnson at Lake George still 120 of them (and 90 of the N.Y. Regiment) were sent to reconnoitre towards Lake George after the din of the battle was heard and they fell in with a large body of Indians at Bloody Pond and routed them. This is the only one of the 3 separate engagements of the day that a detatchment of Rogers Company could possibly have engaged in and it is not very likely that they were even in that for there is no mention of Rogers' Company or his officers: Lieutenant Stark or Ensign Abraham Perry. Stark could not very well have been in this action for he states in later life that 'he was never conscious of taking the life of an individual..' until Jan 21, 1757-C. Stark, *Reminiscenses*, 19. He could not have been in the action at 'Bloody Pond' without at least attempting to kill an Indian for none of the Americans remained idle or gave orders with a sword in this bloody engagement. However Rogers Rangers might have been employed in bringing in the wounded sometime after the 3 battles for Johnson writes Shirley on Sept 30, that '..*A Scouting Party of the N.H. Regt. Brot In yesterday a Wd. Indian of the Penobscot Tribe..he was among the Indians at the late Engagement..The N.H. and Other Scouts daily find numbers of the Enemy Slain in The Woods*'- Johnson Papers, II, 123.

p-27 [11]From the time of the Battle of Lake George, Sept 8, to the close of the year, Rogers Rangers looked in on Ticonderoga five different times and Crown Point three times not to mention engaging with the enemy in two actions on Lake George. At least 11 scouts were performed by other units of Johnson's Army but only 3 of these managed to look in on Ticonderoga from a safe distance (viz: Capt. Dolittle's, James Connor's, and Hendrick and Nicklas's scouts) and these scouts only served to confuse Rogers' accurate information, who viewed the French Forts from their very fortifications. The other 8 scouts (out of the 11) were either recoinnoitres around Johnson's camp or scouts destined for '*Ty*' but never got there-*D.H.N.Y.,IV, 170-200*.

p-27 [12]To help in the reduction of Crown Point was the main reason for the existance of the bulk of Rogers Rangers on the Lake George front for 5 years. In 1731, the French finally fully awoke to the realization of the strategic importance of commanding Lake Champlain and beat the English to erecting a fort at its southern narrows. '*Geographically it is in truth The Gate of the Lake, for such is the narrowness of the lake at this point that the feeblest of armaments might close it to all passage*'; and feeble it was at first for the first work erected by Beauharnois, Gov-General of Canada in 1731, was a small stockade which could accommodate only 30 men. Beauharnois named the fort, '*St.

Frederick', in honor of Frederick Maurepas, the French Secretary of State at that time.

Three years later, in 1734, the stockade was replaced by a 'redoubt a machi coulis' sufficient for a garrison of 120 men. It was constantly enlarged, and in 1742 was, with the exception of Quebec and Louisbourg, the strongest work held by the French in Canada. It's condition in 1749 is described by Kalm: 'Fort St. Frederick is built on a rock consisting of black lime slates' (Chazy Limestone), 'and is nearly quadrangular, has high and thick walls, made of the same limestone, of which there is a quarry about half a mile from the fort. On the eastern part of the fort is a high tower which is proof against bomb shells, provided with very thick and substantial walls, and well stored with cannon from the bottom almost to the very top, and the Governor' (Commandant) 'lives in the tower. In the terre plaine of the fort is a well built little church and houses of stone for the officers and soldiers. There are sharp rocks on all sides towards the land beyond cannon shot from the fort, but among them are some which are as high as the walls of the fort and very near them. Within one or two musket shots to the east of the fort is a windmill, built of stone, with very thick walls, and most of the flour which is wanted to supply the fort is ground here. This windmill is so constructed as to serve the purpose of a redoubt and, at the top of it are 5 or 6 small pieces of cannon.'

Finally, in 1751, the fortress proper was completed, and a ditch was started to surround the fort like a moat. This ditch enclosed the hill referred to by Kalm. Starting at the water's edge about 2 rods north the trench terminated about 15 rods south of the fort. Its greatest distance from the fort in the rear, was 30 rods. This ditch was not yet finished when Rogers and his Rangers boldly slept in it on September 17, 1755. Rogers also notes that an enclosure was erected about 25 rods north-west of the fort which reached to the waters edge and surrounded several buildings used for soldiers quarters. Rogers Rangers were not only the first English to harass the fortress, they were the only body of English to harass the fort while the French remained there; and when they evacuated in 1759 in the face of Amherst's army, it was Rogers Rangers who arrived first at the burning fort and a Ranger Lieutenant raised a British flag over the ruins. At this time (before part of the fort was blown up) Crown Point was a pentagon with bastions at each angle and a strong redoubt 250 yards in advance of each. It was surrounded by a ditch walled in with stone, the walls being nearly 25 feet high; they measured half a mile in circumference. There was an underground passage to the lake. Within the fortress was a level area bounded by long stone buildings. The fortress would accomodate 4,000 men-W. *Murray*, 89; *Palmer*, 48-49; *Kalm* (1750); *D.H.N.Y.*, IV, 259-60; *Rogers* 143; *London Magazine*, Sept 1756 printed a good ground plan; Benj. Stoddart, a prisoner there prior to the War, gives a good description to Johnson in Aug 1755: *Johnson Papers*, I, 891; The *N.Y. Gazette* of Sept 8, 1755, gives *Kalm's* description.

p-27 [13]Fort Carillon (Ticonderoga) was built 11 miles south of Crown Point at the junction of Lakes George and Champlain and became the buffer receiving all the attacks. After Dieskau's defeat on Sept 8, 1755, Vaudreuil, Governor-General of Canada retaliated by ordering Ticonderoga to be built. The Chief Engineer was a Canadian, Chartier de Lotbiniere, assisted by Captain Germain of the Queens Regiment, and Adjutant Joannes of the Languedoc. At first the fort was named Fort Vaudreuil but soon was renamed Carillon, meaning a chime of bells, which the music of the cascade at the outlet of Lake George resembled. The Indian name 'Onderoga' or 'Ticonderoga' is said to describe the noise of these falling waters. At first the fort was square with 4 bastions and defended by a redoubt on a hill commanding the Fort. It was enlarged and strengthened and in 1758 was angular in form, divided into several parts by deep ditches. The communication between them was made by stone staircases placed in the high angles, arranged to make the route circuitous. The walls were high and temporarily covered with timber and earth to protect the barracks. Mortar was poured in the Spring. Hebecourt, the Commandant during the Winter of 1757-58, reports that by Jan 10, 1758, 864 windows had been put on. '*The 20th, the second door of the Fort has been put on and they are working on the barrier, the stairway and the magazine, and after these, the other ramparts, where we must have barriers, to prevent anyone from going there, and so we can keep the doors of the small barracks open without sentinels when the weather is fair. The stairway of the attic of the jail is up and it*

still needs to be picketted. The pump is a success
the cistern is now made of oak plank and we have
made some flagstone to clean the magazine and fill
up the cistern which is made of plank of oak, because it appears that M. Lotbiniere (the Engineer)
does not want this water to be drank. The coal
furnace where there was a fire for two weeks is very good for the forge where there was no fire for
days..'-Hebecourt to Bourlamaeque, Jan 6, 1758, in
Can. Arch: Bourlamacque Coll., IV, Lettres Varium
(translated); Rogers, 76; Hough, 54; S. H. P. Pell.

p-28 [14]Lake George is slightly over 33 miles long
and nearly 4 miles wide at the broadest place; it
is 321 feet above tide water and 225 feet above
Lake Champlain. It is enclosed between ranges of
lofty mountains and contracts into narrows at either end dotted with islands and shadowed by cliffs
and crags; then spreading into a clear and open
expanse. The Iroquois named the lake, Andia-ti-roc
te, 'Where the lake shuts itself'. The French called it 'St. Sacrament', which was given it by Father Jogue, who was bound for a fatal mission to
the ferocious Mohawks in 1646. Reaching its banks
on the eve of the Feast of Corpus Christi (Christ
the King), he apropriately named the lake, 'St.
Sacrament'. The English name of 'Lake George' was
applied by Johnson, who in a letter to Shirley on
Sept 1, 1755, says: 'I have given the name of Lake
George, not only in honor of this Majesty, but to
assert his undoubted dominion here'. For 5 years
Lake George became the chief warpath of Rogers Rangers and they came to know every contour of its
shores and hills. Although most of their traveling
was done by night to avoid being seen by the enemy
-Palmer, 23; Johnson Papers, II, 199.

p-31 [15]Johnson commends the scouting abilities of
Rogers and his men when writing to Governor Wentworth on Oct 6, 1755: 'As Colonel Blanchard is now
oblidged to return with his Regiment..and good Intelligence will still be of the utmost Consequence
to the Security of our Camp..I proposed that Captain Symes and Captain Rogers with a few of their
men should continue here, which they agree to. I
hope your Excellency will approve of their staying
as they will be of a good deal of Service to us in
the Scouting Way..'-Johnson Papers, IX, 247. Johnson did not know exactly how many Rangers staid on
with Rogers, one time he says 4 or 5, another time

6 or 8-Johnson Papers, II, 150, 170. Actually 24
of Rogers' Company staid on with him.
 Rogers' Ambuscade at Isle au Mouton was the first
and last skirmish of Rogers Rangers as the first
Company of Blanchard's N.H.Regiment, for this Company ceased to exist when the Regiment left Johnson's army on Oct 6, to return to New Hampshire.

p-31 [16]Potter, 146-147; 142-143. See Appendice C.

p-32 [17]Ibid.

p-32 [18]John Stark, though he was later to become
second in command of Rogers Rangers and its most
famous Captain, started his first campaign as Rogers First Lieutenant in a very mediocre way, for
there is no record of his even serving on a scout
in 1755. There is no mention of his activities.

p-32 [19]Johnson to Hardy, Oct 13-Johnson Ps, II, 190.

p-32 [20]Johnson Papers, II, 187-188.

p-33 [21]Ibid, II, 190.

p-44 [22]The Banyar-Johnson controversy on Rogers'
veracity are in the Johnson Papers, IX, 251; II,
153*; 162; 190; 205; 287. *Banyar wrote Johnson on
Oct 7, about impeachment of Rogers' reports but it
was destroyed by fire.

p-45 [23]Funk & Wagnall's description of a Partisan
fits Rogers Rangers to a 'T': 'A member of a detached body of troops employed in special service or
in irregular subordinate warfare, such as raids,
forays, and harassing the enemy; a guerrilla.'
 These services were performed by the 'American
Rangers' (who were always associated with Rogers
Rangers by the press) in World War II. A query to
Major Douglas Parmentier, Chief, Publications
Branch, A.U.S., regarding the official existance of
'American Rangers', brought the following reply:
'There are no units in the Army of the United —
States which contain the term, 'American Rangers'
in their title. However, the term, 'Ranger', is
applied to certain American troops specially trained, and was widely publicized following the United Nations' raid on Dieppe, France. The use of
the word, 'Ranger', is not officially recognized by
the War Dept and is used with unofficial approval.'

p-47 [24]Potter, 156-7; D.H.N.Y., IV, 281-283.-

p-47 [25]Rogers, 8.

p-47 [26]Ibid, 10.

p-48 [27]Potter, 153, 150, 152, 156-7, 149, 148, 151 See Appendice C: Rogers' Own Company.

p-48 [28]See Appendice B: Uniforms and Equipment.

p-50 [29]A digest of the events of Rogers Rangers for the first campaign of their existance reveals that 1755 (from April thru December) was full of accomplishments in spite of their small numbers; namely: The building of Ft. Wentworth; building of Ft. Lyman (Edward); convoy duty; reconnaissances around Ft. Edward; Rogers' Hudson River Scout; two skirmishes: A successful Ambuscade at Isle au Mouton; and a pitched engagement near the same place, in which they won their first Battle Honour; another reconnaissance to the Second Narrows; Besides six scouts to the French Forts in which they recoinnoitered (usually by creeping within the very defenses) Ticonderoga five different times and Crown Point three times.

CHAPTER TWO (pp 51-110)

p-61 [30]Boston News-Letter, Feb 26, 1756 copy.

p-61 [31]Massachusetts Archives, IV, 546; The 'gratuity' was voted upon on February 25, 1756.

p-61 [32]Nevins, 47.

p-61 [33]Shirley was so impressed by Rogers' Winter Campaign that he twice urged the Massachusetts Court to make a similar 'gratuity' but they refused. No doubt they remembered Rogers' abduction of the promised recruits in 1755 and were not as willing to forgive as Shirley was-Mass Arch, CIX, 243

p-61 [34]Rogers, 13.

p-61 [35]Ibid, 14.

p-62 [36]Ibid.

p-64 [37]Outside of the New York and Albany 'gratui-

ties' this bounty money of ten Spanish Dollars was the first money that Rogers Rangers felt since their enlistment into Blanchard's Regt. See Appendice B and C. *Rogers*, 14-15; *W.O.34*, Vol 76, p 18: a copy of Shirley's Commission to Rogers, Mar 24, 1756.

p-65 [38]Rogers, in his *Journals*, suppresses the fact that money was paid for every scalp that he or his Rangers might bring in. The 2nd and 6th sections of the English Articles of War were on *Mutiny* and *Desertion*, either offense was punishable by death or at least several hundred lashes with the cat-o'-nine-tails, whichever the Courtmartial and Commander-in-Chief decided upon. *Rogers*, 13-15 Shirley to Winslow, Apr 30, 1756-*LO 1090* (*'LO'* is the call number of the Loudoun Manuscript items in the Huntington Library. They will be cited as such.

p-66 [39]Garty Gilman had gladly left New Hampshire in Sept 1755, when he managed to secure a Corporal's berth in Gilman's newly raised N.H. Regiment sent to Johnson's Army to relieve Blanchard's men. The Regiment served the remaining month of the campaign and Gilman returned with it to New Hampshire, and had been there three months before Rogers signed him up in April-*Potter*, 149, 153; *LO1145*

p-66 [40]*Rogers*, 15.

p-66 [41]*Ibid*.

p-66 [42]*Boston News-Letter*, May 20, 1756 copy.

p-67 [43]*Pouchot*, II, 72; *Parkman*, I, 447-448.

p-68 [44]Jacob's Muster Roll started on May 27, 1756 and ended Nov 11-*Johnson Papers*, IX, 493; *LO 2454*.
The Indian township of Stockbridge, Mass., was incorporated in 1739. In 1750 it contained 53 families, comprising 218 individuals. By 1756 their numbers had increased somewhat but still they could not put over 50 to 75 Warriors in the field. Small as their numbers were, they, and another small tribe, the Mohegans, were more usefull to the British arms than the whole six nations. The Mohegans were a larger tribe than the Stockbridges they were located at Moheek, since Montville, Connecticut, about ten miles north of New London. Over 100 Warriors were recruited from the Mohegans when two Companies of Indian Rangers were raised

for Rogers Rangers in 1758, 59 and 60. Jacob Cheeksaunkun was the principal Sachem of the Stockbridges, and Uncas was the King of the Mohegans. He was a wily old rogue but loyal to the English and a friend of Rogers.

p-68 [45]The Stockbridges did not serve in 1757.

p-69 [46]Pargellis, *Loudoun*, 301-303. When Loudoun asked Abercrombie what he thought of his idea of raising a Regiment of Indians he answered in the negative saying that from the experience they had with Jacob's Company in 1756 they could seldom muster over half of them in camp and even then could not prevail upon them to go out on a scout until after a big pow-wow-Abercrombie to Loudoun in *Loudoun Papers*, Huntington Library.

p-70 [47]The daring activities of Rogers Rangers in 1756, not only established New Hampshire as a province full of skilled woodsmen, but stirred visions in Loudoun's and King George Second's minds of literally Regiments of Rangers ready to be raised: in the other Colonies as well. King George and Loudoun were very explicit in their instructions to their subordinates to try and get as great a number of Rangers as possible into the Provincial troops being raised-*LO 848; LO 933; LO 770*.

Johnson Papers, IX, 439: Johnson to Shirley, Apr 22, 1756: '..In marching thru the Woods in these parts the only way to secure a March is by Indians or experienced Rangers.'

p-70 [48]Over 90% of the names on Robert Rogers Muster Rolls were Scotch or Irish.

p-70 [49]Rogers' *Journals*, 17.

p-74 [50]*Potter*, 156-157; *LO 1145*.

p-76 [51]*Goodenough*, 880: says of Rogers:-He 'was a doughty man and had a reputation as a bold Ranger leader. The men declared that following him was sore service, but that he most always met with great success.'

p-76 [52]The two Privates were James Catto and Peleg Veneys of Robert Rogers' Company. Venays deserted on July 24, and Catto left on the 26th-*LO 2747*.

p-76 [53]Rogers' Journals, 19.

p-79 [54]Bougainville, Montcalm's aide-de-campe, propounded five different hypotheses to account for Rogers' whaleboats being found above Crown Point. Bougainville's Journal. As late as 1757, even Montcalm was questioning Ranger prisoners on the subject: 'The Sergeant told of the manner that the four barges gained admittance to Lake Champlain. Their Commander was the Captain Robert Rogers, the same who commanded the English in the action of January 21st.' (the Ranger Sergt. did not give Rogers' 'secret water-passage' away, instead he concocted the following tall story of two herculean portages that was apparently swallowed by the amazed Montcalm:) 'They went up Wood Creek and made the remarkable feat of a portage at Presquisle opposite to the ground of M. Hocquart; and in order to avoid the Fort of St. Frederic they made another remarkable feat of a portage at the Cape of Damant..' (he apparently meant a portage across Chimney Point, opposite to Crown Point)-Translated from Montcalm's Journal, 183.

p-80 [55]Rogers, 23. Abercrombie did not commission Richard Rogers, Captain, on July 24, for it was Loudoun's place to do so, and he was not yet on the scene. Oddly enough, Loudoun did not commission Richard Rogers, Captain, and Noah Johnson, Lieutenant, until November 2, but he commissioned Caleb Page, Ensign, when the Company arrived in Albany on Aug 29th.

p-80 [56]Boston News-Letter, Sept 2, 1756 states: '..Captain Rogers, has a Brevet for Major..' However this new title was bestowed upon him by the admiring Provincials only, because of the growth of his Corps with the advent of Richard Rogers' Company; it held no legality, and the British officers still called him 'Captain Rogers'. There is considerable doubt as to just who started the 'Brevet for Major' rumor. Rogers might have started it himself in the hope that Loudoun would catch on and officially promote him.

p-80 [57]Shirley Correspondence, II, 453.

p-80 [58]At a Council of War held at Albany on May 25, 1756, Shirley (then acting as Commander-in-Chief) stated that he had raised Robert Rogers'

Company of Rangers 'to harass the Enemy upon Lake
Champlain, and in Scouting Parties by Land as far
as Montreal, and to procure Intelligence..'; and
that he was raising out of Winslow's Provincials
three more such Companies to be employed in the
same service. Shirley also 'proposed to raise four
Ranging Companies of Irregulars consisting of 60
privates each to be employ'd in scouting parties
for keeping open the communication with Oswego,
and harrassing the Enemy's Country between Fort
Frontenac and Montreal..' since he could have no
dependence on the Six Nations for that service.
But Shirley never got around to raising these four
Companies for he was soon superseded by Abercrombie who, in a Council of War at Albany on July 26,
was voted to '..send orders to Johnson to raise
needed Rangers and recommended that Abercrombie
raise another Company (Richard Rogers) for the
Publick Service..' It seems that Johnson's and Rogers letters for more Rangers finally bore fruit
(Rogers had wrote Abercrombie on July 16, suggesting an augmentation of his Rangers and recommended
his brother Richard for the Captaincy of the new
Company). When Loudoun was still in Albany in August he raised one more Ranging Company to be paid
for out of his contingency funds. The Company was
commanded by William Lampson. He completed his
Company by Aug 17, and was stationed at Stillwater
on the Hudson to patrol and protect the environs.
Lampson had originally been commissioned by Shirley, as Captain of a Ranging Company, but he could
not drum up any recruits at that time.
 Out of the 6 Contingency Ranger Companies raised
by Shirley, Abercrombie and Loudoun in 1756, viz:
Robert Rogers', Jacob's, Richard Rogers', Humphrey
Hobbs', Thomas Speakman's, and William Lampson's
Companies. Four of them (all but Lampson's and Jacob's) continued in service and formed Rogers Rangers. However, Jacob Cheeksaunkum's Indian Company
again formed part of Rogers Rangers when they were
revived in 1758-*Shirley Correspondence*, II, 453-59
470, 475-476; *Johnson Papers*, IX, 486-487; *Rogers*,
23; Loudoun's Warrant to pay Lampson 70 pounds
sterling for enlisting and bounty money for raising his Company *LO 1975-1;* Wm. Johnston to Loudoun
Nov 5, 1756 memorandum of cash issued for Warrants
LO 2153; Wm. Lampson to Loudoun, from 'Scantycook'
Sept 13, 1756 *LO 1789;* Loudoun signed a Warrant
appointing Anthony Van Schaick of Albany, Captain
of a Company of Rangers, Aug 13, 1756, but the

Company was never completed-*LO 1400*.

p-80 [59]Richard Rogers' Company marched to Albany by way of Rumford, Derryfield (now Manchester), Litchfield, Monson (now Milford), Peterborough, and Swanzy in New Hampshire then southwest to the Connecticut River they crossed over into Massachusetts to Northfield and south to Deerfield then west to Albany. Richard and Noah Johnson enlisted 20 men at Rumford, New Hampshire; 15 at Litchfield N.H.; 5 at Deerfield, Mass.; 5 men between Deerfield and Albany; and recruiting officers brought in 6 men from Sheffield and 4 from Provinceland (both towns within two days march of Albany). Rogers completed his march from Rumford, N.H., to Albany, N.Y., in thirteen days (Aug 16, to Aug 29, 1756). Starting out with 20 men he arrived in Albany with 50, having enlisted 35 men in New Hampshire, 10 in Massachusetts and 10 in New York-*LO 2504:* Marching expenses for Captain Richard Rogers Company of 50 men from N.H. to Albany. *Boston News-Letter*, Sept 2, 1756, mentions that Richard Rogers and Noah Johnson raised the Company '*in the neighborhood*' of Boston, but they are in error unless they considered southern New Hampshire and western Massachusetts '*the neighborhood*'.

p-80 [60]*Johnson Papers*, IX, 517: Loudoun to Johnson from Albany, August 31, 1756.

p-81 [61]Richard Rogers' Company were on the same establishment as Robert Rogers' with the exception of the Second Lieutenantcy, and the numbers. Richard's Company had no Second Lieutenant until Feb 24, 1757 (Rogers errs in his 'Journals' when he states that Nathaniel Abbot was the Second Lieutenant when the Company was raised in 1756). The new Company had only 50 men whereas Robert's Company now had seventy. However Richard's Company was maintained on the same establishment as Robert's when they were originally raised by Shirley on Mar 24, 1756-*LO 2504; AB 4867-5* ('*AB*' is the call number of the Abercrombie Manuscripts in the Huntington Library); *Rogers*, 23, 14-15, 19.

p-82 [62]Pargillis, *Loudoun*, 89-103; *Parkman*, I, 440 441; *Rogers*, 33-37.

p-83 [63]*Rogers*, 15, 19.

p-83 [64]Surgeon Thomas Williams letter to his Wife from Camp at Ft. Edward, Aug 25, 1756-in *Dawson's Historical Magazine*, April, 1870.

p-84 [65]Wells, *Diary*, Sept 17, 19, 21st entries; Lt Col. Ralph Burton to Loudoun, Aug 5, 1756, *LO 1424*

p-85 [66]*Rogers*, 30-31; *Hervey*, 33: says Lt. Naunauptaunk arrived at Fort Edward on Aug 2, and left there for Ft. Wm. Henry on Wed, the 4th. According to this they must have arrived and joined Rogers Rangers on Thursday, August 5th.

p-87 [67]Loudoun arrived at Albany to take command of his Army on July 29, five days after the berth of Richard's Company. The new Company marched into Albany a month later. The same day in a General Order, Loudoun evidently destined the new Company for the Lake George front for he ordered them to parade at 6 o'clock the next morning (Aug 30th) to escort the Artillery and wagons leaving for Ft. Edward. He changed his mind on the 30th and sent them up the Mohawk-Loudoun's General Orders at Albany, Aug 29-30th *LO 1669;* Loudoun to Hardy, Sep 1

p-87 [68]Webb to Loudoun, from Burnet's Field, 10 'O Clock, Sept 15, 1756 *LO 1815:* states, that it would be difficult for him to keep a lookout for a French invasion force, for he had no Indians and Richard Rogers' Company was very weak and were not much acquainted with the country so that they could scout but a short distance from him. Webb's phrasing of this letter was not a very good boost for Rogers' new Company but then Webb never did have a high opinion of Rogers Rangers. He considered their high pay an affront to the Regulars and their indespensability an exaggeration.

p-88 [69]Loudoun to Webb, from Albany, Sept 16, 1756 *LO 1819;* Loudoun to Hardy, Sept 16, 1756 *LO 1820*.

p-89 [70]Burton to Loudoun, from Saratoga, Sept 16, 1756 *LO 1818; Rogers*, 30.

p-91 [71]Stark, *Reminiscences*, 45 note.

p-91 [72]*Rogers*, 30.

p-91 [73]Rogers' Island was the largest of a group of small islets opposite to Ft. Edward. Off and on for the next two and a half years it served as the base of operations for Rogers Rangers.

p-91 [74]Abercrombie to Loudoun, Ft. Edward, Nov 16, 1756 *LO 2225;* same to same, Nov 12, 1756 *LO 2203*.
It is interesting to note here the cost (to a Ranger officer) of building a hut if a carpenter was engaged. In Sept, 1758, it cost Appy, Loudouns and Amherst's Secretary, 1 pound, 4 shillings; while in Oct, 1759, he paid 3 pounds, 4 shillings, for *'rum, Nails and Carpenters for my hut..'-Appy*, Sept 29, 1758; Oct 30, 1759 entries. No doubt some of Rogers Rangers were among those enterprising individuals who managed to steal plank from the *'King's works'* (namely Ft. Edward) to build better huts with-*Lyman*, Aug 29, 1757, General Order.

p-92 [75]Abercrombie to Loudoun, Ft. Edward, Oct 2, 1756 *LO 1947:* states, that he had out such a vast number of scouts from Fort Edward that he did not think it possible for Montcalm to make a move without him having early notice of it.

p-92 [76]*Rogers*, 30-31.

p-93 [77]See Appendice F, p 298.

p-94 [78]*Rogers*, 33; Loudoun to Fox, Albany, Oct 3, 1756; 'bercrombie to Loudoun, Fort Edward, Oct 2, 1756 *LO 1947; Hervey*, 43.

p-94 [79]*'On Party':* The term, or status, of being out on a scouting party. This term was commonly used by Rogers Rangers.

p-94 [80]*Rogers*, 37.

p-96 [81]*LO 2454:* Loudoun's Warrant for Balance due Jacob's Company, issued Nov 14, 1756.

p-96 [82]*Ibid;* Johnson to Loudoun, Albany, Aug 3, 1756 *LO 1397;* Loudoun to Johnson, Albany, Aug 3, 1756 *LO 1398:* Jacob's Company had already received ten dollars advance money from Shirley and the balance of two months pay (from May 27, to July 27) on Aug 4, by Johnson. In all, 195 pounds, 6 shillings had been paid by Nov 14, and 743 pounds, 12 shillings, N.Y. Currency remained of 938 pounds, 18 shillings, the total estimated cost of the Company for five and a half months service.

p-96 [83]Examination and passing of the Stockbridge Indian Companies Account for 1756-George Croghan to Loudoun, Albany, Nov 14, 1756 *LO 2211*.

p-96 [84]*Ibid;* Loudoun to Abercrombie, Albany, Nov 11, 1756 *LO 2196*. A complete financial adjustment was not made until the Spring of 1757. Captain Jacob personally visited Johnson at Johnson's Hall, and laid the matter before him on Jan 23, 1757, but Johnson had to refer it to Loudoun and it took considerable haggling before the matter was finally settled: *Johnson Papers*, IX, 590-91, 632; II, 678.

p-97 [85]Robert Rogers to Loudoun, Fort Edward, Oct 19, 1756 *LO 2043:* This petition was received by Loudoun the same day for he was at Fort Edward at this time. This was Rogers' first meeting with him.

p-97 [86]Abercrombie to Loudoun, Alby, Dec 6 *LO 2320*

p-98 [87]*Ibid*.

p-98 [88]Shirley to Winslow, N.Y., Apr 30, 1756 *LO 1090;* Winslow's Letter-Book, Orders to Winslow, Apr 30, 1756; *Shirley Correspondence*, II, 453-459, 499-500; Shirley to Winslow, N.Y., Apr 30, 1756 *LO 1091* (his second letter to Winslow on this date).

p-99 [89]Shirley to Winslow, Apr 30, 1756 *LO 1090*.

p-99 [90]*Ibid;* See Appendice B, pp 278-280.

p-99 [91]Shirley to Winslow, Apr 30, 1756 *LO 1090*.

p-99 [92]Shirley originally intended the Companies for the Oswego front, to keep it *'clear of the Enemy's Scalping Parties'*, but by the time Hobbs'and Speakman's Companies were raised and arrived at Albany, Oswego had long since fallen and now that Lake George was the important theater, they were re-routed to that front by Shirley's successor, Loudoun: *Shirley Correspondence*, II, 499-500.

p-99 [93]Winslow's *Letter-Book;* Winslow to Shirley, Apr 24, 1756; Shirley to Winslow, Apr 30, *LO 1091*.

p-100 [94]All four of these men had been Captains in Winslow's own Battalion of Shirley's Massachusetts Regiment, and like Robert Rogers' Company in the N.H. Regiment of 1755, they served on detatched duty (in Nova Scotia) with their Companies as Rangers, distinguishing themselves throughout the Beaujour Campaign and the events following. All of Shirley's Correspondence on the raising of Hobbs' and Speakman's Companies in 1756, reveals that he intended them to be crack Ranging Companies with officers and personnel from his own Province of Massachusetts who had served with distinction in his Provincial Regiment. He intended them to be well clothed, paid, armed and feed. It was through no fault of his that only two skeleton Companies could be raised and it was the raising and dispatching of them to Albany that constituted Shirley's last military efforts as Commander-in-Chief.

p-100 [95]Shirley to Winslow, Apr 30, 1756 LO 1091.

p-100 [96]Same to Same, same date LO 1090.

p-100 [97]Winslow's Battalion left Halifax on Apr 7, and arrived at Boston on the 30th: *Boston News-Letter*, Apr 22, and Apr 30, 1756, copies.

p-100 [98]Shirley even had visions of raising 5 Companies out of his returning Massachusetts Regiment at least he stated as much in a letter to Prime Minister Henry Fox, from Albany, June 14, 1756: *Shirley Correspondence*, II, 466. It is possible that he was endeavoring to curry favour for he was aware that the home office was anxious to employ experienced Rangers. Shirley played safe when he fabricated about giving orders to Winslow to raise five Ranger Companies, for he states in his letter to Fox that he *'did not have returns yet of the progress made in raising them, or whether they can be rais'd; but hope some of them at least will be'* But Shirley overestimated his Regiment's desire to reenlist as Rangers, for the combined strength of the two Companies (Hobbs' and Speakman's) that he finally dispatched from Boston totaled only 72 privates. In a letter to the home office on Sept 4, Shirley attempts to save face by stating that *'soon after my Return hither I sent Lord Loudoun 2 Companies of Rangers consisting of 60 Privates each'*: *Shirley Correspondence*, II, 533.

p-101 [99]*Ibid*, II, 551; 'Notes on Mr. Shirley's Letter to Loudoun Sept 13, 1756' LO 1792.

p-101 [100]Shirley to Loudoun, Aug 23, 1756 LO 1563.

p-102 [101]Secomb, 42, 289, 290, 308, 358, 359, 360, Hist. of Charlestown; Hobbs to Loudoun, Sept 17, 17-56 Account of the River Kennebec LO 1824; Hobbs to Loudoun, Albany, Sept 18, 1756- An Account of the way from No. 4, to N.H. to the mouth of Otter Creek LO 1839.

p-102 [102]Parkman, I, 282-86; Willard, MS Narrative

p-103 [103]Hobbs' and Kennedy's Account of the River Kennebec to Loudoun, Sept 17, 1756 LO 1824.

p-103 [104]Willard's Narrative: mentions Brewer making at least 3 different scouts.

p-103 [105]Shirley to Loudoun, Boston, Aug 23, 1756 LO 1563; Notes on Mr. Shirley's Letter to Loudoun, of Sept 13, 1756 LO 1792: Paragraph Four-Loudoun states Speakman's Company at 21 Privates. He is in error, for Speakman is paid for marching 40 men from Boston to Albany LO 2623-1.

p-103 [106]Ibid.

p-106 [107]Abercrombie to Loudoun, Fort Edward, Sept 28, 1756 LO 1912. However the 2 new Companies were out on some scouts, for Private Thomas Brown of Speakman's, states that during the Fall of 1756: '..I was out upon several Scouts, in one of which I kill'd an Indian..' Brown, 1.

p-106 [108]Abercrombie to Loudoun, Albany, Dec 6, 1756 LO 2320. Private Brown states that he 'enlisted into Major Rogers's Corps of Rangers, in the Company commanded by Capt Spikeman..' Brown, 1.

p-106 [109]Hobbs' and Speakman's Companies came under Rogers' command on Jan 15, 1757.

p-106 [110]Loudoun to Abercrombie, Nov 11th LO 2196.

p-107 [111]Abercrombie to Loudoun, Nov 16th LO 2225.

p-108 [112]Loudoun to Abercrombie, Nov 11th LO 2196.
All of the 4 Companies now received the same pay except the officers of the Rogers's and the new Companies.-See Appendice G, p 304 for difference.

p-108 [113]Abercrombie to Loudoun, Nov 16th LO 2225; Thomas Saul to Loudoun, Albany, Jan 22, 1758 LO

5441; See Appendice B, p 277.

p-108 [114]Loudoun, *Diary,* III, 62, 'pr 25, 1757 *HM 1717.* It is probable that the 2 new Companies arrived at Ft. Wm. Henry on Oct 15, for '*80 Rangers*' formed part of Loudoun's bodyguard when he left Ft Edward for Ft. Wm. Henry on the 14th: *Hervey,* 43. Winslow's Provincial Army left Wm. Henry for home in 2 divisions, on Nov 11, and 17th: *Hervey,* 45.

p-109 [115]Rogers Rangers made 24 recorded exursions in 1756: Five of them were actions, four successful, one, Sergt Archibald's Massacre, the first defeat of Rogers Rangers. Seven were raids to the environs of Ticonderoga and Crown Point. Three, were notable, but bloodless raids to Crown Point and Five Mile Point. Two, were 'Bloodhound Scouts' for British Deserters. Three, were patrols to South Bay and Wood Creek. Four, were scouts to the First Narrows or near Fort William Henry.

p-109 [116]Loudoun to Fox, Albany, Nov 22nd *LO 2263.*

p-110 [117]*Ibid; Hervey,* 43: 'Oct 24, 1756, *Two Companies of the 44th and two of the 48th marched for Fort William Henry to form the Winter garrison.... under the command of Major Eyre of the 44th Regt*'.

p-110 [118]Loudoun to Fox, Nov 22, 1756 *LO 2263 A&B.*

p-110 [119]Loudoun to Hardy, Albany, Nov 9th *LO 2183*

CHAPTER THREE (pp 111-212)

p-111 [120]A daily job of necessity, was that of chopping wood. Alternate details from each Company were sent daily into the neighboring woods. The road between Forts Edward and William Henry had to be kept open, viz: all fallen trees were dragged off the road leaving it clear for sleds to travel on. A daily patrol was made around the two Forts to pick up any tracks of enemy parties.

p-111 [121]Like the Regulars, the Rangers daily ration of Rum was a gill (¼ of a pint). It's potency was increased by 'lacing' it with a pint of boiling water and about an eighth of a pound of melted butter. Drank on an empty stoumach, this potion had a decidedly exhilarating effect.

p-139 [122]Loudoun, Diary, Jan 25, 1757 HM 1717.

p-140 [123]Rogers, 46-7: Rogers to Capt. James Abercrombie, Ft. Edward, Jan 30, 1757; Capt. Abercrombie to Rogers, Albany, Feb 6, 1757. Loudoun's List of Commissions granted in the Independant Ranging Companies, Feb 24-29, 1757 LO 6580.

p-140 [124]Abercrombie to Loudoun, Albany, Jan 27, 1757 LO 2716; Rogers to Loudoun, Albany, Feb 28, 1757 LO 2933; Rogers, 49.

p-141 [125]Rogers, 49-50: General Abercrombie's Instructions for Captain Robert Rogers, Albany, Feb 26, 1757. See Appendice C, p 290.

p-142 [126]Abercrombie to Loudoun, Albany, Jan 27, 1757 LO 2716; Rogers, 52: 'March 5, I was taken ill with the smallpox, and not able to leave my room till the 15th of April following.' See p 304.

p-143 [127]Rogers, 49-50; Men discharged from Rogers Company LO 3708-3; Rogers to Loudoun, N.Y., May 24 1757 LO 3708-2; AB 4867-5; LO 6658-1; LO 6645-1.

p-143 [128]Compiled from the New York Value of Exchange, after the Declaration of War: Wm. Johnston to Loudoun, Aug 10, 1756 LO 1463.

p-143 [129]LO 3061.

p-143 [130]Rogers to Capt. James Abercrombie, Ft. Edward, Jan 30, 1757: mentioned in Rogers' Jrns, 46.

p-144 [131]Although John McCurdy was now the First Lieutenant of Rogers' Company, still he did not receive a new commission from Loudoun. Since all Lieutenants received the same pay, no written commissions were granted when a Second Lieutenant received a First Lieutenant's berth. The difference in Lieutenants being that of seniority only.

p-145 [132]Abercrombie to Loudoun, Jan 27, 1757 LO2716

p-146 [133]Boston News-Letter, June 16, 1757, copy.
Loudoun's and the Prime Minister's opinions and plans of employing Rogers Rangers are in: Loudoun to Fox, Albany, Oct 3, 1756; Cumberland to Loudoun Kensington, Oct 22,-Dec 23, 1756 LO 2065. Although Loudoun was adverse to paying the Rangers such

high wages, still, his opinion of them was higher than that of The Prime Minister: Loudoun to Fox, Albany, Nov 22, 1756 *LO 2263 A&B*.

p-148 [134]Loudoun, *Diary*, III, 62, Apr 25, 1757; Warrant to Lieutenant Charles Bulkeley of Late Capt. Hobbs Independent Company of Rangers for expenses of his men in Recruiting, N.Y, May 26, 1757 *LO 5194-3*. Rogers mentions in his '*Journals*' 51-52 that he '*recommended Lieutenant Bulkeley of Hobbs' Company as a proper person to succeed him in that... command..*' Rogers states that he made this recommendation in his letter of Feb 28th to Loudoun, but in the actual letter he mentions Hobbs' death and that he will endeavour to fill up his Company while he is recruiting for his own, however there is no mention of recommending Bulkeley: Rogers to Loudoun, Albany, Feb 28, 1757 *LO 2933*. Rogers might have recommended him at a later date though, but this is just another example of some of the inaccuracies Rogers made in his printed *Journals*.

p-148 [135]Warrant to Bulkeley, May 26th *LO 5194-3*.

p-149 [136]*LO 3062; LO 3061*. Although for lorn bodies with both their Captains dead, the bulk of the two new Companies stated their desire to continue as Rogers Rangers when the terms of the new establishment were made known to them. Almost two-thirds (47 of: 74 Privates) took the ten dollars bounty money and reenlisted, even though the time of their original enlistment was up on May 27th. The remaining 27 Privates were discharged at intervals from March 12, to May 31, 1757, when recruits had arrived to fill their places pursuant to Abercrombie's orders. Fifteen were discharged out of 45 Private men in Speakman's (now Stark's), while 12 out of 29 Privates were dropped from Hobbs': *LO 6658-1; LO 6645-1*.

p-149 [137]*LO 6580:* Loudoun's Ranger Commissions.

p-150 [138]*LO 3062;* Loudoun makes an interesting entry in his *Diary* on March 8, 1757: He states that Jonathan Brewer was commissioned Lieutenant in place of Samuel Kennedy killed, and on the next line he notes that Lieutenant Jonathan Brewer was '*to be made to Captain*'. B:..... ..... have petitioned Loudoun on the subject (although it is not in the Loudoun Papers), and though Stark had already been given the Captaincy of Speakman's, still, Loudoun was incited to jot down the memorandum that Brewer was 'to be made to Captain' if and when future Ranging Companies were raised.

p-151 [139]Loudoun, Diary, March 8, 1757 entry; Loudoun's Ranger Commissions LO 6580.

p-151 [140]LO 3061-1; LO 3062.

p-159 [141]Gage to Abercrombie, Albany, Mar 28, 1757 LO 3199; Monro to Gage, Ft Edward, Mar 24, LO 3157.

p-159 [142]Eyre to Johnson, Albany, Apr 3, 1757, in Johnson Papers, II, 696-697.

p-159 [143]LO 5194; Ensign Phillips arrived at Albany with his 11 recruits on Mar 22, and was rushed up to Ft Ed. by Gage to join Monro's relief force.

p-159 [144]Loudoun, Diary, Mar 8, entry; LO 6580.

p-160 [145]Ibid.

p-160 [146]Billiting Warrant for Stark's men LO 5194.

p-160 [147]Ibid.

p-160 [148]Warrant to Lt. Charles Bulkeley for expenses of his men in recruiting LO 5194.

p-161 [149]Ibid.

p-161 [150]Loudoun, Diary, III, 62, Apr 25, 1757.

p-161 [151]Loudoun's Ranger Commissions LO 6580. Thomas Cunningham was a Sergt. in Robert Rogers' Company July 24, 1756, while Bill Phillips received his Sergeantcy after Oct 24, 1756 LO 2747, 2570

p-163 [152]AB 4867-5.

p-163 [153]Billiting Warrant paid N.Y., May 24 LO3717

p-163 [154]Ranger Commissions LO 6580; LO 3708-1.

p-163 [155]Loudoun, Diary, Apr-June 18, 1757 HM1717.

p-164 [156]Pargellis, Military Affairs, 269: Dec 1756

p-165 [157]Ibid: 279.

p-165 [158]Rogers, 52.

p-165 [159]Ibid: 52-53; 'Foreign Service', meaning the foreign French *Isle Royale*, where lay the mighty citadel of Louisbourg, Loudoun's 1757 goal.

p-166 [160]Ibid; Abercrombie at N.Y. ordered Webb at Albany on May 2, 1757, to embark Rogers Rangers with all possible expedition for N.Y.: LO 3526.- Consequently the 3 Companies probably embarked on the private sloops at Albany on May 7, or 8th, and arrived in N.Y. on May 10, or 11th.

p-166 [161]Loudoun, *Diary*, III, 23, Feb 8, 1757. Col. Messerve was invaluable to Loudoun from building blockhouses for the Rangers to constructing whaleboats in large numbers. His friend, John Shepherd, was a hardy individual, who, as a Provincial Captain in the N.H. Regiment in 1756, had a smart fight in Aug between Forts William Henry and Edward and was captured, but managed to escape from Montreal and fell in with Rogers' scout Oct 22, 17 56: *Eastburn*, 60-1; *Hervey*, 32-33, 44; *Rogers*, 34.

p-166 [162]Rogers, 53.

p-166 [163]Loudoun's Ranger Commissions LO 6580.

p-167 [164]Wentworth to Loudoun, Portsmouth, Mar 6, 1757 LO 2977; LO 3163.

p-167 [165]Isaac Parker to Loudoun, Hinsdale, N.H., Mar 24, 1757 LO 3161; Ebeneazor Hinsdale to Loudoun, Hinsdale, Mar 24, 1757 LO 3163; Col. Messerve to Captain James Abercrombie, Northfield, N.H., March 18, 1757 LO 3090.

p-167 [166]Messerve to Capt. J. Abercrombie, Flushing Bay, Apr 13, 1757 LO 3352; Loudoun to Wentworth, N.Y., Apr 25, 1757 LO 3462; May 3, 1757, Loudoun's Warrant to pay Capt. John Shepherd 307 pounds, 9 shillings, 2 pence, Sterling, without deductions, for Bounty money and charges attending the raising the said Company. On Shepherd's bill, dated Castletown, May 1, 1757, he states that he was charged 14 pence per man a day while marching through Massachusetts for 'quarters and diet' instead of the customary 4 pence allowed by the Crown-*LO 5091-1*. Loudoun docked the difference though, much to the surprise of the Massachusetts government: Loudoun to Gov. Pownall, N.Y., Jan 9, 1758 *LO 5372*.

p-167 [167]Abercrombie to Webb, N.Y., May 2, 1757 *LO 3526*; Stark, *Memoir*, 30.

p-167 [168]Francis Halkett, Brigade Major, to Loudoun, N.Y., May 25, 1757 *LO 5186*.

p-168 [169]*Cutter*, May 6, 24, 26; June 10-12; July 21st.

p-168 [170]John Titcomb would have been a worthy addition to Rogers Rangers. He marched to the relief of Capt. Shepherd in 1756, and was himself ambushed and wounded. He performed numerous scouts with his Company of Provincials in 1756, and in Apr 17-57, marched to reenforce Number Four, N.H. In May he was ordered down to N.Y., where he arrived on May 13, for the Louisbourg Expedition. On board the Snow, *'St. Peter'*, May 25, Titcomb says he had Lieutenants John McFee, Ephraim Perry, and Ensign James McFee, 8 non-coms, and 76 Privates on board, while 2 men were sick in Connecticut, and 4 men were left at Number Four. Titcomb's Ranging Company were to be equipped by N.H., and Loudoun advanced Titcomb 200 pounds on July 25, to provide hatchets, canteens, etc: *Hervey*, 31-32; *LO 5187, 5186 6640; Cutter*, May 13, 1757. The *Mass Hist Soc Proc* II, 1835-36, 462 states: that a *'Mr. Davis from the first Section, presented a manuscript of Titcomb, a soldier under..Rogers the Ranger in 1756, with a sundry memoranda of subsequent years.'* — The Editor notes that he can find no clue to such a Manuscript or *'Memoranda'* in the Society Library, or in the Donation Book. Titcomb served with Rogers in 1757, not 1756. Maybe some day this interesting Manuscript will come to light.

Another Provincial, George Knaggs, aspired to command a Ranging Company. Raising 50 men he informed Loudoun that if he was encouraged he could raise 50 more. But Loudoun decided he had plenty of *Rangers:* Knaggs to Loudoun, N.Y, May 8, *LO 3581*

p-168 [171]Loudoun's Gen. Orders May 7-Oct 19 *LO3576*

p-168 [172]*Ibid:* May 17th General Order.

p-168 [173]*Ibid:* May 18th General Order.

p-169 [174]Ibid: June 13, Order. Cutter, on May 13, notes that this was a 'field day', for one of the camp women was drummed out of a Regiment. A return of Rogers' Company, dated N.Y., May 24, states that one Subaltern, one Sergeant, and 26 Privates were 'On Command'. They were probably a shore patrol serving as 'Military Police'-LO 5182.

p-169 [175]Loudoun's General Order for June 10, 1757

p-169 [176]Ibid: July 1, Order; Cutter, July 2, 4th.

p-170 [177]Ibid: July 26, 1757, Halifax: 'Captain-Lieutenant Brewer of the Company of Rangers Tryed at the late Court-Martial of which Lieutenant Colonel Gage was President for confining his Captain illegally is found guilty of the Crime laid to his Charge. They therefore do adjudge the said Captain-Lieutenant Brewer to be cashiered. His Excellency the Earl of Loudoun approves of the Sentence but in consideration of his former good services His Lordship pardons him.' The Court-Martial had taken place on July 21st LO 3576. The title of Captain-Lieutenant bestowed on Brewer is interesting. It was thought at first that he might have been an officer in Joseph Goreham's or Benoni Danks' Ranging Companies, for these Corps had Captain-Lieutenants but further study revealed that it was not Jonathan Brewer. The only answer is, that Loudoun had commissioned Brewer Captain-Lieutenant by Brevet, on Mar 8, 1757, to pacify him when Stark had been promoted Captain over him; for Loudoun notes in his Diary on that date: Commissions signed for the Rangers, Jonathan Brewer was promoted to Lieutenant in place of Kennedy. Jonathan Brewer, Lieutenant was to be made to Captain-HM 1717.

While Brewer was under confinement July 1-26, Rogers had placed his most Senior Lieutenant, John McCurdy, over Stark's Company-LO 5186. McCurdy was the Senior Lieutenant present on the Louisbourg Expedition; Noah Johnson, left at Ft. Wm. Henry was the Senior Lieutenant of Rogers Rangers. However, Brewer was in command of Stark's Company before Aug 2, because he was paid by the Paymaster the wages for the Company from May 25, to July 24, 1757 LO 6658-1. Brewer commanded until Aug 20, or 21 when the Company arrived back in New York.

p-170 [178]Stark, Memoir, 417.

p-170 [179]When Rogers Rangers returned to New York, Rogers sent Brewer recruiting with two Rangers into New England until he had time to talk to Stark and smooth things over; A return of Sept 2, LO 6179

p-171 [180]Loudoun, Diary, IV, 21, July 3, 1757.

p-171 [181]Ibid, 25, July 6, 1757; Rogers, 54.

p-172 [182]Rogers, 54: 'On July 3rd, by orders, I commanded a party to Lawrence Town and from thence to Shitzcook; some were left there to cut and make hay in the meadows for the horses intended to be used in an expedition to Louisbourg; others covered the hay-makers, and others were dispatched on scouts to make discoveries..'; Cutter, July 29th.

p-173 [183]Rogers, 54-55; Cutter, Aug 1-2nd. LO1290: Rangers and Messerve's Carpenters were ordered to embark on board the following transports for Louisbourg: 280 men on the Two Brothers, 256 on the Thomas and Mary, 153 on the snow Tartar, total 692.

p-173 [184]Pargellis, Loudoun, 242-243.

p-173 [185]Captain Philip Burgin's Company of would-be-Rangers have often been misconstrued as a Company of Rogers Rangers, actually they never formed part of his Corps. A sketch of Burgin's Company through manuscripts reveals that their Captain, Philip Burgin, was a native of Cumberland County, West New Jersey. In 1756, he had served in Captain Dievantz Company of Batteaumen. Seeking the fame of a Ranger partisan he petitioned Loudoun on Mar 15, 1757, to take into the Ranging Service a Company of Ranger aspirants, most of whom had never been in à woods: Burgin to Loudoun, Mar 15, LO 3064
Loudoun took them into the service on Apr 14, 1757, 'to be forthwith Raised and Employed in His Majesty's Service as Rangers', and to be on the same footing as Rogers Rangers. Captain Burgin, a Lieutenant, an Ensign, and 58 men were in New York ready for service on Apr 14th: Loudoun's Warrant on Abraham Mortier to pay Burgin 244 Pounds N.Y. Currency for Subsistance money for his Company LO 4759; Loudoun, Diary, III, 57, Apr 14, 1757 entry.
Lieutenant Obediah Robins arrived in New York the first week of May with the other 38 men of Burgin's Company, swelling it to it's authorized strength of 100 officers and men: Loudoun's Warrant

May 7, 1757, to pay Lt. Robins 152 pounds subsistance money *LO 6070*. Meanwhile Captain Burgin with: the detatchment that he had raised had been sent to Fort Wm. Henry to be broken in by Richard Rogers. Richard soon learned that Burgin's Dutchmen were unfit for the ardours of Ranging service, and as a further black mark, ten of them attempted to desert the first week of May. Webb informed Loudoun who ordered him to reduce the Company in spite of the Bounty money spent on them, rather than keep them in service on such high pay as one of *'His Majesty's Independant Companies of Rangers'*. Loudoun wrote Webb on May 26, but before Webb received his orders to disband Burgin's Company they performed at least one Scout. After their ineffectiveness had shown up, Webb had ordered them back to Fort Edward and sent Ogden's N.Y. Provincial Ranging Company up to serve with Richard Rogers at Wm. Henry. On May 31, General Orders at Ft. Edward read -: *'That a Detachment of 100 Men Hold them Selves in Readiness To March Tomorrow Morning to ye Lake by Break of Day. -Capt. Putnam & Capt. Burgin's Rangers, 30 Men Each, The Conn Troops one Capt, 1 Subn., & 40 Men.'* Ford, May 31st. Finally, on June 28, 1757, sometime after Loudoun's order of May 26 Webb paid off Burgin's Company and discharged them: *LO 4558;* Loudoun to Webb, N.Y., May 26, 1757 *LO3722* Webb to Loudoun, Albany, May 9, 1757 *LO 3590;* Capt James Abercrombie to Robert Rogers, N.Y., Apr 22, 1757, in Rogers, *Journals*, 52-53. At least one of Burgin's privates was found suitable for Rogers Rangers. He was Job Tecomans, and he entered Richard Rogers' Company on June 25th-*AB 4867-5.*

p-175   [186]*AB 4867-5.*

p-176   [187]Webb to Loudoun, Aug 1, 1757 *LO 4020.*

p-181   [188]Noah Johnson's Memorial to Loudoun, Fort Edward, Nov 10, 1757 *LO 4796:* Lieutenant Johnson says that Webb gave him a verbal order to command Richard Rogers' Company after Rogers' death. Lieutenant Johnson, like other participants at the Siege of Fort Wm Henry, believed that under the circumstances he would be allowed to take up arms again. He hung on until January and accompanied Rogers to New York when he was ordered there in Jan 1758 to discuss augmenting his Rangers. Johnson's case is proof that the English still held to the terms of the Capitulation (until June 25, 1758), for Johnson was not even recommended for a Captain by Rogers at this late date. If there was any chance of Johnson being allowed to break the capitulation Rogers would have done everything in his power to obtain him his rightful promotion, for Johnson was the Senior Lieutenant, and first in line for a Captain's berth, besides being a very good friend of Rogers. Johnson's second petition to Loudoun, N.Y., Jan 12, 1758 *LO 5397*.

p-182 [189]*Rogers*, 55; Loudoun, *Diary*, IV, 99, Aug 10, 1757 entry. Lt. Brewer of Stark's was sent recruiting when the Corps arrived back in New York. Lt. James Rogers of Bulkeley's, and Ensign Samuel Shepherd of Shepherd's, were sent on a packet-boat bound for Boston from Halifax. In Nov, when the Corps was back at Rogers' Island, Sergts Partridge Hamilton of Rogers', and Kelsey of Shepherd's were sent recruiting. By Nov 7, the Corps had 61 sick out of 317 Privates (Stark's had 38 fit men) *LO 6802.*

p-182 [190]James Rogers' receipt to Captain Bulkeley dated *'Halifax; 10th Aug, 1757'*, is the type of 'contract' usually agreed to by Ranger recruiting officers: *'Rec'd of Capt. Chas. Bulkeley three hundred Spanish Mil'd Dollars for inlisting Recruits into His Majesty's Company of Rangers commanded by said Charles Bulkeley at ten Dollars Each Recruit and to appear with Said Recruit at Albany in ye Province of New York in Sixty days from the above date, or to return the above s'd Dollars to Said Bulkeley on Demand.'*-Bulkeley, Aug 10, entry.

p-183 [191]Loudoun to Webb, Halifax, Aug 7, 1757 *LO 4520:* says that he is sending Rogers Rangers thru Long Island Sound to save time. Captain James Abercrombie's *Orderly Book*, Aug 1, 1757 *LO 3993-A*. Surgeon Cutter was so outraged at the precipitous ending of the Expedition against Louisbourg that he abruptly closed his *Journal* and did not make another entry for the remainder of the year. Previous to this, his *Journal* reveals his sentiments: *'July 22d to 28th. The time spent in Councils of war of which we small Folk know little but think a great deal.'* His closing entry for Aug 1, and 2nd, heatedly states: *'The Troops embarking with ye utmost Expedition-just as we were unmoored & ready to sail for Louisburgh-'*.

p-183 [192]*LO 6964*.

p-184 [193]Loudoun, *Diary*, IV, 143, Sept 23, 1757.

p-184 [194]Loudoun to Webb, N.Y., Sept 2, 1757 *LO 43 88*, states: that he is sending four battalions and Rogers Rangers to support him, they were embarking and would sail with the next tide. But there is a discrepancy of time someplace, for Rogers Rangers arrived in Albany on the 14th. It would not take them 12 days to reach there from New York, even with the calmest of winds. Whether the Rangers stopped off on the way or actually did not sail on the 2nd is not known: Abercrombie to Loudoun, Albany, Sept 15, 1757; Same to Same, Sept 18, 1757 *LO 4489*; *Boston News-Letter*, Oct 6, 1757.

p-185 [195]Abercrombie's General Orders, Albany, Sept 14-15, 1757 *LO 3576*; Rogers to Loudoun, Fort Edward, Oct 25, 1757 *LO 4701*; Same to Same, Oct 27 1757, *LO 4707*; *Rogers*, 59-70; See Appendice E.

p-185 [196]*Rogers*, 57-58; Pargellis, *Loudoun*, 305; See Appendice F, p 297:-*Rogers' Cadet Company*.

p-186 [197]Abercrombie's General Orders, Albany, Sept 14-15, 1757 *LO 3576*.

p-186 [198]Chalmers to Loudoun, Albany, Apr 5, 1757 *LO 3287*; Rogers to Loudoun, Sept 13, 1756 *LO 1776*; *Rogers*, 32-33.

p-186 [199]Chalmers' Memorial to Loudoun, *LO 3287*.

p-187 [200]*Rogers*, 57-58; See Appendice E.

p-188 [201]Lieutenant James Pottinger to Loudoun, Halifax, July 21, 1757 *LO 3975*; Loudoun to Cumberland, N.Y., May 11, 1757, in Loudoun's *Letter-Book* to Cumberland, and Pargillis, *Military Affairs*, 349, 332; *Macomb*, Mar 24, 1758 Letter; *Rogers*, 57-58.

p-189 [202]Viz: Edward Crofton, Simon Stephens, Benjamin Bridge, Archibald McDonald, Hugh Sterling.

p-189 [203]*Metcalf*, Sept 21, 1757 entry.

p-189 [204]*Ibid*, Oct 3, 4, 5, 9th; *Rogers*, 55-56.

p-192 [205]Ford, Lyman's-Webb's General Orders, Nov 8, 1757: 'All ye Volunteers belonging to ye Regular Troops and now with ye Rangers are to join their *Respective Corps as soon as they can.*'

p-192 [206]*LO 4900;* also Hugh Sterling and B. Bridge who returned to Stark's and Bulkeley's as Cadets. Rogers does not mention Caesar McCormicj, and Joseph Bolton in his Cadet Company, for they served in that capacity from Nov 24th (after the Cadet Company had been disbanded) in Rogers' Own Company

p-193 [207]*Ford,* Lyman's-Webb's General Orders, Nov 10, 1757: 'Majr Rogers is to order a Guard of Rangers to post proper sentery from it, on ye Live Stock Garden & Fire wood & no Sort of thing to be taken out of ye Garden without proper leave from Col. Haviland & no fire wood to be touched as they will be answerable for it & ye offender punished with the utmost Severity.'

p-197 [208]Joshua Goodenough's *Old Letter.*

p-199 [209]*Ibid.*

p-199 [210]Leech's Court-Martial Proceedings are in War Office 71: 44.

p-199 [211]*Boston News-Letter,* May 1, 1760.

p-202 [212]*LO 4900; LO 4890; Rogers,* 70: Simply says that *'Several of them were dismissed with an allowance of 13 days pay to carry them home, being unfit for immediate service by their past fatigues'* There is no mention of their *'misbehaviour'.*

p-202 [213]Viz: Four men from Rogers' Own; One, from Stark's; Four, from Bulkeley's; and three, from Shepherd's *LO 4893-*Return of the Men to be Discharged from the Rangers and Connecticut Companies at Fort Edward, 24th Nov 1757, signed Wm Haviland; Abercrombie to Loudoun, Albany, Dec 11, 1757 *LO 49 98:* States that Haviland and Capt Abercrombie discharged 14 Rangers.

p-209 [214]See Appendice H, p 304.

p-210 [215]Abercrombie to Loudoun, Dec 26th *LO 5111.*

p-212 [216]*Ibid.* A digest of the recorded Battles, Actions, Sieges, and Scouts of Rogers Rangers for 1757, reveals that they fought one undecisive battle: at La Barbue Creek; Served in three Sieges:

Rigaud's Siege of Ft. Wm. Henry, Siege and Massacre of Ft. Wm. Henry, and Rogers' brief Siege of Ticonderoga; fought in eight actions, in which all but two were victorious; and made at least ten recorded scouts towards the enemy.

CHAPTER FOUR (pp 213-262)

p-213 [217]Abercrombie to Loudoun, Albany, Jan 1, 1758 LO 5311: relates Rogers' 'Thank you Note'.

p-214 [218]Abercrombie to Loudoun, Albany, Dec 11, 1757 LO 4998; Same to Same, Dec 18, 1757 LO 5038; Ibid, Dec 18, 1757 (second letter of this date) LO 5039; Abercrombie to Loudoun, Albany, Dec 30, 1757 LO 5159: '..To whatever numbers your Lordship proposes to augment the present numbers of Rangers, you must settle it with Capt. Rogers whose officers refuse to list a single man under ten dollars of bounty money of which I acquainted your Lordship before. Abating the bounty money I hope its not proposed to increase them to 1,000 men, they seem already numerous enough to govern from their behaviour since they returned to Ft. Edward from the grand scout' (Stark's Misbehaviour Scout) 'and since that their mutinous conduct on the Island which lastly is ever untill your Lordship's pleasure is known. I presume with regard to increasing them your Lordship would propose to carry them no further than to render them good woodsmen & obedient to command which they, far from being at present, as a proof of this, Capt. Abercrombie, acquainted your Lordship that on their march they kept constantly firing at game. That within hearing of the french sentries, both officers and men were asleep on their posts. That they were disappointed in taking prisoners by their firing in the evening themselves; and at the firing of the cannon they all fired up in the air. All this done notwithstanding the repeated exhortations to the contrary. Their behaviour (was) no better in returning..which I was sorry to hear because last year they were a useful and well behaved body & generally succeeded well when they went out in small parties. For these and other reasons, I was neither for augmenting or diminishing them at this juncture, and foreseeing the difficulty and I may say the improbability of rendering them into any order and subordination I suggested the constituting (of) companies from the respective corps (of

Regulars) as the speediest and most likely scheme, free from the embarassment of the new (Gage's) corps and the expence of the old (Rogers Rangers), the latter in a few months might have been dismissed if they did not come into better order after selecting the best woodsmen out of them for conducting and serving as guides to the body collected from the regulars, and I believe there is no officer your Lordship would employ upon any service who would not depend and risk more on a command thus composed, than with any spheres of Rangers that can or will be raised on this continent.'
-Courtesy of the Huntington Library.

p-216 [219]Abercrombie to Loudoun, Jan 2, 1758 *LO5316*

p-218 [220]Ibid.

p-218 [221]Loudoun, Diary, Jan 9, 1758 *HM 1717*.

p-219 [222]Abercrombie to Loudoun, Jan 1, 1758 *LO 53 11*; Loudoun to Abercrombie, Jan 25, 1758 *LO 5459*.

p-219 [223]Rogers' Memorial to Loudoun, Ft. Edward, Oct 25, 1757 *LO 4702*; Same to Same, Oct 27, 1757 *LO 4707*. Rogers, with an ever-watchful eye for likely recruits had taken the names of sixty men from the Provincial troops before they left for home and then asked General Webb if he might enlist them when the campaign ended: Webb to Abercrombie, Ft. Edward, Oct 24, 1757 *LO 4696*. The willingness of these men to enlist showed that New Hampshire was not the only source for Rangers.

p-219 [224]Loudoun, Diary, Jan 9, 1758; *Rogers*, 75.

p-220 [225]*Rogers*, 77; See Appendice B, p 280.

p-220 [226]Rogers to Loudoun, N.Y., Jan 10, 1758 *LO 5379*; *Rogers*, 75-78: Loudoun's Instructions Jan 11.

p-220 [227]Loudoun, Diary, Apr 2, 1758 entry *HM 1717*

p-220 [228]Ibid; Abercrombie to Loudoun, Jan 2 *LO5316*

p-221 [229]*LO 5379*: Loudoun notes on Rogers' original list that 70 men were needed to complete his present Companies. He also jots down Pottinger and Campbell's names and the Province where the proposed Officers are from, and the rank they held at that time. General Webb was with Rogers and Loudoun on the evening of the 10th when Rogers handed Loudoun the list of recommended officers. Loudoun notes that Webb again proposed the raising of 1,000 Indians for service: Loudoun, *Diary*, Jan 10

p-222 [230]Rogers to Loudoun, N. Y., Jan 11, 1758 - *LO 5389 A&B;* Loudoun's List, Jan 14, 1758 *LO 5401;* The five men Loudoun preferred were James Pottinger, Archibald Campbell, James White, Lawrence Smith and Henry Wendell. White and Wendell were the only ones who had not served in Rogers' Cadet Company. Wendell was strongly backed by General Abercrombie, either for a Ranging or Indian Officers berth: Abercrombie to Loudoun, Albany, Dec 26, 1757 *LO 5111*.

p-223 [231]Rogers' Proposal to take Crown Point, N. Y., Jan 13, 1758 *LO 5398*.

p-223 [232]Loudoun, *Diary*, Jan 13, 1758 *HM 1717*.

p-224 [233]*Ibid*, Jan 17, 1758 entry; Loudoun's List of Commissions for the Ranging Companies, Jan 14, 1758 *LO 5401;* Loudoun's Beating Orders to Captain Rogers Jan 11, 1758, authorizing him to raise recruits in any Colony by beat of a drum or otherwhise (to be shown to local Magistrates): *LO 5391*.

p-224 [234]Macomb, *Copy-Letter Book*, Apr 22, 1758 to Greg and Cunningham. See Appendice B, p 281.

p-224 [235]Abercrombie to Loudoun, Albany, Jan 22nd.

p-224 [236]Rogers to Loudoun, Albany, Jan 23, 1758 *LO 5446*.

p-225 [237]Loudoun, *Diary*, Jan 13, 1758; Abercrombie to Loudoun, Albany, Jan 21, 1758 *LO 5436;* Captain James Abercrombie's Proposal to take Crown Point, Albany, to Loudoun, Jan 21, 1758 *LO 5437* (enclosed in Gen. Abercrombie's letter of the same date). Two days later, Capt. Abercrombie's friend, Engineer Matthew Clarke, sent Loudoun his proposal to take Ticonderoga or Crown Point with 500 Regulars and 50 Rangers: *LO 5449*. On the back of Capt. Abcrombie's Proposal, Loudoun jots down in his atrocious scrawl, that he recommends the plan and if the lake freezes it is to be carried on. It was only the complete abandoning of Loudoun's Winter

Expedition in late February that Capt. Abercrombie (not Rogers) was not given the much coveted opportunity. Rogers probably never knew this.

p-226 [238]Lt. Jabez Fitch of Durkee's Conn. Ranging Company at Ft. Edward, records the flood: *'Monday, Jan 2, This is a Vary Stormy Day of Rain Hail and Ise..The Storm was Vary Tedious all Night...-Tues., Jan 3, In ye Morning ye River was So High that it Ran into Many of ye Rangers Hutts and Drove them out..Som of their Hutts were Waist Deep in Water ye River Being So High. This was also a Stormy Day & Vary Slippery Everything Being Covered with Ise. Jan 6, Now ye River Began To Fall.'-Courtesy of the Mass. Soc. of Mayflower Descendants.* Col. Haviland in a letter to Loudoun dated Ft. Ed, Jan 7, LO 5349 gives a similar, but more gleeful, account of Rogers Rangers being floated out of their huts.

p-226 [239]*Fitch*, Jan 2, 1758 entry.

p-226 [240]*Ibid*, Jan 9, March 1, 1758 entries.

p-227 [241]Stark, *Reminiscenses*, 50: Like all of Rogers' utterances and deeds, this bit of witticism spread into New England, and a saying started: *'to pay one's debts as Rogers did that of the nation'*.

p-227 [242]Haviland to Loudoun, Fort Edward, Nov 20, 1757 *LO 4865; Fitch*, Jan 6, 1758 entry.

p-228 [243]*Fitch*, Jan 25, 1758 entry.

p-229 [244]*Ibid*, Jan 28, 1758 entry.

p-232 [245]*Ibid*, Feb 12, 1758 the Artillery arrived; List of Artillery and Ordinance *LO 2731;* 384 horses and 167 Sleighs needed *LO 5514;* Loudoun to Howe Feb 2, 1758 *LO 5523. Levis MSS*, V, pp 213-15.

p-234 [246]Abercrombie to Loudoun, Albany, Feb 14, 1758 *LO 5595;* Loudoun to Abercrombie, Hartford, Feb 22, 1758 *LO 5643 A&B:* Rogers told Loudoun when he was in New York that 200 pair of snowshoes would break a road for any number of men. Howe to Loudoun, Feb 14, 1758 *LO 5584;* Loudoun to Howe, Hartford, Feb 22, 1758 *LO 5638 A&B.* Lt-Col. George Williamson to Loudoun, Albany, Dec 19, 1757 *LO 5043;* There is a photograph of an actual ice-creeper in the N.Y. Hist. Soc. Bulletin, III, Apr 1919, No

1, p 16. Engineer Matthew Clarke to Loudoun, Albany, Jan 23, 1758 *LO 5449*. Abercrombie to Loudoun, Albany, Feb 25, 1758 *LO 5666*: admitted that 300 or 400 men on snowshoes would suffice to make a road.

p-235 [247] It is interesting to note here that the term 'Commando' was applied as earlier as 1758 by the British. Colonel Forbes, a friend of Rogers, and commander of the Pennsylvania front in 1758, wrote Colonel Bouquet from Philadelphia on June 27, 1758: 'I have been long in your opinion of equiping numbers of our men like the Savages..I am resolved upon getting some of the best people in every Corps to go out a scouting in that stile... and all those parties, altho in general they ought to be kept secret from every one but the officers concerned, yet that they may be distinguished and the particulars of each Commando known, each party ought to have some Union Flags, and the particular Indians or Soldiers dressed as such, the Yellow Shallown or Buntin upon their head or remarkable part of their body. This I have recommended to be given out to our friendly Indians in our back frontiers, so pray let your people know as much..' James, 125. At least one of Rogers' Cadets was a protege of Colonel Forbes. He was Archibald Campbell, Jr. Rogers wrote Forbes Nov 5, 1757, from Ft. Edward *LO 4764:* in which he gave Campbell a very favourable recommendation, saying, that he had behaved extremely well, pushing for all scouts and even on one to Ticonderoga. After Campbell received a Commission in the Black Watch he led one of these *Commando* units in Pontiac's War in 1764, imparting Rogers Ranger Rules and tactics to them.

p-236 [248] *Docs.Rel.Col.Hist.N.Y,X,837; Fitch,* Feb 17.

p-236 [249] Howe to Loudoun, Feb 26, 1758 *LO 5671.*

p-236 [250] In regard to the *Uniform* of Rogers' two (Stockbridge and Mohegan) Indian Companies; they were not clothed, instead they wore Indian garb and paint. Abercrombie had recommended to Loudoun: '..I hope they will be dressed Painted like all other Indians, which will·be rather less expence than Common Cloathing and I apprehend will in all respects have a good effect.' Abercrombie to Loudoun, Albany, Jan 2, 1758 *LO 5316-Courtesy of the Huntington Library.* Loudoun followed Abercrombie's advice and instructed Rogers on Jan 11, 1758: '*The*

*Indians to be dressed in all respects in the true
Indian fashion'-Rogers, 77.* Rogers may have tried-
to get them to dye their leggins green to harmon-
ize with the green jackets of his white Rangers.
There is no definite evidence to this effect as yet.

p-236 [251]*Fitch*, Feb 19, 1758 *Courtesy of the Mass.
Society of Mayflower Descendants.*

p-236 [252]*Fitch*, Feb 26, 1758 entry.

p-237 [253]*Fitch*, Feb 27, 1758 entry.

p-237 [254]*Rogers*, 79: 'This gentleman..giving out
publicly at the same time, that, upon Putnam's return, I should be sent to the French Forts with a
strong party of 400 Rangers...'

p-240 [255]*Ibid*, 79-80; Haviland to Loudoun, Ft. Edward, Jan 7, 1758 *LO 5349*.

p-242 [256]Macomb to Greg & Cunningham, Mar 24, 1758

p-261 [257]*Rogers*, 103, 78: '..one of the Captains
dying, to whom I had delivered a thousand dollars
as advance pay for his company, which, agreeable
to the instructions I received, I had a right to
do; yet I was obliged to account with the government for this money, and entirely lost every penny
of it.' The Captain, was John McCurdey. Loudoun
advanced Rogers 1,213 pounds, 6 shillings and 8
pence Sterling to raise the five new Companies:-
Warrant, Jan 12, 1758 *LO 6907*. Rogers' Account a-
gainst the four Louisbourg Companies, dated Jan 24
1758, Albany. Enclosed to Monckton with Appy's explanatory letter of June 30, 1758 *AB 402*.

p-262 [258]Pitt to Abercrombie, Whitehall, Dec 30,
1757, *Pitt Correspondence*, I, 147-8; *Ibid*, Jan 27,
1758, I, 168-9; Re-emphasisis 'the *Execution of
this very material Service..*'; Abercrombie to Pitt
N.Y., Mar 16, 1758, I, 207-8. Abercrombie to Loudoun, Albany, Jan 2, 1758 *LO 5316*.

p-262 [259]Loudoun, *Diary*, Apr 2, 1758: General Abercrombie '..talked to me further of Rogers, that
he had told him that I had promised him rank.'
Loudoun told Abercrombie that when Rogers was with
him in January he 'was very careful when with me
but that I was told by other people he had threat-

ened to give up and take a New Hampshire Provincial Regiment and had talked to Appy in this strain.' (See text, p 220).

p-262 [260]Rogers held the British rank of 'Major' in America only, and only for as long as his Rangers were maintained in service. Rogers, 103-104: 'By his Excellency James Abercromby,..Commander in Chief..in North America. Whereas it may be of great use to his Majesty's service in the operations now carrying on for recovering his rights in America, to have a number of men employed in obtaining intelligence of the strength, situation, and motions of the enemy, as well as other services, for which Rangers, or men acquainted with the woods, only are fit: Having the greatest confidence in your loyalty, courage and skill in this kind of service, I do, by virtue of the power and authority to me given by his Majesty, hereby constitute and appoint you to be Major of the Rangers in his Majesty's service, and likewise Captain of a Company of said Rangers. You are therefore to take the said Rangers as Major, and the said Company as Captain, into your care and charge, and duly exercise and instruct, as well the officers as the soldiers thereof, in arms, and to use your best endeavours to keep them in good order and discipline; and I do hereby command them to obey you as their Major and Captain respectively, and you are to follow and observe such orders and directions from time to time as you shall receive from his Majesty, myself, or any other superior officer, according to the rules and discipline of war. Given at N.Y., this 6th Day of April 1758'.

ADDITIONAL FOOTNOTES (Unique Source Material discovered after this Volume had gone to press):
p-79 [54a]Sergeant James Henry was the Sergeant who told the Paul Bunyan yarn to Montcalm. Henry was captured at La Barbue Creek and was examined on Apr 14, 1757 while a prisoner at Montreal. He escaped two months later. Four of Rogers' five whale boats were discovered by M. de Bleury on Oct 2, 1756. Montcalm records the discovery in his Journal: 'M. de Bleury no sooner discovered the burial of four English barges armed with blunderbusses [Wall-pieces] than he returned with utmost haste the same day to Carillon. The English had gained admittance into the lake Champlain to undertake

the taking of some prizes.'-Translated from Montcalm's *Journal*, October 2, 1756; April 14, 1757.

(Index in Volume II)

www.ingramcontent.com/pod-product-compliance
Lightning Source LLC
Chambersburg PA
CBHW050326230426
43663CB00010B/1755